MW00787356

Military and Veterans Studies

Series Editor
David L. Albright, School of Social Work
University of Alabama
Tuscaloosa, AL, USA

This book series aims to promote a better understanding of the health and well-being of military- and veteran-connected populations, including Active Duty, National Guard, and Reserve Component personnel and Veterans, and its impact on their communities and families. Volumes in the Series include interdisciplinary, international research from researchers, scholars, professional organizations, and NGOs, and incorporate short narratives from real people to ensure their voices are heard.

Mary Ann Forgey • Karen Green-Hurdle

Editors

Military Social Work Around the Globe

 Springer

Editors
Mary Ann Forgey
Graduate School of Social Service
Fordham University
New York, NY, USA

Karen Green-Hurdle
Department of Veterans Affairs
(North Queensland)
Open Arms Veterans & Families
Counselling
Townsville, QLD, Australia

ISSN 2524-3942   ISSN 2524-3950   (electronic)
Military and Veterans Studies
ISBN 978-3-031-14481-3   ISBN 978-3-031-14482-0   (eBook)
https://doi.org/10.1007/978-3-031-14482-0

This Springer imprint is published by the registered company Springer Nature Switzerland AG
The registered company address is: Gewerbestrasse 11, 6330 Cham, Switzerland

Foreword

Military personnel and their families, just like any other group of people, need access to social work services that address their unique needs. Military communities, while diverse across countries with different cultures, norms, and socio-economic status; have many commonalities that differentiate them from civilian communities. Consequently, a unique form of social work is needed for military communities – a form that is rooted in generic social work, but also is responsive and tailored to meet unique military community needs. This book is thus a very welcome and much needed compendium, showcasing the range of military social work services across multiple countries.

There has not been a great deal written on international military social work. In 1999, James G. Daley concluded his book on American *Social Work Practice in the Military*, with a call for an international perspective on military social work (Daley 1999). He followed this in 2003 with the article, "Military social work: A multi-country study," which included only four countries (the US, Finland, China, and South Africa) (Daley 2003). Daley in a 2006 editorial titled, "Building an international military social work focus," points again to the importance of military social work and the need for international comparative research and sharing (Daley 2006).

And so, it is with great delight that we receive the publication of the first international book on military social work, *Military Social Work Around the Globe*, co-edited by Mary Ann Forgey and Karen Green-Hurdle. This book is personally meaningful, as I was employed as a military social worker for the first 17 years of my career; rising to the rank of Lieutenant Colonel and Deputy Director of the Military Health Research Centre, which included a Social Work Research and Development Department, both of which I started. During my years as practitioner, researcher, and manager I saw the great potential that military social work has not only to provide support to military members and their families, but also to shape the way the military thinks about and utilizes its human resources, the nature of military culture, the policies and procedures adopted by the military, and the cultivation of the military community within broader social welfare and human rights discourses. This was particularly evident in my experience of being a military social worker during the transition from the apartheid regime to a democratic, non-racial government (Turton and Van Breda 2020).

This book emerges out of an extensive and creative process of mobilizing a previously rather disconnected and often invisible group of social workers, which could serve as a model for others wanting to do global comparative studies. In 2016, Forgey and Green-Hurdle collaborated on a multinational study on military social work. This promised to be (and indeed is) the largest multi-country study on military social work. The study confirmed the existence of military social work in 25 countries, and interviews were conducted with subject matter experts from 15 countries. In April 2019, a 3-day roundtable conference was convened at the West Point military base in New York, hosted by Fordham University and attended by representatives from 15 countries. This group continues to meet regularly under the title "International Military Social Work Consortium." This book is one of several outputs of this initiative.

This book draws together the approaches to military social work across multiple countries; giving attention to the history of military social work, the settings in which military social workers operate, various approaches to or constructions of military social work, research on military social work, ethical tensions in military social work, the education and training of military social workers, and future directions of military social work services. Each chapter provides an excellent picture of military social work in that country, who is working, and how they work. Together the chapters show various areas of commonality and other areas of difference, and in doing so, point towards ongoing work in the evolution of military social work.

I think it is important for military social workers to define themselves as *military* social workers, and not just social workers who work with military personnel (Van Breda 2012). There is a difference in professional identity when one thinks of military social work as a field of practice requiring a unique knowledge and skill set that is different from, for example, child and family social work. Furthermore, the adoption of an explicit "military social work" professional identity helps position one as a hybrid of a military person and a social worker, both part of the military system and also part of the social work system. These systems may have conflicting values and approaches, which can create ethical dilemmas, as some chapters highlight. A military social work professional identity is important in helping navigate the narrow path between these, as exemplified in the notion of binocular vision that is part of the South African military social work theory (Van Breda and Du Plessis 2009).

This book is an important step towards cultivating an evolving sense of professional identity (Roulston 2020). As each participating country articulates their history, work, personnel, position, and values; they are increasing awareness and consciousness about their form of military social work practice. Articulating one's work is an important step in developing professional identity. Moreover, the co-location of these narratives in one book allows for critical reflection on one's own construction of military social work in relation to the constructions of other countries. We have probably all had that experience of visiting another country or culture and suddenly "seeing" one's own previously invisible or taken-for-granted culture by the difference in this new space. This book offers this opportunity to military social workers, not only in the 14 included countries, but also other countries that are not part of this book.

The comparative analysis that this book offers, which is pulled together by the editors in the final chapter, initiates a larger practice of conceptualizing a global military social work identity. For example, many chapters deliberate on the relative importance of clinical or medical social work versus occupational social work. Some countries are strongly aligned with one or other, and some see the value of both. Teasing out these approaches and weighing their strengths and limitations in each context is an important part of conceptualizing military social work.

Arguably South Africa, more than most countries, has been deliberate in working to develop a theory or model of military social work with its concepts of binocular vision, practice positions, client systems, and a practice model (Van Breda 2012). This is not to say that their ideas are the correct or best ones, but they do illustrate the need for developing the field itself. Most of the research emerging from military social workers has focused on specific issues or treatment approaches, such as trauma, substance use, and domestic violence. What has been lacking is research and writing on military social work per se. This kind of work is important for building the field, with this book making an important contribution to this development by focusing on the de facto construction of the field in various countries. It is hoped that this will precipitate further work on developing, theorizing, and modelling in the field of military social work.

The aim of this book is not to develop military social work as an end in itself, but as a means to a greater end of strengthening military personnel, veterans, military families, and the military community across the world. Military individuals, groups, and communities face considerable stress in their work that can negatively impact their capacity to flourish and embody social justice, compassion, and empathy. A military colleague of mine used to say that the job of military social workers is to humanize the military – I think there is still much truth in this, as military work can be hard on the soul. The global definition of social work (IASSW 2014) emphasizes the "principles of social justice, human rights, collective responsibility and respect for diversities" and states that social work "promotes social change and development, social cohesion, and the empowerment and liberation of people." With its roots in such values, military social work is ideally placed to ensure the full humanity of the military community through working at the micro-macro interface (Olson 2018).

This book will be of interest and value to all military social workers; from the most junior to the most senior, from the countries represented in the book, and from countries not represented. It will also be of relevance to countries that are considering starting up a military social work service, such as Slovakia, which will launch such a service at the end of 2022. The book will be of relevance to academics teaching social work, particularly occupational social work and employee assistance or wellness programs, as well as clinical social work and those teaching or considering teaching military social work. This book furthermore is an invaluable resource for military social work scholars – those who seek to research military social work and build theories and models for military social work. Finally, this book will help to place military social work in the core cluster of fields of international social work practice. Congratulations to the editors and authors for producing this book.

Professor of Social Work, Head of Social Work   Adrian D. van Breda
and Community Development
University of Johannesburg, Johannesburg, South Africa

References

Daley JG (ed). (1999) Social work practice in the military. Routledge, New York
Daley JG (2003) Military social work: a multi-country comparison. Int Soc Work 46(4):437–448. https://doi.org/10.1177/0020872803464002
Daley JG (2006) Editorial: building an international military social work focus: a call for action. Adv Soc Work 7(1):i–iii. https://doi.org/10.18060/115
IASSW (2014) Global definition of social work. International Association of Schools of Social Work. https://www.iassw-aiets.org/global-definition-of-social-work-review-of-the-global-definition/. Accessed 31 Mar 2022
Olson MD (2018) Exploring military social work from a social justice perspective. Int Soc Work 61(1):119–129. https://doi.org/10.1177/0020872815606792
Roulston A (2020) Professional identity in social work. In: Ellis R and Hogard E (eds) Professional identity in the caring professions. Routledge, London, pp 43–56
Turton YJ, Van Breda AD (2020) The role of social workers in and after political conflict in South Africa: reflections across the fence. In: Duffy J, Campbell J, Tosone C (eds) International perspectives on social work and political conflict. Routledge, London, pp 128–141 https://doi.org/10.4324/9781315150833-11
Van Breda AD (2012) Military social work thinking in South Africa. Adv Soc Work 13(1):17–33. https://doi.org/10.18060/1890
Van Breda AD, Du Plessis AW (2009) A model of occupational social work practice: a developmental social welfare critique. Res Soc Work Pract 21(3):316–333

Preface

The purpose of this book is to cultivate an international understanding of military social work, hereafter referred to as MilSW, and how it is practiced by uniformed and civilian social workers within the defense organizations of the countries contributing to this book. This focus on MilSW practice specifically within defense organizations (and not in veteran settings) was deliberate and done out of recognition for the unique aspects of this specific role, and the importance of establishing a more global understanding of fundamental similarities and differences of this field of practice.

The knowledge generated by this book will inform military social workers and defense organizations worldwide about how social workers are assisting service members and their families in dealing with the common challenges that are unique to military life. This comparative international lens will also provide fertile ground for social work students and educators worldwide to consider possibilities of this field of practice in their country, or to develop a deeper and more critical understanding of how MilSW is being practiced within their own country. The international landscape provided within this book will also provide a rich source of ideas for researchers interested in conducting more in-depth analysis of some of the practice issues identified, and in expanding the inquiry of this specialist field to countries beyond those included in this book.

Organization

This book contains a total of 18 chapters. In the first chapter, the co-editors describe the origins of how the idea for collaborating on an international MilSW project came to be, and the developmental steps that enabled this book to become a reality. The strategies used to identify countries practicing MilSW and their subject matter experts are also described, along with the consequential international partnerships that were formed, and that allowed this book to come to fruition.

In Chaps. 2, 3, 4, 5, 6, 7, 8, 9, 10, 11, 12, 13, and 14, representatives from 11 countries describe MilSW practice within their country's defense organization. These chapters are organized alphabetically by country name, and each country, other than the United States of America (US), contributed one chapter to this section. Due to the breadth of MilSW practice and education in the USA, it was deemed necessary to have three chapters from the USA. Two of the chapters address the scope of uniformed and civilian MilSW practice and a third chapter describes MilSW education within the USA. Separating the US contribution into three separate chapters allowed for the necessary detail to be provided; however, it also resulted in some overlap of content in relation to history, uniformed and civilian social work roles, practice settings, and approaches. While much ground was covered within the US chapters, it is important to note that MilSW practice within the Reserves, the National Guard, and the US Public Health Service was not able to be addressed. Given the critical role of military social workers within each of these services, most recently in relation to COVID, this is a critical part of the US MilSW landscape that needs further inquiry.

Within the chapters that describe the scope of MilSW practice within a specific country (Chaps. 2, 3, 4, 5, 6, 7, 8, 9, 10, 11, 12, 13, and 14), the following subjects are addressed:

- History of MilSW
- Practice settings and roles
- Practice orientation and approach
- MilSW role in military to civilian transition (and integration)
- Ethical issues
- MilSW education and training
- Major challenges and future directions
- Conclusion

In general terms, Chaps. 2, 3, 4, 5, 6, 7, 8, 9, 10, 11, 12, 13, and 14 are structured using these subject headings; however, to respect the unique story of each country's MilSW journey, current practice landscape, breadth of services, and the way in which the chapter authors' chose to convey their story, there is some variability with the headings, the sequencing of the topics, and the extent to which each subject is addressed. It is noted that some have also added supplementary material that is significant to the way in which MilSW is practiced in a particular country.

In addition to the aforementioned topics, following the advent of COVID and the reignition of the Black Lives Matter (BLM) movement following the death of George Floyd in the US, chapter authors were given the opportunity after they had submitted their drafts to provide additional content in relation to any specific activities military social workers within their country were doing to address COVID and social justice issues, particularly in relation to racial inequities spotlighted by the BLM movement. In response to this request, some authors provided additional content to their previously submitted drafts.

Chapters 15, 16, and 17, also organized alphabetically, address the status of MilSW in Japan, Slovakia, and Ukraine, countries that do not have MilSW but where there was interest or efforts underway to develop it. In Chap. 15, authors from Japan describe the need and potential for MilSW in Japan, while Slovakia outlines the concrete plans that are in place within their defense organization for MilSW to be established in late 2022 in Chap. 16. In the Ukraine chapter (Chap. 17), the importance of developing MilSW is described; however, it is critical to note that the chapter was written prior to the 2022 Russian invasion. Although the need for MilSW remains extant, the implications of the Russian invasion on its development are not addressed.

The final chapter (Chap. 18) written by the co-editors highlights the most significant similarities and differences described by the authors in the previous chapters. Overall, this international perspective revealed some similar dynamics in the development of MilSW within certain countries and the ethical issues encountered when working as a social worker within a defense organization. Similarities in practice were identified along with some profound differences, particularly in relation to the settings in which it is practiced and how the setting itself can impact the practice that is undertaken. Not surprisingly, some more obvious differences between countries that have conscription (as opposed to an all-volunteer military force) were identified. The extent to which social workers employed by their defense departments are responsible for assisting with the military to civilian transition and integration processes was also found to vary widely across countries. This knowledge may be beneficial to the many countries that are currently grappling with this common challenge.

Editing Challenges

Addressing MilSW from an international perspective involving authors from 14 different countries presented a unique set of editing challenges. Differences in the terminology used for key concepts as well as unfamiliar terminology, language translation difficulties, and spelling variations were all challenges that required time for understanding the difference and for making decisions as to how to address these differences as fairly and consistently as possible.

One of the main terminology differences encountered was the different way in which some countries used the term "veteran." For some countries, "veteran" only referred to former service members, whereas in other countries "veteran" was more inclusive and referred to any service member who had served for a specific period of time. To alleviate confusion for the reader about the meaning of this term, which is central to MilSW, the meaning of veteran in the context of their country is explained by authors within their chapters.

Another key difference identified during the editing process was that not all countries use this term "military social worker" to describe social workers who practice within the military. Some describe this practice as "occupational social work" within the defense forces. Others did not use the term "social worker" in defining these positions and instead defined the role more by job function, e.g.,

Mental Health Officer, Behavioral Health Provider, which were also positions shared by other disciplines. To respect these differences, but also to avoid any confusion on the part of the reader, these differences were made as explicit as possible in each chapter. The implications of these different terms being used for MilSW were also further discussed in the comparison chapter.

Another issue that required resolution when editing an international book in English was the different spelling of words depending on the country's established use of British or American English. To respect each country's choice of English language usage, the spelling used within their country was maintained. As a result, the reader will notice that there are different spellings for the same concept among the various chapters depending on whether the author is using British English, e.g., "defence" or American English, e.g., "defense."

Given that at least six of the chapters were written by authors for whom English was a second language, there were also language translation and interpretation challenges. At times, terms were used that did not necessarily have a common English equivalent. For example, in the Netherlands the term "intervision" was not recognized by the editors as a word used in English and as a result initially was thought to be a typo. After discussion with the chapter authors, we learned that it shares some features of supervision and coaching, but is also a separate and defined process for inter-collegial discussion around a professional service issue. There were also translation difficulties involving the use of a term in English that did not seem to convey the true meaning intended by the author. To ensure that the author's true meaning was conveyed, discussion was sometimes required to understand the underlying meaning of the concept and to find the most accurate English translation. For example, Denmark initially used the term "sparring partner," the meaning of which was unclear to the editors. Clarification with the chapter authors revealed that the term "advocate" was the suitable replacement.

In describing and documenting what exists in relation to MilSW within defense departments worldwide, this book adds significantly to what was a relatively unknown international MilSW knowledge base. However, this book should be viewed as a window to envisage the potential for what more needs to be understood about MilSW from an international perspective in *all countries* that have MilSW since not all contributed to this book. Furthermore, as military forces adapt and respond to new frontiers and challenges around the world from war efforts to pandemics to humanitarian crises and natural disasters, military social workers must also adapt and respond accordingly to ensure that new emerging needs are proactively addressed by thinking globally while acting locally.

There is also much more to MilSW than the practice that happens within defense organizations. While this book sheds necessary light on this unique form of MilSW practice, an understanding of MilSW practice with former military members is a field that warrants a global study similar to what has been undertaken in this book.

This book has been several years in the making. It has required significant commitment and passion for the project from uniformed and civilian MilSW practitioners, educators, and researchers, all of whom have contributed to enabling this book to become a reality. It is a testament to the importance placed on the development and recognition of this field of practice by those involved from around the world, and we hope that the book will serve as inspiration for what can be achieved through connection, collaboration, and commitment to the universal principles that underpin and unite the profession of social work.

New York, NY, USA   Mary Ann Forgey
Townsville, QLD, Australia   Karen Green-Hurdle

Acknowledgments

This book could not have been written without the commitment and collaboration of uniformed and civilian military social work (MilSW) practitioners, educators, and researchers from across the globe. This book has been in progress across a timeline that included a pandemic and numerous unprecedented international conflicts, and subsequently it was very gratifying to work so constructively on building new knowledge and sustainable global partnerships.

First and foremost, we would like to thank all 45 authors who contributed their knowledge and expertise in MilSW for this book. For many, it was the first time that MilSW was officially documented within their countries, and we applaud these authors for taking on such a daunting and groundbreaking task.

We also want to recognize the inspiration that we received from Dr. James Daley. He was the first to recognize the need for this type of international MilSW cross-national exchange, and his insightful vision served as a major building block for our work.

This book would also not have been possible without the support and encouragement of Dr. David Albright, the Series Editor. From the very beginning Dr. Albright expressed his confidence in the valuable contribution that such a book would make for the social work profession, and suggested that we send a proposal to Springer. His thoughtful review and critique of the initial manuscript led to critical refinements and resulted in an enhanced final product.

Special thanks are also extended to the Springer staff who provided guidance throughout the project. Their timely response to our many questions demonstrated their commitment to this project, and their enthusiasm for this innovative area of inquiry in this unique field of practice.

This project was a very long time in the making. From its rudimentary beginnings in 2014, Fordham University supported it through sponsorship of Karen's fellowship in 2016, through the provision of internal research development grants that funded doctoral and master's-level research assistants, and through its sponsorship of the inaugural International MilSW conference at West Point in New York. Special thanks to each member of the Fordham research team that included Yafei Cai, Kundong He, Jonathan Marsh, Marissa O'Connor, Shenae Osborn, Erica

Ponteen, Don Rooks, Brett Sereysky, and Lashawn Smith. Their unending curiosity about MilSW, combined with their tenacity and determination, always invigorated us to keep going.

We also recognize the support and encouragement that we received from Dr. Annamaria Campanini, the President of the International Association of Schools of Social Work (IASSW). Dr. Campanini's belief in the need to develop this type of international knowledge exchange underpinned the decision to apply for an IASSW grant to support the West Point conference, where the idea for this book gained momentum.

Our professional interactions and relationships with clients, colleagues, and students over the course of our careers have also enriched the combined knowledge embedded within this book. Through these experiences, we have gained first-hand knowledge of the sacrifices made by military members and their families, and have been privileged to hear stories of enormous courage, strength, and resilience in the face of adversity.

We also want to especially recognize our colleagues who have participated in the IMilSW Consortium since its inception in 2019. Their enthusiasm for this project, combined with their passionate commitment to achieving positive health outcomes for those that they serve, continually reaffirmed the critical need for this type of book.

On a personal note, we extend our heartfelt gratitude to our life partners, Les Lombardi and Simon Hurdle, for their enduring patience and support, and to our family and friends for their steadfast encouragement.

Individually we have faced several challenging life events since commencing this project. As we weathered these storms, we experienced the gift of a mutually respectful and supportive co-editor and co-authoring partnership, and have come to realize that this kind of relationship may only come along once in a lifetime.

We can see so much potential for all that awaits current and emerging military social workers across the globe, and we hope this book makes the important work that social workers are engaging in within defense systems much more visible and valued.

Contents

About the Editors

Mary Ann Forgey, PhD, LCSW, is a Professor in the Graduate School of Social Service at Fordham University in New York where she has been a faculty member since 1993. Prior to her academic career, she was a civilian social worker within the US Department of Defense and served in the positions of Family Advocacy Coordinator and Army Community Services Director in Wiesbaden, Germany. She has been the Principal Investigator on two research projects related to Intimate Partner Violence (IPV) within the US military, the results of which have been published in the *Journal of Family Violence, Violence and Victims and the Journal of Social Work Education.* As a Fulbright Scholar, Dr. Forgey taught at the University College Dublin, Ireland and conducted research on IPV assessment practices. In 2011, she developed Fordham's first course in Military Social Work. She has been invited to present her work on military social work practice and education at national conferences within the US and internationally in Ireland, Italy, France, and Vietnam. She organized the first roundtable conference on International Military Social Work held at West Point in 2019 and is a founding member and coordinator for the International Military Social Work Consortium, a group of uniformed and civilian military social work practitioners, educators, and researchers from over 15 countries. She is an associate editor of the *Journal of Military Behavioral Health* and a member of the Steering Committee for the Council on Social Work Education (CSWE) Task Force on the Specialized Practice Curricular Guide for Military Social Work.

Karen Green-Hurdle, MPH, AMHSW, BSW, GD Couple Therapy, GC Business, GC Research Methods and Design, Assistant Director with Open Arms Veterans and Families Counselling, is an Australian Accredited Mental Health Social Work professional with over 30 years of senior practitioner, supervisory and executive leadership experience. Since 2000 she has worked in public service roles, in both the Department of Defence and the Department of Veteran's Affairs, delivering and managing mental health counselling, treatment, education, and family support services. Her career highlights include being invited to present on her military social work expertise at forums in Canada, the US, France, Italy, and Singapore, and virtually to the UK and Ukraine. In 2014, she received the Mount Sinai Hospital Icahn School of Medicine (New York) "Enhancement of International Social Work Leadership in Health Care" Scholarship; in 2016, she was awarded a Commonwealth Endeavour Executive Fellowship (sponsored by Fordham University, New York) where she commenced a collaboration with Professor Forgey on a systematic research inquiry exploring the scope of social work practice across international military contexts; and in 2020, she received the Laurie Cowled Women in Leadership Scholarship (QUT Business School). She is a passionate advocate for developing military social work as an international specialist field of practice; has worked as practitioner consultant with Fordham University; is a founding member of the International Military Social Work Consortium; is a member of the Australian Association of Social Workers (AASW) National Advisory Panel on veteran issues; and is an associate editor of the *Journal of Military Behavioral Health*.

About the Contributors

Suzanne M. Bailey, Retired Lieutenant-Colonel, MSM, CD, MSW, is currently the Team Lead in the Road to Mental Readiness (R2MR) Curriculum Development at the Canadian Forces Health Services Headquarters. Having joined the Canadian Forces in 1986, Suzanne Bailey graduated from the Royal Military College of Canada in 1990 and worked as a Military Police Officer prior to completing her Master of Social Work degree in 1996. She enjoyed clinical work for a decade prior to leading the standardization of mental health education and training across the Canadian Forces, for which she was awarded the Meritorious Service Medal by the Governor General. From 2011 until her retirement from military service in 2021 she was the National Practice Leader and Military Occupation Advisor for Social Work in the Department of National Defence.

Ian Barber, BA, MA, AgilePM, PRINCE2, is currently the Project Lead within the Armed Forces Covenant Lancaster Hub in the UK. Following a 28-year service career including working as an Army Welfare Worker in a military capacity while on duty, and upon leaving the Army in a civilian capacity, Ian has worked in several military charitable organizations. In addition to Ian's current role as Project Lead for Armed Forces Covenant Lancaster Hub, he also serves as an Army Reservist welfare worker.

Lene Westergaard Birk, SW, is a Senior Social Worker in Denmark. Lene Westergaard Birk has been trained as a social worker for the past 23 years, and has experience in the municipal and private labor market. Between 2015 to 2021, Lene was employed as a social worker at the Veterans Center where she counseled employees and former employees in the Danish Armed Forces. In this role, she assisted people on sick leave and helped them with issues in relation to the labor market, housing, finances, relationships, and scholarships. Lene has undertaken continuing education as a teacher in the Prevention and Relationship Enhancement Program [PREP], as a psychiatry supervisor, in Solution Focused Therapy, and management training. She has been in a management position at the Psychiatric Center, Copenhagen, since November 2021.

Jennifer Brown, BA (Hons) Social Work, is currently the Senior Social Worker in the Defence Medical Rehabilitation Centre [DMRC] located in Stanford Hall within the UK Ministry of Defence. Jennifer qualified in 2012 and worked at a family support charity in Hull, before moving on to work for an NHS mental health assessment team. In 2016–2017, Jennifer volunteered at refugee camps in Athens and on Lesbos. On her return to the UK, Jennifer worked at a mental health hospital in Coventry, later becoming the senior social worker and safeguarding lead for the hospital while training in dialectic behavior therapy skills. Jennifer has worked at DMRC since October 2020 for the Neurorehabilitation Service, has trained in ACT therapy, and began Best Interests Assessor training in early 2022.

Natacha Cameron, BSW, Registered Social Worker, operates as the New Zealand Defence Force Social Worker at Linton Military Camp in Manawatu. She has been involved in specialist services supporting women and youth within Manawatu prior to working for the military. Natacha has been at the forefront of development of social work services at Linton, additionally bringing the lived experience as a military partner to her role. The success of her work resulted in need to appoint a second social worker at Linton. Natacha is focused on empowering military members and their whānau to be fully functioning through advocacy and access to effective services. Natacha has effectively mentored other military social workers, created programs focused on prevention of common social issues for the Linton community, and is an integral member of the multi-disciplinary team at Linton.

Henriette Dueholm Christensen, SW, is a Specialized Child Counselor in Denmark and in 2022 started serving as a social worker in the Veterans Center's Family Unit. She has been trained as a social worker for the past 28 years, and has worked in the municipal and hospital roles. She has been employed as a social worker at the Veterans Center since 2008 where she advises employees and former employees in the Danish Armed Forces. In this role, she provides support to people on sick leave and assists them with issues in relation to jobs in the labor market, housing, finances, relationships, and scholarships. Henriette has undertaken further education as a children's conversation group leader, systemic appreciative coach, psychiatric counselor, and Solution Focused Therapy.

Liam Cunnah, BSW, Registered Social Worker, is a New Zealand Defence Force [NZDF], PG Cert Health Sciences Endorsed in Family and Systems Therapies, PG Dip Health Sciences Endorsed in Mental Health. Liam is Social Worker at Burnham Military Camp in Christchurch, and has spent years working within the Christchurch community for both government and non-government organizations. With a background in child protection at Child, Youth and Family, and now 5 years as a military social worker, his main skill base and experience lies within the development and facilitation of therapeutic group work. Liam is a highly valued member of the leadership team at Burnham which has contributed to the advancement of military social work within the Army. Liam has led the development of a number of programs tailored to the Burnham environment resulting in systemic change. Liam was the recipient of the NZDF Civilian of the Year award in 2020.

Pavel Czirák, Lt Col, PhDr, PhD, is currently serving as an expert advisor for the Ministry of Defense of the Slovak Republic. Lt Col Czirak is originally from Bratislava, Slovak Republic, and since 1995 has worked in various positions in the field of military social counseling and services and as a military sociologist. At the General Staff, he focused on the development of social policy in the area of care for professional soldiers, their families, and war veterans. He currently works in the Ministry of Defense of the Slovak Republic in the field of social analysis and continues to develop care for the quality of life of professional soldiers and their families.

Colin Fallon, B Soc Sc, DASS, CQSW, M Soc Sc (Social work), MA (Mediation Studies), MA Clin Supervision, Dip. Pers Management (FCIPD), Dip. Criminology, Dip. CBT (BABCP Accred), joined the Defence Forces in Ireland as Principal Occupational Social Worker in 2012. His background in social work was initially in probation, followed by social work managerial positions in the West Midlands Police Service, the Irish Postal Service, Medical Social Work, and the National Education and Welfare Board. Colin is also a Social Work Tutor and Workplace Mediation Practice Assessor.

Christopher Flaherty, PhD, is an associate professor at the University of Kentucky College of Social Work. He is director of the College's Military Behavioral Health (MBH) Research Laboratory, as well the Graduate Certificate in MBH. He serves a primary investigator for the US Army/University of Kentucky Master of Social Work Education Collaborative. Dr. Flaherty's research focus is in the area of behavioral health interventions for military and veteran populations. Prior to joining the College of Social Work, Dr. Flaherty served as a Clinical Social Work Officer within the US Air Force.

Keita Franklin, PhD, LCSW, is currently the Chief Clinical Officer of Loyal Source Government Services in the US. Dr. Franklin has a PhD in social work from Virginia Commonwealth University and holds certificates from Harvard Kennedy School Executive Education on "Leading Large Organizational Change" and "Women in Leadership." She has served as a senior executive in both the Department of Defense (DoD) and the Department of Veteran Affairs (VA) where she served as the principal advisor on all matters related to suicide prevention. Dr. Franklin was responsible for leading a multi-discipline team of experts in the advancement of evidence-based prevention practices for over three million active-duty members, 20 million veterans, and their families.

Dexter R. Freeman, MSW, DSW, is an associate professor and assistant director of the Army at the University of Kentucky Master of Social Work Program within the US Army Medical Department Center of Excellence at Fort Sam Houston, Texas. Prior to his current position, he was an assistant professor in the School of Social Work at Texas State University-San Marcos, and a uniformed social work officer for 20 years in the United States Army. Dr. Freeman earned a Master of Social Work (MSW) from the University of Georgia, and a Doctor of Social Work (DSW) from The Catholic University of America.

Nataliia Gusak, PhD, MSW, is currently an Associate Professor in social work at the School of Social Work, National University of Kyiv-Mohyla Academy (Kyiv, Ukraine). Dr. Gusak has 14 years of experience in teaching social work in Ukraine and internationally. In 2021 she launched the first Military Social Work course in Ukraine for master's students at the National University of Kyiv-Mohyla Academy. She was the leader of the Cyber Veterans Analyst Development and Reintegration Program for Ukrainian veterans, supported by CRDF Global in 2021–2022. Dr Gusak is also a member of the International Military Social Work Consortium, established at West Point in 2019.

Jill J. Henderson, PhD, COL, is an associate professor and the US Army-University of Kentucky Master of Social Work Program Director at Fort Sam Houston, Texas, and the Social Work Consultant to the Army Surgeon General. Prior to her current assignment she served as the senior Army RAND Corporation Fellow in Santa Monica California. Her research interests include program evaluation and development, performance in operational settings, and treatment outcomes. Col Henderson received her PhD from the University of Texas-Austin, MSW from University of Illinois-Champaign Urbana, BS in Psychology (minor Social Work) from Illinois State University-Bloomington-Normal, and a Master of Strategic Studies from the US Army War College.

Majella Hickey, BA, MSc, MSW, NQSW, PG Dip Advanced Field Work Practice & Supervision, PG Cert Systemic Practice & Family Therapy, Dip Human Resource Management (Assoc CIPD), Cert Mediation (MII), joined the Defence Forces Occupational Social Work team in 2016. She has a diverse range of experience working for over 20 years with involuntary and voluntary clients in homelessness, addiction, probation, and criminal justice settings. Majella is a Social Work Tutor and Practice Teacher and presented at the 11th International Practice Teaching and Field Education Conference in 2017 and the 8th European Conference on Mental Health in 2019.

Katherine Hillman, MA (Social Work), BSc. (Hons), is a Personnel Recovery Unit Social Worker within the Army Welfare Service in the UK Ministry of Defence. Katherine qualified as a Social Worker in 2015 and worked in children services before joining the Army Welfare Service in January 2020. She enjoys working with domestic abuse survivors, wounded, injured, or sick serving personnel and their families; particularly in the area of brain injuries, completing field army engagement work, and offering advice guidance and training to the wider army. She has received awards for her role in supporting a domestic abuse survivor and a Commanding Officer's coin for her work throughout the pandemic.

Audrey Hudon, Lieutenant-Colonel CD, MSW, BSW is currently serving as the National Practice Leader/Military Occupational Structure Identification Advisor for the Social Work Directorate of Mental Health at the Canadian Forces Health Services Headquarters within the Canadian Armed Forces. LCol Hudon has been the National Practice leader and Occupation Advisor for the Social Work occupation, and has served in the Canadian Armed Forces for 20 years. LCol Hudon holds a bachelor's and a master's degree in Social Work, and a master's certificate in Healthcare Management. She has 27 years of experience in the Social Work Profession and has worked in different areas as a clinician, such as in Policies and Standards and – Program Development to name a few. Having worked in Cyprus, Poland, Spain, Bosnia, and Ukraine, she has gained a considerable experience as a clinician/team leader.

Rob Hulskamp, MSW, is currently serving as the advisor of employer support of the reserves at the Dutch Ministry of Defence. Lieutenant Commander Rob Hulskamp started his military career as a helicopter mechanic in the Royal Dutch Navy. After obtaining his bachelor's degree in social work, he continued his career as an occupational social worker and in 2010 became an occupational social worker for the Dutch armed forces in Afghanistan. In 2016 Rob graduated with a Master of Social Work, during which he researched how to promote and strengthen the social support of family social networks of military personnel. He has continued his career in supervising occupational social workers, and since 2021 has worked as an advisor of employer support of the reserves.

James F. J. Jamieson, LCol (retired), CD-3, MSW, RSW, began his Canadian Forces career as an Infantry Officer, receiving top marks in infantry training (MGen Kitching Trophy winner). He served with The Royal Highland Regt (The Black Watch) and The Royal Canadian Regt prior to his MSW post-graduate training. Within the Canadian Forces Social Work Services, James was privileged to serve across Canada and Europe and specialized in trauma and addictions issues. James served as Director Social Development Services/ Chief of Social Work and as Director Military Family Services and was awarded a Deputy Minister Award for excellence in this latter role.

Nickalous Korbut, MAJ, MS, is the Behavioral Health Capability Manager within the Medical Capability Development and Integration Directorate (MED CDID) at the Futures and Concepts Center in the Army Futures Command of Fort Sam Houston. Major Korbut is an Active-Duty US Army Licensed Clinical Social Worker and Board Certified Diplomate in Clinical Social Work. He currently works at the West Point Military Academy as an Instructor within the Behavioral Sciences and Leadership Department. He is a 2016 honors graduate from the Army-Fayetteville State University Master of Social Work Program. He was recently awarded the 2020 US Army Social Worker of the Year during the COVID-19 response as a Joint Task Force Commander of a behavioral health medical detachment for providing area support across the northeast region from the Javits New York Medical Station.

Monique Kruishaar, MA, is tactical advisor with focus on vital, safe and healthy work at the Ministry of Finance in Utrecht, the Netherlands. Previously she operated in the position of portfolio holder: Care for soldiers and their families before, during and after deployment within the Occupational Social Work Services Centre of the Dutch Ministry of Defence. Monique started her military career in 1996 and deployed to Kosovo in 2000. Between 2002 and 2009 she worked in youth care child protection. After completing her bachelor's degree in social work in 2009, she continued her career within the Ministry of Defense as a non-uniformed occupational social worker. In 2017 she graduated as Master Healthcare & Social Work and conducted research involving the military family and the assistance of the military after deployment, for which she won the Geralien Holsbrink prize. This prize is awarded to social workers who have developed effective interventions in the field of social support.

Richard Alan Leighton, BSc (Social Work), MSc, PGCert, is a Senior Social Worker currently serving in the Department of Community Mental Health within the Defence Medical Services. Previously he was within the Defence Medical Rehabilitation Centre (Stanford Hall) in the UK Ministry of Defence. After a 27-year Service career, Richard gained a 1st class honors social work degree, followed by a master's in child studies and postgrad certificate in counselling. This informed his practice in the children's workforce, initially in child protection and later as a school social worker, delivering therapeutic counselling to children and families. Richard's practice from 2020 included adults' and children's social work, with Soldiers' and Sailors' Families Association (Gibraltar) providing statutory-social work and safeguarding provision and broader welfare support to Gibraltar's military personnel and their families. More recently, Richard's social work and welfare practices support Service personnel on their physical and psychological rehabilitation journey following complex trauma, limb loss, spinal cord injury, or significant mobility issues.

Clare Low, MA (Social Work), BSc (Hons), is currently a Personnel Recovery Unit Social Worker in Army Welfare Service for the UK Ministry of Defence. Clare qualified as a Social Worker in 2010 and worked in various adult teams across different settings before joining the Army Welfare Service in October 2019. Clare enjoys the range of work involved in the role, particularly working with the diversity of service user needs within day-to-day casework whether it is with wounded, injured or sick Serving Personnel, or their family members. She also enjoys supporting welfare teams (Unit or support to Army Welfare Workers) and other aspects of the role such as delivering briefs about the Personnel Recovery Unit Social Worker role to various Unit Welfare teams and to students on the Defence Specialist Welfare Worker course across the Army. She has received awards for her role in supporting other welfare team within Army Welfare Service and for coordinating the UK's chapter within this book.

Emma Mabbutt, PGDip Social Work (Step Up to Social Work), is a Personnel Recovery Unit (PRU) Social Worker in the Army Welfare Service (AWS) of the UK Ministry of Defence. Emma qualified as a Social Worker in 2017 and worked within statutory children and families' teams before joining the AWS in 2019. Coming from a military family herself, Emma enjoys working within this environment and the unique challenges and opportunities this can bring. Emma has been recognized for her support of new staff members, gaining dual social work registration to provide AWS support in England and Wales, updating AWS policy, and delivering PRU Social Work role briefings and adult safeguarding training. Emma's greatest achievements come from positive impacts she can have for the service users she works with.

Hannu Maijanen, Lic Soc Sc, Captain (in reserve), is a current Social Manager in the Finnish Defence Forces. Hannu completed 11 months of military service in 1985, and has worked in the Defense Forces since 1998. He has studied Social Policy at the University of Lapland (1986–1992) and completed the Licentiate Degree in Social Sciences in 1997. In his current role as a Social Manager in the Defence Command, he is responsible for promoting non-discrimination and gender equality, for both conscripts and salaried personnel, and for developing conditions of service for conscripts.

James A. Martin, PhD, ACSW, LICSW (Retired), Colonel, US Army (Retired), is a Professor Emeritus at Bryn Mawr College. Jim is a retired Clinical Social Worker with 50 years of social work practice, and a recognized leader in the area of military family services. A retired Colonel, Jim's 26-year US Army career included clinical, research, senior management (command) and policy assignments. He was the senior Social Worker in the Persian Gulf during the First Gulf War. Jim was the recipient of the 2014 University of Pittsburgh School of Social Work Distinguished Alumni Award, and the 2015 Distinguished Alumni Award from Boston College School of Social Work. Jim was named a Social Work Pioneer by NASW Foundation in 2016.

Henry G. Matheson, Lieutenant-Colonel (Retired), CD, MSW, enrolled in the Canadian Armed Forces as a social work officer after several years of social work practice with the Province of Nova Scotia. Following enrollment, he provided clinical social work services to air force bases across Canada. He subsequently served as the senior social work officer to Air, Maritime, and Canadian Forces Europe Command Surgeons. In 2001, he undertook the position of National Social Work Practice Leader and Social Work Advisor to the Surgeon General. In this capacity, he also served as the social work advisor in the restructuring of the Canadian Armed Forces Mental Health Services.

Tracy Milward, Dip. Higher Education in Social Work/Applied Social Services UK, Registered Social Worker, is the New Zealand Defence Force (NZDF) Social Worker at Waiouru Military Camp located in the central North Island of New Zealand. She has worked in a range of practice settings both in the UK and New Zealand in disabilities, child protection, corrections, children/families, and military. She is passionate about enhancing the wellbeing of those she works with, along with their whanau (families), by working in a holistic manner. Tracy is a key member of the health team in Waiouru where the primary focus is supporting recruits to complete their initial training. Tracy is also involved in providing social work advice for community agencies due to the isolated geographical location of the camp.

Kazushige Nakano, Master of Social Welfare, is an Associate Professor at Kogakkan University. In January 2022, he published "Basic research on military social work" in Japan.

Antonia Nicholson, BA (Psychology), M App SW, Registered Social Worker, is the National Manager Social Services for the New Zealand Defence Force (NZDF). She received the Chief of Defence Force Commendation in 2022 for work establishing social work capability for all of NZDF. She has worked in a range of practice settings, such as military, health, community support, and statutory welfare. She is passionate about social work services that are holistic and inclusive of whānau (family) and applying a prevention and early intervention framework. She is interested in maturing military social work services, and utilizing research and program development within a complex organization. She feels very privileged to champion military social work in the NZDF and Aotearoa New Zealand with a particular focus on culturally appropriate support. Toni was the recipient of the John Fry Memorial Supreme Award in 2021 for Quality and Innovation in social work.

Craig Richard Pearce, BSc (hons) Social Work 1st Class Honours, is a Social Worker and Casework Manager in Royal Navy Family and People Support within the UK Ministry of Defense. Craig graduated from the University of Portsmouth in 2011, beginning his career as a front-line child protection social worker, and after this, he worked for Shared Lives, an adult placement scheme for vulnerable and disabled adults. Craig began work for the Royal Navy as a social worker in 2015, progressing to the position of Advanced Social Worker in 2017, and later progressing to Casework Manager.

Marie Pichette, MSW, RSW, is a Staff Officer for Social Work Program Development, in the Department of National Defence in Canada. Marie has been employed with the Department of National Defence (DND) since 2000. Over the past 22 years she has been employed in multiple positions with DND including providing clinical services to members of the Canadian Armed Forces (CAF) and their family, Interim Program Manager for the General Mental Health Program at the Ottawa, Ontario clinic, and her current position as the first civilian position within the DND/CAF Professional-Technical network for Social Work. In 2015, she received the Award for Excellence from the Canadian Forces Surgeon General.

Cynthia Apile Pitse, Brigadier General, PhD, MA, is the Director of Social Work in the South African National Defence Force. Amongst her many qualifications, she holds a higher Education Diploma (Cum Laude) at the University of South Africa (UNISA), a Master of Arts (MA) in Social Work Management (Cum Laude) at the University of Pretoria (UP), and a PhD in Social Work in 2010. In her military career she has held a variety of posts from being a unit social worker, social work supervisor, health service manager prior to being appointed Director Senior Staff Officer of Policy and Planning.

Heinrich H. Potgieter, Lt. Col., MA, BA, is the head of the Social Work Research and Development Department at the Military Psychological Institute in South Africa. He holds a BA Social Work and an MA Social Work (Occupational Social Work). During his military career he has been a social worker at a variety of military units. He has deployed in that capacity on several United Nations peacekeeping missions on the African continent.

René J. Robichaux, PhD, LCSW, was commissioned as a social work officer in the US Army Medical Service Corps in 1979. His doctoral work was completed at The Catholic University of America. He retired in 2004 from uniformed service at the rank of Colonel. In 2005, he returned to the Army Medical Command as the civilian program manager for all Social Work Programs, to include the Family Advocacy Clinical Program. He retired from federal service at the start of 2017. His active-duty assignments included three large medical centers, extensive teaching assignments, senior command assignments, and research. In 2015, he was recognized as a Social Work Pioneer, by the National Association of Social Workers, at a ceremony in Washington, D.C.

Pauline Diane Bridgette Ross, CQSW, BSc, is a Specialist Senior Social Worker with the Complex Trauma department in the Defence Medical Rehabilitation Centre (Stanford Hall), within the UK Ministry of Defence. Pauline has worked in health settings for over 20 years as a frontline hospital social worker and in a managerial development position. She has been at DMRC Stanford Hall for over 3 years, gaining experience in neurology and is currently working in the Complex Trauma department. In this specialist field, Pauline enjoys developing communication and interaction with military personnel, their families, and working in partnership with other health professionals to support patients with name recognition, memory recall and retention, and use of IT equipment to promote contact with family members between face-to-face visits.

Kari Seppänen, M Soc Sc, Lieutenant Colonel (in reserve), is the Head of Social Welfare Affairs in the Finnish Defence Forces. Kari Seppänen has worked in the Finnish Defence Forces as a Social Manager in the Eastern Command from 1995 to 2007, as the Head of Social Welfare Affairs in the Army Command in 2008–2013, and since 2014 he has worked as the Head of Social Welfare Affairs in the Finnish Defence Forces in the Defence Command. His main task is to lead the Social Affairs Sector and, particularly, the military social workers in the garrisons. He has also served as a CIMIC officer in the UNIFIL operation in Southern Lebanon in 2013.

Philip Siebler, PhD (Social Work), Research Fellow – Military Families, The Bouverie Centre, La Trobe University, Mental Health Social Worker, had a long career with the Australian Department of Defence as a social worker in a range of settings encompassing military family practice, mental health, and as head of the military family research program which he established. His main research interests include the health and wellbeing of military families, military children and their quality of life, and the protective role of the family in preventing suicide of military personnel.

Kengo Tanaka, PhD, is a Professor at St. Catherine University, Japan where he teaches social work. His thesis was titled "A Study on Military Social Work in the United States: The Significance of Military Social Work and the Professional Development of Military Social Workers." He has presented several papers and a conference report on this topic. Currently, his research focuses on the development of a military social work system based on Japan's Self Defense Force's current situation and a Japanese version of the social work training program.

Adrian D. van Breda, PhD (Social Work), is the Head of the Department of Social Work and Community Development at the University of Johannesburg, South Africa. Adrian worked as a military social worker for 17 years, leaving with the rank of Lieutenant Colonel to join academia. He first worked as a military social worker with the South African Navy, doing comprehensive social work practice as well as research, program design and scale development, and validation on family and organizational resilience. He then moved into military social work and health research, focused on HIV Monitoring & Evaluation, family violence, gender mainstreaming, and theory building on military social work. His current work centers on youth resilience.

Jeffrey S. Yarvis, Colonel (ret), PhD, MSW, MSS, MEd, MSS, LCSW, BCD, ACSW, is Senior Professor of Practice at Tulane University School of Social Work. He is a 35-year US veteran leader in student/soldier affairs, executive medicine, clinician, life-long educator and well-published social work and military scholar in the field of psychological trauma. He was named a 2021 NASW Social Work Pioneer, Diversity MBA's Top 50 Executives Under 50, Uniformed Social Worker of the Year, US Army Social Worker of the Year, Mental Health Professional of the Year, Military Alpha Designator as a Professor & Military Scholar in Social Work, the Bronze Star Medal and Combat Action Badge, and Order of Military Medical Merit Board Certified in Clinical Social Work and Fellow of the APA.

Polly Yeung, BA, MSW(Applied), PhD, is an Associate Professor in the School of Social Work at Massey University, New Zealand. Her research is in ageing, disability, and quality of life.

Limor Zaks Zitronblat is a PhD candidate in the Gender Studies Department and a Lecturer in the Social Work Department at Bar Ilan University Israel. Limor formerly served as a Mental Health Officer (MHO) for the Israeli Defense Forces (IDF) for 25 years in a variety of roles and retired as Head of the clinical unit for military personnel and their families. She continues to serve as a MHO in the reserve forces as a mentor of MHO's. Her research focuses on different aspects of mutual adjustment among couples of combat commanders in the IDF, and she is also associated with the Clinic for Cognitive Behavioral Conjoint Therapy for PTSD.

Chapter 1
Developing Global Collaboration in Military Social Work

Mary Ann Forgey and Karen Green-Hurdle

1.1 Introduction

The broadest and most inclusive conceptualization of the field of Military Social Work (MilSW) encompasses practice with military service members, veterans, and their families (Martin et al. 2017). This book focuses on a sub-category of MilSW, specifically, *social workers who work with military service members and their families and are employed by their country's defense organization* (e.g., Department of Defense or Defense Ministry) in either a uniformed or civilian capacity. These military social workers provide a range of individual, family, and organizational level interventions to active-duty service members and their family members in support of military personnel's functioning within the military work environment and address stressors that may adversely impact the serving members' capacity to support the mission of their country's defense system.

While each nation's military mission may vary, in broad terms the key functions include protecting and defending the nation and its interests through the use of controlled force, providing support to other nations' security activities, and responding to humanitarian crises or natural disasters. In carrying out these functions in relation to their country's military mission, service members and their families may experience some common challenges (Cozza and Lerner 2013). These challenges may be associated with difficulties adjusting to military culture and the hierarchical system that requires strict discipline and uniformity (Soeters et al. 2006); stressors

M. A. Forgey (✉)
Graduate School of Social Service, Fordham University, New York, NY, USA
e-mail: forgey@fordham.edu

K. Green-Hurdle (✉)
Department of Veterans Affairs, Open Arms Veterans and Families Counselling (North Queensland), Townsville, QLD, Australia
e-mail: greenhurdle@gmail.com

© Springer Nature Switzerland AG 2023
M. A. Forgey, K. Green-Hurdle (eds.), *Military Social Work Around the Globe*,
Military and Veterans Studies, https://doi.org/10.1007/978-3-031-14482-0_1

associated with separation from loved ones due to deployments, training activities, and military exercises; and the multi-system impacts of physical, psychological, or emotional injuries that may be incurred when performing military duties (e.g., Williamson et al. 2019). At the completion of their military service, the process of transitioning to civilian status (and integrating into the community) can also pose significant difficulties for service members and their families (Pedlar et al. 2019; Elinsky et al. 2017). These common challenges are shared by many military service members and their families across the world. Military social workers who work with military members and their families play a critical role in responding to these and other systemic issues, and a more comprehensive understanding of this sub-category of MilSW practice across the globe is needed.

Thus, the aim of this book is to develop a more global understanding of the practice similarities and differences among military social workers who are employed by their country's defense organization, including the forms of practice that are unique and perhaps transportable. We hope by focusing on this specific subset of military social workers, this book will contribute to the development of the knowledge base about this specialized field of social work practice from an international perspective and that this knowledge will enrich the ability of military social workers worldwide to respond effectively to the challenges facing military service members and their families.

In focusing on MilSW with service members and their families across the globe, it is also not the intention of this book to elevate this role over the equally important subset of military social workers who work primarily with former military members (commonly referred to as veterans) and their families. The authors highlight that this latter cohort of military social workers provides a range of critical services to support the functioning of former military service members and their families within the civilian world. The decision to focus on MilSW with active-duty personnel (or as some chapter authors refer to this cohort as "current serving personnel") was due to the recognition of what is unique about this type of practice within the field of MilSW, and the belief that a separate focus on this sub-category would consequentially enrich understanding of MilSW practice as a whole.

How this international MilSW project evolved from an abstract idea to an edited book involving 14 contributing countries will now be described. The key milestones along this journey will be reviewed and will include the initial exploratory study, the presentations in Rome, Paris, Dublin, the United States (US), and Australia, and the hosting of the first inaugural international MilSW conference at West Point where the idea for this book was first conceived.

1.2   The Need for an International Perspective of Military Social Work

The most critical factor in the development of this book was the recognition of the need for an international perspective of MilSW. This recognition developed over a period of time for each of the co-editors and was fueled by a multitude of events and experiences. Below are our individual reflections on how we each came to recognize the need for a broader international understanding of MilSW, and what led to our initial meeting in 2014, where we made a commitment to jointly pursue this interest together.

Karen: Due to significant family ties with the military, my interest in supporting Australian Defence Force personnel and their families has been longstanding. As a military partner for over two decades, our family had postings around Australia in both High Readiness Deployable Force Units and Corps-specific training Units in medium to large Defence Barracks environments. Raising a family and managing paid employment whilst my husband was absent from home due to multiple international deployments and service commitments provided me with key insights into the unique challenges and opportunities of the military lifestyle. Postings to new places afforded me exceptional opportunities to work in a variety of social work roles within military-specific support agencies, thus fueling my passion for working with this population. My curiosity about global MilSW was ignited after discovering James Daley's book titled, *"Social Work Practice in the Military"* (Daley 1999), and although the content focused on US MilSW practice, it opened my eyes to an international perspective, and with that, the hope for the potential development opportunities for the specialist field of practice in Australia. In 2008, at the invitation of the Canadian Forces Surgeon General, I travelled to Toronto to present on the scope of Australian Defence social work practice at the inaugural summit in recognition of the sacrifice and service of Canadian military families. Participating in this forum further heightened my interest in multi-country comparisons and the potential for collaboration to increase knowledge about MilSW roles and scope of practice. A series of fortunate events and incidental connections in 2014 during my 8-week scholarship at New York's Mount Sinai Hospital (Icahn School of Medicine) for the *"Enhancement of Social Work Leadership in Health Care Scholarship"* led me to meet with Professor Mary Ann Forgey at the Fordham University in my final week in New York.

Mary Ann: Prior to joining the faculty at Fordham University in 1993, I practiced as a US Department of Defense civilian-military social worker at a US military installation in Wiesbaden, Germany, initially serving as the Family Advocacy Coordinator and then as the Army Community Services Director. This experience left me with a profound respect for our military service members and their families and a deep appreciation for the military social work role. Throughout my career at Fordham, as a result of this experience, I have felt a passion to share knowledge about the strengths and challenges of military life with my students and colleagues and to increase understanding about military social work practice and education through my research. Initially, however, my focus in these areas was completely centered on the US military. It was not until an experience in 2005, while on a Fulbright Scholarship in Dublin, Ireland, that my perspective about military social work broadened. An Irish faculty member, upon learning of my military social work background, recommended that I meet the head social worker for the Irish military. I remember how surprised I was at that moment to learn that there were military social workers in Ireland. Within days, I was on a bus to meet the head Irish military social worker and discuss MilSW similarities and differences. And so, it was really this experience that first sparked my interest in an international perspective and led me to wonder, *"If Ireland has military social workers, what other countries have them and what does their practice look like?"* While the desire to explore this question stayed with me, it was not until my fortunate encounter with Karen Green-Hurdle in 2014, that this question began to be more formally pursued.

During our first meeting, we talked for several hours about what we knew about the role of military social workers in Australia, US, Ireland, Canada, South Africa, and Finland. We also found ourselves consistently asking, *"What other countries have military social workers?,"* and *"How would the roles be similar and different?"* At the conclusion of this meeting, our mutual passion and curiosity for the subject was apparent, and we decided to pursue our interests in learning more about what other countries were doing in relation to MilSW. Practically speaking, we needed to find a way to work together on this topic and to find resources that would assist in our exploration.

1.3   From an Idea to a Concrete Reality

In the year following this remarkable and pivotal meeting, our discussions continued via email and phone calls. Fortuitously, Karen applied for and was granted a 3-month *"Commonwealth Endeavour Executive Fellowship"* to study in New York again in early 2016, and Mary Ann arranged to sponsor her at Fordham University for the duration of the award. During that same year, Mary Ann successfully applied for an internal Fordham research grant that funded a team of doctoral and masters level students to assist with the tasks involved in this exploratory international MilSW research project titled, *"Toward a More Global Understanding of Military Social Work Practice."*[1]

Our shared MilSW interest, the excitement that collaborative academic and practitioner partnerships bring to the mix, along with being able to work together in the same city with a small and dedicated research team, provided the opportunity for us to circle back to the fundamental questions that we pondered during our first meeting. It was in this context that we developed a comprehensive and multi-faceted research strategy that would assist us to learn more about what international MilSW practice may encapsulate.

---

[1] The members of the initial IMilSW research team included Erica Ponteen and Lashawn Smith (Doctoral Research Assistants) and Yafei Cai, Kundong He, Donald Rooks and Brett Sereysky (MSW research assistants).

1.3.1 Process of Identifying Countries with Military Social Work (MilSW)

The identification of the countries that had MilSW in answer to the first research question of *"What countries have social workers working within their defense organizations?"* initially appeared to be deceptively straightforward; however, the process of arriving at a conclusive answer proved to be far more complex. As a starting point, we began to answer this question by first identifying the countries that had trained social work professionals. This was accomplished by obtaining a list of the countries with membership to the International Association of Schools of Social Work (IASSW) as published on their website in January 2016. At that time, 75 countries were listed, and the research team then attempted to contact each country's national social work association via email to inquire about the existence of the MilSW role in their country. If the association was able to affirm that MilSW existed within their country, the name of a subject matter expert was also requested.

If a country did not have an identified national social work organization, or if no response was received from the organization, a subsequent email was then sent to the IASSW representative(s) for that country inquiring as to their knowledge about the status of MilSW in their respective country. Where possible, the IASSW representative would provide contact information for a person(s) at a relevant agency who would have expert knowledge about the role, if it existed, and the research team would make contact with the newly identified person or agency.

In addition to this strategy, a systematic literature search was simultaneously conducted to further identify what countries, irrespective of their IASSW membership, had published literature about MilSW practice. As part of this inquiry, the following databases were searched: Soc Index, Psych INFO, Psych ARTICLES, Academic Search Complete, and Military and Government Collection using the keywords: military social work, military social work practice, international military social work, uniformed social worker, and civilian social worker. In addition, if a country had a specialized social work journal, that journal was also searched using these same keywords.

Through the use of these initial strategies, 25 countries were confirmed to employ social work professionals in civilian and/or uniformed roles within their country's military. Another 22 countries were confirmed as not having any formalized MilSW role within their military, and the MilSW status remained unknown for 28 of the countries investigated. For those countries with an "unknown" status, in addition to the lack of any confirmation from the social work organizations as to the existence of MilSW, no specific MilSW literature was able to be found when this phase of the project ended.

1.3.2 Highlights from the Initial 2016–2017 IMilSW Literature Search

In the initial literature search conducted for the purpose of identifying countries that had the military social work described above, only one article (Daley 2003) was found that described the role of social workers who work directly with military service members and their families in three different countries; US, Finland, and South Africa. In this article, as well as an editorial published several years later, Daley (2006) identified the need for more of an international comparative analysis of MilSW:

> Collation of information and research on Military Social Work development in different countries is needed. Extensive discussion of common military social work technologies is needed to differentiate between country-unique programs and transportable programs useful internationally (Daley 2003, p. 446).

Although no comprehensive cross-country comparative articles other than Daley (2003) or books were found at that time, a growing literature was identified that described MilSW practices within certain countries that had military social work. The majority of the literature found was US based and focused solely on MilSW within the US.

Included in the literature found about US MilSW were four books that describe many facets of US-based MilSW practice. The first book, *Social Work Practice in the Military* (Daley 1999), provides information on the history of MilSW within each of the US military branches and the various roles played by uniformed and civilian military social workers. At the conclusion of this edited text on US military practice, Daley also highlights the need for a more international understanding of military social work. The *Handbook of Military Social Work* (Rubin et al. 2013) builds upon this earlier work with an emphasis on the knowledge and skills currently needed by US military social workers to deal with the problems faced by US service members, veterans, and their families. The text, *Social Work with Military Populations* (Scott et al. 2016), also addresses the current support needs of US service members, veterans, and their families. The social work response to the mental health needs of returning US service members and veterans from combat is the focus of the text, *Advances in Social Work Practice with the Military* (Beder 2012).

Numerous peer-reviewed articles specifically related to MilSW within the US military were also found in this initial literature search, dating as far back as the mid-1940s, with the most productive period occurring between 2008 and 2015. Some of the earlier published peer-reviewed articles found about the MilSW role include Beck 1944; Michaels et al. 1946; Segal 1945; Towle 1950; West et al. 1993.

The majority of the US military social work articles focused on military social work education and training needs: (e.g., Canfield and Weiss 2015; Daley et al. 2015; Daley 1999; DuMars et al. 2015; Esqueda et al. 2014; Forgey and Young 2014; Freeman and Bicknell 2008; Howard 2013; Rishel and Hartnett 2015; Simmons and DeCoster 2007; Smith-Osborne 2015; Whitworth et al. 2012; Williams-Gray 2016; Wooten 2015). Other topics addressed within the US military social work literature include the roles of military social workers within the US military (e.g., Applewhite et al. 1995; Brand and Weiss 2015; Beder 2011; Hoffler et al. 2014; Michaels et al. 1946; Newell 2012; Savitsky et al. 2009; Towle 1950), ethical challenges (e.g., Olson 2014; Simmons and Rycraft 2010), social work with military family issues (e.g., Forgey et al. 2013; Forgey et al. 2011; Kotrla and Dyer 2008; Lowe et al. 2012; Ross and DeVoe 2014; Wichlacz et al. 1975; Wolf et al. 2017), and the importance of military cultural understanding to effective military social work practice (e.g., Hall 2011; Yarvis 2011). Specific military social work practice issues have also been addressed in the literature in relation to deployment-related stressors (e.g., Marquez 2012; Strong et al. 2014; Wooten 2013; Yarvis 2011), substance abuse (e.g., Skidmore and Roy 2011), LGBTQ service members (e.g., Alford and Lee 2016; Pelts et al. 2014), and social worker secondary traumatic stress (Hall 2009).

A much smaller but growing amount of literature was found about MilSW in other countries besides the US in relation to the military social work role, military family issues, and specific issues for practice, some of whom were not IASSW member countries. Interestingly, compared to the extensive literature found in the US, limited information was found specifically in relation to MilSW education in other countries.

To briefly summarize the literature found from countries outside the US, at least one article describing the role of military social workers was found for each of the following countries: Australia (Hughes 2006); Canada (Blackburn 2015); Russia (Surkova 2010); South Africa (Kruger and Van Breda 2001; Van Breda 2012); Taiwan (Jen der Pan et al. 2008); and Zimbabwe (Runesu 2016). Articles were also found that addressed specific practice issues in relation to service members' spouses, e.g., Canada (Sherwood 2009), United Kingdom (Williamson 2011), and issues in relation to the children of service members, e.g., Australia (Siebler and Goddard 2014).

The literature identified and briefly described above not only informed the process of identifying countries that had military social workers or had an interest in developing them, but it also provided valuable insight into the kinds of military social work issues that countries were grappling with and that needed to be more uniformly understood from an international perspective.

Since this initial literature search, additional MilSW literature has been systematically identified with the assistance of subsequent Fordham IMilSW research team members,[2] resulting in an even more comprehensive and up-to-date understanding of the IMilSW knowledge base and its status in several other countries, including Brazil (Silva 2015); China (Yantao and Fang 2017; Yantao 2016); Czech Republic (Laštovková and Brnula 2017); Japan (Nakano and Morikubo 2017); Saudi Arabia (Al-Qahtani 2017); Spain (Martinez-Borrego 2019); Switzerland (Schmid 2019); Turkey (Sahin and Sakarya 2017; Sakarya and Şahin 2019); and Ukraine (Semigina

---

[2]The members of the subsequent IMilSW research team who contributed to the updating of the IMilSW literature included Jonathan Marsh (Doctoral Research Assistant) and Shenae Osborn (MSW research assistant).

and Gusak 2015). As a result of this subsequent literature search, MilSW was able to be confirmed in four additional countries including Brazil, Czech Republic, Spain, and Switzerland. A list of the countries for which the existence of MilSW has been confirmed can be found in Table 1.1. The results of the cumulative IMilSW literature search up to 2019 have also been compiled in an International MilSW bibliography organized by country (Marsh et al. 2022). A narrative review of this IMilSW literature is also in progress.

It is also important to highlight that the edited book titled *"Military Social Work"* has recently been published in Turkey (in Turkish language only) in 2022. One of the co-editors, Hakan Sakaraya, is a member of the International Military Social Work Consortium, and his book makes a significant contribution to the international MilSW literature.

Table 1.1 Countries confirmed to have Military Social Work

Confirmed to have MilSW (From 2016 to 2017 identification strategies including initial literature search)	Confirmed to have MilSW (Identified from subsequent literature search)
[a]Australia	Brazil
Bulgaria	Czech Republic
[a]Canada	Spain
[a]Denmark	Switzerland
[a]Finland	
Germany	
[a]Ireland	
[a]Israel	
Jordan	
[a]The Netherlands	
[a]New Zealand	
Nigeria	
Romania	
Russia	
Saudi Arabia	
Singapore	
Slovenia	
South Korea	
[a]South Africa	
Taiwan	
Trinidad & Tobago	
Turkey	
[a]United Kingdom	
[a]United States	
Zimbabwe	

[a]Countries that contributed a chapter in this book

1.3.3   Identifying Subject Matter Experts (SME)

Of the 25 countries that were confirmed to have MilSW in 2016/2017, at least one Subject Matter Expert (hereafter referred to as SME) from each country was able to be identified. Each of these potential SMEs were contacted and invited to participate in an interview to virtually share information about MilSW practice within their country. Subsequently, SMEs from 15 countries (Australia, Canada, Denmark, Finland, Germany, Ireland, Israel, the Netherlands, New Zealand, South Africa, Taiwan, Trinidad and Tobago, Turkey, United Kingdom, and the US) agreed to be interviewed about the scope of MilSW practice in their country. For various reasons, the following countries where a MilSW role was confirmed to exist, either through confirmation from the social work professional organization or through the literature, did not participate in the interview process: Turkey, Bulgaria, Brazil, Jordan, Nigeria, Romania, Russia, Saudi Arabia, Singapore, Slovenia, Spain, South Korea, and Zimbabwe.

Social work representatives from Italy, Japan, and Ukraine, three of the countries that were confirmed not to have MilSW in their country, also expressed interest in the development of this role in their country or were making efforts to develop it. Similarly, a social work professional from Slovakia also indicated that a MilSW role was currently under development within their military.

1.4   The Exploratory Interviews

Between 2017 and 2018, interviews with identified SMEs were conducted by the co-editors via phone or skype with administrative assistance from the student research team. The purpose of the interviews was to gain a preliminary understanding of the MilSW practices within each country and to explore if there was interest in having a country's representative(s) attend an international forum where each country's approach to MilSW practice could be more fully shared and discussed.

The main areas of inquiry addressed during each interview included the following:

- History and developmental milestones of MilSW
- Organizational structure and roles of uniformed and/or civilian social workers
- MilSW education
- Within-country inter-professional relationships
- Ethical issues
- Cross-country professional social work relationships
- Strengths, challenges, and future directions

1.4.1 Insights Gained from the Exploratory Interviews with Subject Matter Experts

The interviews provided preliminary information and insights into the overall landscape of MilSW within the 15 countries, including the key developmental milestones, the relative size of the MilSW staff, their civilian or uniformed status, the roles undertaken, and the settings in which they worked. Some insights emerged from these interviews about some of the major similarities and differences, particularly in relation to the scope of practice, ethical dilemmas, and the interface between social work practice with active-duty military and veterans.

In terms of the scope of practice, the interviews revealed that the way and extent to which military social workers practiced on each level appeared to be somewhat dependent on the military status (e.g., uniformed or civilian), and the setting in which practice occurred. For example, those whose practice setting was located within the military unit, regardless of their unformed or civilian status, appeared to be practicing quite differently and in a more multi-level way than those uniformed and civilian military social workers whose practice was located in more clinical types of settings (e.g., mental health clinic). The interviews also revealed many commonalities in relation to the types of ethical dilemmas encountered by both civilian and military social workers. The way and extent to which military social workers within a defense organization assisted active-duty service members in their transition to civilian life also appeared to be a major practice difference among the countries.

As a result of these interviews, an enormous amount of valuable and previously untapped international content was obtained, and it became apparent that a more in-depth understanding of each country's MilSW practice approach would have international significance to this specialized field of practice. While it was our initial intention to publish what we had learned from these preliminary interviews, we were humbled by the complexity of what we were learning and realized that the more prudent and respectful strategy that would yield the most accurate descriptions would be to develop a pathway(s) for each country to directly share their approach to MilSW practice.

Fortunately, all of the SMEs interviewed unanimously expressed their enthusiastic interest to attend an international forum where they would have the opportunity to meet their international colleagues and learn from each other.

Another strategy that we utilized to share our emerging findings and garner interest in international military social work was to present at conferences around the globe. These included:

- 2018 International Association of Social Work Schools (IASSW) *Towards a More Global Understanding of Military Social Work Practice* (July). Dublin, Ireland.
- 2017 Australasian Military Medicine Association Conference. *A Multi-National Comparative Analysis of International Military Social Work.* (October). Brisbane, Australia.

- 2017 European Association of Schools of Social Work International Conference. *"Toward a more global understanding of Military Social Work practice"* (June). Paris, France.

In addition, in 2017, we were invited to Rome, Italy, to present to the Italian National Council of Social Work and the National Federation of Social Work at a specially conducted Military Social Work Practice Forum, where we presented the emerging findings to practitioners and senior military personnel.

1.5 Inaugural International Military Social Work (IMilSW) Conference at West Point, NY. April 24–26, 2019

Given the interest expressed by the SMEs, funding for an international MilSW conference was pursued and successfully secured with a grant from the International Association of Schools of Social Work (IASSW) and sponsorships from Fordham University and the University of Alabama.

Thirty invited subject matter experts in MilSW from 16 countries attended the inaugural round table conference at the Thayer Hotel located at the internationally renowned West Point Military Academy in New York, from April 24 to 26, 2019 (IMilSW Consortium 2019). The countries that attended the conference were: Australia, Canada, Denmark, Finland, Germany, Ireland, Israel, Italy, Japan, the Netherlands, New Zealand, South Africa, Trinidad and Tobago, Ukraine, and the United States of America.

The conference provided a range of learning and development benefits for the delegates. It began with a brief presentation of the information and insights gained from the preliminary interviews about the range of social work roles, the ethical tensions experienced, and the extent to which unformed and civilian social workers address the needs of service members as they transition from active duty to civilian status. Three major questions that evolved from the interviews were posed to the delegates for discussion:

1. In what ways does the military social work practice setting (e.g., clinic or military unit, etc.) influence the direct and indirect SW roles (uniformed and civilian) and approach to practice?
2. How do ethical tensions get managed by military social workers in your country?
3. Thinking about the needs of military service members and their families as they transition to civilian life, how can military social work models of practice better support the transition from military service to civilian life?

Delegates commented that discussions with international counterparts were helpful in differentiating the role of MilSW from other helping professionals. Discussions also highlighted the varying levels of importance (or focus) that countries had placed on delivering macro, mezzo, and micro levels of social work practice. For example, some countries were identified to be working within a more clinical model of practice due to a perceived increased medicalization of care, while others had a more clearly defined occupational social work model of practice. In addition, delegates also compared how systems of care relevant to supporting transition from military to civilian life varied greatly across countries.

Prof. Adrian van Breda, from the University of Johannesburg, was invited to give the keynote address based on what the co-editors learned from his interview and publications about the theoretical model of occupational MilSW developed in South Africa (IMilSW Consortium 2019). The keynote address titled "*Military social work developments in South Africa: Practice theory, resilience, and research*" described the occupational social work practice model and Dr. van Breda's research and practice experience while serving as a uniformed military social worker in South Africa. Following the keynote address, participants were broken into small groups and asked to reflect on how their approach to MilSW practice is similar or different from the occupational social work model used in South Africa.

1.5.1 International MilSW Consortium Formed (2019)

During the structured discussion about challenges and future directions, a consensus was reached among conference delegates that it would be essential to have dialogue continue on a regular basis in order to refine and implement the recommendations from the conference around practice sharing, research development, and education initiatives. Thus, the group agreed on a plan to continue to meet virtually every 3 months.

Since the consortium was formed in 2019, the group has worked on some of the conference recommendations, including the refinement of its purpose, aims, and objectives; the development of a prototype for a web page; and the publication of a newsletter with updates from countries on how MilSW has been involved with responses to recent natural disasters, COVID, and racial justice issues. Preliminary planning has also begun for a series of international MilSW webinars in which the work of the consortium will be highlighted and each country's MilSW practice approach showcased.

Since the IMilSW conference at West Point, the co-editors also delivered the following presentations in Australia and the US about the development of International Military Social Work:

- 2019 Australian Association of Social Workers Conference. "*Social Work with military and veteran communities: Global research, emerging evidence and campaigning for specialist recognition.*" (November) Adelaide, Australia.
- 2020 Military Social Work & Behavioral Health Conference. "*International Military Social Work: The Development of a Global Partnership*" (July). Virtual Austin, Texas, US.

A joint panel presentation by IMilSW Consortium participants about the development and activities of the Consortium was also planned for the IASSW conference in Rimini, Italy in July 2020, but was cancelled due to the pandemic.

The idea for a publication of an edited book on International Military Social Work with chapters contributed by representatives from each country was also discussed as a recommendation during the conference and received strong support. Following the IMilSW conference, Dr. David Albright, the editor of the Springer Series on Military and Veteran Studies and a participant at the conference, extended an invitation to the co-editors to submit a book proposal for an edited book on international military social work to Springer Publishing. As part of the proposal process, the conference participants were asked to formally commit to contributing a chapter about MilSW in their country. Fortunately, almost all of the countries who participated in the conference signed on to the book project. In an effort to develop or further strengthen the partnership between practitioners and academic scholars in military social work within each country, lead chapter authors were encouraged to form these partnerships in the writing of their chapters.

1.6   Conclusion

The path to the publication of this international book on MilSW was a very long and winding one, with rich learnings along the way. As co-editors, we are convinced that it would not have come to fruition without the opportunity to form relationships with our international colleagues that were kindled during the interview process and then strengthened by active engagement and face-to-face participation at the West Point conference. These relationships have continued to grow and have been maintained through the ongoing virtual meetings and activities of the Consortium. While differences clearly exist in how each country approaches MilSW, as the chapters of this book will illustrate, all of the contributors share a common goal of creating more of a voice for social work through the documentation of what military social workers do and why the work is important to those we serve and to our profession.

The co-editors and chapter authors anticipate that this book will be of great interest to current and former military social workers as well as social work students and faculty around the globe. We anticipate that our multi-disciplinary colleagues, both civilian and uniformed, will gain insights into the untapped possibilities of MilSW. We also hope that the process used to identify countries with MilSW and to then engage international MilSW practitioners and academics in dialogue through individual interviews, the West Point conference, and the IMilSW Consortium can serve as a model for social work professionals and other disciplines interested in developing a more international perspective in their area of specialization.

Furthermore, the fundamental understanding of MilSW provided in this book creates a platform to strengthen and legitimize the profile of this specialist field of practice in countries where MilSW remains misunderstood or under-valued. As part of this process, we anticipate that the unique perspectives that social work can bring will be re-visioned to ensure that social work can be utilized to its full potential.

We encourage social work degree programs around the world to consider the possibilities of developing a curriculum that is inclusive of the unique challenges and opportunities that military personnel and their families face and to be able to position the learning in the international context.

Ultimately, we are optimistic that a better understanding of the global position of MilSW will provide opportunities for practitioners and academics in multi-disciplinary fields and in different countries to connect, collaborate, and co-design research projects in the MilSW arena as well as develop innovative programs and services for the active-duty personnel and their families.

References

Alford B, Lee SJ (2016) Toward complete inclusion: Lesbian, gay, bisexual, and transgender military service members after repeal of don't ask, don't tell. Soc Work 61(3):257–265. https://doi.org/10.1093/sw/sww033

Al-Qahtani MBA (2017) Professional requirements for applying social service in the military field. Master's Thesis, Naif Arab University for Security Sciences, College of Social Sciences, Department of Psychology. http://repository.nauss.edu.sa/123456789/64850

Applewhite LW, BrintzenhofeSzoc K, Hamlin ER II, Timberlake EM (1995) Clinical social work practice in the US Army: an update. Mil Med 160(6):283–288. PMID: 7659224. https://doi.org/10.1093/milmed/160.6.283

Beck BM (1944) The military social worker. Soc Serv Rev 18(4):461–468. https://www.jstor.org/stable/30014258

Beder J (2011) Preface to special issue: social work with the military: current practice challenges and approaches to care. Soc Work Health Care 50(1):1–3. https://doi.org/10.1080/00981389.2010.517011

Beder JC (2012) Social work in the Department of Defense Hospital: impact of the work. Adv Soc Work 13(1):132–148. https://doi.org/10.18060/1866

Blackburn D (2015) Social work in the military – considering a renewed scope of practice. Can Mil J 16(1):34–43. http://www.journal.forces.gc.ca/vol16/no1/PDF/CMJ161Ep34.pdf

Brand MW, Weiss EL (2015) Social workers in combat: application of advanced practice competencies in military social work and implications for social work education. J Soc Work Educ 51(1):153–168. https://doi.org/10.1080/10437797.2015.979094

Canfield J, Weiss E (2015) Integrating military and veteran culture in social work education: implications for curriculum inclusion. J Soc Work Educ 51(Suppl 1):S128–S144. https://doi.org/10.1080/10437797.2015.1001295

Cozza SJ, Lerner RM (2013) Military children and families: introducing the issue. Future Children 23(2):3–11

Daley JG (ed) (1999) Social Work Practice in the Military. Haworth Press, New York

Daley JG (2003) Military social work: a multi-country comparison. Int Soc Work 46(4):437–448. https://doi.org/10.1177/0020872803464002

Daley JG (2006) Building an international military social work focus: a call for action. Adv Soc Work 7(1):1–3. https://doi.org/10.18060/115

Daley JG, Carlson J, Evans P (2015) Military social work as an exemplar in teaching social work competencies. J Soc Work Educ 51(Suppl 1):S76–S88. https://doi.org/10.1080/1043779 7.2015.1001288

DuMars T, Bolton K, Maleku A, Smith-Osborne A (2015) Training MSSW students for military social work practice and doctoral students in military resilience research. J Soc Work Educ 4:117

Elinsky CA, Blevins CL, Fisher MP, Magruder K (2017) Military service member and veteran reintegration: a critical review and adapted ecological model. Am J Orthopsychiatry 87(2):114–128. https://doi.org/10.1037/ort0000244. Facilitating reintegration for military service personnel, veterans, and their families

Esqueda MC, Cederbaum JA, Pineda DM, Malchi K, Benbenishty R, Astor RA (2014) Military social work field placement: analysis of the time and activities graduate student interns provide to military-connected schools. Child Sch 36(1):41–50. https://doi.org/10.1093/cs/cdt043

Forgey MA, Young SL (2014) Increasing military social work knowledge: an evaluation of learning outcomes. Health Soc Work 39(1):7–15. https://doi.org/10.1093/hsw/hlu003

Forgey MA, Badger L, Krase K (2011) The development of an evidence-based assessment protocol for intimate partner violence in the US army. J Evid Based Soc Work 8(3):23–348. https://doi.org/10.1080/15433714.2011.533946

Forgey MA, Badger L, Gilbert T, Hansen J (2013) Using standardized clients to train social workers in intimate partner violence assessment. J Soc Work Educ 49(2):293–306

Freeman D, Bicknell G (2008) The army master of social work program. US Army Med Dep J:72–75. http://citeseerx.ist.psu.edu/viewdoc/download?doi=10.1.1.884.4815&rep=rep1&type=pdf#page=75

Hall JC (2009) Utilizing social support to conserve the fighting strength: important considerations for military social workers. Smith Coll Stud Soc Work 79(3/4):335–343. https://doi.org/10.1080/00377310903115465

Hall LK (2011) The importance of understanding military culture. Soc Work Health Care 50(1):4–18. https://doi.org/10.1080/00981389.2010.513914

Hoffler EF, Dekle JW, Sheets C (2014) Social work with service members, veterans, and their families. Health Soc Work 39(1):3–5. https://doi.org/10.1093/hsw/hlu007

Howard RW (2013) The Army Internship Program: enhancing mission readiness for uniformed army social workers. J Hum Behav Soc Environ 23(6):812–816. https://doi.org/10.108 0/10911359.2013.795088

Hughes RD (2006) Transforming professions: a case study of social work in the Australian Defence Organisation. Thesis, Australian Catholic University. https://acuresearchbank.acu.edu.au/download/e08df14c0ce08b71f5b33efab41886ea3a79ae1ec1cac260f0e6af120348 3ff7/823462/64923_downloaded_stream_148.pdf

IMilSW Consortium (2019) Fordham University. https://www.fordham.edu/info/28764/international_military_social_work_consortium/

Jen der Pan P, Deng L-YF, Tsai S-L (2008) Evaluating the use of reflective counseling group supervision for military counselors in Taiwan. Res Soc Work Pract 18(4):346–355. https://doi.org/10.1177/1049731507313981

Kotrla K, Dyer P (2008) Using marriage education to strengthen military families: evaluation of the Active Military Life Skills Program. Soc Work Christianity 35(3):287–311. https://www.nacsw.org/Publications/Proceedings2007/KotrlaKMarriageEducationE.pdf

Kruger A, Van Breda AD (2001) Military social work in the South African National Defence Force. Mil Med 166(11):947–951. https://doi.org/10.1093/milmed/166.11.947

Laštovková J, Brnula P (2017) Military social work-possibilities and challenges in the Czech context. Vojenské Rozhledy 26(1):40–51. https://doi.org/10.3849/2336-2995.26.2017.01.040-051

Lowe KN, Adams KS, Browne BL, Hinkle KT (2012) Impact of military deployment on family relationships. J Fam Stud 18(1):17–27

Marquez MR (2012) Not just about posttraumatic stress disorder: a call for military-centric social work. J Hum Behav Soc Environ 22(8):960–970. https://doi.org/10.1080/1091135 9.2012.707942

Marsh JJ, Forgey MA, Green-Hurdle K, Osborn S, Smith L, Ponteen E, Cai Y, He K, Rooks D (2022) International military social work: selected bibliography 1944-2019. [Data set]. https://doi.org/10.13140/RG.2.2.28439.85926/2

Martin J, Albright D, Borah E (2017) Expanding our understanding of military social work: the concept of military and veteran connected populations. J Family Soc Work 20(1):5–8. https://doi.org/10.1080/10522158.2016.1237919

Martinez-Borrego R (2019) The role of social work in the Spanish Armed Forces: needs and resources. Int Soc Work 62(2):518–528. https://doi.org/10.1177/0020872817731149

Michaels JJ, De Bleyker K, Klapper M (1946) Social work in a neuropsychiatric section of a military general hospital. Am J Orthopsychiatry 16(3):496–506. https://doi.org/10.1111/j.1939-0025.1946.tb05408.x

Nakano K, Morikubo T (2017) Introduction of the concept of military social work in the self-defence forces. Kogakkan University. https://www.researchgate.net/publication/306065902_A_study_on_mental_health_and_family_support_in_the_Japan_Self-Defense_Forces_-Focusing_on_Military_Social_Work-

Newell J (2012) Addressing the needs of veterans and military families: a generalist practice approach. J Baccalaureate Soc Work 17(1):53–68. https://doi.org/10.5555/basw.17.1.024662 4pj1051014

Olson MD (2014) Exploring the ethical dilemma of integrating social work values and military social work practice. Soc Work 59(2):183–185. https://doi.org/10.1093/sw/swu010

Pedlar D, Thompson JM, Castro CA (2019) Military-to-civilian transition theories and frameworks. In: Castro CA, Dursun S (eds) Military veteran reintegration: approach, management, and assessment of military veterans transitioning to civilian life. Elsevier Academic Press, pp 21–50

Pelts MD, Rolbiecki J, Albright DL (2014) Wounded bonds: a review of the social work literature on gay, lesbian and bisexual military service members and veterans. J Soc Work 15(2):207–220. https://doi.org/10.1177/1468017314548120

Rishel CW, Hartnett HP (2015) Preparing MSW students to provide mental and behavioral health services to military personnel, veterans, and their families in rural settings. J Soc Work Educ 51(Suppl 1):S26–S43. https://doi.org/10.1080/10437797.2015.1001278

Ross AM, DeVoe ER (2014) Engaging military parents in a home-based reintegration program: a consideration of strategies. Health Soc Work 39(1):47–54. https://doi.org/10.1093/hsw/hlu001

Rubin A, Weiss EL, Col JE (2013) Handbook of military social work. Wiley, New Jersey

Runesu E (2016) An overview of military social work: the case of Zimbabwe. Afr J Soc Work 6(1):14–21. https://www.ajol.info/index.php/ajsw/article/view/148768

Sahin F, Sakarya H (2017) History, development, and functions of the social work in the military. Trakya Univ J Soc Sci 20(1):81–98. http://www.academia.edu/download/57183633/Silahli_Kuvvetlerde_Sosyal_Hizmet_TRAKYA_SOBED.pdf

Sakarya H, Şahin F (2019) In: the army of social service academicians' thought for army and social services in Turkey: the place and future of the field in social service education. Community Soc Work 30(2):538–554. https://doi.org/10.33417/tsh.572220

Savitsky L, Illingworth M, DuLaney M (2009) Civilian social work: serving the military and veteran populations. Soc Work 54(4):327–339. https://doi.org/10.1093/sw/54.4.327

Schmid V (2019) Soziale Arbeit im Militär. Die Schweiz und Kanada im Vergleich, German edn. Social Work in the Military. Switzerland and Canada in Comparison, Grin Verlag, Munich. ISBN-10: 3346070638 https://sites.google.com/site/oplanefusju2/9783346070630-91glutr iGEchide85

Scott DL, Whitworth JD, Herzog JR (2016) Social work with military populations. Pearson

Segal C (1945) Functional aspects of military social case work. Am J Orthopsychiatry 15(4):597–606

Semigina T, Gusak N (2015) Armed conflict in Ukraine and social work response to it: what strategies should be used for internally displaced persons? Soc Health Commun Study J 2(1):1–24. https://www.researchgate.net/publication/299286362_Armed_Conflict_in_Ukraine_and_Social_Work_Response_to_it_What_strategies_should_be_used_for_internally_displaced_persons

Sherwood E (2009) Clinical assessment of Canadian military marriages. Clin Soc Work J 37(4):332–339. https://doi.org/10.1007/s10615-007-0108-2

Siebler P, Goddard C (2014) Parents' perspectives of their children's reactions to an Australian military deployment. Child Aust 39(1):17–24. https://doi.org/10.1017/cha.2013.38

Silva D (2015 August 31) Social work in military aeronautical organizations: analysis of professional practice in the Amazon region. 149 f. Dissertation (Master's) – Federal University of Pará, Institute of Applied Social Sciences, Belém. Graduate Program in Social Work. http://repositorio.ufpa.br/jspui/handle/2011/7464

Simmons CA, DeCoster V (2007) Military social workers at war: their experiences and the educational content that helped them. J Soc Work Educ 43(3):497–512. https://doi.org/10.5175/JSWE.2007.200600054

Simmons CA, Rycraft JR (2010) Ethical challenges of military social workers serving in a combat zone. Soc Work 55(1):9–18. https://doi.org/10.1093/sw/55.1.9

Skidmore WC, Roy M (2011) Practical considerations for addressing substance use disorders in veterans and service members. Soc Work Health Care 50(1):85–107

Smith-Osborne A (2015) An intensive continuing education initiative to train social workers for military social work practice. J Soc Work Educ 51(Suppl 1):S89–S101. https://doi.org/10.1080/10437797.2015.1001290

Soeters JL, Poponete CR, Page JT (2006) Culture's consequence in the military. In: Britt T, Adler A, Castro C (eds) Military life the psychology of serving in peace and combat – military culture. Praeger Security International, Westport, CT

Strong J, Ray K, Findley PA, Torres R, Pickett L, Byrn RJ (2014) Psychosocial concerns of veterans of Operation Enduring Freedom/Operation Iraqi Freedom. Health Soc Work 1:17–24. https://doi.org/10.1093/hsw/hlu002

Surkova I (2010) Social problems in the Russian Army within the framework of social work. J Comp Soc Work 5(2):89–103. https://doi.org/10.31265/jcsw.v5i2.64

Towle (1950) Review of military psychiatric social work. Soc Serv Rev 24(3):424–424

Van Breda AD (2012) Military social work thinking in South Africa. Adv Soc Work 13(1):17–33. https://doi.org/10.18060/1890

West L, Mercer SO, Altheimer E (1993) Operation desert storm: the response of a social work outreach team. Soc Work Health Care 19(2):81–98

Whitworth JD, Herzog JR, Scott DL (2012) Problem-based learning strategies for teaching military social work practice behaviors: review and evaluation. Adv Soc Work 13(1):112–131. https://doi.org/10.18060/1876

Wichlacz CR, Randall DH, Nelson JH, Kempe CH (1975) The characteristics and management of child abuse in the US army-europe. Clin Pediatr 14(6):545–548

Williams-Gray B (2016) Teaching BSW students effective practice with returning military personnel: a strengths-based resiliency framework. J Baccalaureate Soc Work 21(1):1–11. https://doi.org/10.18084/1084-7219.21.1.1

Williamson E (2011) Domestic abuse and military families: the problem of reintegration and control. Br J Soc Work 42(7):1371–1387

Williamson V et al (2019) The impact of military service on health and well-being. Occup Med 69(1):64–70

Wolf M, Eliseo-Arras R, Nochajski T, Brenner M (2017) "This will help your children": service providers' experiences with military families during cycles of deployment. J Fam Soc Work 20(1):26–40

Wooten NR (2013) A bioecological model of deployment risk and resilience. J Hum Behav Soc Environ 23(6):699–717. https://doi.org/10.1080/10911359.2013.795049

Wooten NR (2015) Military social work: opportunities and challenges for social work education. J Soc Work Educ 51(Suppl 1):S6–S25. https://doi.org/10.1080/10437797.2015.1001274

Yantao L (2016) A summary of the research on the social work of the army. J Chansha Civil Administration Vocational Technol Coll 3:36–39. https://www.airitilibrary.com/Publication/alDetailedMesh?docid=csmzzyjsxyxb201603012

Yantao L, Fang Q (2017) Development of Chinese Army social work: connotation, research status, and prospects. Soc Work Manage 17(1):24–30. http://manu49.magtech.com.cn/Jwk3_gdgy/shgzygl/CN/abstract/abstract2353.shtml

Yarvis JS (2011) A civilian social worker's guide to the treatment of war-induced PTSD. Soc Work Health Care 50(1):51–72. https://doi.org/10.1080/00981389.2010.518856

Chapter 2
Military Social Work in Australia: Opportunities for Policy, Practice, and Education

Karen Green-Hurdle and Philip Siebler

2.1 Introduction

This chapter will provide an ecological overview of Military Social Work (MilSW) with Australian Defence Force (ADF) personnel, veterans, and their families across micro, mezzo, and macro levels. The opportunities for the field of practice for the profession in social work policy, practice, and education will be discussed.

Throughout the history of social work in Australia, social workers have occupied many roles supporting active-duty military personnel, veterans, and their families. Unlike in the United States (U.S.), there is no defined Military Social Work (MilSW) field of practice in Australia. Social workers are more likely to describe themselves as 'social workers who work with current serving or ex-serving Australian Defence Force (ADF) personnel, Veterans, and their families'. A professional identity may also be impeded since the organisation that represents social workers, the Australian Association of Social Workers (AASW), has been struggling for some years to achieve national registration and protection of 'Social Work' as a legal title through

---

The opinions expressed in this paper are the authors' and should not be interpreted as the policy or opinions of the Australian Department of Veterans' Affairs and Department of Defence.

K. Green-Hurdle (✉)
Department of Veterans Affairs, Open Arms Veterans and Families Counselling (North Queensland), Townsville, QLD, Australia
e-mail: greenhurdle@gmail.com

P. Siebler
Department of Defence, Defence Family Research, Directorate of People Intelligence and Research, Melbourne, VIC, Australia

The Bouverie Centre, La Trobe University, Melbourne, VIC, Australia
e-mail: philipsiebler01@gmail.com

© Springer Nature Switzerland AG 2023
M. A. Forgey, K. Green-Hurdle (eds.), *Military Social Work Around the Globe*,
Military and Veterans Studies, https://doi.org/10.1007/978-3-031-14482-0_2

the National Registration and Accreditation Scheme (NRAS). As a consequence, social work is not a registered profession in Australia.

Australia has a population of 25.5 million (Australian Bureau of Statistics ABS 2020). The Australian Department of Defence (DoD) comprises the ADF of 58,656 active-duty personnel, 21,694 reserve force personnel, and 18,000 civilian Commonwealth public servants (DoD 2017a). The precise number of Australian veterans is unknown (AIHW 2018). In 2021, the Australian Bureau of Statistics (ABS) noted that around 210,000 veterans received a pension or allowance from the Department of Veterans Affairs (DVA). In addition, more than 100,000 partners, widow(er)s, or children of veterans (known as dependants) were also registered to receive DVA support (ABS 2021).

Traditionally, according to the Australian Institute for Health and Welfare [AIHW] (2018), the term 'veteran' has been used to describe former ADF members who were deployed to serve in war or a war-like conflict environment. In recent years, the definition has broadened, and this chapter uses the term 'veteran' to include current and ex-serving ADF personnel who have served 1 day of full-time service, regardless of whether deployed to active conflict or peacekeeping operations or served without being deployed (Productivity Commission 2019). The term 'veteran community' includes family members of both living and deceased veterans.

Current serving (or active duty) military personnel, veterans, and their families generally seek services, including social work, in the communities in which they live. Thus, most social workers in their careers will provide services to veterans and their families across the non-government service sector in areas such as child protection, family violence, health, housing, homelessness, addiction, and education. It is not feasible that the care of service members, veterans, and their families can be adequately provided for solely by the government. Therefore, the authors agree with the Council on Social Work Education (CSWE) notion that:

> …the social worker providing services to this client base is by definition a military social worker, whether in uniform or not, veteran or not, government service employee, contractor, agency, private practitioner, researcher, or educator (Council on Social Work Education CSWE 2018).

To be consistent with the focus of this text, this chapter will focus more narrowly on military social workers employed by the DoD and DVA who provide services to currently serving military personnel and their families.

2.2 A Brief History of Military Social Work

MilSW has always been provided by civilians throughout social work's long history in Australia. Social work's early history in supporting military personnel and their families had its origins post World War One. Social work education commenced in the 1920s, although it was not until 1940 that a social work programme commenced at the University of Sydney (Camilleri 2001).

The Red Cross Welfare Service played a significant role in the evolution of military social work. As Lawrence (1965) observed, this was a family casework agency and pioneered the development of family casework in Australia (Lawrence 1965). The service was established in collaboration with the Australian Army in 1941 to address family dislocation as a result of the war (Stubbings 1992). The Red Cross appointed medical social workers in military hospitals, rehabilitation programmes, vocational training of soldiers with disabilities, and services for war veterans (Stubbings 1992). However, as Stubbings (1992) has illustrated, the Army continued to refer cases to the Red Cross during the Vietnam War until there was the creation of Army Community Services (ACS) by the Australian Government in the 1970s and the Social Work Information Service (SWIS) for the Air Force in 1988. The Navy employed the first social worker in the Department in 1956.

Modern-day MilSW has evolved extensively in the DoD and DVA, and social workers fulfil a broad range of functions, as the next section will outline. All MilSW practice is underpinned by the Australian Association of Social Workers (AASW) Practice Standards and Code of Ethics, in addition to the Codes of Conduct, with policy and programme requirements detailed by the employing organisation. It is important to note that the major distinction between the services performed by DoD and DVA military social workers is that employees of each respective department are mandated to support their agency's mission or purpose.

2.3 Military Social Work Settings and Interventions

Military social workers occupy many niches in the DoD and DVA and are often employed as part of a multidisciplinary team. As noted in the introduction, and unlike the psychology profession, the term 'social work' is not registered by title in Australia. Consequently, military social workers are often employed in the respective departments in positions without a specific 'social work' reference in the title. Examples of positions include 'counsellor', 'clinician', 'case manager', health service 'coordinator', and Mental Health Promotion Officer. Military social workers encompass micro, mezzo, and macro levels of practice such as individual, family, group, and community. Social workers are also employed at the organisational level in these departments in management and leadership, military family research, and policy-making roles.

2.3.1 Department of Defence Military Social Work

Employees of the DoD, including military social workers, provide targeted services that align with the DoD mission 'to defend Australia and its national interests in order to advance Australia's security and prosperity' (DoD 2021). As will be outlined, the interventions delivered by DoD military social workers ultimately aim to support and maintain the operational capability of the Australian Defence Force.

In Australia, most military social workers are employed in the DoD's military family support organisation, the Defence Member and Family Support (DMFS) branch, formerly the Defence Community Organisation (DCO), which employs over 60 social workers across the nation. Military social workers (DMFS 2020a) assist families with personal, relationship, or military-service-related issues. DMFS MilSW services are delivered from local area offices which are located on or near defence establishments in all states and territories of Australia.

DoD military social workers are expected to have knowledge of military culture and lifestyle issues, benefits and entitlements, and services and resources for personnel and families. However, as there is no formal training or education to prepare a social worker for work in the military and veteran community, the required cultural knowledge is generally obtained through direct practice within the employing organisation. DoD military social workers must be eligible for AASW membership, but there is no requirement for them to be an AASW member.

DoD MilSW interventions include intake and other psychosocial assessments, short-term counselling, referrals for further support, connections to resources in the local community, and advice to the ADF commanders, often via a MilSW report. DoD military social workers offer supportive and informative services to help families prepare for and manage both the challenges and opportunities of military life.

The DoD military social worker must be adept at managing the dual client relationship that exists in supporting the DoD mission, whilst being sensitive to unique individual circumstances of the military member and families. When an issue is identified whereby a military member's personal circumstances may impact operational capability, DoD military social workers undertake comprehensive assessments with the member/family, exploring all options that could alleviate the challenge. Distinctly different from DVA MilSW services, the DoD military social worker works directly within the chain of command and provides comprehensive reports to assist commanders to make informed decisions about issues that may impact operational capability.

In the event of a death of a current serving ADF member, military social workers provide specialised bereavement support services to families on behalf of the Department of Defence. The Bereavement Support Team (BST) consists of a military support officer (who assists with family liaison, funeral arrangements, and navigating military administrative processes) and a military social worker who provides practical and emotional support. It is essential that the BST works collaboratively with the deceased member's military unit and chain of command, chaplains, and other relevant areas of the Department of Defence, in addition to connecting families with the required services and resources in the community. The social worker also consistently monitors the family's needs and wishes to ensure that the BST actions are reflective and respectful of what the family requires. The BST remains active for 6 months, though it can be extended based on the needs of the family. The BST military social worker provides a comprehensive and valuable service that appears to be unique to Australia. The authors suggest that this model for supporting families in a time of significant grief and distress could be of interest to countries where a formalised process for casualty and bereavement support has not been articulated in policy (DMFS 2020e).

Military social workers identify and respond to local needs relevant to the various Army, Air Force, and Navy localities. This results in military social workers supporting community members to develop an innovative and customised range of programmes to help families further enhance their resilience (DMFS 2020a). Subsequently, community work functions can be broad, and this is where, as Westhuis (1999) describes it, social workers get out of their counselling role and into the military community.

In addition to roles in the Defence Member and Family Support, military social workers employed by the DoD are also employed in military health centres in mental health or rehabilitation teams. As part of a multi-disciplinary team, military social workers provide clinical, mental health, and drug and alcohol interventions such as conducting intakes, assessments, and providing treatment for current serving personnel. In addition, military social workers also deliver military mental health prevention and promotion training programmes to ADF personnel, which include suicide prevention, drug and alcohol treatment services, and face-to-face or online resilience training (Australian Association of Social Workers AASW 2016).

2.3.2 Department of Veterans Affairs (DVA) Military Social Work

The purpose of the DVA is 'to support the wellbeing of those who serve or have served in the defence of our nation, and their families, and commemorate their service and sacrifice' (DVA 2019). Within the DVA, military social workers provide services that align with the organisational purpose and are employed in the two key directorates; Open Arms Veterans and Families Counselling (hereafter referred to as Open Arms), and Client Coordination and Support.

Open Arms provides free, confidential, nation-wide counselling and support to current and former ADF personnel and their families. It has an integrated, 24/7 service delivery system that includes high-quality mental health assessment, evidence-based, trauma-informed, recovery-orientated treatment, clinical counselling (individual, couple, and family), group programmes, case management, and after-hours telephone support. Military social workers occupy roles in Open Arms service delivery teams that include titles such as counsellor, care coordinator, group programme facilitator, and first-line contact officers in the 24/7 national call centre. Military social workers may also hold key executive leadership and clinical oversight roles in the organisation.

Whether employed within an Open Arms service centre or contracted as an Outreach Provider Counsellor (private practitioner), it is mandatory for all social workers employed or contracted by Open Arms to maintain AASW membership and Mental Health accreditation (Open Arms Veterans and Families Counselling 2020).

In DVA's Client Coordination and Support Directorate, the Client Support Framework has been implemented to provide holistic, coordinated support for veterans with complex care needs and high levels of vulnerability (Collie 2019). Experienced allied health professionals, including social workers, are employed in all divisions of the framework. The DVA Veteran Mental Health and Wellbeing Strategy and Action Plan 2020–2023 (DVA 2020a) outlines the services that are available via the 'Triage and Connect' gateway and indicates that referrals can be made to other sections of the framework, including:

(i) 'Coordinated Client Support' programme which provides specialised case management services for veterans with complex and high-needs clients, enabling them to access benefits and services in a timely and professional manner. It is noted that there is also a specialist programme to support ADF members (under 30 years of age) who are transitioning on medical or administrative grounds (Collie 2019); and a,

(ii) 'Wellbeing and Support Programme' which provides high-intensity, face-to-face community-based, case management services.

In addition, 'social worker wellness checks' are available for veterans who wish to make a compensation claim or access treatment for an injury, which occurs when an 'Initial Liability Assessment and Needs Assessment' is conducted, though a referral can be made for a wellness check at any time in the veterans DVA journey (Collie 2019). DVA 'wellness checks' are comprehensive, person-centred, psychosocial assessments that provide early insights about heightened risk factors for vulnerable veterans—thereby resulting in timely supportive interventions for those needing access to health services counselling, crisis accommodation, financial support, or home care assistance (Creyke 2019).

Through the DVA Allied Health programme, the two provider categories for social workers are 'generalist' and 'Mental Health Social Workers' (AASW 2020a). These military social workers operate in private practice clinics providing services in the community to veterans via specific DVA contracts. In order to provide services for DVA, social workers must hold AASW membership and meet other criteria relevant to the category. Generalist social work services include counselling, case management, care coordination, referral, advocacy, and family therapy with a focus on veteran wellbeing, vocational and employment counselling, or rehabilitation. Mental Health Social Worker services can only be provided by those who have AASW mental health accreditation and who are registered with the Australian government's universal health insurance scheme, Medicare. Their services include assessment, psychoeducation, cognitive behavioural therapy, relaxation strategies, skills training, interpersonal therapy, and counselling (DVA 2020d). DoD military social workers liaise with DVA social workers on a case-by-case basis, although formal policy practice could enhance current inter-departmental collaboration.

2.4   Overview of the Australian Military Social Work Approach

The approach of Australian MilSW practice is undefined, in that there is no available literature that formally articulates the Australian MilSW framework as clinical, occupational, community capacity building, or another approach in either the DoD or DVA systems. It is the author's opinion that the framework in which MilSW practice operates is dependent on the setting and objectives of the employing organisation. For example, having a clinical understanding of signature military health conditions and associated systemic issues are essential in the provision of assessment, case formulation, and treatment planning for individuals, whilst theoretical knowledge of family and community systems is imperative in both therapeutic work and community capacity development.

Assessing compassionate circumstances (and how these may be mitigated) whilst ultimately ensuring that military operational capability is maintained by the military member, or responding to critical incidents within a military unit (such as death by suicide), is specific to DoD MilSW and requires a coordinated occupational social work approach informed by both comprehensive clinical judgement and systems knowledge. It is further suggested that military social workers delivering case management and care coordination services need to be well versed across all approaches in order to effectively deliver services.

Legislation, Acts, Regulations, Directions, and Rules underpin all activities and tasks of employees of the DoD and DVA and therefore directly influence the MilSW approach. Australian Public Servants and those contracted to provide services on behalf of the Commonwealth must commit to support the directions and policies of the government of the day (Australian Public Service Commission APSC 2018; DoD 2020; DVA 2020c).

The Defence Force Discipline Act [DFDA] (1982) ensures that current serving military members are held accountable for actions that occur in the environment in which they perform their duties. However, civil crimes, including intimate partner violence, child safety and protection issues, physical and sexual assault, drug offences, and other potentially criminal acts are managed in accordance with relevant state/territory legislation and may include mandatory reporting provisions by civilian statutory authorities. Mandatory reporting requirements vary across states and territories, and it is therefore essential that DoD military social workers are aware of their professional and organisational responsibilities in relation to legal matters.

It is imperative for Australian MilSW to remain abreast of emerging issues and the strategies that are implemented to address social, health, economic, and political issues. The field of Australian MilSW must also be proactive in foreshadowing issues that may require systemic responses and contribute to policy development.

An example of DoD Defence Member and Family Support (DMFS) efforts to raise the profile of the importance of families in supporting military members in maintaining operational capability occurred in 2009 when the 'Australian Defence

Families Covenant' was officially endorsed by the Chief of Defence Force (CDF). The Covenant articulates the valued contribution of DoD families in supporting the military mission and has been endorsed by each incoming CDF since that time, reaffirming the ADF's commitment to military families (DMFS 2020b). The authors suggest that the CDF endorsement and implementation of the Covenant have assisted in maintaining the profile of the military family, leading to a greater emphasis being placed on family inclusive practice and its incorporation into policy.

In addition, the 'Defence Family and Domestic Violence Strategy 2017–2022' was implemented in 2017, and DoD DMFS military social workers have an important role in operationalising the objectives of the strategy. This includes direct service provision with those impacted by family and domestic violence. Providing ADF personnel with knowledge and skills to identify and effectively respond to this issue promotes an accurate understanding of the impacts of family and domestic violence in the occupational setting (DoD 2017a, b).

DoD's cultural reform priorities are embodied in the 2017–2022 'Pathway to Change – Evolving Defence Culture' and include a focus on leadership accountability, capability through inclusion, ethics, workplace behaviour, health, wellness, and safety. The recommendations from several high-profile reviews into issues such as allegations of sexual and other forms of abuse in the DoD, the use of alcohol in the ADF, social media and Defence, and treatment of women have all informed the current strategy.

In the veteran community, the Veteran Mental Health and Wellbeing Strategy and Action Plan 2020–2023 (DVA 2020a) provides guidance for how allied health workers, including military social workers, can help to improve the wellbeing of veterans and their families, with a focus on suicide prevention strategies and transition and reintegration issues.

The Australian Census is conducted every 5 years, and for the first time, the 2021 Census will include an Australian Defence Force service topic. It is anticipated that the data obtained will help to guide policy and service delivery responses to veteran issues that include health, housing, and employment (DVA 2020e). It is the authors opinion that this knowledge will provide social workers in research, policy, programme design, and direct practice programming with a greater potential to understand how many veterans are in the community in which they serve and identify service delivery gaps that social workers (and related organisations) could be meeting.

2.5 Australian Military Social Work Research

Both Departments have research organisations that focus on ADF personnel, veterans, and the military family, with the DoD launching a Military Family Research Programme in 2020. The Defence Family Research Programme will provide translatable research to inform the Australian community, both Departments of Defence and Veterans Affairs, policymakers, practitioners including military social workers, military associations, the University sector, and family advocacy groups. There is a strong interest in ADF and veteran research in academic settings and the ex-serving charitable sectors that could be better harnessed for the benefit of the military population. This rich research community could be better integrated and coordinated to develop a coherent research agenda and optimise use of the pool of research funding.

The DVA and DoD commission research of utility for MilSW. The Transition and Wellbeing Research Programme (DVA 2020b) is the most comprehensive study undertaken of serving and ex-serving ADF personnel and their families. A series of reports have been released in relation to prevalence, pathways to care, physical health status, family wellbeing, technology use, mental health changes over time, and the impact of combat. Of particular relevance to the systemic framework of MilSW is the Family Wellbeing Study, which focused on the impact of military service during service and in the early year's post discharge from military service (Daraganova et al. 2018; Muir 2018). Broadly, the issues explored in the study included residential and educational mobility, financial wellbeing and employment, and personal and family wellbeing. Whilst, the insights obtained were generally positive, the study found some subgroups that may benefit from more targeted assistance in future.

A small number of academic researchers external to the DoD and DVA have contributed knowledge in relation to policy and practice to support young children, post-traumatic stress disorder and the family, and children and deployment (Rogers 2020; McGaw et al. 2019; MacDonald 2016; Rogers 2016).

To date, a small number of military social workers have completed higher-degree research at PhD or master level with a focus on current serving personnel, veterans, and their families. This research has undergone an ethics approval process within the DoD. Other disciplines such as psychology, medicine, education, and nursing also conduct research. Thus, in comparison to the US, there is a paucity of Australian social work research to inform policy, practice, and education in relation to deployment, MilSW, and Intimate Partner Violence (Siebler, 2009; Siebler and Goddard 2014; Siebler 2015; Siebler and Karpetis 2019). It is futher noted that Siebler created an ecological model of the military family for social work (Siebler and Karpetis 2019).

2.6   Military to Civilian Transition Support

The Transition and Wellbeing Research Programme (TWRP) is a comprehensive, collaborative Australian study that was undertaken by DVA and the DoD. The research incorporated three major studies that explored the impact of military service on the health and wellbeing of ADF members, veterans, and their families (Van Hooff et al. 2019). The 'Mental Health Prevalence Report' was one of the reports produced from the TWRP and it revealed that an estimated three in four ADF members who transition from military service have met the criteria for a mental health condition during their lifetime (Van Hooff et al. 2018). This research highlights the importance of MilSW remaining abreast of military and veteran health issues and the challenges that may be faced during the period of transition that may include heightened levels of stress responses.

As part of routine MilSW duties, DMFS social workers can assist individual current serving military members and their families to prepare for the emotional challenges and practical aspects that can be associated with significant change, including transitioning from military to civilian life. This may include assistance with practical planning, emotional support, short-term counselling, goal setting, psychoeducation, referrals to relevant community resources, and reinforcing the importance of maintaining positive health and wellbeing (DMFS 2020c).

The DMFS-Australian Defence Force Transition Centre (ADFTC) branch conducts regular 'ADF Member and Family Transition seminars' throughout the year. The seminars aim to provide practical information about services provided by ADFTC transition coaches, DVA, financial and superannuation services, and a broad range of key support services, including Open Arms. The previous face-to-face format has been electronically adapted to the COVID-19 environment, and participation is now remotely accessible with opportunities for individual consultation with a wide range of stakeholders. Transitioned members are able to access support via the ADFTC for a period of up to 24 months post-transition (DMFS 2020c).

Open Arms recognises the unique challenges associated with transitioning to civilian life. In addition to individual support, couple and family support is also provided by the 2-day Stepping Out workshop that examines the process in both practical and emotional terms for members and partners (Open Arms Veterans and Families Counselling 2020).

There are a range of Commonwealth government and non-government initiatives that are designed to support veterans and families in the transition process. These include educational seminars that cover issues of education, employment, income support and benefits, health, meaningful engagement, and the importance of social connectedness. There are also staff employed in the ADF Transition Centres that offer life coaching and DVA staff that work on bases providing an advisory service prior to discharge from service. Community and peer advisers are also employed in Open Arms (and other veteran-centred agencies) to provide guidance on options that may make transition smoother.

Of significance, there is no publicly available information to suggest that social work has an integral role in transition support services in either DoD or DVA. Given the diverse and potentially complex systemic challenges that are presented at this juncture in the members' and families' lives, and the potential value of specialised MilSW assessment and coordinated support services, the authors identify that this is an area of social work practice that could be bolstered to better support transitioning members and their families. For example, policy focussing on family health and wellbeing, in addition to transitioning members, could be developed to formalise a collaborative partnership between DMFS military social workers and DVA to ensure case management is available to all who may benefit from this service, further optimising positive outcomes in the transition phase. MilSW could develop evidence-informed educational skills-building packages aimed at increasing the military cultural competence of emerging (students) and current health professionals. This would result in staff in non-veteran-specific services being better equipped to assist veterans and their families to manage the challenges that may emerge in any location across Australia.

2.7   Ethical Issues and Challenges

Entering into a relationship with a serving member of the Australian Defence Force (ADF) means entering into a relationship with the ADF itself. (DMFS 2020d)

This statement is arguably intrinsic to the most typical ethical tensions that Australian military social workers may face when working within the current serving military community. Olson (2014) suggests that social workers, including those working with military communities, must often function in systems that are underpinned by competing yet co-existing philosophies. The complexities of an environment with such a dichotomy may result in challenges that include managing dual clinical and organisational responsibilities and whether 'informed consent' is realistic given the power differential in rank structure.

In the military context, it is essential to understand the unique superior-subordinate command structure and the issues of implicit coercion and undue influence that may exist in order to pay careful attention to whether military personnel are fully informed about consent in research (McManus et al. 2005). Similarly, the opinion of the authors is that military social workers in both DVA and DoD are ethically responsible for ensuring that current serving military clients are fully informed at the commencement of their engagement with the service of the provisions and limitations of privacy and consent that may be present in the military setting. For example, disclosure of the imminent risk of harm to self or others, or involvement in the criminal activity requires active management. When a currently serving military member's disclosure results in determining that due to duty of care provisions that DoD must be informed, the military social worker is ethically obliged to discuss the reasons for disclosure with the client and to address any issues of concern that the military member may have. Wherever possible, the current serving member would be actively involved in discussing the issues with his or her treating military medical team.

Daley (2013) suggests that 'dual role' or 'dual loyalty' dilemmas are more evident for uniformed military social workers in combat settings but may also be present in non-combat environments. Whilst the authors concur that dual role and loyalty issues are more attuned to uniformed military social workers in the Australian context, where there are only civilian-military social workers employed, the dual client tension is noteworthy. Within the DoD, a military social worker may encounter 'dual client' ethical tensions when supporting clients to balance individual and family needs with the overarching organisational mandate. The military social worker is responsible for delivering services that support and sustain the capability of ADF members to offer unrestricted service in order to achieve the mission of the ADF, which is to 'Defend Australia and its' national interests' (DoD 2021). Unrestricted service means that the ADF member must be able to serve in any location, at any time, in accordance with the ADF requirements. The systemic impact of the demands of ADF employment may result in conflict between the military member and the needs of his or her family, against the backdrop of command requirements and the organisational mandate (DMFS 2020d).

Regardless of organisational settings, or holding membership with the national professional association, all Australian social workers are required to uphold the values and responsibilities of the Australian Association of Social Work (AASW) Code of Ethics (2020). Where ethical tensions arise due to legal or organisational requirements that are not deemed to be compatible with the AASW Code of Ethics, the Code advises that guidance may be sought from competent professionals (which may include the AASW Ethics Consultation Service) to work toward resolution of the dilemma.

2.8   Education and Training

Military social workers have the same level of undergraduate preparation as any other practicing social worker in Australia. Military social workers employed by the DoD must be eligible for membership of the AASW in addition to having several years of post-qualifying social work experience for employment.

As previously noted, Open Arms requires social workers to be accredited as mental health social workers to work as either centre-based counsellors or as Outreach Provider Counsellors. DVA employs generalist and mental health accredited social workers within the Client Coordination and Support Directorate and as contracted service providers in the DVA Allied Health programme (DVA 2020d). Aside from having several years of practice experience, there are no other explicit perquisites for the employment of military social workers by either organisation.

The Australian Social Work Education and Accreditation Standards (AASW 2020b) set the principles and graduate requirements for social work education. The Standards form the criteria for the accreditation of professional social work courses, with the AASW accrediting both Bachelor of Social Work and Master of Social Work (Qualifying) courses for entry into the profession. Graduates from these programmes are eligible for membership of the AASW.

The Australian Social Work Education and Accreditation Standards (AASW 2020b) outline a required curriculum, although do not specify any content in relation to MilSW. The authors are aware that a number of Departments of Social Work have invited military social workers to present classes on MilSW to students; however, it is unknown as to what extent, if any, social work departments include core content on MilSW in their courses.

The AASW has a range of credentialing titles including accredited social workers, accredited mental health social workers, accredited family violence social workers, and accredited clinical social workers. At the time of writing, there was no MilSW credential, and this concept will be discussed in the final section of this chapter.

Whilst desirable, advanced training in family therapy, relationship counselling, Cognitive Behaviour Therapy (CBT), and/or other specialisations depending on the role and setting is not a requirement for employment. As previously outlined, military social workers are employed in a variety of roles in both departments and employment is role specific. Thus, a military social worker employed in a research setting would most likely have a higher research degree, relevant experience, and research knowledge—whereas a military social worker in a military family support or mental health role would be employed on the basis of their experience, skills, and knowledge in a relevant direct practice role.

The AASW Scope of Practice for social workers in relation to Australian Defence Force (ADF) Service Members, Veterans, and their Families (AASW 2016) provides an overview of the role, scope, contribution, and evidence base of social work in this practice setting. Given there is no professional accreditation or education requirement specific to MilSW, there is no competency measurement provision. This has implications for MilSW education, which the next section will address.

2.9   Next Steps—Opportunities for Military Social Work in Australia

MilSW presents the profession, academia, and Social Work Departments in universities with significant opportunities. We agree with the Council on Social Work Education (CSWE) that the field of MilSW practice is important to both advance social work and respond to the needs of military personnel and their families:

> Military social work, as a field of practice and research, is critical to our relevance as social workers, to the advancement of new career options, and in our leadership among the helping professions. This does not mean that we endorse war or aggression, but rather that we extend meaningful help to those who have been affected. (CSWE 2010)

Given that there is a defined and long-standing field of MilSW that is developing internationally as this text demonstrates, we contend that the AASW could adopt this nomenclature and consult widely to advance the field (Bevilacqua and Darnauer 1977; Council on Social Work Education 2018). These areas of advancement encompass international, including the National Association of Social Workers (NASW), the membership base, including the major social work employers of DVA and the DoD, and the tertiary education sector. Furthermore, the AASW has laid the groundwork to establish MilSW by recently creating a Veterans National Advisory Panel to '…provide expertise, leadership, and strategic focus on key issues that the AASW is engaged in to further the social policy and advocacy priorities of the Association, and the profession of social work' (AASW 2020c).

As mentioned previously, university courses are not required to offer units of study in military social work, although some have informally provided content via military social workers providing guest presentations to students. To that end, social work education could include content regarding MilSW as a field of practice. Similar to the U.S. Council on Social Work Education [CSWE] (2010) standards, we argue that Australian social work courses need to include '...some infusion of content relative to service members, veterans, their families, and their communities...', as the CSWE does. This would integrate with the extant core Australian Social Work Education and Accreditation Standards (ASWEAS) curricula notably in areas such as: constructions of social work purpose, place, and practice; power, oppression, and exploitation; culture, identity, and discrimination; and psychosocial health and wellbeing across the life cycle (AASW 2020b). Social work departments share responsibility in preparing social workers to serve the above population by addressing their needs in the development of curricula. The needs of service members, veterans, and their families are enduring. Given the interest, as evidenced by large enrolments in social work by international students, a range of mechanisms are possible, such as including a small trial of both national and international MilSW curriculum content.

The AASW has responded to its membership base and created specialised accreditations in relation to family violence, clinical social work, mental health, disability, and child protection. At the practice level, credentialing of MilSW by the AASW would be a significant first step to build upon the AASW Scope of Practice framework for social workers (AASW 2016) in relation to working with military personnel, veterans, and their families. Credentialing could be undertaken in tandem with DVA and DoD and would enable quality assurance, empower employers to recruit staff according to a requisite skill set and create career advancement opportunities. In addition, it is conceivable that if the AASW were to achieve national registration by title, new vistas would be afforded social work credentialing, particularly in multidisciplinary teams in the health setting in the DoD and advanced MilSW practice domains.

Advanced study in MilSW is important, and this could be achieved by offering electives and/or higher postgraduate–level academic study, creating MilSW competencies and curricular resources that reflect accreditation standards for master's and higher programmes.

Social work departments could create partnerships with the DoD and DVA to foster field placements with a focus on the full gamut of MilSW interventions, including direct practice and research placements. Options could be explored with research organisations within the departments at master and PhD levels for mutual benefit and to grow the next generation of researchers. Social work research is a core curriculum in Australia and opportunities exist in a range of organisations for career researchers.

2.10   Conclusion

Without the fanfare, MilSW has long made an important contribution in assisting Service members, veterans, and military families across the life course. Australian Social Work has a range of opportunities to advance the field of MilSW in Australia, with the concomitant outcome of a professional identity both in Australia and internationally. We contend that change at the macro level to advance the field of MilSW will be challenging given there is no collective of military social workers to initiate and coordinate the AASW/profession, academia, and social work departments. The support of organisations such as the International MilSW Consortium may be helpful in placing the important work that is done in Australia in a global context. Whilst past efforts to raise the profile of MilSW in Australia resulted in the AASW supporting the production of the 2016 '*Scope of social work practice: Australian Defence Force Service members, veterans, and their families*' document, and the establishment of a Veterans Advisory Panel in 2020 (AASW 2020c); more robust advocacy in collaboration with the AASW will be required to further develop the MilSW identity and make it a higher priority for the profession. At the time of writing, a Royal Commission into Defence and Veteran Suicide is underway, and it is hoped that the role and value of social work in the public health and micro levels of suicide prevention, assessment, treatment, and safety planning will be articulated during this very important inquiry.

Applying a social work lens to the myriad of tasks that transitioning members and their families face in reconciling and adjusting to civilian life after a lengthy career, or one cut short due to medical or disciplinary issues, may help improve health outcomes for those members and families. DoD, DVA, and/or private practice military social workers with a passion to enhance quality of services would be well placed to lead the development and delivery of interactive and educational programmes in local communities across Australia (along with a veteran peer), in order to raise the awareness of health professionals to the issues and challenges that veterans and families may face at various points in their lives where significant change, loss, or adjustment is inevitable. These experienced military social workers would also be able to tailor and deliver interactive online programmes for communities that would help to provide and promote opportunities for meaningful growth, hope, and connection for military and veteran communities.

There is still a long way to go to establish a MilSW identity in Australia. A number of passionate practitioners and academics across our nation will advocate to advance the field of Military Social Work both nationally and internationally. We contend the future is positive for the specialisation and advancement of the profession, and ultimately for members of the military and veteran communities in Australia and across the globe.

References

Australian Association of Social Workers [AASW] (2020) Code of ethics. Canberra, Australia
Australian Association of Social Workers [AASW] (2016) Scope of social work practice: Australian Defence Force Service members, veterans, and their families. North Melbourne, Victoria
Australian Association of Social Workers [AASW] (2020a) Department of Veterans Affairs and Social Work. https://www.aasw.asn.au/practitioner-resources/department-of-veterans-affairs-and-social-work. Accessed 3 Oct 2020
Australian Association of Social Workers [AASW] (2020b) Australian social work education and accreditation standards. https://www.asn.au/document/item/6073. Accessed 3 Oct 2020
Australian Association of Social Workers [AASW] (2020c) Department of Veterans' Affairs National Advisory Panel. https://www.asn.au/social-policy-advocacy/national-advisory-panels. Accessed 3 Oct 2020
Australian Bureau of Statistics [ABS] (2020) Australian demographic statistics. https://www.abs.gov.au/ausstats/abs@.nsf/lookup/3101.0Media%20Release1Jun%202019. Accessed 3 Oct 2020
Australian Bureau of Statistics [ABS] (2021) Department of Veterans' Affairs. About the census. https://census.abs.gov.au/about/census-stories/DVA. Accessed 31 Aug 2021
Australian Institute for Health and Welfare [AIHW] (2018) A profile of Australia's veterans 2018. Canberra, Australia
Australian Public Service Commission [APSC] (2018) Working with the government and parliament. https://www.apsc.gov.au/section-1-working-government-and-parliament. Accessed 17 Dec 2020
Bevilacqua J, Darnauer P (1977) Military social work. In: Encyclopaedia of social work, 17th edn. National Association of Social Workers, Washington DC, pp 927–931
Camilleri P (2001) Educating for social work: facing the new century. Aust Soc Work 54(1):16–20
Collie A (2019) The mental health impacts of compensation claim assessment processes. Insurance Work and Health Group, School of Public Health and Preventive Medicine, Faculty of Medicine Nursing and Health Sciences, Monash University. https://www.dva.gov.au/sites/default/files/independent-study-mhiccap.pdf. Accessed 13 Feb 2020
Council on Social Work Education [CSWE] (2010) Advanced social work practice in military social work. Alexandria, Virginia
Council on Social Work Education [CSWE] (2018) Specialized practice curricular guide for Military Social Work. Alexandria, Virginia
Creyke R (2019) Independent review of the implementation of the recommendations of the joint inquiry into the management of Jesse Bird's case. https://www.dva.gov.au/sites/default/files/report_-_independent_review_-_jesse_bird_joint_inquiry.pdf. Accessed 19 Feb 2021
Daley JG (2013) Ethical decision making in military social work. In: Rubin A, Weiss EL, Coll JE (eds) Handbook of military social work. Wiley, New Jersey, pp 51–66
Daraganova G, Smart D, Romaniuk H (2018) Family wellbeing study part 1: families of current and ex-serving ADF members: health and wellbeing. Department of Defence and Department of Veterans' Affairs, Canberra
Defence Force Discipline Act [DFDA] (1982) Compilation No. 33. https://www.legislation.gov.au/Details/C2019C00107. Accessed 14 Dec 2020
Defence Member and Family Support [DMFS] (2020a) About DMFS. https://www.defence.gov.au/members-families/About/Default.asp. Accessed 3 Oct 2020
Defence Member and Family Support [DMFS] (2020b) Australian defence force family covenant. https://www.defence.gov.au/members-families/About/Covenant.asp. Accessed 11 Dec 2020
Defence Member and Family Support [DMFS] (2020c) ADF member and family transition guide. https://www.defence.gov.au/members-families/_Master/documents/Transition/ADF-member-transition-guide.pdf. Accessed 28 Dec 2020

Defence Member and Family Support [DMFS] (2020d) Your family and the Australian Defence Force. https://www.defence.gov.au/members-families/Family/Default.asp. Accessed 28 Dec 2020

Defence Member and Family Support [DMFS] (2020e) Death and bereavement. https://defence.gov.au/members-families/Military-life/difficult-times/death-bereavement.asp. Accessed 7 Mar 2022

Department of Defence [DoD] (2017a) 2016–17 Defence annual report. Canberra, Australia

Department of Defence [DoD] (2017b) Defence Family and Domestic Violence Strategy (2017–2022) https://www.defence.gov.au/members-families/fdv-strategy.asp. Accessed 11 Feb 2020

Department of Defence [DoD] (2020) Legislative framework. https://www.Defence.gov.au/payan-dconditions/adf/Frameworks.asp. Accessed 15 Dec 2020

Department of Defence [DoD] (2021) Our mission and purpose. https://www.defence.gov.au/about/at-a-glance. Accessed 14 June 2021

Department of Veterans Affairs [DVA] (2019) DVA corporate plan 2019–2023. https://www.dva.gov.au/sites/default/files/dva-corporate-plan-2019-23_0.pdf. Accessed 14 June 2021

Department of Veterans Affairs [DVA] (2020a) Veteran mental health and wellbeing strategy and action plan 2020–2023. https://www.dva.gov.au/documents-and-publications/veteran-mental-health-and-wellbeing-strategy-and-national-action-plan. Accessed 19 Oct 2020

Department of Veterans Affairs [DVA] (2020b) Transition and wellbeing research programme. https://www.dva.gov.au/about-us/overview/research/transition-and-wellbeing-research-programme. Accessed 2 Sep 2020

Department of Veterans Affairs [DVA] (2020c) Legal resources. https://www.dva.gov.au/about-us/overview/legal-resources/recent-changes-our-legislation. Accessed 19 Dec 2020

Department of Veterans Affairs [DVA] (2020d) Notes for allied health providers. https://www.dva.gov.au/providers/notes-fee-schedules-and-guidelines/notes-providers/notes-allied-health-care-providers. Accessed 17 Feb 2021

Department of Veterans Affairs [DVA] (2020e) Veterans to be counted on 2021 census [Media Release]. http://minister.dva.gov.au/media_releases/2020/feb/va016.htm. Accessed 2 June 2021

Lawrence R (1965) Professional social work in Australia. Australian National University Press, Acton, Canberra

MacDonald G (2016) School-based support for students with a parent on military deployment. Child Aust 42(1):57–65

McGaw VE, Reupert AE, Maybery D (2019) Military posttraumatic stress disorder: a qualitative systematic review of the experience of families, parents and children. J Child Fam Stud 28:2942–2952

McManus J, Mehta S, McClinton A et al (2005) Informed consent and ethical issues in military medical research. Acad Emerg Med 12(11):1120–1126. https://doi.org/10.1197/j.aem.2005.05.037

Muir S (2018) Family wellbeing study: part 2: military family approaches to managing transition to civilian life. Department of Defence and Department of Veterans' Affairs, Canberra

Olson MD (2014) Exploring the ethical dilemma of integrating social work values and military social work practice. Soc Work 59(2):183–185. https://doi.org/10.1093/sw/swu010

Open Arms Veterans and Families Counselling (2020) Get support – treatment program and workshops. https://www.openarms.gov.au/get-support/treatment-programs-and-workshops#stepping-out. Accessed 27 Dec 2020

Productivity Commission (2019) A better way to support veterans, Report No. 93. Canberra, Australia

Rogers M (2016) Narrative, acculturation and ritual: themes from a socio-ecological study of Australian Defence Force families experiencing parental deployment. Child Aust 1(2):1–13

Rogers M (2020) Recommendations to support young children from Australian military families: a report for policy makers, family and social workers, and educators. J Manage Policy Pract 21(2):1–26

Siebler P (2009) 'Military people won't ask for help': experiences of deployment of Australian Defence Force personnel, their families, and implications for Social Work. Dissertation, Monash University

Siebler P (2015) 'Down under': support for military families from an Australian perspective. In: Moelker R, Andres M, Rones N (eds) Military families and war in the 21st century: comparative perspectives. Routledge, New York, pp 287–301

Siebler P, Goddard C (2014) Parents' perspectives of their children's reactions to an Australian military deployment. Child Aust 39:17–24

Siebler P, Karpetis G (2019) "In the cross-fire": intimate partner violence in military families. In: Moelker J, Andres M, Bowen G, Manigart P (eds) The politics of military families. Routledge, New York, pp 233–252

Stubbings L (1992) Look what you started Henry! History of the Australian Red Cross Society. Australian Red Cross Society, East Melbourne

Van Hooff M, Lawrence-Wood E, Hodson S et al (2018) Mental health prevalence, mental health and wellbeing transition study. The Department of Defence and the Department of Veterans' Affairs, Canberra

Van Hooff M, Lawrence-Wood E, Sadler N et al (2019) Transition and wellbeing research Programme key findings report. Department of Defence and Department of Veterans' Affairs, Canberra

Westhuis D (1999) Working with military families during deployment. In: Daley JG (ed) Social work practice in the military. Haworth Press, New York, pp 275–290

Chapter 3
Military Social Work in the Canadian Armed Forces

Suzanne M. Bailey, Henry G. Matheson, James F. J. Jamieson, Marie Pichette, and Audrey Hudon

3.1 History of Military Social Work (MilSW)

While the profession of social work has existed as an enduring occupation in the Canadian Armed Forces (CAF)[1] since 1952, its origins can be traced back more than a decade earlier. Upon hearing that Canada had joined the allied war effort in September 1939, a civilian social worker by the name of Stewart Sutton wrote to the Prime Minister to advocate for the development of some type of social service in the army that would help soldiers to manage preoccupations from home. Mr. Sutton anticipated that the distance between Canada and the front lines in Europe would create some unique challenges for military personnel and their families, and that additional resources and channels of communication would be helpful in addressing issues that could contribute to morale problems (Hanson n.d.). He envisioned, "some kind of a service whereby, in addition to any other channel a man might wish to use, there would be some well organized (sic) way that he could report a problem in full confidence and get some assurance, an honest assurance, as to what could be done about it, if anything" (Hanson n.d.).

---

[1] Under the National Defence Act, the terms Canadian Forces (CF) and Canadian Armed Forces (CAF) are interchangeable (Canada 1985). The abbreviation CAF, which has been more commonly used since 2013, will be used in this chapter except when referring to organization titles.

S. M. Bailey (✉) · H. G. Matheson · J. F. J. Jamieson · M. Pichette · A. Hudon
Canadian Forces Health Services Headquarters, Ottawa, ON, Canada
e-mail: Suzanne.bailey@forces.gc.ca; lhmath@magma.ca; liznjimj@gmail.com;
marie.pichette@forces.gc.ca; Audrey.Hudon@forces.gc.ca

© Springer Nature Switzerland AG 2023
M. A. Forgey, K. Green-Hurdle (eds.), *Military Social Work Around the Globe*,
Military and Veterans Studies, https://doi.org/10.1007/978-3-031-14482-0_3

After an initial acknowledgment to his letter, Mr. Sutton was contacted in 1942 and asked if he would be willing to help create the organization he had written about in 1939. Mr. Sutton joined the army, later achieving the rank of Lieutenant-Colonel, and was instrumental in the establishment of the Division on Special Services in May 1942, marking the beginning of MilSW in the CAF. Despite some initial uncertainty in the Army about the role of social work and its mandate, Captain Sutton's early information indicated that soldiers' concerns about family problems were prevalent; however, there seemed to be a lack of coordination, uniformity, or direction about how to manage these situations. There needed to be a clearly identified point of contact to assist with these issues, and those who were appointed to assist needed to be properly trained for the role (Sutton 1942). The role of the first uniformed military social workers during the war was primarily as consultants and advisors to commanding officers on matters related to social services, in addition to coordinating referrals and liaising with community service agencies. Uniformed social workers were also involved in the screening of new recruits, assessing them for mental health and psychosocial problems that could interfere with military service. Initially associated with Personnel Services and then Auxiliary Services, it was quickly recognized that social work should be affiliated with Medical Services. The Director General Health Services, Major-General Chisolm, in a memorandum to the Adjutant-General, advocated that,

> ... failure to provide adequate Social Service results by far most commonly in psychosomatic symptoms and consequent increase in sick parades, disabilities and loss of training time. The work done by these Social Workers is actually Mental Hygiene and ... it is impossible to have an adequate Health Service for the Army without the inclusion of such workers (Chisolm 1943).

The Directorate of Social Science, part of the Royal Canadian Army Medical Corps, became official on 17 July 1944 with a mandate for hiring uniformed social workers, providing professional guidance and supervision, developing social policy, completing professional assessments on compassionate matters, and providing advice to Commanding Officers (Letson 1944). These are many of the same roles that Canadian military social workers continue to perform today.

By 1944, there were seven uniformed social workers in the army, a number that grew to more than 60 by the end of the war to assist with the rehabilitation of troops returning from overseas, the integration of war brides into Canadian society, and other post-conflict social issues. In reflecting back on these early years, Lieutenant Colonel Sutton highlighted two key strengths of the social work occupation. The first was that confidentiality regarding the service member's concerns was maintained, including a stipulation that no social work documentation or correspondence would be placed on the individual's personnel file (Hanson n.d.). The other area where uniformed social workers excelled was in building relationships within communities across Canada, despite their small number in an army of 500,000. Their ability to establish networks with community agencies, clergy, police departments, and local governments was key to arranging for resources for military members and their families (Hanson n.d.).

As with many capabilities established to meet wartime needs, the Directorate was disbanded at the end of World War II, and all social workers were released from the military. A social work capability was re-established in 1952 in response to recommendations by Professor Charles Hendry of the University of Toronto, who had been commissioned to complete a study on the social work and recreational needs of the Armed Forces. Professor Hendry observed that military families experienced many of the same challenges as civilian families and that the experience of World War II had demonstrated the benefit of having social workers to augment the other regimental and community resources to assist military members and their families (DND 1964). When he submitted his report in 1949, he recommended that the Armed Forces recruit professionally trained social workers into uniformed service to help manage the "special problems of social well-being" (DND 1964), citing the benefits of having a single resource with experience in conducting interviews and assessments, coordinating referrals, providing skilled assistance in handling difficult cases, and maintaining confidentiality (DND 1964).

In 1952, the Royal Canadian Air Force established the Social Welfare Branch with four squadron leaders and eight flight lieutenants, marking the official beginning of a continuous presence of uniformed social workers in the CAF. These social workers were all professionally trained and had at least 2 years of experience working in a civilian agency. A civilian social work presence in the Royal Canadian Navy followed shortly thereafter, and social work was expanded to all elements when the CAF unified into a single command structure in 1968 with 24 uniformed and two civilian social work officers and became Canadian Forces Social Work Services.

3.2 Military Social Work (MilSW) Role and Settings

3.2.1 Evolution of Social Work Role in Response to Organizational and Societal Factors

Canadian MilSW in the 1970s was largely practiced in small social work offices on large military establishments across the country, with a presence on Canadian bases in Germany as well. These social work offices, usually comprised of a uniformed social work officer and sometimes a civilian social worker, had responsibility for smaller military establishments in their area and would regularly travel between locations to provide services. While focused primarily on individual case work, group work, community organization, and consultation and liaison; social work services in these years also became more involved in preventive programmes and family services. They provided educational sessions to members and supervisors about available services and resources and worked closely with the other helping professionals in local military and civilian communities.

As the 1970s came to a close, the practice of MilSW within the CAF entered a period of considerable change. For the CAF at large, the period was characterized by significant geopolitical shifts; a marked increase in deployments; a greater emphasis on incorporating social changes such as the inclusion of women into CAF policy and practices; new recognition of the contributions of families and their needs within the various CAF roles; and consequently, new expectations for the evolving role of social work practice in a military environment. The growing awareness and appreciation for the clinical mental health skills that social workers brought to the table contributed to military social workers becoming affiliated once again with Medical Services. In 1979, the Directorate of Social Development Services led by a social work Lieutenant Colonel was once again transferred to the Surgeon General Branch, and social work became a specialist occupation within Canadian Forces Medical Services (CFMS). This move was brought about by both necessity, as occupational alignment was changing for a number of professions, and philosophically, to keep with a growing societal recognition of the effectiveness of a holistic model of health that integrated the physical, psychological, and social circumstances of the person. Over time, it would formalize the working relationship between medical personnel and social workers at the base level, while the expansion of social work capability within Family Services would enhance the services available to military families and the wider community.

Following the move to CFMS, social work officers continued to provide a combination of occupational and clinical services, including administrative assessments such as deployment and overseas screenings; addiction assessments; compassionate posting requests; consultations with other service providers and commanding officers; and counselling services directly to members and, on occasion, to their families in isolated locations and foreign postings. Through the 1980s and 1990s, the role of the social worker became even more multifaceted with opportunities for employment in a variety of roles including teaching at military colleges, working in health promotion and prevention programming, being part of a treatment team in alcohol and drug treatment centres, and collaborating with the expanding network of Military Family Resource Centres (MFRCs). The closure of in-patient treatment facilities and restructuring of health services would affect some of these roles in future years but would be offset by novel roles in special operations command and enhanced support to deployed operations.

In 1994, with the Cold War coming to an end, the CAF launched a restructuring and deficit reduction initiative that included a review of medical services. The intent was to provide a more operationally focused medical service that could achieve its objectives with fewer uniformed members. While the initial recommendation was to dismantle the MilSW occupation and retain a civilian capability, strong resistance from Commanders and other military occupations outside Health Services contributed to the decision to retain the occupation (Clay 1996). The rank of Lieutenant Colonel, however, was not restored to the occupation until 2001.

3.2.2 A New Concept for Mental Health Care Delivery

The 1990s and early 2000s also saw an unprecedented emphasis on the mental health of military personnel in Western nations amid greater societal understanding and acceptance of mental health. Within the CAF, there was increased effort to identify and support the mental health needs of those returning from deployment, and a concurrent effort to review and modernize the delivery of health care within the CAF, including mental health care, under the auspices of a project called Rx 2000 (DND 2013). In order to identify the prevalence of mental illness in the CAF and determine the resources required to provide care, Statistics Canada conducted the CAF Mental Health Supplement to the Canadian Community Health Survey in 2002. This was the first large-scale population-based mental health survey of Canadian military personnel. The findings from this survey were instrumental in establishing a way forward for restructuring the delivery of mental health care by indicating that while CAF members were more likely than their civilian counterparts to access care, there remained a considerable percentage who delayed or simply did not access care. The results also showed that mental health and mental illness were not well understood in military personnel and that more needed to be done to increase awareness and access to resources (NDCAF 2014).

Of the many initiatives stemming from Rx 2000 that affected the way social work was practiced, the most significant was the Mental Health Care Model (DND 2003). The new model of care was multi-disciplinary and collaborative in nature and included social workers, mental health nurses, psychologists, psychiatrists, addiction counsellors, and clinical chaplains in the provision of team-based care for both psychosocial concerns as well as diagnosed mental health conditions. Stand-alone social work offices ceased to exist and were replaced by teams comprised of social workers, mental health nurses, and addiction counsellors. CAF personnel continued to have direct access to social workers through what was now called the Psychosocial Services Programme, and while they continued to perform many of the traditional occupational functions such as screenings and compassionate assessments, social workers were also expected to take on a more active clinical role in this new model. This expectation extended to social workers' participation in the other mental health programmes such as the General Mental Health Programme and the Operational Trauma Stress Support Centres, which provide assessment and treatment for a broad range of mental health conditions. There was also an increased emphasis on family inclusion in the member's care by all mental health disciplines. By 2009, the implementation of the Rx 2000 Mental Health Care Model had been completed and the number of mental health clinicians had more than doubled, with social workers representing the largest single group of mental health providers. The Directorate of Mental Health was formally established in 2009, with the senior social work officer becoming the National Practice Leader for Social Work and responsible for the professional technical oversight of the profession in Canadian Forces Health Services (CFHS).

3.2.3   Social Work Support to Deployed Operations

Military social workers have been active participants in domestic and international operations for decades. They have supported military operations, disaster response, and humanitarian missions during incidents such as the Suez crisis of 1956–57, the conflicts in the former Yugoslavia in the 1990s, the Gulf War, Afghanistan, Mali, Haiti, and Sri Lanka. Military social workers have also provided mental health support during domestic operations, including the response to the Swiss Air 111 crash off the coast of Nova Scotia in 1998 and recently the COVID-19 pandemic in 2020. The deployed role includes supporting members coping with a variety of stressors either at home or in the theatre of operations, providing preventive education to deployed units, working with other helping professionals, and delivering reintegration services prior to soldiers' return home. The importance of outreach and networking is especially important in the deployed setting to ensure that personnel at all levels of the chain of command know that social work support is accessible and are familiar with the services available.

Military social workers have been actively involved in pre- and post-deployment screening and education, with uniformed social workers often deploying to ships or into active theatres of operations to facilitate post-tour transition and reintegration for military personnel. While some form of pre- and post-deployment screening processes focused on identifying psychosocial factors that could impact a member or their family during a deployment have been in place for several decades, a more comprehensive post-deployment screening process was implemented in 2002 in response to the growing understanding of the potential impact of deployment on mental health (DND 2013). This enhanced process was aimed at increasing early identification of post-deployment difficulties, decreasing the delay to care, and included completion of standardized questionnaires and a semi-structured clinical interview. Further, a robust pre-and post-deployment education programme was established in 2008 (DND 2013) to provide standardized evidence-based training to assist military personnel to manage the demands of operations and the challenges of reintegration after their mission. This contributed to uniformed and civilian social workers becoming an integral component of the Third Location Decompression programme that has been provided to international missions since 2006 (Garber and Zamorski 2012).

3.2.4   Fundamental Military Social Work (MilSW) Roles

As the occupation has evolved, there has been a growing understanding that the problems of social well-being have an impact on military personnel and military readiness. The demands of service such as mobility, isolation, separation, and training can create psychosocial issues or exacerbate existing situations and require specialized support and resources. Despite the changes in mandate and affiliation over the decades, the types of concerns addressed by CAF uniformed and civilian social workers throughout the years have remained fairly consistent. Since 1942, when Captain Sutton stated that "men's worries over family problems is prevalent and a source of serious concern" (Sutton 1942), social work in the CAF has addressed such matters as marital problems, compassionate issues, financial distress, substance use, family adjustment, intimate partner violence, and a range of mental health problems. The systemic approach of traditional social work was recognized in the 1964 Staff Paper on the Establishment of a Social Work Service in the CAF that stated that "people require consideration as individuals and groups" (DND 1964) and continues to be reflected in the most recent Defence Policy for Canada, which recognizes the incredible contribution of families to the operational effectiveness of the Forces and places "an unprecedented focus on ensuring our people and their families are well-supported, diverse and resilient – physically, psychologically and socially" (Government of Canada 2017). In addition to providing direct services to members and their families, social workers continue to act as consultants to commanding officers and career managers to develop and maintain collaborative relationships with local resources and helping professionals, to arrange referrals for more specialized services, and to make recommendations to inform policy development.

In the years since the transition away from standalone social work offices to the integration into the multi-disciplinary mental health model, interventions have gradually become more clinically focused at the individual level, with less of a community development role. Social workers in the psychosocial level of services typically provide short-duration interventions for personnel exhibiting symptoms of anxiety, depression, adjustment to stress, or relationship distress—employing evidence-based treatment approaches such as cognitive behavioural therapy.

The changes of the past two decades have also affected social work charting and documentation in a number of ways. Since the initial establishment of Social Work Services during World War II, social work client files were kept separate from each member's health records or other military records and could only be accessed by social workers. In order to enable team-based inter-disciplinary care, social work files were integrated into the health care record with access by other members of the care team. Further integration followed when all mental health notes became part of the electronic health record in 2014, and standardized charting templates were developed, through a collaborative process, for all mental health encounters (DND 2014). For many mental health clinicians, this represented a significant shift in how care was delivered, resulting in closer integration between primary care providers and mental health clinicians as they deliver care to military personnel.

The other aspect of the social work role that has changed in the past two decades is the gradual increase in leadership and management responsibilities as the size of the mental health teams has expanded. The implementation of multi-disciplinary team-based care brought with it requirements for supervision, coordination, communication, and management of departments that had more than doubled in size. As a result, most uniformed social workers and many civilians transitioned into team lead or programme manager positions with additional responsibilities, thereby decreasing the number of hours available for clinical practice.

3.2.5 Military Social Work Role in Military to Civilian Transition

In addition to the mental health clinicians employed within CFHS who provide care for military personnel, there are social workers in other parts of DND, namely, Military Family Services (MFS) and the Canadian Armed Forces Transition Group (CAFTG), who support military and veteran families as well as members who are nearing the end of their career in uniform. MFS works to ensure that the Canadian military family community is well supported in order for military families to lead positive and nurturing family lives comparable to other Canadian families while supporting the operational effectiveness of the CAF. Through its MFRCs, as well as virtual programmes and 24/7 telephone support services, they promote and facilitate community-based services and programmes to enhance the well-being of military and veteran families. The Veteran Family programme was expanded in 2018 to support veterans and their families by helping them navigate the complex process of releasing, the challenges that may arise, and the sometimes unexpected impact on social, emotional, and financial wellbeing (Canadian Forces Morale and Welfare Services 2020). Canadian Armed Forces Transition Group [CAFTG] was established in 2018 to significantly enhance the support provided to military personnel and their families as they transition from active duty to post-military life (CAFTG 2018; Therrien et al. 2021). While the social workers in these organizations are in a chain of command separate from Health Services, there is collaboration at the local and national levels to ensure that services are coordinated and complementary.

3.3 Practice Orientation and Ethical Issues Encountered

Despite many of the aforementioned changes, the practice orientation continues to be a balance of occupational and clinical social work. Some of the traditional occupational social work tasks such as compassionate assessments, screenings, and advocacy have remained as part of the policy-based mandate. These tasks, which require the social worker to balance the needs of the individual with those of the organization, can be challenging and require careful consideration in making recommendations that can impact a member's career. The social worker must ask themselves, in these types of situations, who the client is and who is requesting the service being provided. While the objective is to determine if an individual or family's situation can be accommodated with a view to retaining highly trained personnel, each situation must be assessed against the needs of the organization. These challenges are not unique to MilSW but do require clear policies and guidance, such as not completing screenings or compassionate assessments on members with whom one has a prior relationship, as well as frequent reflection and professional technical consultation through an established network.

Wearing the uniform can also contribute to tension regarding boundaries and confidentiality when the military social worker is part of the small community and chain of command in which and for whom they are providing services. Situations will arise throughout one's career that require reflection on the question of whether one is a professional military officer first or a professional social worker. As military officers, they must act in accordance with the Queen's Regulations and Orders, which includes a duty to report any infringement of the pertinent statutes, regulations, rules, orders, and instructions governing the conduct of any person subject to the Code of Service Discipline (Canada 2019), while also adhering to their professional Standards of Practice and Code of Ethics (MacKay 2015). They may find themselves in situations where they question whether they are required to report certain transgressions, or which of their roles takes priority. In the early years, social workers received little guidance on how to deal with these sorts of tensions and relied on clinical judgment, common sense, and consultation with other care providers. Policies clarifying professional ethics and strengthening patient confidentiality have alleviated many of these concerns in recent years, but emerging policies such as the duty of all uniformed personnel to report sexual misconduct bring these tensions to the forefront and re-invigorate the discussion regarding the balance of loyalties of uniformed care providers (MacKay 2015).

For both uniformed and civilian social workers in the military, the hierarchical nature of the command structure can also appear to conflict with social work values and compound the existing power imbalances in the clinician-client relationship. Improvements to human rights legislation, privacy protections, and codes of ethics have significantly ameliorated this aspect of MilSW—but given the nature of the role and the organization in which it is carried out, it will never completely disappear. Within this framework, social workers remain advisors to the chain of command and make recommendations based on their assessment; however, they must accept that the final decision rests with someone else in the chain of command.

3.4 Military Social Work (MilSW) Education and Training

In his 1943 recommendations to establish the original capability of MilSW, Captain Sutton recognized that a combination of education and experience was required for uniformed military social workers. He advocated that Canadian Army social workers be graduates of a recognized School of Social Work, be approved by the Canadian Association of Social Work (CASW), and that they be in "possession of necessary maturity of personality, emotional poise and tact" (Strathy 1943). While those particular attributes may have been difficult to identify in applicants, the official criteria included a balance of professional social work education and experience. For many years, social workers who joined with a Bachelor of Social Work (BSW) degree could apply to complete their Master of Social Work (MSW) through sponsored post-graduate training. In 1998, a clinical Master's degree became the basic occupational requirement for all uniformed military social workers, and those applying with a BSW were eligible for a subsidized education programme to complete their MSW upon entry.

Subsequent to some of the other changes in 1979, there was an increased focus on preparing social workers to work in a military and medical setting. Unlike other military specialists, there were no setting-specific courses designed to prepare social workers for military practice. Beginning in the early 1980s, uniformed social workers who joined the occupation undertook a formal 1-year on-the-job training programme to prepare them to practice social work within the military. The 1-year structured training requirement, which continues today, would evolve over time to include formal supervision and mentorship from a senior social work officer and would expand to include an increased focus on clinical management and leadership as social workers were placed in those roles following the implementation of the mental health model. Social work officers also attend second language training as part of their occupational training to enable them to provide a basic level of services in both English and French.

Military social workers attend accredited Canadian universities to complete their MSW and follow the clinical pathway to prepare them to practice in an adult mental health setting. While each university must meet the criteria of the Canadian Association of Social Work Education, there is significant variation in the courses and content of each social work degree programme. As a result, the skill sets that individuals possess upon graduation vary widely and can have a significant impact on their ability to practice in a multi-disciplinary military setting. The structured, on-the-job training programme aims to level this playing field to some extent, with training modules focused on the CAF occupational social work role and additional clinical training in evidence-based treatment modalities, such as Cognitive Behaviour Therapy, offered if they were not part of the degree courses. While there are American universities that have degree programmes that focus specifically on delivering care to military personnel and veterans, the number of social workers in Canada delivering care to this population is not large enough to warrant a separate course or degree specialty.

3.5   Major Challenges and Future Directions

In his foreword to the 21st First Anniversary Newsletter in 1974, Major Ken Jacobs observed that "many of the problems confronting us in the early days are still with us: the isolation from colleagues, the limited career possibilities, and too few people to do a proper job". Almost 50 years later, despite the years of growth and change, those factors remain. A social work officer can spend many years working in clinics where they are the sole uniformed member of their occupation, with the nearest colleague several hours away. Modern technology has helped to some extent, but there is often a sense of isolation and perhaps feeling misunderstood in a healthcare setting where other professions are often represented in larger numbers and their roles are familiar and well understood. As the social work role can vary greatly across health care and community settings, there is frequently a lack of understanding of the MilSW role and where it fits in the larger health care team. The integration into multi-disciplinary care and closer collaboration with primary care providers has contributed to greater insight into the social work role.

The small size of the occupation, with 42 uniformed positions, also limits career progression as the senior rank remains a single Lieutenant Colonel position. Pathways to transition into other health service roles that open up additional pathways to career progression are being explored and would offer choices to social work officers who wish to continue to serve the organization and continue their career progression.

As it approaches its 80th anniversary, the social work occupation in the CAF continues to grow and evolve. The past decade has seen new positions established to support specialized units; a significant increase in the demand for social work support on deployed operations; and increased demand for clinical care as mental health education and societal awareness have contributed to decreased stigma and increased recognition of distress. Social workers have and will undoubtedly continue to make significant contributions towards the wellbeing of the men and women of the CAF and their families as they face the challenges and opportunities of military service.

References

Canada (1985) National Defence Act R.S.C. 1985, c N-5. https://laws-lois.justice.gc.ca/eng/acts/n-5/. Accessed 29 Nov 2020

Canada (2019) Department of National Defence Queen's Regulations and Orders for the Canadian Forces. https://www.canada.ca/en/department-national-defence/corporate/policies-standards/queens-regulations-orders/vol-1-administration.html. Accessed 25 Mar 2022

Canadian Armed Forces Transition Group [CAFTG] (2018) My transition guide: transitioning from military to civilian life. https://www.canada.ca/en/department-national-defence/corporate/reports-publications/transition-guide.html#guide. Accessed 30 May 2021

Canadian Forces Morale and Welfare Services [CFMWS] (2020) Services for military and veteran families: the 2020+ Strategic Framework. Ottawa

Chisolm GB (1943) Department of National Defence Memorandum H.Q.S.8877-2, Welfare Officers, Internal document, Ottawa

Clay WA (1996) Chief of Health Services memo 1243-1. Military Social Work Service, Internal document, Ottawa

Department of National Defence [DND] (1964) A staff paper on the establishment of a social welfare service for the Canadian Forces. Internal document, Ottawa

Department of National Defence [DND] (2003) Concept for Canadian Forces mental health care. Annex A to Canadian Forces Mental Health Initiative, Ottawa

Department of National Defence [DND] (2013) Surgeon General's Mental Health Strategy: an evolution of excellence, Ottawa

Department of National Defence [DND] (2014) News release: Canadian Armed Forces launch electronic mental health notes, Ottawa

Garber BG, Zamorski MA (2012) Evaluation of a third location decompression program for Canadian Forces members returning from Afghanistan. Mil Med 177(4):397–403

Government of Canada (2017) Strong, Secure, Engaged: Canada's Defence Policy, Ottawa

Hanson J (n.d.) LCol (Ret'd) Sutton's personal account of the origins of social work in the Canadian Army, Ottawa, Canada. Unpublished document

Jacobs K (1974) Foreword to social work newsletter twenty-first anniversary, Ottawa

Letson HFG (1944) Department of National Defence Memorandum H.Q.S. 8877-2. Directorate of Social Science, Internal document, Ottawa

MacKay HC (2015) Commander Canadian Forces Health Services Group 1234-1 (D Surg Gen). Operation Honour DSG Frag Order, Internal document, Ottawa

National Defence and the Canadian Armed Forces [NDCAF] (2014) The CF 2002 Supplement of the Statistics Canadian Community Health Survey, Ottawa

Strathy JGK (1943) Department of National Defence Memorandum H.Q. 54-27-7-270 (Trg 3) Appointment, qualification and promotion of officers non-medical general list, RCAMC (A) CA. Internal document, Ottawa

Sutton S (1942) Department of National Defence Memorandum BDF 650-99-21 Morale implications of worry over personal and family problems of O.R.'s. Internal document, Ottawa

Therrien M, Coulthard J, Green K (2021) Canadian Armed Forces Transition Group: leading the way for a smooth transition. J Veterans Stud 7(1):55–58. https://doi.org/10.21061/jvs.v7i1.231

Chapter 4
Social Work in the Danish Defence

Lene Westergaard Birk and Henriette Dueholm Christensen

4.1 Background: Overview of the Danish Military

The Danish armed forces engage in a wide range of operations in Denmark,
Greenland, and the Faroe Islands. Internationally, Denmark has a longstanding tradition of participating in military international cooperation and operations at the
world's trouble spots. The Danish Defence maintains the sovereignty of the Danish
Commonwealth and forms part of society's overall emergency readiness (the so-
called total-defence concept). Since 1948, more than 60,000 Danish service members have served in trouble spots all over the world in UN and NATO missions, or
through Danish participation in international coalitions (Danish Defence 2021). At
the end of 2021, the strength of the Danish Armed Forces was some 21,231 military
personnel including conscripts, supported by about 5386 civilians
(Forsvarsministeriets personalestyrelse 2022).

Military conscription is mandatory for all physically fit men older than 18.
Women may participate but are not obligated to do so. Military service is typically
4 months. There is an exemption for conscientious objectors, including on religious
grounds, allowing conscientious objectors to instead perform alternative civilian
service, which also has a period of 4 months. An individual wishing to perform
alternative service as a conscientious objector must apply within eight weeks of
receiving notice of military service. The application is adjudicated by the
Conscientious Objector Administration and must show that military service of any
kind is incompatible with the individual's conscience. The alternative service may

L. W. Birk (✉)
Veterans Center, Danish Armed Forces, Gentofte, Region Hovedstaden, Denmark
e-mail: lene.westergaard.birk@regionh.dk

H. D. Christensen (✉)
Veterans Center, Danish Armed Forces, Høvelte, Region Hovedstaden, Denmark
e-mail: vetc-fa502@mil.dk

© Springer Nature Switzerland AG 2023
M. A. Forgey, K. Green-Hurdle (eds.), *Military Social Work Around the Globe*,
Military and Veterans Studies, https://doi.org/10.1007/978-3-031-14482-0_4

take place in various social and cultural institutions, peace movements, organizations related to the United Nations, churches, ecumenical organizations, and environmental organizations throughout the country (Global security n.d.).

4.2   History of Danish Military Social Work

As early as 1943, the Royal Danish Navy set up a consulting company for serving personnel, and thus the first step was taken toward a final plan for social services in the Danish Defence. In 1951, the Royal Danish Navy hired their first trained civilian social worker (Bjerg 1991).

With the Defense Act of 1951, the work was legislated, and the institution was named the Army Welfare Service. The institution was placed directly under the Danish Ministry of Defence and in the following year, the Army Welfare Service set up a committee of experts to prepare a proposal for a permanent social worker plan for the entire personnel of the Danish Defence. Following the committee work and various pilot projects, the social worker plan commenced (Bjerg 1991).

In 1960, the Danish Parliament passed a new settlement for the Danish Defence programme. The institution changed its name to the Information and Welfare Service of the Danish Defence (IWS) but was still under the Ministry of Defence. In 2011, the Danish Veteran Centre was established, one year after the government at that time had adopted Denmark's first Veteran Policy, which included the idea of one single entry for veterans and their relatives in the form of a Veteran Centre covering the entire Danish Realm (Denmark, Faroe Islands, and Greenland). It is also important to note that in Denmark, *a veteran may be an active duty military member or a former Defence member,* as a veteran is defined as a person who has been deployed in an international mission at least once on the grounds of a decision made by the parliament, the Danish government, or a minister (Forsvarsministeriet 2016). Therefore, the term "veteran" in this chapter is inclusive of both current and former military personnel. The Veteran Centre social workers work with both active-duty members and former military members.

With the creation of the Veteran Policy (Forsvarsministeriet 2016), the goal of the Veteran Centre became to work for recognition and support for veterans (both current and former military members) and their relatives through 19 new initiatives. By bringing together all relevant disciplines in the same organization, the initiatives that the Danish Defence already had for physically and mentally injured veterans were strengthened.

Today, the Veteran Centre is a well-established part of the Danish Defence and is organizationally part of the Ministry of Defence Personnel Agency (DDPA). The DDPA is an agency under the Ministry of Defence. The Ministry of Defence and its subordinate authorities solve tasks that contribute to peace and security. The tasks are solved nationally as well as internationally.

4.3   Requirements for the Job as a Social Worker in the Danish Defence

To be able to work as a social worker in the Danish Defence, one must hold a degree in social work. This 3.5-year professional bachelor's programme consists of seven semesters, with the fourth semester including an internship period of 5 months. An additional requirement for being employed as a social worker in the Danish Defence is having practical experience in either municipal administration or the field of psychiatry.

All social workers receive continuing education as psychiatric counsellors to learn concrete tools for dealing with the challenges that arise in conversations with the mentally vulnerable, providing insight into key considerations and how to make demands, as well as increase insight into the various mental illnesses and conditions. In addition, there are regularly held theme days with social topics such as social legislation, operation of the 24-hour telephone, and other relevant topics.

All social workers also receive Solution Focused therapy training (Sikkerhedskonsulenterne 2022). This training enables social workers to have solution-focused conversations with veterans and enriched networking meetings to ensure the development of a network around the veterans and their relatives for improved future-focused, health, and wellbeing outcomes.

4.4   Military Social Work Practice

4.4.1   Organizational Framework

The Veteran Centre is a part of the ministerial department of the Ministry of Defence. Administratively, the Veteran Centre is connected to the Danish Ministry of Defence Personnel Agency (DDPA) and, as an independent authority, reports directly to the director of the DDPA (Fig. 4.1).

The Veteran Centre has the following four departments: Administration, the Research and Knowledge Centre, the Department of Military Psychology (DMP), and the Department of Rehabilitation (DR) (Veterancentret 2020a).

The head office and management of the Veteran Centre is located in Ringsted. Military and civilian staff members work in different locations around Denmark. The primary locations are Aalborg, Holstebro, Fredericia, Slagelse, and Høvelte.

The Research and Knowledge Centre and staff are placed in Ringsted together with the management. Each primary place of duty has employees from the Department of Military Psychology (DMP) and from the Department of Rehabilitation (DR). The DR consists of social workers, employment counsellors, outreach counsellors, and family counsellors. The family counsellors are either social workers or psychologists. There is a strong focus on interdisciplinarity among the employees.

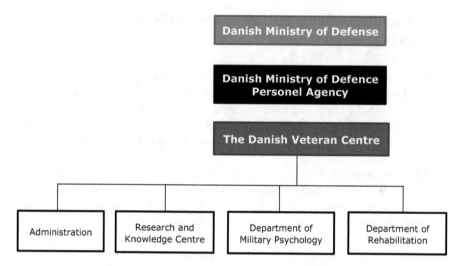

Fig. 4.1 Ministry of Defence – Veteran Centre Structure

The Veteran Centre employs both military and civilian personnel. The management consists primarily of military members who are officers. The social workers employed at the Centre have always been civilian employees, and all social work positions within the Veteran Centre require a degree in social work.

Over the years, the social workers have supported the Danish Defence military members and their relatives through information, counselling, and preventive activities. Furthermore, they help create a good workplace for the members of the Danish Defence with visible and dynamic participation in change processes. Their efforts are specifically targeted at groups and individuals whose problems are caused by their military service. This also applies to former military personnel. Thus, the social workers of the Danish Defence provide lifelong access to counselling and guidance as long as the case is related to deployment.

4.4.2   Social Work Practice Settings

Since the opening of the Veteran Centre in 2011, the total number of employees dealing exclusively with veterans and their relatives has increased. In May 2012, there were 111 on the permanent staff, and in October 2020, there were 142; 22 were social workers who worked in barracks spread over five regions.

The reason for this is that the social workers must be visible and easily accessible to the staff, which ensures fast and smooth case processing. By working at the barracks, the social workers also gain a greater understanding and insight into the military reality.

Due to the social workers' accessibility by being located within the barracks, military personnel often come to social workers for advice and guidance either in relation to their work situation or private life. Military personnel often come by the social work office unannounced and sometimes at the request of their superiors or colleagues. They also know the social workers from the presentations given in connection with deployments and from their participation in meetings at the barracks.

The Veteran Centre has a 24-hour telephone service that is answered by a social worker outside normal opening hours, who is trained in providing counselling and support over the phone. The purpose of the 24-hour telephone service is to ensure that soldiers, veterans, and relatives can talk to a social worker at any time and receive telephone support and assistance in relation to their current situation. The social worker is not doing face-to-face visits but may contact the police or emergency services, if necessary, when a life-threatening crisis is identified. The social worker can also be helpful in contacting an emergency doctor or the psychiatric emergency room. The vast majority of interventions involve the person needing to talk to a professional about their issues.

4.4.3 Practice Orientation and Approach

The social workers provide counselling and guidance to current and former military personnel and their relatives, as well as provide counselling for military commanders regarding social issues and social legislation. The social workers play a coordinating role in addition to providing guidance to both current and former military personnel.

The social workers work from a holistic perspective, illuminating each case from all angles and involving relevant professionals such as employment counsellors, outreach counsellors, family counsellors, psychologists from the Veteran Centre, military commanders, contact officers, infirmary, and partners outside the Danish Defence. The social workers collaborate with municipalities, psychiatrists, hospitals, general practitioners, trade unions, voluntary organizations, substance abuse centres, and so on. The primary task is to ensure that both current and former military personnel and their relatives are supported in the best possible way before, during, and after deployment.

The social worker's practice orientation is inspired by Solution Focused Therapy (Sikkerhedskonsulenterne 2022). With this approach, the focus is on the military member and their opportunities to bring forward their own resources, desires, and ability to develop measures that can fulfil their goals. In using this approach, the social workers' assumption is that the person in question possesses solution measures that are important to investigate, and the focus is on strengthening and building on what works well for the individual. The following case example illustrates a social worker using a solution-focused approach:

A Danish former military member lives in a cottage where he has isolated himself and feels anxious and unsafe in his home. Due to his PTSD and anxiousness, he has deliberately chosen to live in secrecy. He expresses that he wants to change his situation, which is why he is invited to participate in a Solution Focused Therapy session. During the session, the military member talks with the social worker about his hopes for the future. He wants to find a new home where he can feel safe. To him, feeling safe means that he would no longer feel a pressure on his chest. He is asked to describe his future apartment; where should it be located, what should it look like inside, what furniture should it contain and so on. By imagining and describing this, it becomes clear to him what his future should be like. When he was offered a new home by a housing association, he was ready to move in and furnish it. He could then start a new life, being aware of what it takes to get a safe base and thus ensuring better well-being in his everyday life. Today, he knows that he is thriving because he is gathering strength and energy in his home, something he has not been able to do before and was appreciative of the role of social work in supporting him to achieve his practical and psychosocial goals.

4.4.4 Social Work Roles with Military Service Members and Former Members

Social workers have a role in supporting conscripts given that all men over the age of 18 years of age must serve a four-month period of conscription. Women over the age of 18 years old may participate but are not obligated to do so. The social workers talk with conscript soldiers about their well-being during their service, domestic conditions, mental health issues, and general well-being.

When military personnel are deployed on an international mission, the counselling consists of preparing the soldiers and their relatives on wills, practical and mental preparation, insurance plans, and identifying a network of people who can help and support the relatives while the soldier is deployed. During the deployment, there are relatives' events with presentations by social workers regarding preparation for leave-taking, mental reactions, and homecoming.

If a soldier returns home from a mission prematurely, they are obliged to participate in an interview with a social worker. The reasons that a soldier may return home prematurely can be because of sickness in the family, injury, death in the family, or children's response to the deployment. The purpose of this is for the veteran to be informed about the support opportunities in the Veteran Centre as well as in the civilian sector, offer psychologist sessions, contact the employer with the aim of starting work again, and refer to treatment and concrete services available within the municipality. For example, if the service member is on sick leave, the Danish Defence receives a refund of his or her salary in the form of sickness benefits from the municipality. The person on sick leave is obliged to cooperate with the municipality regarding the course of the illness. The social workers (in collaboration with their employer) support military personnel when they are on sick leave due to mental or physical challenges. Social workers also participate in meetings with the public system in order to ensure that the member on sick leave returns to work as best and as quickly as possible.

In collaboration with the veteran, who may be a currently serving military member or former member, the social workers provide support and advice in occupational injury cases. The social workers can help with filling out insurance questionnaires and ensuring that all relevant documents are included in the case. If the veteran receives compensation, the Veteran Centre offers financial counselling, and the social workers ensure that the veteran receives this offer. If the veteran does not already have an occupational injury case, social workers talk to them about the option of reporting the injury and help them with the process.

If a soldier with a deployment-related mental or physical injury can no longer do their job, they can be referred to a rehabilitation course provided by the Veteran Centre. In such cases, the social worker's task is to conduct an assessment and a social case history that describes the veteran's challenges. Usually, the rehabilitation course extends over three years and includes retraining for roles outside of the military to ensure that the veteran can get a job in the civilian sector. During the course, the social workers work closely with employment counsellors, psychologists, psychiatrists, and the municipality. The veteran receives full pay during the course and is terminated from employment when the course ends. Subsequently, the veteran still has the opportunity to seek counselling and guidance from the Veteran Centre following discharge from the military, as the Veteran Centre serves both currently serving and former military members.

In collaboration with the veteran, the social workers can prepare an application for a service dog, which may assist veterans with mental challenges. Service dogs can relieve isolation, loneliness, and help get the veteran out of their home. The service dog service is aimed at veterans diagnosed with PTSD and a long-term treatment history behind them. Veterans, therefore, need to meet a number of criteria to be considered for the service (Veterancentret 2021).

Social workers have the opportunity to apply for grants for veterans offered by private foundations, and it is often the social workers in the Danish Defence who apply for these since veterans cannot apply themselves due to the rules of the funding programme. The grants are used for housing, vacation with children, dental treatment, medicine, and financial counselling.

Two examples are provided below that illustrate the social work role within the Veteran Centre when working directly with a currently serving service member (Case 1) and a former military member (Case 2):

Case 1: A military member is on long-term sick leave from his job as a constable in the Army. He has been on sick leave for the last three months due to depression. It is unknown whether his condition is related to his previous deployment. He is offered an interview with one of the social workers at the barracks. He is also referred to the psychologists of the Danish Defence, who can help to shed light on whether his condition is related to his deployment and provide him with the relevant coping strategies/tools. In addition, the military member is required to meet with his/her immediate superior to make a potential plan for their return to work. The social worker is in charge of the return-to-work process and works in collaboration with the military member, the psychologists of the Danish Defence and the military member's immediate superior to prepare a plan including specific goals for the person's return to work.

During the process, the social worker will follow up continuously until the member is back at work full time. If it is determined that they cannot return to work, then they can remain a part of the rehabilitation program until discharged.

Case 2: A veteran deployed in the 1990's is applying for help and support in reporting a work-related injury. The veteran has post-deployment mental health issues from his deployment to the Balkans and wants assistance in clarifying this. The social worker 's role entails helping him to report the case. Together with the veteran, the social worker can further assist with the completion of the questionnaires for the Labour Market Insurance, so that the case can be resolved. This can be a lengthy process during which the social worker is in continuous contact with the veteran who may also suffer from other issues including problems with general care, loneliness, housing, lack of relationships and the like. Here, the social worker can be an advocate for the veteran and ensure that the case is properly managed by overseeing the management of the case and supporting the veteran from the start to the end of the process.

4.4.4.1   Roles with Family Members

The social workers within the Veteran Centre participate as teachers in a Danish-adapted version of the Prevention and Relationship Enhancement Programme (PREP) relationship courses, as well as in children's discussion groups (Veterancentret 2020b). The PREP approach was developed in the US and is based on more than 30 years of research and is used in the American, Swedish, and Norwegian defence (Veterancentret 2020b). The PREP is a weekend course, where couples receive preventive tools to improve communication. The couples are presented with nine different themes, including love, security, communication, communication challenges, problem-solving, sex, reconciliation, the way forward, knowledge, and support. The course combines presentations and practical exercises to inspire couples to develop their relationship and to offer a helping hand for couples who want to increase the quality of their relationship and their family life. Annually, six to eight courses are offered throughout the country. It is free of charge to participate. In these courses, everyone participates on an equal footing regardless of rank, and the courses are in great demand.

Together with the family counsellors in the Veteran Centre, the social workers are group leaders in the children's discussion groups. The groups consist of eight 2-hour sessions, where the main theme revolves around having a father or mother who has been deployed and has mental challenges as a result. In the groups, the children get the opportunity to talk to other children in the same situation as themselves. They talk about their worries and experiences of having a parent who has been deployed and do various activities such as exercises and games. While the children are in the groups, the parents have the opportunity to exchange experiences with each other. There are presentations for the parents on how they support their children in their everyday life, among other things.

In 2020, the Veteran Centre set up a new Family Unit with specialized child counsellors, supplementing existing efforts for relatives of service members and former members. Some of the typical themes that many relatives come to the Family Unit with are challenges in connection with deployment, development, reactions of children and young people, cohabitation issues, divorce and contact with children, life with PTSD in the home, and being a parent or sibling to a veteran.

Social workers do interviews with current and former military personnel and relatives at a place of duty, at home visits, or at a partner agency of the Danish Defence. Most often, the interviews take place with the veterans alone, but where relevant, their partners are also invited along. The social worker provides the framework for networking meetings where the veterans can invite family and friends. The networking meetings are an opportunity for the veterans to talk about their situation and build a safety net with support from family and friends. This work with the veteran and their family and friends is also inspired by the Solution Focused Approach.

4.5 The Influence of the Danish Veteran Policy on the Work of Social Workers

Every four years, the parties in the Danish Parliament negotiate the budget of the Danish Defence, the tasks to be solved, and what the Veteran Centre should focus on in the next 4 years.

In 2010, a Veteran Policy was adopted, which is regularly adjusted (Forsvarsministeriet 2016). The Veteran Policy sets out the general principles and overarching objectives for the recognition and support of veterans and their relatives. The policy creates the framework for the specific initiatives in the veterans'area. The Veteran Policy is based on evaluations made by the Veteran Centre and adjustments to the initiatives set out in the first Veteran Policy from 2010 (Forsvarsministeriet 2016). This has contributed to the addition of further financial resources to the veterans'area (Forsvarsministeriet 2016).

In Denmark, citizens can receive cash benefits from the state. To receive cash benefits, one must be without financial means and be available for the labour market. Many veterans have received financial compensation in connection with a physical or mental injury. This generally means that they will not be able to receive cash benefits. However, veterans are exempt from this stipulation as a special section has been introduced in the legislation of the Active Social Policy Act (Lovtidende 1998). This section disregards compensation for occupational disabilities paid as a result of personal injury in accordance with the Compensation and Reimbursement Act to previously deployed soldiers and other government employees with a post-traumatic stress disorder (danskelove.dk/aktivloven/14 n.d.).

4.6   Social Work Role in the Military to Civilian Transition

4.6.1   Defence Employment Contracts

Previously, the Danish Defence employed their military personnel on a so-called K35 contract (Lyk-Jensen and Pedersen 2019). This means that personnel are on contract until the age of 35 years old. After being employed for 18 months, personnel subsequently earn the right to 1 week of training with a salary per month, which is called Civil Education. The purpose of this is to ensure that the person in question can receive an education that can contribute to getting a job in the civilian sector, and thus facilitate the transition from the military. Most bring together their training weeks so that they can get a longer education period with pay before they turn 35 years old.

In connection with the Danish Defence Agreement 2013–2017 (Danish Ministry of Defence 2020), the parties of the Danish Parliament decided that K35 contracts should no longer be used, and military personnel are now employed on general contractual terms. K35 contracts are expected to be phased out in 2030, which reduces the educational benefits for those who serve.

4.6.2   Rehabilitation Course

Veterans who are currently serving in the military can be referred to a rehabilitation course if they suffer from a mental or physical injury that occurred during an international mission, causing permanent impairment, a significant loss of work ability in relation to previous functioning, and the veteran is deemed to be unfit for international service. An occupational injury report must be made at the same time. In Denmark, all employees, regardless of occupation, are covered by the public Labour Market Insurance covering physical and mental injury. In addition, deployed Danish Defence military personnel are covered by the Work Injury and Compensation Office of the Danish Defence. The Danish Defence has chosen to have its own insurance plan since deployed personnel do not have the opportunity to insure themselves privately during missions. They are thus double insured, partly through the public Labour Market Insurance and partly through the Danish Defence. Rehabilitation of the physically and mentally injured was included in the Veteran Policy in 2010 and has been part of the Veteran Centre's efforts since its establishment in 2011 (Forsvarsministeriet 2016).

The social workers often receive inquiries from a commander or military member in connection with a longer course of illness. They can also be contacted by an employment counsellor or the legal department of the Ministry of Defence Personnel Agency. The reason why the legal department makes inquiries is so that no one is discharged until the current situation of a given military member has been clarified from all angles.

After conversations with the military member, the social worker assesses whether they are in the target group for a rehabilitation course. The target group for rehabilitation in the armed forces are employees who during deployment in international service have sustained a physical and/or mental work injury resulting in a permanent disability with a significant loss of ability to work in relation to their previous functioning. If this is the case, the social worker will write a report on personal and family conditions, educational and occupational conditions, housing, finances, health, and summarise the issues. The report is sent to the approval unit in the Veteran's Centre together with medical documentation such as a doctor's note from a psychiatric specialist as well as documentation that a work injury has been reported. The approval unit then decides whether the criteria are met. If the military member is a candidate for a rehabilitation course, the case is created along with an interdisciplinary team consisting of a social worker, employment counsellor, and, if relevant, a psychologist from the Veteran Centre to support the member. The military members will be moved from their unit to the Veteran Centre, which will be their nearest employer from this moment on.

In collaboration with the military member, the employment counsellor who is now in charge of the case will co-create a plan with the aim of supporting the member's capability of finding a job in the civilian sector. Often, the plan will be civilian education for up to 3 years with pay from the Veteran Centre. Some personnel will have the right to civilian education that can extend the period during which they can gain an education with pay.

Since 2013, a total of 317 veterans had completed a rehabilitation course. In 2017, the Veteran Centre conducted a study of a total of 74 of these completed rehabilitation courses. The study showed that 63% of the participants had become self-sufficient in either a full-time or flex job after completing a rehabilitation course, 15% had been granted an early retirement pension, while 19% had been transferred to courses in the municipality. The latter is not a rehabilitation goal, but it illustrates how some courses may require a long-term and sustained effort due to the complexity of the veteran's problems.

4.7 Support of Former Military Members

The social workers at the Veteran Centre also help former military service personnel, often getting in touch with veterans who are in jobs but who can no longer do their job due to physical or mental illness. They can self-refer or sometimes a family member will reach out for them. Provision of counselling and guidance to clarify their work ability and their further connection to the labour market in close collaboration with relevant internal and external partners are services provided by the social worker.

From 1 January 2017, a job programme for veterans was introduced as part of the recognition of veterans. Veteran Centre social workers can refer veterans to this job programme which aims to get more mentally and physically injured veterans into work, with the target group being veterans who have been deployed on at least one international mission under the Ministry of Defence or the Ministry of Justice (Veterancentret 2020c). At the same time, the veteran must have particular difficulty in maintaining a permanent connection to the labor market due to deployment-related mental or physical injuries. The job programme includes two aspects: the possibility of prioritizing veterans for public positions and the possibility of receiving a premium of DKK 50,000 as a private employer if injured veterans are employed. Private employers who employ veterans can apply for a premium of DKK 50,000 with the Job Scheme Act. Payment of the premium presupposes that the veteran is within the target group of the law and that the veteran has been employed for at least 26 weeks without interruption. It is also required that the average working time during the period has been at least 15 h per week. In the period 2017–2019, a total of 34 premiums were awarded (Forsvarsministeriet 2016).

4.8   Ethical Issues

The social workers in the Danish Defence Forces are bound by professional confidentiality that is maintained towards the military commanders regardless of rank. Professional secrecy is important in order to establish a confidential space where military personnel and former military members can talk openly about their problems. If it is assessed that the social worker has to break the duty of professional secrecy, the person concerned is informed in advance. This may occur if there is a concern that a person is a danger to themselves or others.

The professional knowledge of social workers is highly respected, and social workers are included in relevant military contexts. Previously, it was considered problematic to talk to social workers due to the fear that their colleagues will find them weak and that their reputation will be ruined, but now employers ask military personnel to contact the social worker. Furthermore, collaboration partners such as the public system, doctors, and psychiatrists now also turn to social work for advice and guidance or advocacy support.

Ethical dilemmas may also arise in the collaboration between the veterans (both currently serving and former members) and the municipality. Veterans may have an expectation that the social workers will focus exclusively on their best interests, regardless of the law. At the same time, the social workers must appear professional to our collaboration partners outside the military. Social workers employed by the defence force are the link between the veterans and the municipality and act as "translators" for both parties. The veterans speak one language and the municipality another. The veterans may have an expectation that their service to their country will be taken into account in the municipality; however, this is not always the case as veterans are subject to the same law as all other Danish citizens.

In relation to the social workers' collaboration with other bodies, it is important that the social workers are able to cooperate and clarify their role in each case. A matching of expectations is important from the start. This means that social workers must be very aware of their role, both professionally and ethically.

Social workers are often asked to help apply for a scholarship for veterans who are currently serving or former members. In responding to these requests, social workers often face the dilemma of being asked to support an application that they cannot ethically vouch for, such as when a veteran has the funds to support his own education but will not prioritize it despite his needs. In this case, it is important that the social worker honours professionalism and assessment and give the veteran a professional, well-founded reason for not being able to ethically assist him in his application for scholarship funding.

4.9   Major Challenges and Future Directions

Although Denmark has made a great effort for many years to reach out to all Danish veterans, this work is not yet done. The number of veterans applying for help is increasing, and as it becomes more acceptable to seek help, there will most likely be a greater number of inquiries going forward. With the increased focus on family work and thus support and help for relatives, more and more veterans, including both currently serving and former members, are expected to seek counselling and guidance. In 2020, with the Family Unit being established on March 1, the unit received an additional 231 cases which would normally have been handed over to the social workers. In addition, more veterans are now coming to social workers for help with their work-related injury cases.

In the fall of 2020, compensation for physically and mentally injured veterans was the focus of attention as it has often been difficult for this group to get an occupational injury recognized. A recent case in the courts of Denmark will probably set a precedent and lead to the reopening of many occupational injury cases. In this scenario, the social workers will be ready to provide support and guidance.

Since the Veteran Policy was adopted in 2010, there has been an increased focus on supporting and recognizing veterans and their relatives (Forsvarsministeriet 2016). The establishment of the Veteran Centre in 2011, where all relevant professional groups were brought together to serve both current and former service members and their families, has led to a more targeted and qualified effort with an interdisciplinary focus on the tasks necessary to assist the veterans. Going forward, there will need to be significant effort expounded by social workers and other members of the interdisciplinary teams to meet the growing needs of Danish veterans, both currently serving and former military members, and their relatives, as well as a continual development and improvement of professional competencies, to ensure an effective response.

References

Bjerg HC (1991) Folk og værn gennem 50 år. Forsvarets oplysning og velfærdstjeneste 1941–1991, 43–47

Danish Defence (2021) Facts and figures. https://www.forsvaret.dk/en/roles-and-responsibilities/international-role/. Accessed 3 Mar 2022

Danish Ministry of Defence (2020) Danish defence agreement 2013–2017. https://www.fmn.dk/en/topics/agreements-and-economi/agreement-for-danish-defence-2018%2D%2D-2023/danish-defence-agreement-2013-2017/#:~:text=The%20agreement%20implicates%20that%20the,financial%20latitude%20for%20development%20initiatives. Accessed 20 May 2022

Danskelove (n.d.) Aktivloven §14. https://danskelove.dk/aktivloven/14. Accessed 15 Jan 2022

Forsvarsministeriet (2016) The veteran policy of Denmark. https://www.fmn.dk/globalassets/fmn/dokumenter/strategi/veteraner/-the-veteran-policy-of-denmark-2016-pdf. Accessed 21 Nov 2020

Forsvarsministeriets personalestyrelse (2022). http://www.forpers.dk

Global Security (n.d.) Denmark-total defence-conscription. https://www.globalsecurity.org/military/world/europe/dk-conscription.htm. Accessed 25 Feb 2022

Lovtidende A (1998) Active social policy act no. 455 of 1997. 141(707):4104–4123 https://www.ilo.org/dyn/natlex/natlex4.detail?p_isn=51409&p_lang=en. Accessed 20 May 2022

Lyk-Jensen SV, Pedersen PJ (2019) Introduction. In: Soldiers on international missions. Emerald Publishing Limited, Bingley, pp 1–4. https://doi.org/10.1108/978-1-78973-031-920191002

Sikkerhedskonsulenterne (2022) Sikkerhedskonsulenterne vi smarbejder om sikkerhed. www.sikkerhedskonsulenterne.dk. Accessed 20 May 2022

Veterancentre (2021) Servicehunde kan støtte veteraner. www.veterancentret.dk/da/arbejdsomraader/veteraner/socialradgivning/servicehunde. Accessed 21 Nov 2021

Veterancentret (2020a) Organisation. https://www.veterancentret.dk/da/om-os/organisation/. Accessed 20 May 2022

Veterancentret (2020b) Evaluering af kommunikationskurset PREP. www.veterancentret.dk/da/viden/forskning/forebyggelse/evaluering_af_kommunikationskurset_prep. Accessed 20 May 2022

Veterancentret (2020c) Jobordning for veteraner. www.veterancentret.dk/da/arbejdsomraader/veteraner/nyt-job/jobordningen/. Accessed 20 May 2022

Chapter 5
Military Social Work in the Finnish Defence Forces

Kari Seppänen and Hannu Maijanen

5.1 Background

5.1.1 Finnish Defence Solution and Conscription System

The primary task of the Finnish Defence Forces (FDF) is the military defence of Finland. This task includes monitoring the land and sea areas of Finland as well as its airspace; ensuring the country's territorial integrity; securing the livelihood of the population; as well as providing military training and education. The military defence of Finland is implemented based on the principle of territorial defence. In territorial defence, the sites and functions of importance for military activities are protected in cooperation with other authorities (FDF 2021a).

General conscription is the foundation of the Finnish Defence solution and applies to all male Finnish citizens. The responsibility for military service begins at the age of 18 and continues until the age of 60. The country is defended with a large reserve of 280,000 wartime troops, of which around 95% are reservists and the rest are salaried personnel (FDF 2020). According to the Defence Forces Annual Report in the peacetime organization of the Defence Forces, the number of salaried employees is 12,520, of whom approximately 8000 are soldiers and 4000 civilians (FDF 2020). Women comprise 18.7% of the salaried employees (FDF 2020).

The military service period begins with conscript service and, after this, continues in the reserve with occasional training. Military service can also be performed as non-military service, which is an alternative for conscripts who, due to conscientious grounds, are prevented from carrying out military service. Conscription occurs between the ages of 18 and 29, in general closer to the ages of 19–20. Approximately 20,000 people are conscripted each year (Finnish Defense Forces 2021c).

K. Seppänen (✉) · H. Maijanen (✉)
Defence Command Finland, Finnish Defence Forces, Helsinki, Finland
e-mail: kari.seppanen@mil.fi; hannu.maijanen@mil.fi

© Springer Nature Switzerland AG 2023
M. A. Forgey, K. Green-Hurdle (eds.), *Military Social Work Around the Globe*,
Military and Veterans Studies, https://doi.org/10.1007/978-3-031-14482-0_5

Military service can last for 165, 255, or 347 days. Individuals trained to be reserve officers, non-commissioned officers, and those in the most demanding special duty positions in the rank-and-file serve for 347 days. Those trained for rank-and-file duties requiring special skills and professional competence serve for 255 days. Other conscripts trained for rank-and-file duties serve for 165 days (FDF 2021b).

In 2021, conscripts were paid a per diem allowance of EUR 5.20/day for their military service. The per diem allowance increases according to the length of service –EUR 8.70/day for a period exceeding 165 days and EUR 12.10/day for a period exceeding 255 days. The Defence Forces provide free accommodation, clothing, and meals to conscripts (FDF 2021b).

Women are not subject to conscription, but women have the opportunity for voluntary service. The requirements for being accepted into women's voluntary military service include Finnish citizenship, the need to be between the ages of 18–29 years at the start of military service, and suitability for military training in terms of health and personal qualities. As the military service is voluntary for women after entry into service, women have the opportunity after a few weeks to consider whether they would like to complete the service. After the reflection period, women are subject to the same conscript regulations as men. After military service, under the Conscription Act, women are also in the reserve until the end of the year until they reach the age of 60 (INTTI.FI n.d.).

5.1.2 Nordic Welfare State as a Guardian of Citizens' Well-Being

Finland is among the Nordic welfare states where the public sector, the state, and municipalities play a very important role as a provider of welfare services and social security. As a rule, social security provided by public sector institutions is free, or almost free of charge, and offered to all citizens on an equal and fair basis; hence the higher Nordic tax rate compared to other welfare models. Thanks to public welfare services, the Defence Forces do not need to organize all support services, but instead can rely on the services provided by the public sector.

5.1.3 Social Work and Education of Social Workers in Finland

In Finland, social work generally refers to a social worker who has received a Master's degree in Social Work. Social workers are used in a variety of settings, but most often they are seen working in social offices, municipal social services, schools, health care, services for the mentally handicapped, family counselling, substance abuse care, and rehabilitative work both in the public sector and in private service organizations.

The Bachelor of Social Services is a university of applied sciences degree, with the standard period for completion being 3.5 years. The Bachelor of Social Services degree prepares professionals for positions requiring social welfare expertise in both the public and private sectors and can include various guidance and education social welfare tasks.

The military social workers in the Finnish Defence Forces all have attained a Bachelor's degree in Social Services or a Master's degree in Social Work. No university provides specific education for the position of a military social worker, nor does the National Defence University provide this education. Therefore, orientation to the work, the operating environment, on-the-job training, and continuing education play a key role for educating social workers for military social work (MilSW) services.

5.2   History of Military Social Work

In Finland, the idea of MilSW originated in World War II. In World War II, the Finnish Armed Forces had special education officers (soldiers) tasked with supporting the soldiers' mental performance and will to defend the country (Heikkilä 2007).

In addition to education, in 1942, the Civil Affairs Advisory Office for Soldiers was launched. This office was tasked with providing written information and advice on issues of concern to soldiers, such as their own livelihoods or that of their family/ widows, work opportunities after the war, wage issues, and compensation issues related to disability after war (Nummela 2015).

The first actual social welfare position was aimed at addressing housing issues of salaried personnel and was established at the Defence Forces after the war in 1948. Questions related to housing, such as the production of housing, were an important social issue during the post-war reconstruction. The Finnish Defence Forces did not have actual military social workers before the 1970s, but the responsibility for supporting the well-being of salaried personnel and conscripts was mainly created by the medical workers and chaplains (Nummela 2015).

The turning point in the development of social welfare issues in the Defence Forces came towards the end of the 1960s. Social welfare committees, operated by volunteers, were established in the garrisons to develop the well-being and service conditions of the personnel and conscripts. The social welfare committees discussed issues related to the housing of salaried personnel and everyday issues of conscripts related to, for example, food, among other things (Nummela 2015).

In the early 1970s, conscripts and personnel issues were separated from each other, and a separate participation system, the conscript committee, was set up for the conscripts. The conscript committee gave all conscripts performing their military service the opportunity to participate in the development of their service conditions. A conscript committee operating under the unit commander with members selected from among the conscripts was established in every military unit that trains conscripts. The purpose of their activities was to participate in the development of the conscripts' service conditions and in the promotion of general well-being and leisure activities. Conscript committee activities are part of the social welfare organization and an important cooperation instrument between the commander and conscripts of a military unit.

In 1973, the organization and management of the Defence Forces' social activities were centralized to the Social Office of the Defence Command. At that time, there were no trained social welfare professionals working at the social office. In 1974, social welfare services were extended to regional organizations when four civilian social secretary positions were established in military districts (Nummela 2015).

In the 1970s and 1980s, health care, judicial matters, ecclesiastical work, and social affairs were separated into their own fields in the Finnish Defence Forces. At this time, professionals with special qualifications within their respective fields were hired. Finland's first military social worker, who worked in a garrison, was employed in 1976. The duties of this first military social worker were similar to those of today, and she worked in collaboration with the Social Welfare Committee and the Conscript Committee (Nummela 2015).

In the 1990s, various military units started hiring military social workers using so-called employment appropriations, granted for a period of two years at a time. As a rule, when the period ended, the units made the positions permanent, as the military social worker services had proven their necessity through their practical actions.

Currently, the Finnish Defence Forces employ 22 military social workers in garrisons in Finland, with one additional uniformed military social worker working in the Finnish contingent in the UNIFIL operation in Lebanon. The military social worker deployed abroad is currently the only uniformed social worker in the Finnish Defence Forces.

In the garrisons in Finland, as all military social workers are civilian employees of the Defence Forces, they do not wear a uniform. The Defence Command directs MilSW and employs a head of social welfare affairs, social welfare manager, and senior planning coordinator to steer all social welfare activities in the Defence Forces. These are also civilian positions.

5.3 Military Social Work (MilSW) as Part of the Framework of Human Performance

The Education and Training Division (J7) of the Defence Command is responsible for the development and steering of the Defence Forces' education and training section. MilSW and other social affairs are part of the human performance section of the education and training division. At the local level, the military units are responsible for supporting and maintaining the human performance of the salaried personnel and conscripts. The purpose of occupational and in-service safety measures is to protect people from the hazards caused by physical and mental risk factors.

The MilSW professionals, together with the physical education professionals, the chaplains, and the occupational and in-service safety personnel, form the entity of Human Performance in the Defence Forces. The Human Performance section is tasked with maintaining and developing the psychological, social, physical, and ethical performance of the salaried personnel and conscripts, as well as the integrity and safety of operations (Defence Command 2015 pp. 16–18).

Within this framework of human performance, MilSW is responsible for matters related to psychological and social performance (Fig. 5.1).

Psychological performance is about an individual's resources, which he or she needs for coping with everyday challenges, including mentally stressful situations. A mentally fit person feels well, appreciates themselves, trusts their ability to cope with everyday situations, is able to make decisions, and is realistically confident about the future and surrounding world.

Social performance is understood as the ability to perceive oneself and others as part of a group, with the capabilities and will to act in a proper manner in a group. Interaction skills, human relationships, cooperation, group integrity, and taking others into consideration are integral parts of social performance.

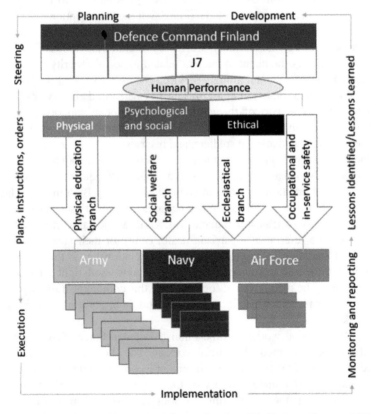

Fig. 5.1 Human Performance System according to directive of the Defence Command Education and Training Division

Physical performance is linked to the individual's health and other areas of human performance. With the help of good physical fitness, a person stays healthier, able to cope with the physical requirements posed by work or service tasks without overburdening oneself.

Ethical performance refers to the ability to act fairly, respecting human dignity. A key aspect related to it is the ability to justify one's own actions to oneself and others, awareness of one's own values and the values of the Defence Forces, perception of right and wrong, and the ability to distinguish between them.

5.4   Military Social Work (MilSW) Practice Settings and Roles

5.4.1   MilSW in Garrison

The work of military social workers is based on law. In matters associated with social security during military service, a conscript is entitled to relevant professional assistance in accordance with Section 106 of the Conscription Act 1438/2007 (Ministry of Defence 2008). In their work, military social workers support conscripts in performing their military service by social work means. The military social worker guides the client in matters related to social security, studies, work, housing, financial affairs, and military service. The military social worker supports the mental and social fitness of conscripts as they perform their services. The military social worker is part of the garrison's psychosocial support group and is involved in the organization of crisis work. Services are also provided to salaried personnel in garrison, deployed soldiers, and reservists.

In individual client service situations, the focus is on encountering the client, listening carefully, and assessing the situation. This work requires professional ability to generate interaction and trust in client relationships. Building a confidential client relationship is an important competence area in a military social worker's task.

A conscript may seek an appointment with a military social worker on their own initiative, or by a referral of a garrison health centre or their superiors. For conscripts, the foundation for establishing a client relationship is that they become familiar with the services provided by military social workers right at the beginning of their service. The methods used for achieving this communication include a lesson given to new recruits which include a presentation of the work done by military social workers.

The military social workers in the Finnish Defence Forces favour a solution-oriented approach as a method of social work and social counselling. This is due to the specific nature of the operating environment in which young conscripts, coming from civilian life, are trained as reservists that master military skills at a rapid rate. In this environment, there is no time for long-term support measures or deeper therapy-level treatment. For example, if conscripts have serious mental health issues, the service is interrupted for a fixed period of time or the person is fully exempted from peacetime service. MilSW also provides career guidance services for conscripts. Military social workers and conscript committees work in close collaboration to provide information and counselling on work and study matters for conscripts. The relatives and family members of the conscripts and salaried personnel are mainly supported by the social security and services provided by the civilian society (Lehtinen 2013).

The aim of cooperation between the Defence Forces and other authorities is to provide conscripts with the kind of service conditions that allow them to concentrate on their service without civilian matters distracting them too much. Below are some of the key authorities outside the Defence Forces whose services are available to conscripts.

Kela (Social Insurance Institution of Finland) For the duration of the military service, conscripts, women carrying out voluntary military service, as well as their next of kin, are paid a conscript's per diem allowance. In addition, Kela can pay a person performing their military service a housing allowance or the interest on student loans. A conscript's family may also receive assistance for family expenses.

Time Out! The Time Out activities are carried out at conscript call-ups and when someone drops out of the military service. The operating model is nationwide and is currently in use in almost all municipalities in Finland (FDF 2021c).

The Time Out activities are a support service intended for all young men and women of call-up age or in military service. The service assigns a personal counsellor for each young person, provides support in examining the life situation, and guidance in seeking different services. The counsellors are professionals who have been given an introduction to the operating model and offer young people an opportunity to assess their own life situations and optional courses of action at a low threshold. Young people can seek Time Out services before the call-up, at the call-up, or with a military social worker's referral if their service is interrupted. The intention is to prevent the beginning of a potential spiral of exclusion. The Time Out activities are voluntary, of a comprehensive and solution-oriented nature, and aimed at supporting young people's personal resources (Appelqvist-Schmidlechner 2011).

The Time Out counsellors are mostly municipal employees educated in youth work. The Time Out counsellors have been given introductory training in the operating model and implement the Time Out support service as part of their basic work.

State Treasury – Issues Related to Military Injuries and Service-Related Illnesses During military service, the Defence Forces' health care system is responsible for any health care and treatment costs. After the military service, the State Treasury covers the treatment costs caused by an in-service injury sustained or service-related illness acquired during military service and takes care of any other compensations according to the Compensation for Military Injuries Act. If necessary, the military social worker assists with preparing the accident report to the State Treasury.

5.4.2 Role of Military Social Worker in Crisis Management and Peacekeeping Operations

During crisis management operations (deployments), a uniformed military social worker deployed with the troops works in the position of a Social Welfare Officer and supports the force commander in the maintenance of the troops' human performance in cooperation with other experts (doctors, nurses, chaplains). It is noteworthy that most of the soldiers on operations are reservists. Personnel may turn to the Social Welfare Officer in issues that are causing them concern, either during the operation or in their civilian life. The Social Welfare Officer can help with practical arrangements and provide discussion support.

As determined by leadership of the operation, the social welfare officer is responsible for organizing lessons on social welfare services available during the deployment and demobilization discussions, and participates in their implementation together with the chaplain, medical staff, and other personnel. In addition, as specified by the command, the social welfare officer participates in the implementation of working atmosphere surveys and feedback events arranged during each rotation in collaboration with the chaplain, health care personnel, and other personnel. The social welfare officer on deployment keeps in contact with the military social worker counterpart in Pori Brigade in Finland, and informs them of the personnel who may be discharged in the middle of their service period and of any support measures they may need.

5.4.3 Role of Military Social Worker for Psychosocial Services of Crisis Management Operations at Pori Brigade in Finland

The Pori Brigade provides pre-deployment training. The military social worker for crisis management operations (deployments) who works at the Pori Brigade in Finland provides advice and guidance on all matters related to psychosocial support for crisis management soldiers before, during, and after the operation, working together with the deployed Social Welfare Officer.

Before the operation, the Pori Brigade military social worker for crisis management soldiers participates in the pre-deployment training by giving lessons and, during this training, arranging the so-called family day for the family members of those being deployed to an operation. The event addresses issues related to the time of operation from the perspective of family members.

In the event of a potential interruption of service during an operation, the military social worker for crisis management soldiers may have individual support and guidance discussions with the people involved. If necessary, they will take care of arranging psychosocial support in Finland or assist in the management of injury cases.

In addition, the Pori Brigade military social worker for crisis management operations organizes information and discussion events for family members, which focus not only on the same content as the above-mentioned family day but also on peer support. These events offer family members an opportunity to network and share experiences of the impacts of crisis management services on their everyday lives.

5.4.4 The Support System After Crisis Management Operations and Role of the Military Social Worker

The post-operation support for crisis management veterans consists of a number of services and other measures provided by the Defence Forces, the State Treasury, the Peacekeepers Association Finland, and the Association of Crisis Management Veterans with Disabilities, aimed at providing concrete support for the welfare of veterans and improving their appreciation in society. Long-term support is paid for by the State Treasury and provided by public or private social welfare and mental health services.

The military social worker for crisis management at the Pori brigade bears the main responsibility for the two day discharge from service event organized for all those returning from operations 2–5 months after they return home. The event is part of service, and the military social workers of other garrisons also participate in the events when soldiers are demobilized (discharged), as moderators of group conversations and holders of individual discussions.

The discharged crisis management personnel participate in lessons on the impact of operations and potential traumatic events on their adaptation to everyday life and mental well-being. The most important part of the discharge from service training are the group and individual discussions led by experts, in which the entire duration of crisis management service and possible events that may have caused stress or post-traumatic symptoms are addressed. As an advanced task, the participants of discharge from service training respond anonymously to a survey that examines, their mental and social fitness, the events during the operation, and any potential psychological symptoms. If a person's score in the survey exceeds the risk threshold, they may contact the military social worker for crisis management to find out what kind of support is needed.

The support offered to the family members and crisis management veterans themselves after the operation also consists of a telephone helpline provided by the Peacekeepers Association Finland, and the possibility to participate with crisis management veterans in peer support meetings organized by the Peacekeepers Association. On the helpline provided by the Peacekeepers Association, it is possible to discuss post-operation problems encountered or the coping problems of a family member who has served in a crisis management operation. The family members and veterans can also always contact the military social worker for crisis management in Pori Brigade.

5.4.5 Role of Military Social Work (MilSW) During Wartime

The task of the Defence Forces training system is to ensure that the development, maintenance, and restoration of the human performance of personnel and troops continue in emergency conditions and wartime.

When raising readiness and during wartime, the military social workers in the units work together with civilian authorities to help maintain the performance of the troops. With the wartime strength of the Finnish Defence Forces being 280,000 people, it is clear that there are not enough peacetime military social workers to carry out wartime tasks. Reservists from the social welfare sector are also needed. Refresher training is also organized for social welfare professionals needed in emergency conditions and wartime.

5.5 Ethical Issues

In Finland, the trade union of social workers has been developing ethical principles for social work. The organization sees the basic task of social welfare professionals as follows:

> Social welfare professionals have the duty to stand by groups in the weakest social position, to support people in difficult life situations and to provide information on unreasonable situations and discriminatory structures to political decision-makers. Social welfare work is regulated by legislation, but meeting statutory requirements does not always guarantee fairness. Therefore, the everyday choices need to be guided by strong professional ethics.

In the Defence Forces, the military social worker is tasked with supporting the performance of military service, even though conscripts may at some point feel that the service is in conflict with their own objectives. Coping with conscript service or the hard training may be tiring. The place of service may be transferred to another location in the middle of military service, which may cause changes in travel and civilian life. A conscript may not find any friends when everyone is transferred to a new unit. In such matters, the task of the military social worker is to motivate the conscripts both to cope and to take care of their civilian affairs so that they remain able to function and continue service. Difficulties may also arise due to not seeing the closest people, such as a girlfriend or boyfriend, often enough during the time of service. A military social worker may encounter difficult professional ethics situations where the easiest solution to the conscript's problems, under the Conscription Act (Ministry of Defence 2008), might be to drop out of military service. This creates the question, "should the social worker support the Defence Forces' goals or the client's wishes?"

In Finland, as an alternative to military service, it is possible to carry out non-military service if reasonable grounds prevent a person from performing military service. Although military social workers may understand that for some conscripts, non-military service may be a better alternative than military service, or perhaps some conscripts want to switch in the middle of their service to non-military duty; military social workers are employed by the Defence Forces; therefore, it is their duty to support people to carry out their military service. Even though the law very clearly defines non-military service as an alternative to military service, military social workers may experience ethically conflicting feelings when discussing with conscripts the possibility of transferring to non-military service.

5.6   International Cooperation

In the social welfare sector, most of the international assistance done by the Defence Forces focuses on developing support activities for crisis management veterans. In practice, the international cooperation related to the development of the support system is conducted in the NORDEFCO (Nordic Defence Cooperation) Veteran Issues working group. In addition to the Nordic countries, the Baltic countries also participate in the working group whose chairmanship rotates between the countries involved. The group exchanges information on the implementation of support for veterans in different countries through proven practices and studies. Practices proven successful are transferred to the line organizations in various countries. In addition, as agreed, the working group implements different research and report projects aimed at generating new information on the physical and mental health of coping veterans, focusing on succeeding to provide the much-needed support. It is also one of the focuses in Nordic conscript cooperation, to exchange good practices and results of studies and reports on conscripts.

Regarding gender issues, key modes of cooperation are currently being implemented under the auspices of the NCGM (Nordic Centre for Gender in Military Operations) (Swedish Armed Forces [SAF] n.d.), NATO and Partnership of Peace. The work and collaboration consist of seminars, working groups, and the development of training on gender-related issues. The implementation of the United Nations Security Council Resolution 1325 is also promoted together with UN and EU gender actors.

The latest form of international cooperation is participation in the meetings of the International Military Social Work Consortium. This alliance enables the global exchange of information in MilSW.

5.7   Major Challenges and Future Directions

MilSW has already established its position in the Finnish Defence Forces, which provides excellent opportunities for developing the content of the work for the future. The activities are based on the values of fairness, equality, tolerance, client orientation, and cooperation. Special attention will be paid to the harmonization of work among garrisons. The legal status of MilSW will be strengthened, and client documentation and reporting will be improved.

There is room for improvement in the visibility of MilSW. The aim is to develop and enhance communication on MilSW services and psychosocial support through the Defence Forces communication and on social media channels (i.e. Defence Forces intranet, Instagram, Twitter, Facebook, etc.).

All of these goals need every military social worker and their supervisor's strong commitment for development. The aim is that services provided by military social workers are sufficient, meet the needs of clients, and are delivered with a high standard.

References

Appelqvist-Schmidlechner K (2011) Time out! Getting life back on track: a psychosocial support programme targeted at young men exempted from compulsory military or civil service. Dissertation, University of Tampere

Defence Command (2015) Directive of the Defence Command Education and Training Division, Finland

Finnish Defence Forces [FDF] (2020) Defence forces annual report, 2020 https://puolustusvoimat.fi/asiointi/aineistot/henkilostotilinpaatokset. Accessed 31 Aug 2021

Finnish Defence Forces [FDF] (2021a) About us. https://puolustusvoimat.fi/en/about-us. Accessed 16 Jun 2021

Finnish Defence Forces [FDF] (2021b) Conscription – a finnish choice. https://puolustusvoimat.fi/en/finnish-conscription-system. Accessed 15 Feb 2021

Finnish Defence Forces [FDF] (2021c) Conscript 2021: a guide for you who are getting prepared for your military service. https://puolustusvoimat.fi/documents/1948673/59593990/Varusmies_2021_englanti_saavutettava.pdf/d87c6a1e-ffbe-5d33-924a-5e244a51671c/Varusmies_2021_englanti_saavutettava.pdf?t=1612789811133. Accessed 11 Aug 2021

Heikkilä T (2007) Valistustyöstä sotilassosiaalityöksi – Puolustusvoimien valistustyön kehittyminen 2 maailmansodan aikana sotilassosiaalityön näkökulmasta. Master's Thesis, University of Tampere

INTTI.FI (n.d.) Voluntary military service for women. https://intti.fi/en/voluntary-military-service-for-women. Accessed 15 Feb 2021

Lehtinen V (2013) Varusmiespalveluksen aikainen tuen tarve ja puolustusvoimien sotilassosiaalityön palvelu kotiutuvien varusmiesten ja varuskuntien sosiaalikuraattorien näkemänä. Master's Thesis, University of Turku

Ministry of Defence (2008) Conscription act. https://www.finlex.fi/fi/laki/kaannokset/2007/en20071438.pdf. Accessed 11 Jan 2021

Nummela T (2015) Sosiaalityö varuskunnassa – varusmiesten kokemukset sosiaalikuraattorityöstä peruskoulutuskauden aikana. Master's Thesis. University of Turku

Swedish Armed Forces [SAF] (n.d.) Nordic center for gender in military operations. https://www.forsvarsmakten.se/en/swedint/nordic-centre-for-gender-in-military-operations/. Accessed 10 Jun 2021

Chapter 6
The Approach to Military Social Work in the Republic of Ireland

Colin Fallon and Majella Hickey

6.1 History of Occupational Social Work in the Irish Defence Forces

In an attempt to trace the origins of occupational social work in the Irish Defence Forces, it is useful to look at the issues that gave rise to its existence. Poor economic performance and a prolonged recession from 1980 to 1987 resulted in poor living conditions, rising unemployment, and emigration in Ireland. In response to the issues of low pay and conditions, the National Army Spouses Association (NASA) was established in 1988 to highlight the poor conditions of serving soldiers, sailors, and airmen (Martin 2010). Through a sustained public campaign involving the use of protests, media, and political lobbying, the government responded by setting up the Gleeson Commission on Remuneration and Conditions of Service in July 1989 (Martin 2010). Its role was to carry out a major review of remuneration and conditions of service of the Defence Forces, including manpower and personnel, pay and allowances, and welfare conditions, which include welfare funds and validity of a counselling service.

Running alongside this was an Internal Board set up by the Adjutant General in December 2009 to review welfare in the Defence Forces (Óglaigh na hÉireann 1990). Up until this period, religious chaplains had been involved in the welfare needs of personnel and their families. Through the medium of their annual conference, the chaplains had been expressing concern since 1981 regarding the growing number and diversity of problems affecting the lives of service personnel and the

C. Fallon (✉)
Irish Defence Forces, McKee Barracks, Dublin, Ireland
e-mail: colin.fallon@defenceforces.ie

M. Hickey
Irish Defence Forces, Air Corps, Casement Aerodrome, Baldonnell, Co. Dublin, Ireland
e-mail: majella.hickey@defenceforces.ie

© Springer Nature Switzerland AG 2023
M. A. Forgey, K. Green-Hurdle (eds.), *Military Social Work Around the Globe*,
Military and Veterans Studies, https://doi.org/10.1007/978-3-031-14482-0_6

failure of those in authority to adequately address the solution (Óglaigh na hÉireann 1990). In a submission to the Board Report on Welfare in The Defence Forces (Óglaigh na hÉireann 1990) and the Report of the Commission on Remuneration and Conditions in the Defence Forces (Gleeson 1990), the chaplaincy service high-lighted the need for a Defence Forces policy on welfare; suggesting that all aspects of the person be enshrined within it, including the soldier's family and his environment. They recommended a code of confidentiality be formulated at all levels and ranks with the introduction of "qualified personnel into the Defence Forces in an attempt to provide a better support for the soldier and his family" (Óglaigh na hÉireann 1990: B-1).

6.1.1 Formation of the Personnel Support Service

In response to the findings and recommendations of the Commission and Internal Welfare Board, the Personnel Support Service (PSS) was formed in May 1991. A Military Director (DPSS), Command Personnel Support Services Officers (CPSSO), and a Civilian Head Social Worker were appointed during the period from May 1991 to January 1992. Five civilian social workers were recruited in March 1993 to work alongside trained Non-Commissioned Officers, known as Barrack Personnel Support Service Officers (BPSSO), to provide a confidential support service to serving members and their families (Óglaigh na hÉireann 1995).

Acting as a service for confidential information, education, support, and referrals; the PSS was designed to give Irish Defence Forces Personnel access to information and services both from within the military community and outside. In many ways, it combined the functions of a Citizens Information Centre (CIC) and an Employee Assistance Programme (EAP) within each Barracks.

Each of the brigades were assigned a civilian Social Worker whose tasks were to provide both support and assistance on a preventative and curative basis to service personnel and their families and to provide professional guidance, where required, to the CPSSO and BPSSO (Óglaigh na hÉireann 1995).

Having undergone organisational restructuring in 2013, The Irish Defence Forces is now a two-brigade structure consisting of three main branches: the Army, Air Corps, and the Naval Service. It is a small, well-integrated force with a combined establishment of 9500 permanent personnel and 1484 reserve personnel (Commission on Defence Forces 2022). Its primary role is to provide military defence of the state from armed aggression and to act as an aid to the civil power. Since 1958, the Irish Defence Forces have contributed to multinational peacekeeping missions, crisis management, and humanitarian relief operations in many parts of the world (O'Brien 2019).

6.2   Social Work Practice in the Irish Defence Forces

6.2.1   Practice Settings and Roles

Located within the PSS, the role of the occupational social work team is to provide a social work service to serving personnel and their families, civilian-military staff, veterans, and military reserve personnel on duty. Occupational social workers are civilian employees co-located with Barracks PSS Officers in both military barracks and formation locations. They conduct home visits to families of serving personnel and travel on short deployments to overseas missions in Lebanon (United Nations Interim Force in Lebanon) and Syria (United Nations Disengagement Observer Force) (Fallon et al. 2021).

The occupational social work service in the Irish Defence Forces comprises six full-time social workers, two part-time, and one principal social worker (Fallon et al. 2021). From a service delivery perspective, occupational social workers aim to deliver a service that supports military and civil operations and values the unique contribution of each serving member through promoting diversity, positive mental health, and the general well-being of personnel.

Occupational social workers deal with a range of personal, work, and family issues, including:

- Mental health
- Bereavement (including deaths in service, family members, miscarriages, and stillbirths)
- Repatriation of personnel from overseas
- Physical health issues (coping with injury, disability, long-term and life-threatening health conditions)
- Trauma and support for those involved directly or witness critical incidents
- Bullying, harassment, and sexual harassment
- Relationship, sexuality, and gender issues
- Budgeting and financial /debt management
- Child safeguarding /child welfare concerns
- Domestic violence
- Interpersonal communication
- Fertility matters, perinatal and post-natal complications
- Separation custody and access issues
- Consensual workplace advocacy within the Chain of Command (Fallon et al. 2021)

6.2.2 Factors Influencing the Contemporary Irish Defence Forces Social Work Approach

Social work in the Irish Defence Forces is orientated to both clinical and occupational social work and underpinned by national legislation, policies, and military regulations. Occupational social workers bring a range of core counselling skills to their clinical practice which includes psychotherapy, cognitive behavioural therapy (CBT), narrative therapy, addiction therapy, person-centred therapy, crisis intervention, strengths perspectives, and task-centred social work approaches. In addition, the team offers a range of practical psychosocial interventions and self-care techniques around mental health promotion & well-being. They deliver evidence-based programmes such as Safe-Talk (programme for suicide awareness), mental health first aid, mindfulness, Critical Incident Stress Management (CISM), and Wellness Recovery Action Plan (WRAP) (Fallon et al. 2021).

The implementation of a comprehensive and progressive Mental Health and Wellbeing Strategy for the Defence Forces 2020–2023 (Óglaigh na hÉireann 2020) provides a structured format for streamlining care pathways within a multidisciplinary framework. Eight supporting objectives and time-defined milestones seek to coordinate support to personnel in a manner that is evidence-based, universal, and coherent. The eight supporting objectives are: governance, resilience, suicide, stigma, critical incident stress management, a comprehensive approach, military families, and a model for clinical support. Objective eight, *a model for clinical support,* refers to the development of an effective person-centred model for clinical support that provides for the timely identification, referral, treatment, and reintegration of personnel suffering from mental illness or disorder (Óglaigh na hÉireann 2020). The strategy highlights the importance of appropriate use of multi-disciplinary care teams, the identification of effective care pathways, and training and education of mental health professionals.

The occupational social work interventions are influenced by the Safety, Health and Welfare at Work Act (Minister for Enterprise, Trade, and Employment 2005), which regulates the welfare of employees at work. This act details the employer's duty of care and obligations in relation to substance abuse, accidents, bullying and harassment, and informs the employee's own duty of care to each other.

Section 13 of the Safety, Health and Welfare Act (Minister for Enterprise, Trade, and Employment 2005) and Military Instruction Admin A7 deal with bullying and harassment. Occupational social workers are cited in the Defence Forces Military Instruction Admin A7 as the appropriate personnel to support persons experiencing bullying or harassment, or those who may be the subject of a complaint.

For serving members victimised by bullying/harassment, social work support focuses on:

- Counselling to counteract any self-esteem issues as a result of the negative experience

- Facilitating the service-user to find their "*voice*" and a safe place from which to process their experience
- Information on the rights of all parties to a complaint and the informal and formal options open to parties under A7 Admin Instruction
- Access to further internal or external supports as appropriate
- With consent, empower the service user in relation to the option of formulating a complaint, formally or informally (Óglaigh na hÉireann 2014)

In 2013, as part of a military social work (MilSW) initiative, an internal mediation service was established with Personnel Support Service staff receiving certified training in mediation practice. Following on from this training, the role of mediation in interpersonal conflict within the organisation was endorsed in Irish Defence Forces policy under Military Admin Instruction A7 (Óglaigh na hÉireann 2010) and in practice through referral of cases for workplace mediation. The provision of an internal mediation service by accredited workplace mediators complies with the Mediation Act 2017, offering parties informal resolution channels as an alternative dispute resolution mechanism. The provision of mediation is endorsed by the principle of voluntary participation and is utilised to resolve interpersonal conflict/relations, prevent escalation of conflict, and avoid absenteeism or consequent litigation issues.

Serving members refer voluntarily to the occupational social work service. At times, the service user may avail of the service on the recommendation of a colleague, Non-Commissioned Officer (NCO), or Commanding Officer to address issues that are interfering with their ability to either cope on a personal level and/or that compromise their performance. In all cases, attendance is voluntary, though service users may be referred for formal reports to command at any time as part of a rehabilitation programme from the Medical Corps or on direction from the Military Court.

6.2.3 Social Work Practice Interventions

Social work practice in the Irish Defence Forces is constructed from an eclectic mix of formal and informal knowledge and skills, as well as professional ethics and values. Occupational social workers bring a range of diverse skills to their practice.

One-to-One Counselling The diversity of practice within a military setting requires a high level of clinical knowledge and expertise to deal with a broad range of issues. Cognitive Behavioural Therapy (CBT) for the treatment of depression, anxiety, and other psychological disorders is well documented (Beck 1970; Ellis 1962; Butler et al. 2006). This vignette demonstrates the use of a one-to-one CBT for the treatment of depression:

> Jack was a thirty-eight-year-old serving member who enjoyed a rewarding career in the Irish Defence Forces. A qualified mechanic and instructor, Jack slipped on spilt oil suffering

a severe hip injury. He self-referred to the occupational social work service, having been diagnosed with depression and anxiety, and was placed on illness leave following the accident.

An assessment revealed pre-disposing factors of key losses in his life including the absence of a relationship with his father and the death of a grandfather who had a profound influence on his sense of self-identity during adolescence and adulthood.

Following assessment, the therapy goals of treatment were to improve his mood and self-esteem, learn to express difficult feelings, address processing loss, manage pain associated with his back condition, and manage self-blame and anger over the accident.

Using a CBT approach, behavioural experiments were collaboratively set to challenge negative predictions in relation to the expression of feelings and to help process bereavement and loss in his life. Targeting distorted cognitions helped him work on core beliefs and rules for living. As the sessions progressed, a combination of thought records, pain self-efficacy questionnaires (PSEQ) (Nicholas 2007), weekly activity sheets, and homework facilitated a positive change in his mood, which was reflected in updated scale results. Following his return to work on a phased basis with light duties, the therapy ended at session fifteen. The outcome of therapy was that Jack now had the tools to offset low mood and manage his pain threshold more effectively, having improved his level of self-esteem and given himself permission to process his losses.

Group Work Occupational social workers are trained as Well-being Recovery Action Plan (WRAP®) facilitators, developed by Mary Ellen Copeland in 1997. WRAP® is an evidence-based programme of self-management and recovery for those experiencing mental health difficulties (Copeland 2018). Designed to facilitate awareness and support for personnel with mental health issues, WRAP® groups have been instrumental in promoting the use of wellness tools and strategies and developing peer support networks amongst serving personnel in the Irish Defence Forces (Fallon et al. 2021).

The key concepts of WRAP® are hope, personal responsibility, education, self-advocacy, and support (Copeland 2018). Modules focus on decreasing and preventing intrusive feelings and behaviours, improving quality of life, increasing personal empowerment, and achieving individual life goals through the creation of a wellness toolbox and daily maintenance plan. The purpose of the maintenance plan is to monitor early warning signs for distressing and uncomfortable behaviours and feelings, recognise triggers, and modify behavioural responses. The occupational social worker is not delivering the group as an expert with all the knowledge and skills; they are part of the group, holding space for shared learning and giving permission for vulnerability and authenticity.

A separate health promotion and well-being initiative is the delivery of smoking cessation groups to serving personnel. Smoking cessation groups are facilitated by a small team of medical officers and occupational social workers. They address the psychosocial and dependency aspects of smoking, with a shift from the focus on the individual's treatment to positive peer group interaction and reinforcement. The use of motivational and psychoeducational approaches enhances learning for participants and maximises the unique competencies, skills, and efficacy of sharing specialist knowledge and clinical resources.

Family Work Occupational social workers are available to support families of serving personnel through home visits and office appointments at military installations. During deployment, this work involves providing support with parenting, isolation, and stress. Hoare (2016) states that while there is a lower risk of injury and death associated with multinational peacekeeping and humanitarian operations, the burden of managing the stressors placed on the family during the deployment cycle are the same.

Critical Incidents Irish Defence Forces personnel frequently encounter critical and traumatic incidents as part of their work, either at home or while deployed overseas. Occupational social workers are a key part of the critical incident response team as the model requires the presence of a mental health professional. They carry out debriefing interventions under the Critical Incident Stress Management Model (CISM) (Mitchell 1983; Mitchell and Everly 2001), under the umbrella of the International Critical Incident Stress Foundation (ICISF). CISM is rooted in Crisis Intervention Theory (Lindemann 1944; Caplan 1961, 1964), and occupational social workers are trained and experienced in delivering group work and supporting people through crisis situations. CISM interventions require on-scene support, structured individual and group responses, and follow-up counselling. These responses are intended to mitigate psychological trauma and accelerate recovery.

Restorative Practices Certified by the International Institute for Restorative Practices (IIRP), occupational social workers are trained to provide restorative justice conferencing to the Military Court. Restorative Practices are also used to resolve issues relating to bullying, disrespectful/inappropriate behaviour, and interpersonal communication difficulties amongst serving personnel.

Pre and Post Deployment Psychosocial Education As the Irish Defence Forces respond to our country's obligations to the European Union, United Nations, and NATO in respect of peacekeeping missions overseas, there is a continuous cycle of deployment groups, specifically UNFIL (Lebanon), UNDOF (Syria), KFOR (Kosovo), and Mali (EUTM MALI) (Óglaigh na hÉireann 2022). Occupational social workers promote the psychological welfare of all serving personnel by cofacilitating briefs with BPSSO's at pre- and post-deployment briefings. The briefs focus on preparation for separation from family members/spouses/partners and children, and the provision of information on resources available to serving members and their families within the Irish Defence Forces.

6.3   Ethical Issues

Occupational social workers in the Irish Defence Forces must comply with a "Code of Professional Conduct and Ethics" devised by CORU, the Social Work Registration Board in the Republic of Ireland (CORU 2019). CORU is a derivative of the Gaelic word "coir" meaning care. The registration board, established in 2010 (CORU 2019), was set up to protect the public by promoting high standards of professional practice, education, training, and competence amongst its registrants. The Code of Professional Conduct and Ethics (CORU 2019) ensures that social workers maintain a high standard of ethics by demonstrating ethical awareness, respecting the rights and dignity of service users, avoiding conflicts of interest, undertaking research in an ethical manner, and ensuring that any advertising is truthful, accurate, lawful, and not misleading.

The code includes responsibilities specific to social workers which concern professional and personal boundaries, legal responsibilities, and potential consequences of non-cooperation and engagement with supervision in professional practice (CORU 2019). Social workers should promote social justice in their practice by challenging negative discrimination and unjust policies and practices. They should respect diversity, different cultures, and values, advocate for the fair distribution of resources based on identified levels of risk/need, and work towards social inclusion (CORU 2019). Under the Health and Social Care Professionals Act (Minister for Health and Children (MHC) 2005), breaches of the code for poor professional performance or misconduct can result in a fitness to practice inquiry and imposition of disciplinary sanctions up to and including withdrawal of professional licence.

6.3.1   Ethics of Dual Relationships

Occupational social workers face ethical dilemmas which are unique to practice within a military culture. Ethical tensions often arise for social workers when they enter into dual relationships with service users. According to Kagle and Giebelhausen (1994), "a professional enters into a dual relationship whenever he or she assumes a second role with a client". This can happen before, during, or after the social worker relationship commences. Section 27.1 (a) of the CORU Code of Professional Conduct and Ethics (2019) states that: "you must not knowingly work with a service user with whom you have or have had a personal relationship that may compromise your professional practice". The development of personal relationships with fellow comrades is somewhat inevitable and unavoidable in a closed military community. The CORU code of ethics does not acknowledge this implicit capacity with the role of the occupational social worker for "dual relationships" or address the complexities they can create.

6.3.2   Boundary Issues

One significant concern is the ongoing management of relationships outside of the social workers' office. Within the closed military system, occupational social workers are fellow comrades to serving members—for whom they may later be engaged in a professional social work relationship, and then subsequently encounter them within various military contexts (gym, dining hall, military courses, shared transport, military exercises, social events, etc.). Occupational social workers manage boundary issues at the initial assessment by making it explicit to the service user that they may have ongoing, unavoidable contact with each other outside of the therapeutic space. In preserving the integrity of the therapeutic relationship, social workers facilitate discussions with service users on scenarios that might undermine their privacy by problem solving and exploring ways of dealing with them. Scenarios might include the possibility of meeting publicly with other colleagues in public spaces or during operational activities. Facilitating this type of discussion is imperative to building and maintaining trust with military personnel within a closed community. Complicated ethical issues and challenges related to boundaries, privacy, and confidentiality are also explored in supervision.

The following vignettes capture the ethical tensions and boundary issues experienced by occupational social workers in the Irish Defence Forces:

> I remember being overseas and how awkward it felt trying to manage my relationship with a service user outside the therapeutic space. I was asked to join a group of comrades in a military swimming pool. I had come from a background in child and family social work, and felt completely unprepared for a scenario such as this.

> I was collected with a fellow comrade in military transport from the barracks, I quickly realised that the driver was attending counselling with me. I had to be very careful in managing this unanticipated meeting and in protecting the service user's privacy and confidentiality.

6.3.3   Trust and Rapport

As the occupational social worker and the serving member both operate within the same military closed system, prospective service users are often assessing and determining whether the social worker is someone they would trust in the future. The occupational social worker will be aware that the serving member may one day be their client, and the serving member knows that social work services will be administered by that same social worker. Serving personnel often assess the social worker based on their sociability, humour, social and conversational skills, and reaction to others. The following vignette captures a social worker's experience:

> Each December I would be pretty much the only civilian at the Barracks Christmas party. It had been tough finding my feet in a totally unfamiliar setting, but I was beginning to understand something of military culture – quietly and carefully building a social work presence.

I was chatting with a couple of guys at my second Christmas party when, out of the blue, one of them said: 'we've been watching you since you came, and you've passed the test.'

'What test was that?'

'Trust'.

6.3.4 Confidentiality

Occupational social workers in the Irish Defence Forces must adhere to the standards of confidentiality as set out by CORU Code of Professional Conduct and Ethics (2019). Sections 2.1 and 2.2 of the code state that service user information is only shared with others to the extent necessary to give safe and effective care or where disclosure is mandated by law. Social workers must obtain consent from the service user before discussing confidential information. As standard practice, all service users are informed of the exceptions to confidentiality and where a breach has to be instigated. These include disclosure of a crime or intent to commit, substance misuse, or a threat to their own or another's life (suicide intent or homicide intent). The occupational social worker has a duty to inform the Unit Commander when a person presents as either a risk to themselves or another, for example, experiencing suicidal thoughts, contemplating suicide, or engaging in illicit drug taking.

Occupational social workers comply with standard mandatory reporting laws relating to child abuse and the protection of vulnerable children and adults. A social worker is not required to report disclosures of child abuse or domestic violence to a service member's command. Data protection legislation governs all interventions with service users. As a result, military personnel do not have access to social work case files, for which the reporting relationship on all clinical and data retention matters is to the principal occupational social worker.

6.4 Role in Military to Civilian Transition

The Defence Forces Personnel Support Service provides Transition to Civilian Life Courses for military personnel. Occupational social workers present on the psychosocial aspects of leaving the military and adjusting to civilian life. Social workers help prepare serving members for retirement through assistance with career planning and identification of transferable skills, information, and referral to community services.

This case study demonstrates a serving member's transition from military to civilian life:

John was a 49-year-old enlisted soldier referred to the occupational social work service by a medical officer. The referral was prompted by presenting symptoms of insomnia, anxiety, and low self -esteem. The medical officer attributed these feelings to John's imminent retirement from the military and recommended counselling. John described how he had always been a carefree, easy-going person and that his anxiety had only increased in recent weeks. The social worker explained that it was not uncommon to experience grief and anxiety in the lead up to a major life change such as retirement. Learning about grief reactions and change helped him to acknowledge and normalise his feelings.

John described the transition to civilian life as challenging, despite having obtained some valuable and transferable skills in the military. He described how his self-identity and self-worth were attached to his career. Using a strengths perspective, the social worker helped him to identify core strengths of teamwork, networking, time management, analytical and decision-making skills, self-discipline, and self-motivation. A significant amount of work centred on career planning and resetting goals. A major turning point came in session four when John secured an interview for a management role in a civilian setting. The provision of psychoeducational tools and a holistic client centred and strengths-based approach played a key role in helping him to understand his reactions, reduce anxiety, and ultimately regain his confidence. John secured the position as manager at the interview, and a number of months later made contact to relate that he had adjusted successfully to his new role.

6.4.1   The Friday Club

As a means of strengthening and supporting the linkages between serving and veteran members, the General Staff established Barrack Drop-in Centres in April 2015 (Óglaigh na hÉireann 2015) known as *"The Friday Club"*. The Friday Club provides a welcoming and relaxed environment where Irish Defence Forces veterans of all ages can visit barracks and installations in a structured manner. This enables veterans to establish or strengthen existing contacts with serving members on a monthly basis. Where requested, meetings are facilitated for veterans with BPSSO's/social workers in a discreet location during the Friday Club. Direct social work interventions with veterans include assistance with accommodation, welfare entitlements, physical health issues, mental health, and bereavement counselling.

A number of barrack locations have their own dedicated office areas for veterans, with this area expanding in service provision and accommodation for homeless veterans. The Organisation for National Ex-Service Personnel (one-veterans.org) also employ two Veteran Support Officers to respond to veteran's issues.

6.5   Educational and Training for Occupational Social Workers in the Irish Defence Forces

There are six third-level educational institutions providing qualifying social work education at both Master's and/or Bachelor's level in the Republic of Ireland. While different areas of social work practice are addressed in graduate training, to date there is no specific training module on military/occupational social work offered in these courses. Effectively, the law of supply and demand applies to this area of interest. There are few, if any, openings annually into the military/occupational social work fields. The opportunities and growth areas of employment for the 4983 registered social workers (CORU 2021) are within the public service in the areas of children and families, medical and community-based mental health, primary care, older persons services, disability services, and probation. Securing employment as an occupational social worker in the military is challenging due to limited employment opportunities and low staff turnover.

Social workers come to the Defence Forces with knowledge and experience in diverse social work settings, with some having gained post-graduate qualifications prior to entry. There are also opportunities for students to seek social work placements in the Defence Forces. Social workers employed by the Department of Defence in government public service positions obtain the knowledge and skills to perform the duties of the role through induction, on-the-job training, peer support, and supervision. They may utilise in-house training and are also provided with study assistance for continuous professional development post-entry. In terms of essential criteria for recruitment, evidence of working in adult settings/adult mental health is required. The current social work team holds a range of desirable post-graduate qualifications (as specified in job description) in areas such as bereavement, cognitive behavioural therapy, narrative therapy, psychotherapy, addiction counselling, advanced fieldwork practice, supervision, human resource management, adult education, social policy, and mediation.

6.5.1 Challenges Faced in Occupational Social Work Education and Training

The current position of occupational social work in Ireland, which is the formal approach used within MilSW in the Defence Forces, has declined nationally in its presence and prevalence over the past 30 years as a social work specialism. This is reflected in the absence of organisations employing occupational social workers and the consequent absence of occupational/MilSW as a module in professional training. The Defence Forces are the only Irish organisation that has retained recruitment of occupational social workers since its inception in 1992. Hughes et al. (2018) comment on similar difficulties in the United States with the spread of alternative Employee Assistance Programmes (EAP) and outsourcing of welfare/assistance programmes, which has been an international trend since the 1980s. The authors acknowledge the difficulties in constructing a pathway that will deliver on the re-emergence of occupational social work as a distinct viable field of practice when no consistent outlets for employment actually exist in the Irish context.

Halton and Wilson (2013) highlight challenges within the postgraduate social work training system in Ireland where there is no tradition of collaborative working between universities and employers. There is no national continuous professional development policy or post-qualifying frameworks and no state funding for post-graduate education, with most social workers undertaking post-qualifying pro-grammes at their own expense (Halton and Wilson 2013). Halton and Wilson (2013) state that "social work practitioners need to be prepared to work in more complex challenging and diverse practice situations, where high levels of both technical proficiency and creativity are necessary". Recruitment of social work professionals with knowledge and skills relevant to an occupational and military context is challenging in the absence of specialised postgraduate social work counselling and employee assistance programmes in Ireland.

6.6   Conclusion

From service inception, the social work role within the military setting has evolved into a generic service that encapsulates both clinical and occupational social work approaches in the delivery of a support service to serving personnel and their families.

Social work is a generic profession where graduates are prepared in their professional education to transfer knowledge and skills from one context of practice to another. Occupational social workers come to the Defence Forces with postgraduate qualifications, knowledge, and experience from a range of social work backgrounds and settings. As lone workers, the role involves a high level of responsibility, organising, managing social work service within military installations, the ability to make effective decisions regarding prioritisation of cases, service development, planning, policy, and programme development. Developing good working relationships with the chain of command is critical, as is the ability to communicate, influence, negotiate, and make complex, timely decisions in resolving or mediating problems. The process of recruiting social workers with experience of working with adults in a clinical and organisational setting has strengthened and enhanced the quality and diversity of service delivery. The key to reinforcing the diversity of future practice lies in the continuation of current recruitment practices and the continued investment in postgraduate and evidence-based training and continuous professional development opportunities for team members.

The implementation of the Mental Health and Wellbeing Strategy for the Defence Forces (Óglaigh na hÉireann 2020) yields a very positive direction for occupational social work to have professional impact in a multi-disciplinary context. The strategy enables the occupational social work team to continue to influence, contribute, and advocate for the mental health and wellbeing of serving personnel in the Irish Defence Forces.

References

Beck AT (1970) Cognitive therapy: nature and relation to behaviour therapy. Behav Ther 1(2):184–200

Butler AC, Chapman JE, Foreman EM, Beck AT (2006) The empirical status of cognitive behavioural therapy: a review of meta-analyses. Clin Psychol Rev 26(1):17–31

Caplan G (1961) An approach to community mental health. Grune and Stratton, New York

Caplan G (1964) Principles of preventative psychiatry. Basic Books, New York

Commission on the Defence Forces [CDF] (2022) Report of the commission on the defence forces. https://military.ie/en/public-information/publications/report-of-the-commission-on-defence-forces/. Accessed 24 Mar 2022

Copeland ME (2018) Wellness recovery action plan for veterans, active service members, and military in transition. Human Potential Press, Sudbury

CORU (2019) Code of professional conduct and ethics social work registration board. https://coru.ie/files-codes-of-conduct/swrb-code-of-professional-conduct-and-ethics-for-social-workers.pdf. Accessed 12 Nov 2020

CORU (2021) Registration statistics December 2021. https://coru.ie/news/news-for-health-social-care-professionals/coru-registration-statistics-december-2021.html. Accessed 22 Mar 2022

Ellis A (1962) Reason and emotion in psychotherapy. Lyle Stuart, New York

Fallon C, Davis J, Hickey M, Murtagh G, Twomey S (2021) Occupational social work in the Irish Defence Forces. Irish Soc Worker J Winter 2021:82–92

Gleeson D (1990) Report of the commission on remuneration and conditions in the defence forces. https://iarco.info/wp-content/uploads/2020/09/GLEESON-COMMISSION-REPORT-31-July-1990.pdf. Accessed 28 Oct 2020

Halton C, Wilson G (2013) Changes in social work education in Ireland. Soc Work Educ 32(2):969–971

Hoare R (2016) Ireland to the Lebanon and back: a case study of the use of child-centred play therapy and parental psychoeducation to reduce the separation anxiety of a pre-school child during his father's military deployment. Irish Soc Worker J Spring 2016:18–27

Hughes D, Olsen MC, Newhouse C (2018) Occupational social work education for employee assistance practice. J Teach Soc Work 28(4):379–397

Kagle JD, Giebelhausen PN (1994) Dual relationships and professional boundaries. Soc Work 39(2):213–220

Lindemann E (1944) Symptomology and management of acute grief. Am J Psychiatr 101:141–148

Martin M (2010) Breaking ranks: the emergence of representative associations in the Irish armed forces 1989–1992. PhD thesis, University College Cork

Mediation Act (2017). https://www.irishstatutebook.ie/eli/2017/act/27/enacted/en/print. Accessed 31 Mar 2022

Minister for Enterprise, Trade, and Employment [METE] (2005) Safety, health and welfare act. https://www.irishstatutebook.ie/eli/2005/act/10/enacted/en/print. Accessed 12 Nov 2020

Minister for Health and Children [MHC] (2005) Health and social care professionals act. https://www.irishstatutebook.ie/eli/2005/act/27/enacted/en/html. Accessed 12 Nov 2020

Mitchell JT (1983) When disaster strikes – the critical incident stress debriefing process. J Emerg Med Serv 8:36–39

Mitchell JT, Everly GS (2001) Critical incident stress debriefing: an operational manual for CISD, defusing and other group crisis intervention services, 3rd edn. Chevron Publishing, Maryland

Nicholas MK (2007) The pain self-efficacy questionnaire: taking pain into account. Eur J Pain 11(2):153–163

O'Brien T (2019) The evolution of defence forces peacekeeping operations. Ir Stud Int Aff 30:119–129

Óglaigh na hÉireann (1990) Board report on welfare in the defence forces. Defence Forces Printing Press, Dublin

Óglaigh na hÉireann (1995) Personnel support services internal briefing document. Defence Forces Headquarters, Dublin

Óglaigh na hÉireann (2010) Administrative instruction A7 discipline. Defence Forces Headquarters, Dublin

Óglaigh na hÉireann (2014) Occupational social work policies. Defence Forces Printing Press, Dublin

Óglaigh na hÉireann (2015) Instructions to officers commanding barracks and installations on the establishment of defence force veteran drop in centres "The Friday Club". Defence Forces Headquarters, Dublin

Óglaigh na hÉireann (2020) Mental health and wellbeing strategy for the defence forces 2020–2023. Defence Forces Printing Press, Dublin

Óglaigh na hÉireann (2022). https://www.military.ie/en/overseas-deployments/current-missions/. Accessed 22 Mar 2022

Organisation for National Ex-Service Personnel. https://www.one-veterans.org/services/. Accessed 22 Mar 2022

Chapter 7
Military Social Work in the Israel Defense Forces (IDF)

Limor Zaks Zitronblat

7.1 Background: Military Service in Israel – Uniqueness and Challenge

The State of Israel is unique because it is a Western state involved in violent conflicts with an ongoing struggle for its existence. Since its inception, Israel has known seven wars, two intifadas, multiple waves of terror, and has been involved in many military operations, retaliatory operations, military confrontations, and rounds of fighting not defined as wars. The concept of existential threat has a deeper meaning because it is based not only on the experience of conflict with the Arabs but also on the collective memory of Jewish history. The perception of the security threat is also reflected in the national distribution of resources; about 15% of the state budget is directed to security needs. There is no other country in the world that, during all its years of existence, has spent on security such a large share of the national product (Bartal and Carmi 2012).

This complex reality leaves a significant imprint on life. The State of Israel is one of the few democracies in the world where there is a conscription obligation and reserve service. The obligation to report for military service applies to every citizen or permanent resident who has reached the age of 18 and is enshrined in the Security Service Law. Conscription into the Israel Defense Forces [IDF] is a normative and integral part of Israeli life, and everyone understands that after graduating from high school they are expected to enlist. Women are also committed to conscription, unlike all the armies of the world (except North Korea). Mandatory service takes place in democracies when there is a security threat and a national ethos that

L. Z. Zitronblat (✉)
School of Social Work, Bar Ilan University, Ramat Gan, Israel

Reserve Forces – Israeli Defense Forces, Ramat Gan, Israel
e-mail: Zitronl@biu.ac.il

© Springer Nature Switzerland AG 2023
M. A. Forgey, K. Green-Hurdle (eds.), *Military Social Work Around the Globe*,
Military and Veterans Studies, https://doi.org/10.1007/978-3-031-14482-0_7

supports the duty of service. Israeli youth experience security tensions that emphasize their duty to protect through their military service directly, the security of their
country, their family, and sometimes their home (Scherer 1997). This is a unique
challenge that adolescents around the world are not required to confront, as the following vignette demonstrates:

> Amit, who lives in Sderot, a city surrounding the Gaza Strip, grew up with Qassam rockets
> falling on the city. Today, as a soldier serving five minutes away from home, he guards his
> home. As a combat soldier engaged in day-to-day operations, he is proud to do so. Knowing
> that I am directly guarding my home has an impact. When I see the streetlamp next to my
> parents or my neighbor's house. I understand that I was chosen to be the one who protects
> my home, and it is an indescribable feeling

The prevailing approach in the State of Israel is that IDF service is based on the
"People's Army" model. This model emphasizes the principles of uniformity, equality between recruits in opportunities, realizing potential and reward, statehood, representing the diversity of Israeli society, and emphasizing individual contribution to
the collective in the field of security (Tishler and Hadad 2011).

Regular service is a formative experience in the lives of most Israelis as human
beings and as citizens of the country. Service in the military is a complex intersec-
tion for those enlisted and a particularly demanding system which tests personal
values and qualities, exhausts individual abilities, and prepares those enlisted to
bear a burden not previously placed on their shoulders.

Military service in Israel, with its unique characteristics, is one of the main
stressors for Israeli adolescents. The encounter between the young Israeli and the
military framework is a unique interaction. The 18-year-old recruit encounters typical challenges of this age centered around the conflict between dependence and
independence, identity, and autonomy. The period of adolescence, which allows a
gradual process of solving these inner conflicts, is interrupted in a forced and sharp
manner by conscription into the military. The military framework dictates uncom-
promising and demanding conduct. Soldiers are detached from their familiar and
supportive environment and must rapidly adapt to a new, sometimes foreign and
threatening organization that dictates clothing, identification marks, and behavior
patterns. He or she may be confronted, for the first time, with a tough authority
figure that demands obedience (Bleich 1990). Soldiers are asked to deal with unfamiliar conditions, demands, physical challenges, and mental stress. In addition,
later in service, the intensive activity requires long-term operational alertness while
demonstrating a high level of professionalism, task load, and sometimes dealing
with life-threatening situations on the battlefield during combat.

The mental health challenges that combat soldiers face from the very participation in combat are understandable, but it turns out that even soldiers who are not
directly exposed to combat in the field face mental stress challenges caused by their
indirect involvement as a combat supporter (Svetlitzky 2017).

Zohar et al. (2004) researched pressure from service without distinction between
units and positions and found, through a factor analysis, five significant areas of
pressure for service members. The strongest factor found was the requirements of
the military role. The next factor was homesickness, followed by negative life events

(death of a family member, divorce, or threat to sexual identity), friction with authority (especially one that is perceived as rigid), and dissatisfaction with placement in a role experienced as unchallenging.

These stressful situations may apply to both men and women serving in the military. Although women's service is common in various armies worldwide, the IDF is one of the only militaries in the world that recruits women to its ranks under a compulsory conscription law. Initially, with the establishment of the State of Israel, the conscription of women served the security needs of the young Hebrew state that needed all possible manpower to protect the home country, and women even participated in the fighting during the War of Independence; but later, in the Compulsory Service Law enacted in 1952 (Security Service Law 1952), they were exempted from combat and positioned in education or administrative positions. In 2000, the law was amended (Security Service Law Amendment No. 11 2000), and about 90% of the positions in the IDF became open to women. However, the military's commitment to the principle of equality has remained in conflict to this day, and the IDF is gendered (Sasson-Levy 2011). Thus, in addition to all the stressful situations involved in the service described above, the female soldier may encounter frustration about her military role and aspirations to advance, while at the same time may feel conflicted between her female identity and image and the IDF's demands on appearance, behavior, and male professional image (Bleich 1990).

This chapter will focus on the IDF Mental Health Array as the organization that provides mental health services in these stressful situations through professionals, most of whom are social workers who are titled Mental Health Officers.

7.2   History of Military Social Work and the Mental Health Array

The Mental Health Array is a multi-professional team served by a unique Israeli profession, Mental Health Officers (MHOs). Approximately 250 professionals including social workers, psychologists (who engage the same role), and psychiatrists serve in the array. These professionals are "uniformed" and allocated to all military units, including recruitment centers, training bases, military prisons, regional clinics (for soldiers who are stationed in the military home front), and all deployed units. In wartime, there are professionals who join the MHOs to support the regular forces.

The IDF Mental Health Array was established to provide routine and emergency care. The mission of this array, which is part of the IDF Medical Corps, is to provide optimal mental health care for IDF soldiers in war, ongoing operational activity and routine time; by improving mental resilience, preventing mental disorders, and promoting mental health. There is a community emphasis in this professional work - a focus and emphasis on health and its promotion, and on problem solving and assistance in the military community, as opposed to the medical model that focuses on morbidity and psychopathology. This array fulfills many roles and provides mental health care to all those serving in the military in compulsory, career, and reserve service during routine times and operational activity, setting policy in the areas of mental health, and providing professional training for mental health officers. Additionally, there are roles such as consulting with medical and human resources commanders on mental health issues, placing personnel and professionals to enable optimal utilization of human effort, and developing prevention and intervention programs on various issues.

The Mental Health Array was founded about 15 years after the establishment of the IDF and the Medical Corps. The delay in the establishment of the array may have reflected the naive notion that Israeli soldiers are mentally resilient Military social work. In addition, for many years, there was a shortage of professionals in these fields (Nadav 2000), and only a handful of psychiatrists constituted the IDF mental health field whose worldview was clinical and whose main occupational focus was mental diagnosis and screening regarding the suitability of soldiers for military service (Sheklar 1990).

In November 1962, a military psychiatrist asked a social worker he knew to join the mental health branch of the IDF, which at the time consisted only of psychiatrists, to explore the possibility of a different perception of intervention and treatment in the military mental health field. The suitability of the social work profession, which was perceived as a solution for the needy and weak, was questioned in a forceful organization such as the military. This social worker, Gabi Weissman, became the first social worker in the IDF. At the beginning of his professional career, he was called to provide interventions only in cases of extreme crisis, but he later realized that the military organization requires adapting social work perceptions to enable more effective coping with the expectations of the military environment.

Gabi Weissman, the first MHO tells:

> I am the only member of my family who survived the Holocaust. At the end of the war, I immigrated to Israel and studied Social Work. The Mental Health Officer concept was invented by me with the understanding that we are officers representing the military system and people who care and deal with the well-being of the individual... The goal in the early years was to care for the individual. In time, we combined counseling for commanders... In combat, the goal was to address the unit's vision as a unit, to strengthen the commander because his strengthening strengthened all the soldiers in his command. That is why it is so important for the MHO to be a military therapist who knows the characteristics of the military system and be a part of it (G. Weissman, personal communication, June 30, 2020).

7.3 Practice Orientation and Approach

Initially, Mental Health Care included (and still includes) a systemic community approach, as such, advising commanders to be agents of change to assist their subordinates. Later, considering the success of this professional concept, more social workers were stationed in potentially high-stress units, such as training bases and military prisons.

The new name for the profession of Mental Health Officers (MHOs) emphasizes that these professionals are officers dealing with health. Wars in Israel have influenced and established professional standards and grew the number of professionals in the mental health system. After the Six-Day War (1967), the concept of emergency intervention began to develop.

The focus of this practice is prevention, training, and advising commanders on various issues of individual care. At the same time, MHOs joined the recruitment centers with the idea of preliminary mental health screening for service in the IDF. In the 1970s, MHOs also joined a special project promoting and absorbing special populations that were not yet recruited to the military, such as people who come from criminal backgrounds or from low-income families with a minimum level of education. The Yom Kippur War (1973) and its aftermath was a turning point for the concept of deployment of social workers, including the function and therapeutic approach to PTSD, and the newly formulated concept that mental health care must be performed in the field, as close as possible to the combat zone and not in hospitals. This idea required a large increase in the number of professionals. Thus, the mental health branch of the IDF grew by hundreds of professionals in the reserve forces and dozens in the compulsory service and became a department in charge of all mental health care in the IDF (Sheklar 1990). In 1982, the department turned into an array headed by a psychiatrist with a Colonel rank. The department continued to grow when two unique clinics were added; the first one in 1982, after the Galilee War—the Combat Stress Reaction Unit, and the second in 1984—the Institute for Counseling and Care for career personnel and their families. This was based on the understanding that military service as a way of life presents challenges, difficulties, and stress.

In recent years, continuous improvement and expansion of therapeutic care for soldiers began. The Mental Health Array sought to expand and deepen the operating method of care and of MHOs embedded in front units (Lubin 2009). In 2008, additional MHOs were added, especially in the combat units, and the training numbers doubled. Another step to emphasize therapeutic organicity at the deployed level was taken in 2015 in the Mental Health Care Forward Program where MHOs were embedded in the level of the brigade and became a part of the brigade's headquarters. This move increased the availability and accessibility of mental health care services, reduced the stigma, and helped to reduce dropouts.

7.4   Military Social Work Education and Training

As mentioned, there are approximately 250 MHOs in the mental health array, and 60% are social workers (Fig. 7.1). MHOs enlist in the military, typically after completing a Bachelor of Arts degree in social work and after military service. Most of them have served full compulsory service, and some have even served as combatants and officers. They are drafted as officers, work as part of a military unit, and wear uniforms. MHOs are deployed in a variety of positions in the Army, Navy,

Fig. 7.1 MHO profession
(Rofe 2019). (Reproduced
with permission)

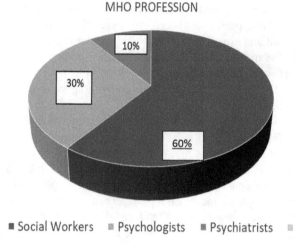

Airforce, and Intelligence Branches. They are stationed at training bases, brigades and divisions, military prisons, recruitment bureaus, and clinics.

MHOs receive the rank of Lieutenant and can advance to the most senior rank of Lieutenant Colonel. New recruits participate in professional orientation and a comprehensive training program with their peer group. During the first 3 years, the basics required to fulfill the profession/job are taught, including interview theory, intervention, psychiatric diagnosis, self-harm and suicide, PTSD, community approach to psychotherapy, and mental fitness (Rofe 2019). All of this is part of the "School for mental health officers." After the first 3 years of obligatory studies and upon earning a master's degree while serving, MHOs may enroll in the next level of studies to maintain professional competence. University courses in cognitive behavioral therapy (CBT) technique, approaches for individual psychotherapy, group therapy, and couple/family therapy are offered. In addition, MHOs benefit from weekly supervision sessions with an experienced professional and from involvement in research with the best researchers in Israel and around the world. Also, approximately 30 civilian social workers, who are not drafted nor uniformed, are placed in certain positions in military home front bases, such as recruitment centers and clinics. The rationale for civilian status is to retain these professionals in the same position for a longer period of time as a source of knowledge for this position.

7.5 Practice Settings and Roles

The role of the MHO includes interventions during wartime, routine treatment and prevention, training and counseling for commanders and other professionals. The MHO uses a variety of interventions to provide optimal medical care to soldiers before enlistment and through compulsory and reserve service. Care can be facilitated at the individual, group, and community levels. When dealing with career military personnel, couple and family therapy is also included.

Prior to enlistment, the MHOs in the recruitment centers are also engaged in occupational social work by implementing mental screening to the candidates for recruitment to match the service in the IDF designed to enable quantitative and qualitative utilization of manpower and prevent harm as a result of maladaptation (Kron 1990). An index of adjustment difficulties based on experiences over the years makes it possible to assess a soldier's ability to adapt to military service and to recommend adapted roles and conditions.

When recruited, the complex encounter between soldiers and the military can create and cause adjustment disorders and various crisis situations. The nature of the intervention of MHO at this stage, especially at training bases, will usually be individual and supportive. Dan, a soldier who completed combat training in armor tells:

> I have always thought of enlisting to a combat unit. The problem was my anxieties. I always had anxieties. Two years ago on an annual trip, I had terrible anxiety and really felt I was disconnected from reality. I'm really afraid of sleeping outside the house and now I am a combat soldier in training. I was really, really scared the first days and nights of training. I would stay awake most of the night and get up the next day tired and less functional. I asked myself if this is my place at all... my commander noticed and talked to me then offered me to contact the MHO. When I entered his office, I was afraid, but he was really understanding and helpful. He tried to get to know me and was very tolerant. We agreed to talk during the training, and he taught me some breathing to calm down. We talked every week and from conversation to conversation I felt better. He also talked with my commanders. Now I have finished my training and I feel much better, sleeping better, functioning. Glad I did not give up and received help (Dan, personal communication July 17, 2020).

The MHO must intervene to assist the soldier in building coping tools while addressing the community aspect of recruiting supportive elements in the military environment, especially commanders.

There is ongoing assistance to junior commanders on dealing with soldiers in distress through education, training, supervision, and staff preparation. In addition, there are open and ongoing discussions with senior commanders, which help promote unit resilience and legitimacy of mental health treatment (Lubin 2009).

In cases of severe crisis, disconnection from the source of military pressure and consulting on adequate service conditions may also be considered. Individual treatment during the service may include short-term dynamic and cognitive-behavioral therapies, which are appropriate for anxiety and depression disorders. For cases of sexual assault, domestic violence, or unplanned pregnancy during military service or before enlistment, there is a special center, Coping and Supporting Center, that provides psychological assistance to male and female soldiers by MHOs who specialize in dealing with cases of harassment and violence. Referrals to that center can be confidential and does not necessarily require filing a complaint. MHOs also offer group therapy on adjustment disorders, eating disorders, and more. Group therapy is provided by the unit MHO and in the mental health clinics. Group therapy is also provided to specific professionals such as doctors, medics, and military rabbis.

In 2017, as part of the Mental Health Array, a new mental fitness branch was established to engage in health promotion, realizing the IDF philosophy that human resources are key to success in military missions. The term "Mental Fitness" refers to the soldier's entire skills and capabilities to effectively deal with mental challenges on the battlefield and in other military missions. This branch studies the manifestations of mental fitness and develops programs to increase mental fitness among soldiers to provide coping resources and resilience that will help soldiers deal with distress situations with the goal of prevention.

There are several programs that build resilience and enhancement from stress. Gradual Mental Training Scale (Zohar et al. 2004) deals with situations that gradually intensify during training. Another program is *Back to Future,* where mental decompression tracks that are designated for combat soldiers to process the transition from their demanding combat service to their release from service. Additionally, body-brain training includes attention bias training (Wald et al. 2016) and neurofeedback (Keynan et al. 2019). A unique training that was recently developed by the Israel Defense Forces is *Magen,* the Hebrew word for shield, a psycho-educational preparation for combat events that leads to mental resilience (Svetlitzky et al. 2020). To assist a friend in time of need for example, in battle response situations, a special technique designed to bring the soldier back to function is being taught. This technique includes a number of actions that convey an expectation of returning to effective functioning, such as giving the soldier a feeling that you are with him until he returns to function, encouraging him to perform simple tasks, and building the sequence of the events that occurred while emphasizing that the event has ended and the threat has been removed. On the ground, the need for this skill has risen because of the damage that a functional collapse that accompanies a combat response may cause in unit morale, functional continuity, and mental disability. This technique is also taught to doctors and medics as a part of the scheme of treatment.

Special attention is given to suicide prevention. The suicide rate of IDF soldiers has decreased by more than 50% since 2006 (Shelef et al. 2018). In 2006, the IDF began implementing a suicide prevention program. The program includes:

1. Reducing access to weapons – a move that led to an immediate 40% decrease in soldier suicides while on holiday or during weekends at home;
2. Expanding the learning from any suicide incident, with a significant reduction in the period required to draw lessons;
3. Development and implementation of training and education tools for training the gatekeepers – commanders, unit members, doctors, and supervisors;
4. Recruiting the MHO as an organic member of the unit, reducing the negative label, increasing the soldier's accessibility to mental health care, and maintaining the chain of care (Shelef et al. 2019).

In recent years, efforts have been made to further prevent suicides by conducting research in the field, including a study of the perception of general and military pressure among IDF soldiers who attempted suicide and ongoing research of the overall plan to prevent soldiers' suicides (Ginat et al. 2019).

Additional projects deal with career personnel because they have a unique lifestyle and working conditions (Dagan and Margalit 1990). A variety of individual, couple, and family treatments are offered in the special clinic for mental health care for career personnel. The unique population of combat commanders are also offered individual therapy for their spouses and children. Spouses can also participate in support groups. In this unit, most of the caregivers are civilian social workers.

A special interest of social workers working in the IDF is posttraumatic stress disorder (PTSD). Based on principles of interventions of acute stress reactions in World War I, Proximity, Immediacy, Expectation (PIE) remain the basis of the forward care for an acute stress reaction in war times (Ginat et al. 2019). Experience gained in wars led to the understanding that it is recommended to treat casualties within the unit and that initial prevention must be provided on the battlefield by strengthening the resilience tools. It is also recommended to start intervening immediately after the traumatic event (early secondary prevention). A military staff that has experienced an exceptional combat event undergoes a special group intervention whose primary purpose is to produce a common narrative to support the identification of soldiers with potential for injury.

At the home front, there is a special clinic, the Combat Stress Reaction Unit, which aims to prevent mental health disabilities that can result from chronic posttraumatic stress disorder. The MHOs of this unit treat soldiers who have already completed their compulsory service and have been diagnosed with post-traumatic stress disorder. Soldiers with PTSD during their service are treated by the MHOs of their unit. The individual therapy practices of this unit are Prolonged Exposure (PE), Eye Movement Desensitization (EMDR), and Reprocessing and Hypnosis. Cognitive Behavioural Conjoint Therapy (CBCT) for couples and group therapy are also practiced.

7.6   Other Welfare Projects

There are some other welfare projects in the IDF. For example, soldiers who come from low-income families, also known as "welfare soldiers," are taken care of by female soldiers who play a unique role in regular service. This seems to be unique as it is not seen in any other part of the world at this time. This position in Hebrew is called "*Mashakit Tash*." It is very similar to the roles of a social worker in the community welfare services, especially when considering the family and socioeconomic situation of each soldier. Adjustments to the conditions of service are important to support maximum military service without harm. Some adjustments that may be seen include, but are not limited to, increased monthly salary, family assistance, work permits, and hours of work. This may include releasing a soldier to visit home for regular vacations to support their family in times of sickness. Soldiers receiving relief are monitored during the service to examine their adjustment. Men can also fill this job position in units where ultra-orthodox men serve for their country.

Another project is The Array of Casualties, established to teach about wars like the Yom Kippur War, where many casualties occurred. This is a special unit that cares for wounded soldiers and families with soldiers killed during service. The unit consists of social workers who are trained in preparation for this position. Training topics include methods to inform bad news to families, while being aware of cultural aspects in mourning customs which are seen in various denominations.

There are also several programs to promote the integration of vulnerable populations into the IDF. Since its establishment, the IDF has performed state-social tasks such as recruiting and nurturing vulnerable populations (Cohen and Amrani 1989). Over the years, the populations defined as vulnerable include detached youth, new immigrants (especially from the former Soviet Union and Ethiopia), those who have not yet completed the process of socialization to the State of Israel and Israeli society, and minority populations – citizens whose language is Arabic-Druze, Bedouin, Circassians, Muslim Arabs, and Christian Arabs. To this day, social workers and other professionals tailor programs for these populations which enforce strict discipline, while considering potential adjustment problems that can arise during their military service. These programs create a bridge between the members of these groups and society as a whole, and thus, strengthen the social fabric in Israel (Ben Yosef Azulay et al. 2017).

7.7 Ethical Issues

There are some ethical issues that stand at the doorstep of MHOs when dual loyalty arises, especially in the Israeli reality in which the service is mandatory. MHOs must examine themselves when evaluating whether they put military readiness above the well-being of the individual, for example when a combat soldier expresses fear (which is an understandable reaction), but with no symptoms of a diagnosis; or when a soldier exhibits adjustment problems, but the problems are not related to a mental health diagnosis. There are also issues of confidentiality/privacy concerns, which include sharing information with their commanders when the soldiers ask to meet an MHO, or when the MHO must inform a soldier's parents during a premature discharge without the ability to provide a diagnosis or the circumstances surrounding discharge. In these situations, it remains at the reporting level without sharing details with both the commanders and the parents.

7.8 Conclusion

Military social work in the IDF has been practiced in the Mental Health Array by MHOs for over 50 years. MHOs provide mental health care in both routine and wartime operations for a variety of populations including compulsory, career, and reserve forces with an assortment of methods adapted for the challenges of military service in Israel. MilSW also touches on other unique projects outside the Mental Health Array and related to the well-being of soldiers. MHOs are considered ground-breaking, both in Israel and around the world, especially as related to frontline care. Daily, they serve with professionalism, humanity, compassion, and creativity. The contribution of MilSW supports IDF soldiers and their commanders for continued functioning and optimal compliance with the task of protecting the security of the State of Israel.

References

Bartal E, Carmi N (2012) Environment in the shadow of war – the relationship between the perception of the security threat and the perception of the environmental threat, and the effect of the relationship on attitudes and environmental behaviors. Ecol Environ 3(4):304–311. https://doi.org/10.1080/10807039.2013.798217

Ben Yosef Azulay N, Gilat I, Sagi R (Eds.). (2017) When I wear uniform – I'm a king. Unique populations and social integration in the IDF. Ma'arachot

Bleich A (1990) The unique interaction between the Israeli youngster and the military framework: Adaptational crisis, psychopathological features, and expressions of distress. I.D.F Med Corps J 32:10–12

Cohen A, Amrani N (1989) The effect of the "Basic Education" course in the IDF on the self-image of conscripts in need of care. Megamot 32:75–83

Dagan R, Margalit H (1990) The career military personnel and his family – normal aspects and clinical characteristics. I.D.F Med Corps J 32:22–24

Ginat K, Fruchter E, Lubin G, Knobler H (2019) Military psychiatry in Israel challenges and achievements. Medicine 158(7):473–477

Keynan JN, Cohen A, Jackon G et al (2019) Electrical fingerprint of the amygdala guides neurofeedback training for stress resilience. Nat Hum Behav 3:63–73. https://doi.org/10.1038/s41562-018-0484-3

Kron S (1990) Mental health assessment and screening for military service in the IDF. I.D.F Med Corps J 32:13–14

Lubin G (2009 Dec 15) IDF mental health system – where to? The Medical, Israel Doctor's Website. http://www.themedical.co.il/Article.aspx?f=17&s=2&id=2680. Accessed 3 Mar 2022

Nadav D (2000) White and Khaki: history of the medical corps in the years 1949–1967. Ministry of Defense Publication

Rofe N (2019) Mental health professionals in the field in the IDF. The International conference on disaster and military medicine (DimiMed), Dusseldorf, Germany, 18–19 November 2019

Sasson-Levy O (2011) The military in a globalized environment: perpetuating an extremely gendered organization. In: Jeanes E, Knights D, Martin PY (eds) Handbook of gender, work, and organization. Wiley, Hoboken, pp 391–411

Scherer M (1997) Full, partial service and non-recruitment of underprivileged members of the IDF – The problem and its consequences. Soci Welfare 17(1):7–33

Security Service Law (1952)

Security Service Law (Amendment No. 11) (2000)

Sheklar (1990) Mental health in uniform – the development of the mental health system in the IDF. I.D.F Med Corps J 32:5–7

Shelef L, Paz N, Ben Yehuda A (2018) Suicides and suicidal attempts among IDF soldiers. J Arch Military Med 15:14–22

Shelef L, Nir I, Tatsa-Laur L, Kedem R, Gold N, Bader T, Ben Yehuda A (2019) The effect of the Suicide Prevention Program (SPP) on the characteristics of Israeli soldiers who died by suicide after its implementation. Eur Psychiatry 6:74–81. https://doi.org/10.1016/j.eurpsy.2019.08.007

Svetlitzky V (2017) "The missing squad" – mental fitness – an essential ingredient In the construction of the soldier, and the commander. Maarachot, pp 468–469:60-65

Svetlitzky V, Farchi M, Ben Yehuda A, Start AR, Levi O, Adler AB (2020) YaHaLOM training in the military: assessing knowledge, confidence, and stigma. Psychol Serv 17(2):151–159. https://doi.org/10.1037/ser0000360

Tishler A, Hadad S (2011) Compulsory army versus professional army – the effect of the recruitment method on the military power of the State of Israel. Caesarea Israel

Wald I, Fruchter E, Ginat K, Stolin E, Dagan D, Bliese PD, Quartana PJ, Sipos ML, Pine DS, Bar-Haim Y (2016) Selective prevention of combat-related post-traumatic stress disorder using attention bias modification training: a randomized controlled trial. Psychol Med 46(12):2627–2636. https://doi.org/10.1017/S0033291716000945

Zohar A, Shen G, Dycian A, Pauls D, Apter A, King R, Cohen D, Kron S (2004) The military life scale: a measure of perceived stress and support in the IDF. Isr J Psychiatry Relat Sci 41(1):33–44

Chapter 8
Occupational Social Work Within the Netherlands Armed Forces

Monique Kruishaar and Rob Hulskamp

8.1 The History of Occupational Social Work Within the Netherlands Armed Forces

The origins of military social work (MilSW) in the Netherlands date back to the end of the Second World War. In mid-April 1945, Prince Bernhard, in his capacity of Commander of the Interior Forces, added Section IX to his staff. Section IX focused on the social care of members of the interior forces upon their return to society (Sun 2008).

In March 1946, Section IX was transferred to the Social Services Department of the Ministry of War. This department was intended for conscripts and regular personnel of the army and air force (Sun 2008). The Royal Netherlands Navy had already established a Social Services Department in 1935 (Hooiveld 1986). From 1948 until the early 1950s, the Social Services Department was responsible for the social care of military personnel returning from Indonesia (Sun 2008). The Social Services Department was subsequently further expanded and became part of the Social Services and Personnel Care Department (SZP). The work was extended to include the care of former and disabled military personnel.

M. Kruishaar
Department of Vital, Safe and Healthy working, Ministry of Finance, Utrecht, The Netherlands

Occupational Social Work Services Centre, Dutch Ministry of Defence, Amsterdam, The Netherlands
e-mail: monique.dec78@gmail.com

R. Hulskamp (✉)
Employability and Reservist Department, Dutch Ministry of Defence, Amsterdam, The Netherlands
e-mail: robhulskamp@hotmail.com

© Springer Nature Switzerland AG 2023
M. A. Forgey, K. Green-Hurdle (eds.), *Military Social Work Around the Globe*, Military and Veterans Studies, https://doi.org/10.1007/978-3-031-14482-0_8

In 1955, the department changed its name and became the Department of Social Affairs (SZ). The SZ department was responsible for the social care or welfare of conscripts, regular military personnel, and former and disabled military personnel. In concrete terms, this meant drawing up and implementing policy based on the service regulations for social care and healthcare. Other activities of the SZ department included occupational social work, rehabilitation and disability care, social services, and personnel care in military criminal law and probation. In addition, the SZ department was also responsible for the maintenance of military graves for a short period of time (Sun 2008).

In the early 1970s, the Military Social Services Department (MSD) was set up to provide assistance to the individual armed forces services. The MSD provided assistance to members of the military in the event of problems at work due to personal problems, including financial difficulties (Sun 2008).

The MSD and the Department of Occupational Social Services for Civilian Personnel were merged in 1989, bringing all social care of military and civilian personnel together in a single department (Sun 2008). In 2021, this situation remains intact. The department is now called the Occupational Social Work Services Centre.

8.1.1   The Development of Occupational Social Work

The approach to MilSW at the Netherlands Ministry of Defence is mainly based on occupational social work (Ministerie van Defensie 2021a). As previously noted, the end of the Second World War and the aftercare for deployed members of the interior forces, was the starting point of today's MilSW in the Netherlands. Several national developments contributed to the current form and set-up of MilSW in the Netherlands armed forces, in the shape of occupational social services, and these will now be outlined.

The first of these developments was that from the second half of the nineteenth century onwards, the Dutch government became increasingly involved in the social care of the people of the Netherlands. This increased involvement formed the basis of the Dutch welfare state (van der Linde 2008).

Secondly, the need for social care for military personnel deployed as part of the Netherlands armed forces from the end of the Second World War was acknowledged. This development occurred in parallel with a third development, namely, a further national expansion and professionalisation of healthcare, and thus of social work, in the Netherlands (van der Linde 2008). At that time, there was also a growing focus within organisations on personnel care and the social welfare of personnel (Schaafsma 2001). As a result, social workers also started working for organisations. These employees, now known as occupational social workers, focused on the problems experienced by personnel working in these organisations (Schaafsma 2001). In 1955, Sun (2008) explicitly referred to occupational social work as part of the Social Services Department within the Netherlands armed forces.

8.2 Current Occupational Social Work Within the Netherlands Armed Forces: Practice Settings and Roles

8.2.1 Occupational Social Work Services Centre

In 2021, the Ministry of Defence occupational social workers work from one organisation: the Occupational Social Work Services Centre (OSWSC). The OSWSC is available to all defence personnel (uniformed and non-uniformed defence personnel), *active and post-active veterans,*[1] military war and service victims, and the families of defence personnel (Ministerie van Defensie 2021a).

In all circumstances, defence personnel and their families can request the services of the OSWSC. This can be done by making a personal appointment with an occupational social worker. Defence social workers also work at units themselves, where they are in contact with commanders and members of personnel. A blended form of social work is also possible: a mixture of face-to-face and online (e-mail) contact. In addition, in the event of a crisis, a telephone call can be made to the Ministry of Defence's emergency services hotline. This line can be reached 24/7 and is manned by personnel from the OSWSC (Ministerie van Defensie 2021a).

In 2021, the OSWSC of the Defence organisation employed 51 uniformed and 30 non-uniformed social workers. Eight of these 81 social workers were available specifically to post-active service veterans and their families.

8.2.2 Core Tasks

In practice, occupational social workers have to deal with a variety of psychosocial and work-related problems, such as adjustment problems after a deployment, dealing with too high a workload, conflicts with supervisors or colleagues, coping with bad news, and dealing with changes in the defence organisation.

Problems in someone's personal situation that can or may influence their employability at work are also addressed, such as relationship problems, problematic debts, parenting problems, coping with bereavement, and intensive family support or informal care for loved ones.

The core tasks of the OSWSC (Ministerie van Defensie 2021a):

- Provision of psychosocial assistance to defence personnel (uniformed and non-uniformed), veterans (on active duty and post-active) and to the families of

---

[1] A veteran is an actively serving soldier who has been deployed and is still working within the Defence organisation. Veterans who have left the service are called post-active veterans. These terms refer to both male and female veterans.

defence personnel in the case of psychosocial problems, at work or in their personal lives
- Provision of care during deployments and special missions
- Advising commanders on the deployability of defence personnel: verbally or by a written advisory report
- Providing deployment-related psychosocial care to military personnel and their families
- Provision of training courses and workshops aimed at improving the psychosocial functioning of defence personnel
- Participation in a Social Medical Team: a multidisciplinary team focused on the deployability of defence personnel
- Notification of incidents and crisis intervention

8.2.3 Practice Settings

Uniformed and non-uniformed occupational social workers mostly work in a clinical setting at an office on a base, airfield, or naval station; they are distributed throughout the Netherlands, Germany, and the Caribbean. They also join units during exercises. Only uniformed military occupational social workers join units on missions/deployments. Because occupational social workers work closely with the units and accompany them on exercises and missions, the threshold for military personnel seeking help is lowered.

Defence personnel live off-base and if necessary, occupational social workers visit defence personnel and their families off-base at their homes. This is particularly the case for post-active service veterans and their families, because these veterans are no longer on active duty.

Ministry of Defence occupational social workers work closely with (among others) doctors, psychologists, and chaplains of the defence organisation. If necessary, they also work together with aid organisations outside the defence organisation. This cooperation aims at establishing a joint assistance plan. If the problem lies outside the specific expertise of the occupational social worker, he/she will refer it to the relevant aid organisation. Examples of these are municipal debt assistance agencies, the Youth Care Office, housing associations, agencies dealing with domestic violence, and agencies for legal assistance and legal aid.

8.3 Practice Approach and Type of Interventions

8.3.1 Interventions Focused on Defence Personnel and Their Work Environment

Occupational social workers focus their interventions, especially on the individual employee, in the context of their work (Schaafsma 2012). In doing this, they work methodically. The aim of the MilSW in the Netherlands Armed Forces is to ensure that defence personnel (uniformed and non-uniformed personnel) achieve their full potential in their social functioning within the work environment. In this context, military social workers also pay attention to the social context of the personal situation of the defence employee and provide support if necessary (Schaafsma 2012). Military social workers are occupational social workers and, in this way, they contribute to the deployability of defence personnel (Ministerie van Defensie 2021a).

During the first interview with a member of defence personnel, an exploratory conversation is held based on a number of topics (Scholte 2002). Subsequently, a problem analysis and an assistance plan are drawn up and discussed with the defence employee or client (Scholte 2002). The working principles are to keep it short and simple to start with, aim at organising support close to the defence employee's (or client's) day-to-day life, empowering the defence employee/client and his or her networks, and making connections between those involved in the network.

Defence occupational social workers advise commanders and management on social welfare topics to prevent problems within the unit or department. They also provide care for members of personnel who have experienced traumatic events; this involves the use of low-threshold preventive interventions, such as group discussions. During these discussions, military personnel are given the opportunity to share experiences among themselves. They can find it difficult to share experiences with family and friends and often look for like-minded colleagues who can relate to the experiences they have had. Making low-threshold preventive interventions is important for recognising psychosocial stress symptoms at an early stage and offering help where necessary. In addition, sharing experiences contributes to better preparation for future activities of a similar nature (Elmqvist et al. 2010). These (group) interventions are also in line with the 'Guideline on psychosocial support for uniformed persons' (ARQ Nationaal Psychotrauma Centrum 2021). This guideline states that good employership starts with ensuring psychosocial support, with attention for factors that enhance psychosocial well-being.

Occupational social workers also provide further training and workshops for departments or groups on subjects such as stress management, aggression regulation, and learning how to deal with the consequences of change in the defence organisation. Commanders consult occupational social workers if there is a suspicion of psychosocial problems among personnel, or whenever these problems have been identified.

Social Medical Team Each unit has a Social Medical Team (SMT). This SMT is a multidisciplinary team consisting of the unit commander, an occupational health physician, a personnel consultant, a chaplain, and an occupational social worker (Ministerie van Defensie 2021a). The SMT aims to support the commander in his/ her tasks in the field of occupational health and safety, as well as well-being. Through multidisciplinary collaboration, a plan of action is drawn up for defence employees who are sick or unavailable due to medical, social, psychological complaints, or a combination of complaints. In the case of doubts regarding deployability, the SMT provides advice to the unit commander, orally or by means of an assessment report. In order for care provision to run efficiently during deployment, the SMT is required to meet on a regular basis before, during, and after deployment.

8.3.2 Interventions Focused on the Families of Defence Personnel

When a member of defence personnel experiences personal problems that may affect their deployability, family members are involved in the assistance provided by defence occupational social workers (Ministerie van Defensie 2021a). This provides an insight into the functioning of the family and allows a better assessment with regard to the deployability of the member of personnel, which is the basis for an assessment report to the commander. This applies to the deployability in the workplace, during both exercises and missions. Occupational social workers are also available to the family itself if problems related to the service member's work arise in the personal sphere (Ministerie van Defensie 2021a).

Notification of Incidents and Crisis Intervention In the event of a crisis or emergency, such as the death or injury of service personnel, a hostage situation, or a serviceman or woman missing in action during military service, it is important that the family is notified. The commander is responsible for ensuring that the message is passed on to the service member's family and is assisted in this by an occupational social worker (Ministerie van Defensie 2021a). For practical reasons, the choice is often made for only the occupational social worker to convey the message to the family instead of the commander. This would be the choice if, for example, the commander is deployed. Five occupational social workers are available 24/7 in the event of a crisis or the requirement to notify families with regard to incidents.

This notification process also applies vice versa. In the event of a family incident at home, an occupational social worker informs the relevant service member of the military unit in the deployment area (Ministerie van Defensie 2021a). The occupational social worker assists both servicemen and women and their families in dealing with bad news and their bereavement (Ministerie van Defensie 2021a).

8.3.3 Care Around Deployment

Since 2006, care surrounding deployments has been laid down in policy within the defence organisation. In addition to internal policy, the care process around deployments is also laid down in legislation. After the introduction of the Veterans Act in 2013, the government now monitors the implementation of proper care for veterans. This Act gives veterans rights to recognition, appreciation, and proper care (Nederlands Veteraneninstituut 2015). The care process regarding deployments consists of three elements: care before, during, and after the deployment.

Before the Deployment Prior to a deployment, a serviceman or woman's suitability for deployment is determined. A Social Medical Team (SMT) advises the commander on the medical, psychological, and social suitability of military personnel. During their pre-deployment training, military personnel are also informed about the care available, including occupational social work. In addition to general information about the deployment and the deployment area, topics related to personnel care are also presented; defence occupational social workers present the support that can be offered to military personnel and their family during the deployment.

Prior to the deployment, the families of military personnel are invited to a family information day. On this day, the families and friends are given information on the various care options within the defence organisation that they can fall back upon. For the well-being and functioning of military personnel, a sound family situation is very important. A lack of support for the family from the defence organisation during deployments can have a negative impact on the psychosocial well-being of deployed military personnel (Mulligan et al. 2012).

During the Deployment During the deployment, an SMT can be present to provide military personnel with professional support. The presence of the team depends on the nature and size of the mission. Only uniformed occupational social workers are members of an SMT during the deployment. The SMT advises the commander in the deployment area about the deployability of military personnel and offers medical and psychological assistance to the military personnel involved.

The defence organisation involves the family of the employed personnel during the deployment. For instance, defence sets up a so-called Home Front Committee where family and friends can ask practical questions. In addition, the defence organisation arranges contact days or 'home front days' during the deployment period. During these days, occupational social workers are present to provide assistance and support.

After the Deployment After the deployment and before returning home, deployed personnel follow a decompression programme. The initial focus of this programme is on preparing them for their return to the Netherlands and to their home and work situations (Ministerie van Defensie 2021b).

The decompression programme takes place at a location between the deployment area and the Netherlands, such as Greece, Cyprus, Portugal, or the Canary Islands. During the decompression programme, there are group discussions about the group's experiences during the mission and their transition to the home situation. In addition, information is provided on issues that military personnel commonly face in the transition from the deployment to the home situation. These group discussions are led by an occupational social worker and an experienced serviceman or servicewoman. During the decompression programme, there are also possibilities to relax before returning home.

About 3 months after their return to the Netherlands, military personnel have a post-deployment interview with an occupational social worker (Ministerie van Defensie 2021b). This is a way for the defence organisation to be able to offer assistance to military personnel at an early stage, particularly if there are deployment-related problems. This enables them to return to their homes, work, and society in the best possible way. The post-deployment interview gives a good indication of whether complaints decrease, remain stable, or increase over time (Gersons and Olff 2005). Research by Hanson et al. (2013) shows that deployment-related issues affect not only the service member but the whole family. Servicemen and women are given the option of bringing their family with them to the post-deployment interview, meaning a joint post-deployment interview. The purpose of the joint post-deployment interview is to get a better picture of the return of members of the military to the family situation, in order to identify and limit possible problems. By involving the partner in the post-deployment interview, possible changes in the service member's behaviour can be acknowledged and identified. Research by Rie et al. (2013) shows that partners are often more aware of the problems experienced by service members after deployment than the service member themselves. Problems such as stress, being constantly on high alert, being irritable, sleeping badly, and hiding problems are often noticed and identified by partners. In addition, support from the family and a good partner relationship appears to reduce the chance of developing PTSD symptoms (Cozza et al. 2010; Khaylis et al. 2011).

During the meeting, participants jointly look back and reflect on the experiences of the service member and their relatives with regard to the period of deployment and the period of return to the family situation after deployment. Telling the story and generating mutual understanding is helpful. These aspects are important against stress complaints, which benefits the integration for both the service member and the family (Hopman 2008). Possible complaints and/or problems can be discussed with an occupational social worker. If required, appropriate help can be offered, psychoeducation can be employed, referrals can be issued for relational therapy, for example, and specialist help can be sought for children. Talking about and dealing with joint problems allows for better preparation for future deployments. With this approach, the Occupational Social Work Services Centre is keeping with societal developments with a shift towards system-oriented work, i.e. the involvement of the social networks of members of the military in providing assistance.

Six months after the return from deployment, servicemen and women and their families[2] are sent a questionnaire (Netherlands Ministry of Defence 2015). The questionnaire is not mandatory and is therefore filled in on a voluntary basis. Military personnel can indicate beforehand to which member of the family the questionnaire may be sent. Both questionnaires are used as screening instruments for medical and psychosocial complaints that have arisen as a result of the deployment.

The questionnaire for military personnel asks about experiences during deployment that may have had an impact on their daily functioning, both at home in carrying out tasks and at work. In addition, military personnel are asked if there are concerns about their own psychological and physical condition, such as changes in their thinking, feelings, and conduct, and they are asked if there are concerns about their family.

The family questionnaire focuses specifically on the family's experiences during the deployment of their loved one, since a deployment does not only have an impact on the deployed soldier but also on his or her family and household. As with the questionnaire for military personnel, the well-being of the family in terms of physical, psychological, and social functioning, and, if applicable, the well-being and functioning of the children are addressed. The questions focus on a comparison of situations before and after deployment; situations such as the interaction between the children and the service member and the state of the relationship between the partner and the service member.

The answers to the questionnaire may indicate the need for a telephone call by an occupational social worker in order to offer support to the serviceman/woman or their family (Ministerie van Defensie 2021b). In addition, the outcomes of the questionnaires are meant to improve the care for future deployed colleagues and their families wherever required.

8.3.4 Special Missions: COVID-19 Deployment Care Plan

From March 2020 to July 2021, the defence organisation was deployed to assist in the fight against coronavirus. The numerous activities for which defence assistance was sought consisted of both providing urgent care to COVID-19 patients and deploying support services which includes the surveillance of border areas, the provision of logistical support and transport, undertaking planning activities, and supporting activities in rapid testing facilities.

It is well known that the organisation, the work environment, and the work tasks are factors that can influence the psychosocial well-being of the employee (Giorgi et al. 2020). Due to the nature of their work, professional groups such as healthcare workers and military personnel run an increased risk of developing psychological

---

[2]The Ministry of Defence sees the people who mean a lot to military personnel on deployment, such as the partner, children, family and friends, as an integral part of personnel care for military personnel on deployment (Netherlands Ministry of Defence 2015).

complaints or burnout. In particular, employees who perform tasks other than their usual job are seen to be at extra risk. This can have far-reaching consequences for their own well-being, that of their loved ones, and their employability in the workplace (Brooks et al. 2019). In order to limit possible negative psychosocial consequences for deployed defence employees, the care plan for COVID-19 deployment was drawn up during the first Corona crisis.

The aim of the *'Zorgplan inzet COVID-19'* (Care plan for COVID-19 deployments) was to be able to identify any psychosocial stress at an early stage and, where necessary, to provide adequate care to prevent any problems in the future. The families of deployed personnel were also included in the care plan, as the deployment of personnel could have an impact on the home situation (Lester et al. 2016).

The defence organisation has a substantiated care plan for deployments, as described in paragraph 4.1, and has gained positive experiences with this plan in the past few years. Based on these experiences, the interventions and products from the deployment care plan were adapted and redirected to the COVID-19 deployments, involving care before, during, and after the deployment.

8.4 Interventions Focused on Post-active Veterans

Post-active veterans can use the National Care System for Veterans in the case of problems related to their previous deployments (Nederlands Veteraneninstituut 2021). This National Care System for Veterans includes military and civilian aid agencies that specialise in providing assistance and care to veterans and their relatives.

The OSWSC is part of the National Care System for Veterans (Nederlands Veteraneninstituut 2021). Eight of their occupational social workers are available specifically and only to post-active-veterans. These occupational social workers assist post-active veterans if they are experiencing difficulties in their psychosocial functioning, at work or privately, or if there is a relationship between the problem and their previous deployments. In doing so, occupational social workers work together with other military aid agencies and civil aid organisations affiliated to the National Care System for Veterans (Nederlands Veteraneninstituut 2021). This collaboration is necessary because post-active veterans can have multiple complex problems with psychological, psychosocial, and physical complaints being interconnected.

8.5 Ethical Tensions

Occupational social workers may be faced with conflicting interests (Schaafsma 2012). They have to deal with the interests of the defence organisation that wants occupational social workers to contribute to the deployability of defence personnel. Defence personnel expect occupational social workers to provide expert and professional help, and possibly also to represent their interests (Schaafsma 2001).

Based on the professional profile of the social worker, occupational social workers provide assistance with the aim of enabling people to achieve their full potential in their social functioning, both at home and at work (Jagt 2017). In practice, occupational social workers have to deal with requests for help from defence personnel arising from problems in their family situation that may affect deployability at work. The assistance of occupational social workers is aimed at solving these problems or making them manageable so that defence personnel remain deployable. This will at least serve the interests of the organisation. But the problems can also be so serious and time-consuming regarding a certain member of personnel that deployment of that person would be unwise, for example, then the personal interest of the defence employee prevails. In such situations, occupational social workers advise commanders on deployability, weighing up organisational interests against the personal interests of the defence employee.

In recent years, due to a sharp increase in healthcare costs, the Dutch government has explicitly stated that people should help each other as much as possible instead of relying on government-funded aid and care. That same government expects defence personnel to be fully deployable. If they are deployed to exercises or missions, this means that Defence personnel are less able to provide informal care to, for example, their elderly or sick parents or their children with special needs. In practice, occupational social workers have to deal with these conflicting interests when it comes to requests for support in combining work and informal care. In doing so, occupational social workers must weigh up the interests of the organisation, the interests of society, and the interests of defence personnel against each other.

8.6 Education and Training of Occupational Social Workers

Occupational social workers who are employed by the OSWSC have completed a bachelor's degree in social work. They have subsequently followed a postgraduate course in occupational social work.

Internally, additional training is provided in terms of a course in 'care after traumatic events' and a course in how to pass on bad news to the next of kin in the event of a crisis or emergency, such as death, injury, a hostage situation, or a service member missing in action during military service.

The quality of the occupational social workers is guaranteed by means of periodic training that is compulsory for members of the National Professional
Association of Social

Work and for registration (Beroepsvereniging van professionals in sociaal werk
2021). This means that registration points must be earned every 5 years through
attending courses regarding further education, training, supervision, and intervision.

8.7   Major Challenges and Future Directions

Within the defence organisation, an increasing number of initiatives are focusing on
care or assistance within the psychosocial domain of occupational social work.
Examples are the assistant practitioner for mental health care (general practice mental health worker), lifestyle coaches, mediators, the Defence Colleagues Network,
and the Defence Centre of Expertise for Leadership Development (ECLD). In order
to cope with the increase in the number of other disciplines in the psychosocial
domain within the defence organisation, the Defence OSWSC is looking for cooperation with these disciplines. Efforts are also being made to make occupational
social work a more distinct area through the delivery of high-quality and more scientifically substantiated occupational social work.

Another challenge is that an internal evaluation among occupational social workers shows that not all the necessary knowledge and the competencies to be developed for the professional practice of occupational social work are addressed during
the bachelor's degree programme for social work and the post-higher professional
education training programme for occupational social work. This challenge is
acknowledged by other large social work organisations in the Netherlands.
Collective improvements are being made in this area through the national professional association.

8.8   Conclusion

This chapter first provides a description of the history of occupational social work
in the Netherland's armed forces. The sources consulted show that the aftercare of
the Netherland's internal armed forces deployed during the Second World War
formed the basis for occupational social work within the Netherland's armed forces
in its current form.

The current occupational social work organisation of the Netherlands armed
forces is located in an Occupational Social Work Services Centre. Defence personnel (civilian and military) and their family members can get psychosocial help there.
The assistance provided by the occupational social work organisation is aimed at
ensuring and increasing the deployability of defence personnel. They advise commanders and supervisors with regard to deployability. This subject is regularly

discussed in a Social Medical Team. Occupational social workers also work in a preventive manner by, among other things, providing information and workshops to improve psychosocial functioning.

Occupational social workers have completed a Bachelor's degree in social work and attended a post-higher professional education course in occupational social work. In addition, they have to follow periodic training in order to remain registered in the occupational social work register.

The occupational social work organisation also provides care before, during, and after deployments. Veterans, both active duty and post-active, can call on occupational social workers if needed. There are also occupational social workers available specifically to post-active veterans; they work closely with military and also civilian aid organisations.

In their work, occupational social workers work in the interests of both defence personnel and the defence organisation as a whole. These interests may conflict with one another, requiring the social worker to weigh up these interests.

Future challenges within occupational social work are related to the fact that other disciplines offer similar roles to occupational social work. In order to continue to develop in terms of quality, the occupational social work domain explicitly focuses on improving scientifically substantiated occupational social work.

Acknowledgements We would like to thank a number of people for making this chapter possible.
First, we would like to thank the editors, Mary Ann Forgey, PhD, LCSW and Karen Green-Hurdle MPH, MHSW, for the valuable feedback we have received in writing this chapter.
We would like to thank the Occupational Social Work Services Centre of the Netherlands Ministry of Defence for the opportunity to write this chapter. Our thanks also go to colleagues from the Occupational Social Work Services Centre for their professional support. Finally, we would like to thank the translators of the Dutch Defense Language Centre for their cooperation in carefully translating the original Dutch text into English.

References

ARQ Nationaal Psychotrauma Centrum (2021) Richtlijn psychosociale ondersteuning geünifor-meerden (3ᵉ druk). https://www.impact-kenniscentrum.nl/nl/producten/richtlijn-psychosociale-ondersteuning-geuniformeerden. Accessed 30 Sept 2021

Beroepsvereniging van professionals in sociaal werk (2021) Beroepsregistratie. https://www.bpsw.nl/professionals/maatschappelijk-werkers/beroepsregistratie/. Accessed 30 Oct 2021

Brooks SK, Rubin GJ, Greenberg N (2019) Traumatic stress within disaster-exposed occupations: overview of the literature and suggestions for the management of traumatic stress in the workplace. Br Med Bull 129(1):25–34

Cozza J, Guimond JM, McKibben BA, Chun RS, Arata-Maiers TL, Schneider B, Maiers A, Fullerton CS, Ursano RJ (2010) Combat-injured service members and their families: the relationship of child distress and spouse-perceived family distress and disruption. J Trauma Stress 23:112–115

Elmqvist C, Brunt D, Fridlund B, Ekebergh M (2010) Being first on the scene of an accident-experiences of 'doing' prehospital emergency care. Scand J Caring Sci 24(2):266–273

Gersons PR, Olff M (2005) Coping with the aftermath of trauma. Br Med J 330:1038–1039

Giorgi G, Lecca LI, Alessio F, Finstad GL, Bondanini G, Lulli LG, Arcangeli G, Mucci N (2020) COVID-19-related mental health effects in the workplace: a narrative review. Int J Environ Res Public Health 17:7857

Hanson S, Brockberg D, Gewirtz A (2013) Development and evaluation of a web-enhanced parenting program for reintegrating National Guard and Reserve families: after deployment, adaptive parenting tools/ADAPT. Am Psychol Assoc 1:52–62

Hooiveld I (1986) Militaire Sociale Dienst, 40 jaar helpende handen. Uitgeverij onbekend

Hopman BEM (2008) En dan kom je thuis…. Bijblijven 24:27–34

Jagt N (2017) Beroepsprofiel van de maatschappelijk werker (12ᵉ druk). BPSW, Utrecht

Khaylis A, Polusny MA, Erbes CR, Gerwit A, Rath MR (2011) Posttraumatic stress, family adjustments, and treatment preferences, among National Guard Soldiers Deployment to OEF/OIF. Mil Med 176:126–131

Lester P, Liang L, Mogil C, Woodward K, Nash W, Sinclair M, Semaan A, Klosinski L, Beardslee W, Saltzman W (2016) Evaluation of a family-centered preventive intervention for military families: parent and child longitudinal outcomes. J Am Acad Child Adolesc Psychiatry 15(1):14–24. https://doi.org/10.1016/j.jaac.2015.10.009

Ministerie van Defensie (2021a) Bedrijfsmaatschappelijk werk helpt. https://www.defensie.nl/onderwerpen/personeelszorg/bmw. Accessed 17 Sept 2021

Ministerie van Defensie (2021b) Zorg tijdens en na missies. https://www.defensie.nl/onderwerpen/gezondheidszorg/tijdens-en-na-missies. Accessed 17 Sept 2021

Mulligan K, Jones N, Davies M, McAllister P, Fear N, Wessely S, Greenberg N (2012) Effects of home on the mental health of British forces serving in Iraq and Afghanistan. Br J Psychiatry 201(3):193–198. https://doi.org/10.1192/bjp.bp.111.097527

Nederlands Veteraneninstituut (2015) Veteranen. Onze missie. http://www.veteraneninstituut.nl. Accessed 10 Jan 2016

Nederlands Veteraneninstituut (2021) Veteranenloket. https://www.nlveteraneninstituut.nl/veteranenloket/. Accessed 17 Sept 2021

Rie S, de la Mooren T, Schok M, Andringa S, Weerts J, Driessen T (2013) Uw mening, onze missie: het perspectief van veteranen en hun partners/gezinsleden met betrekking tot kwaliteit van zorg. Een cliëntgericht initiatief om opvattingen in kaart te brengen over de zorg en hulp ten behoeve van het welzijn na een uitzending. Eindverslag vfonds

Schaafsma B (2001) Bedrijfsmaatschappelijk werk. Hulpverlening, begeleiding en advies voor medewerker en organisatie. Uitgeverij Bohn Stafleu Van Lochum, Houten/Diegem

Schaafsma B (2012) Bedrijfsmaatschappelijk werk in ontwikkeling. Uitgeverij SWP, Amsterdam

Scholte M (2002) Psychosociale screening in de arbeidshulpverlening (3ᵉ druk). NIZW Uitgeverij, Utrecht

Sun X (2008) Inventaris van het archief van de Afdeling Sociale Zaken van het Ministerie van Oorlog/Defensie 1941:1952–1985. https://www.nationaalarchief.nl/onderzoeken/archief/2.13.198?query=sun%20x&search-type=description. Accessed 24 Mar 2020

van der Linde M (2008) Basisboek geschiedenis sociaal werk in Nederland (2ᵉ druk). Uitgeverij SWP, Amsterdam

Chapter 9
The Approach to Military Social Work in Aotearoa New Zealand

Antonia Nicholson, Natacha Cameron, Liam Cunnah, Tracy Milward, and Polly Yeung

9.1 Emergence of Military Social Work in Aotearoa New Zealand and Its Foundations

Military Social Work (MilSW) has existed within the Royal New Zealand Navy (RNZN) for around 25 years and was initially based on the Australian Defence Force (ADF) model of social work (Australian Association of Social Work 2016). The New Zealand Defence Force (NZDF) – *Te Ope Kātua O Aotearoa* – "The personnel of the main defensive stockade of New Zealand" structure is shown in Fig. 9.1 to highlight the leadership arrangements of the three single services in which the military social workers are employed within.

A. Nicholson (✉)
Social Services, New Zealand Defence Force, Wellington, New Zealand
e-mail: antonia.nicholson@nzdf.mil.nz

N. Cameron
Linton Regional Support Centre Linton Military Camp, New Zealand Defence Force, Manawatu, New Zealand
e-mail: natacha.cameron@nzdf.mil.nz

L. Cunnah
Southern Regional Support Centre Burnham Military Camp, New Zealand Defence Force, Selwyn, New Zealand
e-mail: Liam.Cunnah@nzdf.mil.nz

T. Milward
Waiouru Regional Support Centre Waiouru Military Camp, New Zealand Defence Force, Waiouru, New Zealand
e-mail: tracy.milward@nzdf.mil.nz

P. Yeung
Massey University School of Social Work, Palmerston North, New Zealand
e-mail: P.Yeung@massey.ac.nz

© Springer Nature Switzerland AG 2023
M. A. Forgey, K. Green-Hurdle (eds.), *Military Social Work Around the Globe*,
Military and Veterans Studies, https://doi.org/10.1007/978-3-031-14482-0_9

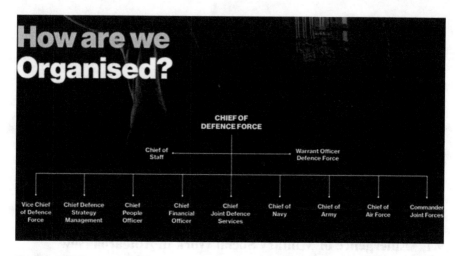

Fig. 9.1 NZDF structure (NZDF Annual Report 2019). (© Crown Copyright)

When military social work was first established, there was a lack of clarity about the role of social work in the military and how these services integrated with existing health and well-being support. As a result of the benefits from the Navy social work service, Defence Health, in 2016, implemented a pilot to test the feasibility of expanding the social work service in the New Zealand Army (NZ Army) and the Royal New Zealand Air Force (RNZAF). The outcomes sought from an expanded MilSW service in NZDF were to support personnel resilience and well-being through the provision of integrated and quality social work practice. The intended results for the pilot were to improve the operational readiness of uniformed members and improve access to support services for families. The evaluation of the pilot social work programme demonstrated effectiveness and a positive impact from enhanced ease of access to social work services in meeting the important outcome of enhancing the welfare of members and their families (Wilson and Hardie-Boys, personal communication, 6 June 2017).

Another critical consideration in the establishment of the MilSW service within the NZDF is the strong link with *tikanga Māori*, the customs and traditional values of the indigenous people of New Zealand. This relationship with culture is highlighted with the integration of family/*whānau* systems, tribal variances, and a warrior ethos. MilSW in Aotearoa New Zealand is committed to implement a culturally appropriate practice framework (Wepa 2015), which will be discussed in more detail in the following section. The framework also needed to be responsive to the unique demographics of the organisation, which is largely a male-dominated population, as shown in Table 9.1.

The existing scope of social work guided by Aotearoa New Zealand Association of Social Workers (ANZASW Te Rōpū Tauwhiro i Aotearoa) and Social Work Registration Board (SWRB) in Aotearoa New Zealand has provided a strong foundation to support the establishment of MilSW in the NZDF. Social work skills and

Table 9.1 Gender Representation of NZDF population (Ministry of Defence 2014)

Service	Female (%)	Male (%)
Navy	24	76
Army	14	86
Air Force	20	80
Civilian	46	54

knowledge have assisted NZDF Health to move from a bio-medical to a more holistic model of well-being. MilSW includes the provision of direct services to members, their families, NZDF civilians, and for the community, with brief education as well as support for commanders with their duty of care to their personnel. NZDF is a relatively small-scale military organisation, and the benefits of social work services are therefore more readily visible to command at all levels. Military social workers in the NZDF are employed as civilian members.

Two founding documents for social work (and the relationship between the Crown and Māori) in this country are *Te Tiriti o Waitangi* (Māori version) and the Treaty of Waitangi (English version), 1840, (Ministry of Culture and Heritage 2019), which shape how social workers engage with clients and provide a culturally safe environment. The Aotearoa New Zealand Social Workers [ANZASW Te Rōpū Tauwhiro i Aotearoa] Code of Ethics (2019) is based on principles that acknowledge the status of the Treaty document and the collaboration between *Tauiwi* (people who are not Māori) and the Māori population in this country about social work association structures, policies, procedures, and sharing of aspirations for both groups.

The model of MilSW in NZDF uses a person-centred focus of support based on holistic well-being and aligns well with the ANZASW Te Rōpū Tauwhiro i Aotearoa Code of Ethics (2019) in relation to the principle of *"Rangatiratanga"*, which promotes client empowerment and self-determination. Social work within the NZDF is seen as a professional service implemented by social workers who are trained by accredited institutions and governed by the Crown regulatory body, the SWRB *"Kāhui Whakamana Tauwhiro"*. Thus, NZDF members and command are assured that when using the social work service, a safe and competent standard of service delivery is being provided under the Social Workers Registration Board's Code of Conduct and Competence Standards (2019, 2020).

Military Social Work (MilSW) in the NZDF focuses on working with the complexity of a military organisation, potential occupational hazards associated with military service, and the military-related stressors on individuals within the military organisation and their families. It also provides micro-level social work with individuals, such as brief intervention therapy and problem solving, which takes into account the impact of the military environment and broader social systems on presenting issues. The importance of cultural identity, both military and bi-cultural on well-being, is woven through this work.

9.2 Structure of Military Social Work (MilSW) in NZDF and Underpinning Laws and Regulations

According to 2020 statistics, the NZDF has 13 full-time military social workers who support a total of 15,463 (NZDF 2020) military and civilian members (excluding reserves) and their families. These social workers are based at individual camps and bases across NZ: five Army – *"Ngāti Tūmatauenga"* – ("Tribe of the God of War") camps, three Air Force – *"Te Tauaarangi O Aotearoa"* – ("NZ Warriors of the Sky") bases, and one Navy – *"Te Taua Moana o Aotearoa"* – ("Warriors of the Sea of Aotearoa") base. Military social workers participate within health settings as members of multi-disciplinary teams (MDTs) alongside other military health professionals and, at times, with external community-based organisations, such as – *Oranga Tamariki* – Ministry for Children (for child protection).

Each camp and base is structured differently, and the location of the military social workers varies. Since the military social workers are employed by the different single Services (Navy, Army, or Air Force), the single service decides where the social worker is to be located and what structure they become a part of. The National Social Services Manager provides the technical support and professional guidance for the social work team and will also recommend changes for the resourcing of the social work team based on evidence of service demand and collated data.

Some of the social workers are based in a Defence Health Centre, which is located within the camp or base, alongside other medical professionals, such as medical officers and nurses. Alternative settings for other military social workers are in Community Support Hubs located inside or outside the camp or base alongside other military professionals, such as chaplains, transition coaches, complex case coordinators, defence community facilitators, and defence community coordinators. Camp and base locations are sometimes located near populous centres (refer Fig. 9.2), but may also be geographically isolated, reinforcing the importance of internal social work support networks.

Establishing any new function can be challenging. At the grassroots level, the establishment of the social work role required an initial focus on the "ground up" delivery through resourcing, role design, operating practice, and the development of practice guidelines. However, the strategic aim of this new function was to enable an integrated and holistic health service, which supported the psycho-social-spiritual domains of member well-being. The focus on roles needed to be tailored to camp and base-specific needs, and this required military social workers to navigate the challenges of delivering services while continuing to shape and refine process and practice. Focus includes clarifying roles within multi-disciplinary teams, building consistency of service delivery, refining foundational practice documents (to enable consent, assessment, and intervention phases), resourcing, and the organisational structure and positioning of social work services.

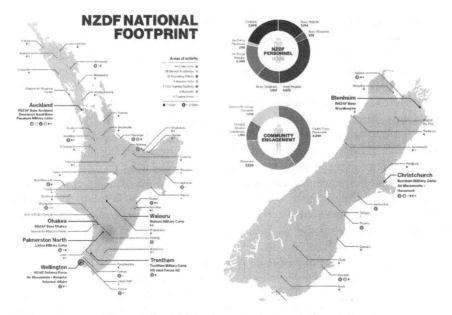

Fig. 9.2 NZDF National Footprint (NZDF Annual Report 2019). (© Crown Copyright)

9.2.1   Laws and Regulations Underpinning the NZDF Military Social Work Approach

Military social workers have a complex, multi-layered system to work within which adds to their professional responsibility as military social workers when coupled with the Defence Legislation. The Defence Act (DA) 1990 (Parliamentary Counsel Office [PCO] 1990) applies to all members of the NZDF, both military and civilian. It sets out the makeup, functions, and conditions of service for all members and volunteers. The Armed Forces Disciplinary Act (AFDA) 1971 (PCO 1971) stipulates the responsibilities for maintenance of discipline and adherence to customs and practices of single services or joint operations. Offences under this Act are either service or civil (whereby an offence is committed against any other Act which is outside the AFDA 1971). If the matter is civil then jurisdiction is shared with the relevant civil authority. Currently, all military social workers are civilian members and while they report directly to NZDF, there is no professional obligation to report under the AFDA. This context at times allows more flexibility to work with service users to engage in a safe environment to ensure confidentiality. Despite this, military social workers have formed and consolidated a strong and trusting relationship within the organisation and continuously encourage service users to engage with command to seek for a collaborative, supportive, and therapeutic relationship to deal with any issues.

At the heart of the MilSW practice, the social workers balance the client and *whānau* (extended family), safety, and self-determination with the requirements of the organisation and those of their professional duties and obligations. At times, there can be tension over which takes precedence, and navigating potential conflicts can be challenging. Nevertheless, if matters concerning the immediate safety of children arise, social workers' priority is to meet their statutory requirements to report these matters to the responsible government agency, *Oranga Tamariki* – Ministry for Children – (New Zealand Family Violence Clearinghouse 2020). The duty for this reporting is enshrined in legislation (PCO 1961, *Oranga Tamariki* Act, and Children's Act 2014) and takes priority over any other organisational circumstances.

The military social workers are required to obtain and maintain their professional accreditation and practicing certificate through the SWRB as prescribed in the Social Workers Registration Act 2003 (Ministry of Social Development [MSD] 2021). The SWRB have a range of regulatory instructions that outline standards for social work practice, as well as providing an avenue for members of the public to find out what standards social work services should adhere to. The SWRB is responsible for the application of the Social Workers Registration Act, 2003. This level of regulatory oversight provides assurance for other health professionals and the public about the standard of work delivered to clients. The Health and Disability Commissioner [HDC] Act 1996 (HDC n.d.-a) and the Code of Health and Disability Services Consumers' Rights (HDC n.d.-b) stipulate obligations on health providers for the delivery of safe health services. This has been particularly advantageous for processes like multi-disciplinary case management meetings, where other health professionals have come to seek and respect the input of the military social workers about client outcomes and goals (National Advisory Committee on Health and Disability 1998). From the military social workers' perspective, one of the most important pieces of legislation they work with is the Privacy Act, 1993 (PCO 2020). The NZDF adheres to all New Zealand legislation. The Privacy Act 1993 together with the Health and Disability Commissioner Act 1996 provides social work clients with the assurance that their personal information will be managed in accordance with the law and principles stipulated. One example is where social work clients need to be advised why their personal information is collected, who will have access to the information, whether it is voluntary to provide the information, and what will happen if the information is not provided. The practice of protecting client privacy applies equally in a military environment as in the public domain, unless there are security aspects that override these laws and principles. These Acts, together with the SWRB regulations, mean the clients' privacy is safeguarded as much as possible within a highly regulated military environment. As military social workers in NZDF are not uniformed personnel, it is important to navigate this potentially contested relationship carefully between service users and command when requests for information about clients arise. To facilitate this relationship requires not only a good understanding of the complexity of the defence force system, but also relational practices where social workers can support service users directly and provide command with support and guidance to help the uniform personnel to manage their issues in a respectful and constructive way.

9.3   Overarching Framework Underpins Military Social Work Practice in the NZDF

In order to deliver services across the micro, meso, and macro systems, the social work service draws on a holistic well-being model. The NZDF have chosen to utilise an indigenous framework that encompasses a holistic approach to the well-being of all NZDF personnel and their wider *whānau*/family as, "NZDF recognises the deepening significance of an individual's mental, spiritual and social well-being, and not just that of their physical health" (NZDF 2018b). This model is called *"Te Whare Tapa Whā"* (the house with four walls), which provides a framework for a holistic view of a client and their *whānau*/family, and can be applied to develop a culturally responsive and inclusive sense of practice which is relevant to the whole NZDF community for all of the issues described earlier.

Te Whare Tapa Whā is based on four dimensions or cornerstones of well-being developed by Sir Mason Durie in 1984 to provide a Māori perspective on health. The four dimensions are: *Taha Tinana* (physical health), *Taha Hinengaro* (mental health), *Taha Wairua* (spiritual health), and *Taha Whānau* (family health). The model illustrated in Fig. 9.3 is relevant to all populations in NZ and underpins the military Social Work practice framework in the NZDF.

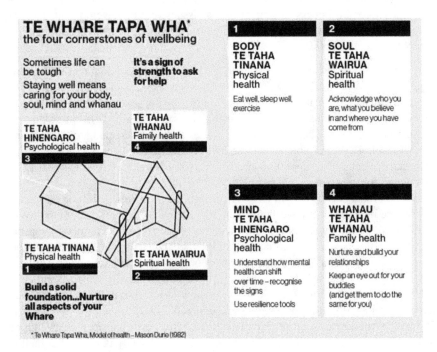

Fig. 9.3 *Te Whare Tapa Whā* model of well-being (Durie 1998) as depicted in the NZDF (2018a, b). (*Staying on the Top of Your Game* publication © Crown Copyright)

At times, military social workers are called upon by an individual commander or their command teams to provide advice on an array of different well-being or wellness matters, from the social impacts of physical injury or illness to unit culture or morale connected to operational demands. A collective positive outcome is pursued for command, the organisation, and the individuals and their families. The social workers endeavour to navigate a mutually beneficial, respectful, and interconnected outcome that meets the needs of the service member, their *whanau,* and command. These can often involve reinforcement of current plans and/or actions that have been put in place in support of NZDF personnel. Other times, this can be in response to certain trends or themes identified within a particular unit, and support and guidance can be offered in response to this.

9.4   Putting Theory into Practice in Military Social Work in NZDF

The MilSW service in the NZDF was set up with the intention of creating different levels of service delivery including the following:

(a) Micro-level interventions with individual clients and their families.
(b) Meso- and macro-level interventions. This incorporates the delivery of education and/or awareness raising on social issues, policy development, and the implementation of prevention programmes to support the strategic intent of the NZDF health service.

The services provided are based on both clinical and occupational modes of delivery. Clinical social work in NZDF is defined when social workers are "involved in the assessment and 'treatment' of mental distress and/or involved in counselling or therapeutic work to enhance client wellbeing" (Appleby et al. 2020). An example to illustrate this point is when a social worker uses a clinical screening tool, for example, an alcohol use tool, to evaluate the level of distress a client is experiencing in their daily life and plan supportive intervention (for example, a drinking safety plan) that works for the client.

Occupational social work in NZDF draws on the following definition as a "field of practice in which social workers attend to human and social needs of employees in the work milieu by designing and executing appropriate interventions to ensure healthier individuals and environments" (Googins and Godfrey 1985). An example of occupational social work is the provision of education and awareness activities that support NZDF members to know how to respond to family violence and child safety issues, so that they become aware of how to respond in the course of their duties. Specifically, this training has equipped NZDF members working in COVID-19-managed isolation facilities to identify and take appropriate action when they become aware of family violence and child safety issues in the facility that they are managing.

9.4.1   Micro-Level Interventions with Individual Clients and Their Families

Military social workers engage mainly with military members and their families on a range of military-related and social issues. These can include posting cycle stressors, work-life balance, personal relationships (including prolonged absences from family/*whānau*), health and well-being, finances, parenting, family violence, and child safety. The social worker also has a close connection and network with the wider community and can make referrals for civilian members working in the NZDF for support when required.

There are four primary pathways for the NZDF community to engage with the MilSW service for individual support. These are self-referral, command referral, and an internal or external provider referral. An individual will self-refer or be referred for a wide range of presenting issues. The MilSW service has developed a bio-psych-social tool that is underpinned by the four domains of *Te Whare Tapa Whā* (see discussion and Fig. 9.3) as a means of developing a holistic assessment. The assessment tool seeks to identify the individual's personal and environmental strengths and challenges from a holistic perspective rather than focusing solely on the presenting issue. The broader assessment process supports the social worker to identify a plan for either social work brief intervention or for the completion of a referral to a specialist provider externally (e.g. clinical psychologist or counsellor) or other internal health provider such as a medical officer or organisational psychologist. The assessment process draws on information about the military member and their family well-being, as well as resilience and strengths of their community interactions (Sudom 2012; Saleebey 2013; Hom et al. 2020). It incorporates potential impacts of service (Alrutz 2017; Blueknot Foundation 2020) to ensure the intervention is relevant for the client. To create tailored intervention plans with clients, social workers draw on a range of health and well-being tools and resources.

Social workers provide advocacy for NZDF personnel by providing a clinical lens to commanders and managers to ensure they are well-informed and to support their duty of care obligations when making decisions that pertain to both the individual and wider unit. This is particularly relevant around risk assessments when it is necessary to consider both the specialist knowledge and training that occurs within the military – such as weapons or close combat training, which would generally not be taken into consideration for non-military people living within the civilian community.

Clinical Social Work Interventions   When working with individual service members and their families, military social workers utilise intervention processes (outlined as follows) to support member and *whānau* well-being, while at the same time supporting the organisations' objectives.

During the initial meeting with the client for clinical social work intervention, the social worker uses evidence-based practice to establish a therapeutic alliance (Rogers 1977; Parker and Bradley 2014; Coulshed and Orme 2006) as well as knowledge of the unique military culture and setting (culture and structure, policy settings, health and well-being guidance, unit cohesion, and morale) (Ministry of Defence 1987). These factors include the allegiance the service member has to their unit or team, the close relationships that develop within the unit comparable to those of personal family, the importance placed on continued career progression, and medical grading for deployability. The social worker is mindful of the clients' cultural heritage and how they may self-identify (Durie 1998, E Tū Whānau Māori Reference Group 2019, Aotearoa New Zealand Association of Social Workers Te Rōpū Tauwhiro i Aotearoa Code of Ethics 2019); as a member of an *iwi* (tribe), the importance of this identity together with their *whānau* (extended family) of origin, and the need to provide a culturally safe environment. They will ascertain if children are in the family and work with the family to ensure that children's' well-being is paramount (Alrutz 2017; Ministry of Social Development [MSD] 2017).

Once the social worker has completed the bio-psycho-social assessment and screening tools, the social worker works alongside the client to determine the next steps. If the outcome of this meeting is that the presenting issues are identified as complex, severe, or high risk; the social worker will seek specialist referral services through the Medical Officer. However, if the outcome of the assessment/screening sits within the realm of brief intervention therapy (a mild-moderate level of impact from the issue), then the social worker may undertake this work alongside the client. The social worker will apply clinical reasoning (American Board of Examiners in Clinical Social Work 2020) to tailor the intervention plan to the individual client. For example, when the history of the client indicates the need for a trauma-informed model of practice (Van der Kolk 2014; Blueknot Foundation 2020), the social worker is equipped to use this approach and create opportunities for the client to rebuild a sense of control and empowerment (Kassam-Adams et al. 2014).

The social worker may additionally draw on culturally informed practice to provide an effective assessment that acknowledges, respects, and integrates the clients' and their families' cultural values and beliefs, and practices (Banks and Kelly 2015). This is particularly important in the NZDF context where the population broadly represents the NZ demographic data for ethnicity (Environmental Health Indicators New Zealand [EHINZ] 2020) for Māori and people from the Pacific region.

The military social worker will adopt a strengths-based collaborative process with the client. This process will be supported by working together to determine an outcome that draws on the clients' current strengths and assets (Saleebey 2013). In addition, as military personnel identify with completing tasks to achieve operational requirements, the social worker may alternatively focus by redirecting them to "imagine life without the problem" (Joubert and Guse 2021), rather than completing a detailed analysis of the problem itself. The aim here is to enable the service member to identify specific goals and create practical strategies or actions for them to achieve those (Connie and Metcalf 2009) within military and family systems. Adopting a wider macro-level lens means the social workers integrate the ecological systems theory/framework within their practice. Here, the relevance of the military community and setting for the individual's relationships within that community and wider society (Bronfenbrenner 2005) are analysed to assist with intervention plans.

Using a variety of interventions, the social worker may provide psychoeducation for individuals, which may draw on Cognitive Behavioural Therapy (CBT) processes (Beck Institute for Cognitive Behaviour Therapy 2020). The social worker may assist the client to reframe their thought patterns to enable positive emotional or behavioural actions rather than detrimental ones (Beck Institute for Cognitive Behaviour Therapy 2020). Another model of intervention being utilised is that of Acceptance and Commitment Therapy (ACT) (Harris 2019). Social workers may work with mindfulness and acceptance techniques mixed in different ways with commitment and behaviour change strategies (Harris 2019) for positive client outcomes.

Military social workers are called upon to provide risk assessment and safety planning for clients which is based on a holistic model and includes their family/*whānau* for support, but also discussion around other family/*whānau* challenges. Crisis intervention work associated with risk issues may result in onward referrals to specialist Mental Health Services following an assessment. Using the crisis intervention model, the social worker may draw on a range of community-based services as well as involving their direct command chain. The command chain is involved with soldier consent, or when immediate safety issues are identified. Balancing the needs of the service members with the sometimes-conflicting needs of the military unit is an important issue faced by military social workers. Sharing personal information can be an ethical challenge in an institution that is heavily grounded on discipline and hierarchy. Therefore, building relationships with defence force, command, and its community have been paramount.

Unlike other countries such as the United States where "Military Social Work" is more developed, social work in the NZDF is still developing and maturing. Recent changes as stated earlier have shown that MilSW has become an important field of practice with significant development of regulatory and social measures in relation to the well-being of the military. This demonstrates a flexible relationship with the organisation and highlights the recognition gained due to the ability to provide a wrap-around support service. Social work knowledge, values, and skills are transferrable across client populations and situations. Ethical challenges and dilemmas occur in MilSW, as within other social work fields of practice, that require advanced critical and analytical skills. Social workers are able to draw on their level of organisational knowledge and can assist external services to better understand these specific military environmental nuances to enable completion of more thorough and comprehensive risk assessments and safety plans. This information may include factors such as isolation or being disconnected from *whānau*, training, access to weapons, and the obligation for holding a security clearance within NZDF, thus providing better outcomes not only for the individual service member but also for the organisation.

9.4.2   Meso- and Macro-Level Interventions

The social workers may also work at the organisational level to deliver education on a broad range of social and wellness topics. They do this by utilising tailored presentations, group work for units, or education for the wider defence community. A demand for these packages can also be identified by the local well-being team, wider community, and command teams.

Topics for the education packages can include alcohol and drugs, mental health, parenting, and family harm. One recent example is where command had identified through an influx of alcohol-related incidents that a negative culture underpinned by problematic alcohol use may have been present. Due to the identified trend, the commander chose to engage the military social work service to discuss how best to effect change on a macro level. On advice from the social workers, the next step chosen (to understand the level and type of intervention required) was the completion of a formation-wide survey about alcohol. The findings identified key themes for interventions that were subsequently introduced; alcohol awareness education, efforts to tackle boredom, and increased support for those providing host responsibilities.

Alongside these interventions, the social workers provide support for service members and facilitate access to community-based services. Social workers provide education about the military culture, environment, and population to these community-based services to ensure they understand the unique challenges faced by service members and their *whānau*. This is completed to enable best outcomes and responsive service delivery.

Social workers also provide social work directly to individual units or larger formations as required. From the outset of the service, there has been a need to demonstrate the "value add" of the service as social work was not well understood. This has been easily quantifiable when focusing on the micro level of service delivery, with the one-on-one sessions with service personnel. As the service has become more accepted and understood, this has led to micro-based themes and trends informing meso- and macro-level interventions. These can be responses to social, economic, geographical, political, and environmental challenges in specific regions (EHINZ 2020), for example, on the macro level the availability of affordable housing in particular areas and the financial repercussion on service members and their dependants/*whānau*, or natural disaster responses. On the meso level, social workers may be called upon by units to discuss self-care, how to maintain work/life balance, managing stress, and healthy relationships. Furthermore, social workers deliver "what is NZDF Social Work" to new recruits and newly posted NZDF personnel. Often, this education is provided by social workers at a unit level, which leads to the service personnel becoming self-aware of individual issues and where they may go on to engage one-to-one with a social worker. The key message in any of the social work education or training presentations is raising self-awareness for prevention, early identification, and intervention.

9.5   Social Work Ethical Tensions

As a social worker in NZDF, there are a number of unique ethical tight ropes that require recognition and navigation in order to deliver best practice outcomes for individuals, families, and ultimately Command (Tallant and Ryberg 2007). First, it is important to acknowledge that the social workers in the NZDF are ultimately employed by the same organisation as most of their clients. This can cause challenges for social workers around the capacity to remain impartial and client-centred (Aotearoa New Zealand Association of Social Workers Te Rōpū Tauwhero i Aotearoa 2019) when the performance and outcomes sought by the organisation are not necessarily aligned with the outcomes sought by the service member (Hall 2011). Command tasking may have an impact on the service members' access to social workers, and they may also seek information to enable their responsibilities for the welfare of their personnel. At times, this can create an ethical tension between the command's need for information to manage people effectively, and the social worker's responsibility for maintaining the confidentiality of personal information. Civilian social workers in a military setting do not hold rank and are therefore able to advocate for a service member across all ranks without tension or fear of consequences from this hierarchical system.

Through focusing on the building of mutually respectful relationships and commitment to the intent and purpose of the organisation, the social work service is further being embedded and trusted as a key enabler by local and higher command. The social workers demonstrate this commitment by attending parades, field exercises, and being ever ready to respond to command requests. As the service continues to grow, the number of positive outcomes being witnessed by command for their service personnel increases.

The service that is provided by military social workers is a voluntary service, which means a service member may choose to engage through a process of written informed consent, whereby the parameters of confidentiality and the extent of disclosure of information are made explicitly clear with individual coming through the service (SWRB 2020). When service personnel are faced with uncertainty or something that is unknown, they can often look to their peers and/or the command chain for guidance and recommendations.

Using a process of informed consent, the social worker must inform the client of the limits of confidentiality and the requirement to complete documentation. As a form of documentation, case notes that are written by social workers may be accessed by the medical officers who are also providing the client with support. This can pose ethical tensions between the self-determination and help seeking of the client when compared to the organisation using the information to minimise organisational risk (Hom et al. 2020). At times, this can be at the detriment of the service members' particular engagement goal, but ultimately mitigate any foreseeable or unforeseeable risks.

A service member's role is to follow a commander's order or intent. When a service member is ordered to attend a command-referred social work appointment, it is imperative that the social worker ensures the serving member is engaging out of their own free will and choice by going through a rigorous consent process.

In isolated locations, it is not uncommon for ethical tensions to arise when both parties in a professional relationship context seek individual support services via a sole social work practitioner. At times, this may involve working with commanders alongside members of their unit. This effect may be experienced more frequently in the NZ context due to the smaller size and inter-connectedness of the military population. The social worker will navigate these ethical tensions through a mix of reflective practice, peer consultation, supervision, and practice guidance (Aotearoa New Zealand Association of Social Workers Te Rōpū Tauwhero i Aotearoa, 2019). The social worker must be initially aware of the identified conflict and manage this accordingly (Brand and Weiss 2015).

9.6 Transition Support

When considering the veteran population, social workers are unlikely to become involved with supporting their transition to civilian life unless it is a complex matter. The military social workers may be called on to provide an assessment and link veterans with external support services to assist their transition. NZDF has a Veterans' Affairs Unit, *Te Tira Ahu Ika a Whiro*, that provides services for veterans as mandated under government legislation named the Veterans Support Act 2014 (PCO 2021). The social workers will draw on knowledge of risk and protective factors, including service type and era, and the impacts (or benefits) on mental well-being as a result of service experience and lifestyle (Yeung et al. 2018). Having social workers available within the NZDF who understand the culture, context, and structures is an advantage for this work with veterans.

9.7 Preparation for the Role as a Military Social Worker in NZDF

As described earlier, there are broad-ranging social issues found across the NZDF population that are mirrored by those identified in the U.S. military population (National Association of Social Workers 2012). In addition, the nature of the military environment means there may be after-hours demands at times. There are few comparable social work roles, which prepare a social worker for the breadth or complexity of the MilSW as noted by Daley (1999). In addition, academic social work education in NZ does not currently include modules on MilSW as a field of practice as it does in some other countries (Brand and Weiss 2015).

The induction process for new military social workers includes preparing for social work practice in the military environment (tools, technology, meetings, processes), education on the military structures and service culture at their location, familiarity with different units and key personnel at location, and learning about key documents relating to social work service delivery (policies, standards, and standard operating procedures). It is expected to take an experienced social worker a year to be fully embedded in the role.

Much of the occupational social work knowledge is acquired through on-the-job experience. Although there is good evidence that by providing training and education on military culture and context increased social workers' preparedness for response and intervention (Hall 2011), the MilSW practice relies heavily on the social worker building strong relationships with key defence stakeholders.

As many of the military social workers are the sole social worker on-site, a number of processes have been implemented to support them in their role. These include peer support via informal connections, a routine fortnightly virtual meeting, a quarterly face-to-face social work conference, regular liaison with the social work technical lead, access to ongoing continuing professional development, and military and social work practice notes that support service delivery. In addition, the social workers will use peers to review cases and discuss social work issues that occur at all locations and participate in multi-disciplinary health processes with other health professionals as well as their external professional supervision.

9.8   Major Challenges and Opportunities

MilSW has been a developing service within the NZDF for the past 4 years following a social work pilot. This has led to a number of challenges as the service has been tested and adjusted over this period. From its inception back in 2016 (excluding Navy), there have been many challenges faced around the extent and potential limitations of the service.

At present, due to the evolving nature of MilSW as a field of practice in Aotearoa New Zealand, the service has drawn on individual social workers from an array of social work backgrounds. The result is a broad generic platform of knowledge and skills. This may well be different to other militaries who are able to draw on preparatory courses tailored for social workers in a military environment (Forgey and Young 2014; Wooten 2015) that are not yet available in Aotearoa New Zealand. Future development of the service includes discussion on the inclusion of New Zealand MilSW into the academic syllabus as a specific field of social work practice, and the inclusion of social work student placements.

Another unique challenge for military social workers is that the delivery of primary health care is only funded for uniformed personnel and does not extend to *whānau* or dependants of uniformed personnel. Family members are funded through public health systems on a capitation basis. At times, a social worker may assess that a family member needs access to specialist public health services, which requires social workers to use their specialist and local knowledge to connect and signpost possible options. Public services can have long waitlists due to also serving and supporting the wider community. Family members do have access to 24/7 well-being phone support, which does include access to counselling services if appropriate. Timely access to targeted and responsive care enhances family well-being and operational readiness; however, the availability of some public services can be challenging.

Future opportunities for the MilSW functions include further development of the social work team, scope of practice and framework, closer ties with other MilSW services, research into outcomes from social work interventions in NZDF, adaption to new or emerging military service operations (for instance more focus on natural disaster response), and benchmarking with other militaries in this field.

In conclusion, while the MilSW service in NZDF is still in the developmental phase, consistent benefits, not only for the organisation but also for individual members and families, are delivered. Drawing on a culturally responsive and competent workforce, these advantages include a greater level of support for social issues for *tangata whenua*, individuals, and commanders, as well as a strengthened focus on holistic support for members and their families. This in turn enables operational readiness for uniformed members and continues to actively promote the value of social work service in the military context.

References

Alrutz A (2017) What happens at work goes home: investigating secondary traumatic stress and social support among the partners of New Zealand's police, fire, ambulance, and defence personnel. Dissertation, University of Auckland

American Board of Examiners in Clinical Social Work (2020) Professional development and practice competencies in clinical social work. A position statement of the ABECSW. https://www.abcsw.org. Accessed 23 Apr 2018

Aotearoa New Zealand Association of Social Workers Te Rōpū Tauwhero i Aotearoa (2019) Code of ethics. https://anzasw.nz/code-of-ethics-2019. Accessed 5 Sept 2019

Appleby J, Staniforth B, Flanagan C, Millar C (2020) Clinical social work in Aotearoa New Zealand: origins, practice, and future implications. Aotearoa New Zealand Soc Work 32(4):103–115

Australian Association of Social Work (2016) Scope of social work practice: Australian Defence Force (ADF) service members, veterans, and their families. https://www.aasw.asn.au/document/item/8706. Accessed March 2018

Banks L, Kelly M (2015) Cultural safety and the nursing council of New Zealand. In: Wepa D (ed) Cultural safety in Aotearoa NZ, 2nd edn. Cambridge University Press, Cambridge

Beck Institute for Cognitive Behaviour Therapy (2020) Cognitive behavioural therapy. https://beckinstitute.org/. Accessed 14 Nov 2020

Blueknot Foundation (2020) Supporting adult survives of childhood trauma & abuse. https://blueknot.org.au/. Accessed 4 Feb 2020

Brand MW, Weiss EL (2015) Social workers in Combat: application of advanced practice competencies in military social work and implications for social work education. J Soc Work Educ 51(1):153–168. https://doi.org/10.1080/10437797.2015.979094. Accessed 2 Dec 2021

Bronfenbrenner U, Ecological Systems Theory (1992). In Bronfenbrenner U (2005) Making human beings human: bioecological perspectives on human development Sage Publications

Connie E, Metcalf L (2009) The art of solution focused therapy, 1st edn. Springer Publishing Company, New York

Coulshed V, Orme J (2006) Social work practice, 4th edn. Palgrave Macmillan, Basingstoke

Daley JG (1999) Social work practice in the military. Haworth Press, New York

Durie M (1998) Whaiora Māori health development. Oxford University Press, Auckland

E Tū Whānau Māori Reference Group (2019) E Tū Whānau Mahere Rautaki framework for change 2019–2023. https://www.msd.govt.nz. Accessed 26 Aug 2020

Environmental Health Indicators New Zealand [EHINZ] (2020) Environmental health indicators. https://www.ehinz.ac.nz/. Accessed 17 Nov 2020

Forgey M, Young S (2014) Increasing military social work knowledge: an evaluation of learning outcomes. J Health Soc Work 39(1):7–15. https://doi.org/10.1093/hsw/hlu003

Googins B, Godfrey J (1985) The evolution of occupational social work. Social Work 30(5):396–402. https://doi.org/10.1093/sw/30.5.396

Hall LK (2011) The importance of understanding military culture. J Soc Work Health Care 50(4):4–18. https://doi.org/10.1080/00981389.2010.513914

Harris R (2019) ACT made simple: an easy-to-read primer on acceptance and commitment therapy, 2nd edn. New Harbinger Publications Inc, Oakland

Health and Disability Commissioner [HDC] (n.d.-a) Code of health and disability services consumers' rights. https://www.hdc.org.nz/your-rights/the-code-and-your-rights/. Accessed 26 Apr 2022

Health and Disability Commissioner [HDC] (n.d.-b)) Health and disability commissioner act 1996 health. https://www.hdc.org.nz/about-us/history/#:~:text=The%20Health%20and%20Disability%20Commissioner,and%20efficient%20resolution%20of%20complaints. Accessed 26 Apr 2022

Hom MA, de Terte I, Bennett C, Joiner TE (2020) Resilience and attitudes toward help-seeking as correlates of psychological well-being among a sample of New Zealand Defence Force personnel. Military Psychol 3(4):329–340. https://doi.org/10.1080/08995605.2020.1754148

Joubert J, Guse T (2021) A solution-focused brief therapy (SFBT) intervention model to facilitate hope and subjective wellbeing among trauma survivors. J Contemp Psychother 51:303–310

Kassam-Adams N, Vega G, Marsac M, DiBattista N, Schneider S, Kazad A (2014) Culturally-sensitive trauma-informed care. Healthcare toolbox. Center for Paediatric Traumatic Stress. https://www.healthcaretoolbox.org/culturally-sensitive-trauma-informed-care. Accessed 6 Oct 2020

Ministry for Culture and Heritage (2019) Treaty of waitangi February 6th 1840. New Zealand history Nga korero a ipurangi o Aotearoa Treaty of Waitangi February 6th 1840. https://nzhistory.govt.nz/politics/treaty-of-waitangi. Accessed 10 Jan 2019

Ministry of Defence [MOD] (1987) The army wives study. Ministry of Defence, Wellington

Ministry of Defence [MOD] (2014) Maximising opportunities for Military Woman in the New Zealand Defence Force, Wellington. https://www.women.govt.nz/inspiring-action-for-gender-balance/maximising-opportunities-military-women-new-zealand-defence. Accessed 21 Apr 2022

Ministry of Social Development [MSD] (2017) Families commission families and Whānau status report. https://www.msd.govt.nz/documents/about-msd-and-our-work/publications-resources/corporate/superu-annual-report.pdf. Accessed 21 Apr 2022

Ministry of Social Development [MSD] (2021) Social worker registration. https://www.msd.govt.nz/about-msd-and-our-work/work-programmes/social-worker-registration/index.html#:~:text=Changes%20to%20Social%20Workers%20Registration,SWRB)%20from%2027%20February%202021.&text=These%20changes%20will%20ensure%20greater,the%20professionalism%20of%20social%20workers. Accessed 26 Apr 2022

National Advisory Committee on Health and Disability (1998) The social, cultural and economic of health in New Zealand: action to improve health. https://www.health.govt.nz/system/files/documents/publications/det-health.pdf. Accessed 8 Nov 2018

National Association of Social Workers (2012) NASW standards for social work practice with service members, veterans & their families. https://www.socialworkers.org/LinkClick.aspx?fileticket=fg817fIDop0%3D&portalid=0. Accessed 21 Apr 2022

New Zealand Defence Force [NZDF] (2018a) Defence health strategy 2025 – a better, stronger, healthier NZDF. http://health.nzdf.mil.nz/assets/Uploads/Defence-Health-Strategy-FINAL.pdf. Accessed 1 Aug 2018

New Zealand Defence Force [NZDF] (2018b) Staying on top of your game. NZDF, Wellington. https://health.nzdf.mil.nz/assets/Documents/Staying-at-the-top-of-your-game.pdf. Accessed 20 Aug 2019

New Zealand Defence Force [NZDF] (2019) NZDF annual report 2019. http://www.nzdf.mil.nz/search/SearchForm?Search=annual+report. Accessed 24 Nov 2019

New Zealand Defence Force [NZDF] (2020) Public information https://www.nzdf.mil.nz. Accessed 2 Oct 2020

New Zealand Family Violence Clearinghouse (2020) Data summaries. https://nzfvc.org.nz/our-work/data-summaries. Accessed 23 Oct 2020

Parker J, Bradley G (2014) Social work practice, 4th edn. Sage Publications, London

Parliamentary Counsel Office [PCO] (1961) New Zealand Legislation, Crimes Act 1961. https://www.legislation.govt.nz/act/public/1961/0043/137.0/DLM327382.html. Accessed 26 Apr 2022

Parliamentary Counsel Office [PCO] (1971) New Zealand Legislation, Armed Forces Discipline Act 1971. https://legislation.govt.nz/act/public/1971/0053/latest/DLM401063.html. Accessed 26 Apr 2022

Parliamentary Counsel Office [PCO] (1990) New Zealand Legislation, Defence Act 1990. https://legislation.govt.nz/act/public/1990/0028/latest/DLM204973.html. Accessed 27 Apr 2022

Parliamentary Counsel Office [PCO] (2020) New Zealand Legislation, Privacy Act 1993. https://www.legislation.govt.nz/act/public/1993/0028/latest/DLM296639.html. Accessed 26 Apr 2022

Parliamentary Counsel Office [PCO] (2021) New Zealand Legislation, Veteran's Support Act 2014. https://www.legislation.govt.nz/act/public/2014/0056/latest/whole.html. Accessed 26 Apr 2022

Rogers CR (1977) Carl Rogers on personal power. Delacorte, New York

Saleebey D (2013) The strengths perspective in social work practice (advancing core competencies), 6th edn. Pearson Publishers, New York

Social Workers Registration Board (2019) Code of conduct. https://swrb.govt.nz/practice/code-of-conduct/#:~:text=The%20Code%20requires%20social%20workers%20to%3A&text=respect%20the%20cultural%20needs%20and,responsible%20for%20your%20professional%20development&text=respect%20the%20client's%20privacy%20and,openly%20and%20respectfully%20with%20colleagues. Accessed 9 Jan 2020

Social Workers Registration Board (2020) Competence standards. https://swrb.govt.nz/practice/core-competence-standards/. Accessed 3 Dec 2020

Sudom K (2012) Impact of military life on families and single canadian forces members current state of knowledge and research gaps. Canadian National Defence. https://www.cfmws.com/en/AboutUs/MFS/FamilyResearch/Documents/DGPRAM/Quality%20of%20Life/TM%202012008%20Impact%20of%20Military%20Life%20on%20Families%20and%20Single%20CF.pdf. Accessed 23 Sept 2020

Tallant SH, Ryberg RA (2007) Social work in the military: ethical dilemmas and training implications. In: Daley JG (ed) Social work practice in the military. Haworth Press, New York, pp 179–204

Van der Kolk B (2014) The body keeps the score; mind, brain and body in the transformation of trauma. Penguin Books, New York

Wepa D (ed) (2015) Cultural safety in Aotearoa NZ, 2nd edn. Cambridge University Press, Cambridge

Wooten N (2015) Military social work: opportunities and challenges for social work education. J Soc Work Educ 51(1):6-25. https://www.ncbi.nlm.nih.gov/pmc/articles/PMC4469218/. Accessed 25 Mar 2020

Yeung P, Allen J, Godfrey HK, Alpass F, Stephens C (2018) Risk and protective factors for wellbeing in older Veterans in New Zealand. J Aging Mental Health 23(8):992–999. https://doi.org/10.1080/13607863.2018.1471584

Chapter 10
Military Social Work in South Africa

Heinrich H. Potgieter and Cynthia Apile Pitse

10.1 History of Military Social Work in South Africa

In South Africa, a united Military Social Work (MilSW) service came into being on 27 April 1994 with the creation of the South African National Defence Force (SANDF). Prior to this date, seven military forces existed within the South African context. The seven military forces included the Transkei, Bophuthatswana, Venda, and Ciskei (TBVC) defence forces; the armed wing of the Pan-Africanist Congress (PAC) known as the *Azanian People's Liberation Army* (APLA), the armed wing of the African National Congress (ANC) better-known as *uMkhonto we Sizwe*, and the South African Defence Force (SADF).

All of the military forces that preceded the SANDF provided healthcare services to their members, with the nature and scope of the services being determined by the resources available to the respective organisations. So-called "welfare services" were provided by many role players, including trained social workers in the various organisations inside South Africa, as well as in countries where members of the various organisations found themselves in exile or receiving military or other training (De Klerk and Kruger 1999).

As the best resource of the organisations, SADF, as far as is known, was the first of these organisations to formally introduce social work services. The first qualified social worker was appointed in the SADF in 1968 (Eatwell 1982). From the

H. H. Potgieter (✉)
Social Work Research and Development Department, Military Psychological Institute, South Africa National Defence Force, Pretoria, Republic of South Africa
e-mail: milsocworksouthafrica@gmail.com

C. A. Pitse
Directorate of Social Work, South African Military Health Service, South African National Defence Force, Pretoria, Republic of South Africa
e-mail: pitsecynthia@yahoo.com

© Springer Nature Switzerland AG 2023
M. A. Forgey, K. Green-Hurdle (eds.), *Military Social Work Around the Globe*, Military and Veterans Studies, https://doi.org/10.1007/978-3-031-14482-0_10

mid-1970s up to 1994, much of the focus of the social work service fell on providing social work services to conscripts along with services to regular force members. At present, there are 146 military social workers in the SANDF, of which nearly all are uniformed military personnel, with a limited number being appointed in a civilian capacity.

Note should be taken of the development and implementation of the Psychological Integration Programme (PIP) during the first years of the existence of the SANDF. The aim of this programme was to ease the transition of amalgamating seven military organisations into one. Social workers and other specialists from the organisations that amalgamated participated in the development and implementation of this programme. In spite of numerous challenges, the programme was an overall success that eased the transition process for members of all the forces who were previously in opposition (South African Military Health Service 2009).

10.2 Military Social Work Practice Settings

In South Africa, social work practice can occur in many settings, including hospitals, work organisations, schools, government departments, and non-government organisations. Of importance is the distinction between primary and secondary settings of practice. Primary settings refer to organisations where social work functions are the reason for the existence of the organisation, for example, a welfare organisation. Secondary settings refer to institutions where social work exists in a supportive capacity. The military serves as an example of a secondary setting of social work practice.

Military organisations are complex entities that are divided into multiple sub-entities such as services, divisions, and units. These entities have many features in common, such as hierarchy, command and control, and overall military culture (with different subcultures such as the navy culture and the air force culture). These entities must function in a coordinated manner in order to fulfil the mandate of the organisation. In the case of the SANDF, the mandate is contained in section 200(2) of the Constitution of the Country (Constitution of the Republic of South Africa 1996), which states: "The primary object of the defence force is to defend and protect the Republic, its territorial integrity and its people in accordance with the Constitution and the principles of international law regulating the use of force". The mandate and functioning of the SANDF are further expanded on in the Defence Act No. 42 of 2002 (Department of Defence 2003).

The size of military units can vary from a handful of staff to thousands of personnel. All units, and the people who work there, face multiple challenges. As unit size increases, the complexity of functioning in a coordinated manner also increases. At the same time, a range of human needs are present. The provision of services to military units tends to focus on services from the occupational social work perspective of MilSW. In South Africa, occupational social work is "a specialised field of social work practice which addresses the human and social needs of the work community within a developmental approach through a variety of interventions which aim to foster optimal adaptation between individuals and their environment" (Department of Social Development 2020a).

Military Social Work (MilSW) in the SANDF is hosted within the South African Military Health Service (SAMHS). The SANDF is comprised of four services; the Army, Air force, Navy, and the SAMHS, as well as several divisions, for example, the Intelligence division. Within the SAMHS, MilSW is headed by a director with the military rank of Brigadier General. The Director of Social Work has functional control of all military social workers in the Department of Defence. From the auspices of the Directorate of Social Work, MilSW services are provided to all the services and divisions.

Military health care facilities include military hospitals (tertiary level facilities), specialised institutes (having some primary care functions as well as some specialist functions), and what is colloquially known as "the sick bay". The sick bay describes a facility that provides primary health care services and is usually the first port of call for those seeking health care services in the SANDF, with characteristics of both the military organisation and health care organisation. Those that are in need of specialised health care services are referred to tertiary facilities. Military social workers provide services at tertiary and primary health care facilities and directly at units under the command of various services and divisions.

Within the sick bay, the military social worker must be prepared to provide services leaning towards the health care or medical spectrum of social work service delivery, as well as services that relate more to occupational social work. At the sick bay, the variety of other health care professionals encountered as healthcare team members is limited when compared to tertiary leveltertiary-level healthcare facilities.

In military hospitals, military social workers form part of a fully-fledged multi-professional team. Approximately 15% of military social workers are staffed in military hospitals. The MilSW service is primarily approached from the health care spectrum of military social work service delivery. All the military social workers not staffed in military hospitals can be expected to function in the sick bay setting, as well as in other military units. Concurrently, the military social workers in military hospitals must be able to fulfil functions related to the occupational social work spectrum of MilSW.

Health care social work, or social work in health care as it is phrased in South Africa, is well described by Carbonato (2019). Although not specifically defined, Regulation 3(1) (Department of Social Development 2020b) describes the scope of practice of social work in health care as follows: "Social work in health care as a field of speciality in social work, provides social work services within the national health system, including, but not limited to, health establishments, rehabilitation programmes, community-based programmes, and private practise".

10.3 The Military Social Work Practice Model: Social Work Roles and Interventions

The Military Social Work Practice Model (MSWPM) was introduced in the SANDF in 1998 (Radebe 2009) and has been revised several times. The model serves as a framework for understanding the approach to MilSW service delivery within the SANDF and serves to guide and assist military social workers in navigating through the *various roles and interventions* that can be employed.

The development of the MSWPM (Kruger and Van Breda 2001) was a reaction to the existing models of occupational social work. Due to limitations in existing models, such as conceptualising the development of occupational social work in terms of stages and phases (Van Breda 2012), this model was developed to suit the needs of MilSW in the SANDF.

The model signified a shift towards a typology of interventions that allowed for all methods of social work intervention to be viewed as valid, as opposed to viewing services as developing on a continuum from micro, through meso to macro practice. In the latter instance, one stage or phase of practice appears to be held as more valid or more appropriate than others. In this model, methods of practice can be employed in parallel, depending on the needs that are present. The model hinges on two key concepts, namely, binocular vision and positions of intervention.

Binocular vision is a metaphor aimed at helping military social workers with difficulties in operationalising ecosystemic thinking in practice. The metaphor establishes an integrated person-in-environment perspective (Van Breda 2012). Once binocular vision is achieved, the military social worker can focus on the military organisation, soldiers, and their families simultaneously, thereby seeing the system as one, rather than viewing components separately. This allows for an understanding of the transactions between people and their environments (Germain and Gitterman 1980), creating opportunities for these complex interactions to become a point of leverage for service delivery.

Rather than stages or phases of intervention, the term "position" of intervention was introduced (Kruger and Van Breda 2001). Assuming an initial stance of methodological neutrality, the military social worker assesses the nature of needs or problems being experienced by the client system from an ecosystem perspective. The client system can include individuals, groups, units, and the military organisation as a whole. Once the client's needs and problems are defined, the military social worker selects roles and appropriate interventions to utilise in the process of service delivery. This culminates in the military social worker assuming one or more appropriate positions of service delivery.

Figure 10.1 illustrates that the military social worker assumes methodological neutrality, analysing and defining presented needs or problems. The military social worker can move into any position of intervention based on an analysis of the presented need, problem, or situation.

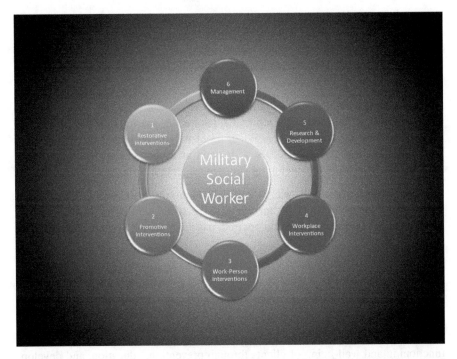

Fig. 10.1 Military social work practice positions (Directorate of Social Work 2021). (Reproduced with permission)

In what follows, each of the positions will be outlined according to four dimensions, namely, the definition of the client, the role of the social worker, the nature of problems targeted by the military social worker, and the forms of interventions used.

10.3.1   *Position 1: Restorative Interventions*

From this position of military social work, a problem-solving service is provided to military employees and their families. It is aimed at restoring their problem-solving and coping capacities. These interventions address people and their non-work-related problems.

Definition of Client
The client is defined as an individual, couple, family, group, or community who has a problem. The size of the client system is not relevant. People who have not yet developed a problem that needs to be resolved are not defined as clients in this position. The employees of the SANDF are viewed in their role as people and not primarily in their role as employees.

Role of the Military Social Worker
The military social worker takes on the role of therapist, enabler, advocate, facilitator, and problem solver. The exact nature of this role is dependent on the social worker's preferred theoretical framework and therapeutic models and the number of people who own the problem.

Nature of Problems
Clients present with problems of a personal nature, e.g. marital distress, adjustment difficulties, housing concerns, etc. When problems are presented that involve the workplace, the social worker deals with them at a personal level, for example, assisting the individual in developing stress management skills.

Forms of Intervention All case, group, and community work interventions, which focus on problem resolution, are appropriate. The social worker uses their preferred models and techniques, e.g. person-centred, psychodynamic, systems, behavioural, task centred, etc.

10.3.2   *Position 2: Promotive Interventions*

In this position, the military social worker aims to promote or enhance the social functioning and well-being of clients through prevention, education, and development. These interventions address the needs of people at a non-work-related level.

Definition of Client
Here, the client is still defined as an individual, couple, family, group, or community. These people have a psychosocial need which they desire to fulfill.

Role of the Military Social Worker
The military social worker takes on the role of educator, trainer, facilitator, enabler, guide, and coordinator.

Nature of Problems
The social worker addresses a broad range of human needs. They may also work with clients who have a problem, but who desire to live more fully despite the problem. The social worker may also work to prevent the development of problems that would require restorative interventions. Interpersonal needs in the workplace may be addressed but at a personal level.

Forms of Intervention
The social worker may make use of casework, group work, community work, psycho-education, workshops, seminars, pamphlets, exhibitions, community organising, etc.

10.3.3   Position 3: Work-Person Interventions

In this position, the military social worker focuses on what happens between people and systems in the workplace, which requires a shift in thinking from the personally oriented to the occupationally oriented. These interventions address people who have work-related problems or needs.

Definition of Client
Here, the client is defined as the systems or patterns of interaction between employees in the workplace. The employee is defined in occupational terms as a worker and a person with a rank and status in the organisation. The family and the broader community are also clients in as much as they relate to the workplace.

Role of the Military Social Worker
The military social worker takes on the role of negotiator, mediator, facilitator, arbiter, etc. The social worker aims to ease the interactions between employees and is a specialist in interpersonal relations in the workplace and in community building. The military social worker seeks to assist employees and families to fit better with the organisation and with other employees in the organisation.

Nature of Problems
The military social worker shifts their focus to problems within the workplace, such as conflicts between peers, conflict between employees', the organisation's values, morale or productivity-related issues, etc. The social worker also focuses on the interface between the military system and the family system, facilitating greater communication and cooperation between the two systems and promoting the family's capacity to deal with job demands. The social worker may also facilitate civil-military relations.

Forms of Intervention
The military social worker may make use of case, group, and community work techniques, problem-solving processes, experiential exercises, community development, team building, community building, negotiation, mediation, participation in committees, workgroups, etc.

10.3.4   Position 4: Workplace Interventions

In this position, the military social worker focuses on the workplace, that is, on the unit or organisation which comprises policies, structures, hierarchies, procedures of working, etc. These interventions address the workplace itself.

Definition of Client
The organisation, workplace, or unit itself is defined as the client. The military social worker focuses on the impersonal structure or processes of the workplace, within which employees' function. While there may be a complete turnover of employees in a particular workplace, its structure and processes may remain the same. The employee is seen as a part of the organisational structure and processes at this point in time.

Role of the Military Social Worker
The role of the military social worker in this position is that of social engineer, policy maker, systems analyst, researcher, organisational development consultant, etc. The military social worker endeavours to assist the workplace in developing processes and structures which promote optimal productivity, effectiveness, morale, and social well-being among employees. The military social worker is an integral part of the management of the workplace, being a specialist on the interface between an impersonal organisation and a personal workforce. In focusing on this interface, the social worker humanises and may serve as the social conscience of the organisation.

Nature of Problems
The military social worker focuses on problems in the structure of the workplace, such as unit standing orders, policies, hierarchies, organisational culture, procedures of working, utilisation of personnel, etc.

Forms of Intervention
The military social worker can investigate the effect of certain structures on the workforce and develops policy proposals to enhance the structure and functioning of the organisation. The military social worker participates in workgroups that are tasked with addressing structural and procedural issues in the workplace and may develop structures or forums for cooperation between the military and the civilian community.

10.3.5   Position 5: Research & Development

In this position, the military social worker views the military system with a specific interest in identifying and addressing knowledge and service delivery technology shortfalls. This position addresses everything related to developing knowledge as to any dimension of human and organisational needs and the development of technology towards more effective and efficient MilSW service delivery.

Definition of Client
The development of knowledge and service delivery technology is defined as the client. The improvement of service delivery by means of developing knowledge and interventions related to any other position in the model is the focus.

Role of the Military Social Worker
The military social worker is an investigator, scientist, researcher, and developer.

Nature of Problems
The military social worker focuses on identified knowledge, theory, and technological deficits that impact on MilSW service delivery. The problem takes the form of one or more questions to which a satisfactory answer is not available.

Forms of Intervention
Informal to formal research can be undertaken. The scale of the research can vary from small, focused units of analysis to unit-based and organisation wideorganisation-wide inquiry. Approaches ranging from qualitative to quantitative to mixed methods can be employed. Development activities can range from designing service delivery protocols, to developing measurement and assessment instruments, to developing information communication and technology-related systems.

10.3.6 Position 6: Management

In this position, the military social worker focuses on the MilSW service delivery system and the context within which the service is provided. This position addresses everything that impacts on the provision of organisationally relevant services.

Definition of Client
The social work service delivery system and the provision of organisationally relevant services is the client. The military social worker focuses on the MilSW service delivery system itself in order to ensure that a system capable of delivering services is created or sustained and continuously developed in response to environmental changes.

Role of the Military Social Worker
The military social worker is a manager and leader who manages and leads the social work service itself. Not all military social workers will focus on management exclusively, but all military social workers will contribute to management functions in some way. Military social workers in defined management posts will focus more on activities from this position than military social workers in direct service delivery posts.

Nature of Problems
The military social worker focuses on ensuring the provision of relevant MilSW services in a particular context, be it a unit, an area, province, or hospital. The central challenge (management problem) is to provide an integrated and relevant service in the context of resource constraints, multiple and often conflicting client demands, human resource and organisational considerations, and taking into consideration requirements from the profession of social work.

Forms of Intervention

All management functions must be performed; these include planning, organising, staffing, directing, and controlling. Examples of sub-functions include, but are not limited to, budgeting, personnel development and training, social work supervision, monitoring and evaluation, social work policy development, leadership, and performance appraisal.

In the SANDF, the MSWPM has forged the development of a MilSW service delivery system that is not defined or based on any specific social, family, or organisational problem or need. For example, there is no specific focus on post-traumatic stress-related issues. It is expected of military social workers and the MilSW system itself to adapt service delivery in reaction to and in anticipation of environmental dictates.

10.4   Practice Orientation and Approach

South Africa is unique in its adaptation of the developmental approach to social welfare and social work as a national government policy in 1997. The White Paper for Social Welfare (Ministry of Welfare and Population Development 1997) provides the national policy framework for the transformation of South African social welfare towards the developmental social work approach. Patel and Hochfeld (2013) describe the developmental approach as "pro-poor and informed by a rights orientation." The rights orientation refers to the human rights orientation enshrined in the Constitution (Constitution of the Republic of South Africa 1996). The emphasis in the White Paper for Social Welfare was placed on social interventions that were generalist in that they involved the use of multiple methods of intervention. It is also concerned with the promotion of active citizenship, participation in development, and individual and collective empowerment.

Clinical social work has not had the prominence in South Africa that it has in the United States. This is likely due to two factors. Firstly, specialisations within social work are relatively new in South Africa, with draft regulations for registration as a clinical social worker published in 2020 (Department of Social Development 2020c). Secondly, the White Paper on Social Welfare has resulted in a social work orientation that was initially generalist in nature in South Africa. Only two tertiary institutions have been identified as offering post-graduate training in clinical social work, namely, the University of Johannesburg and the University of Cape Town.

Against the above background, it is suggested that the three major influences on the formation of MilSW in South Africa have been generic social work, occupational social work, and health care (medical) social work. The influence of the three sources on the formation of MilSW in South Africa is illustrated in Fig. 10.2.

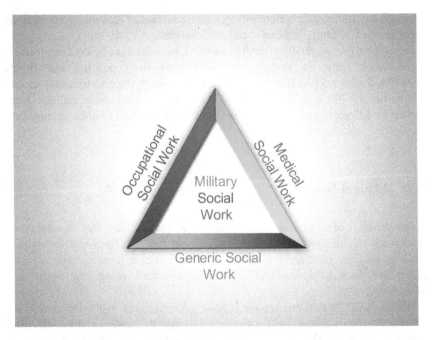

Fig. 10.2 Military Social Work (Directorate of Social Work 2021). (Reproduced with permission)

10.5 MilSW Role in Military to Civilian Transition and Integration

Services to military veterans are provided by the Department of Defence as well as the Department of Military Veterans.

The Department of Military Veterans was established in 2011 (Department of Defence and Military Veterans 2011) by means of the promulgation of the Military Veterans Act. The Military Veterans Act provides for a set of benefits for military veterans that include, among others, compensation for combat-related injuries or illness, counselling services, education and training opportunities, and facilitation of employment placement (Department of Defence and Military Veterans 2011).

Within the SANDF, the Directorate of Human Resources Separation manage the separation or exit of members from the SANDF. The Directorate provides opportunities for members separating from the SANDF to access work and education, as well as skills development opportunities within the civil society. MilSW is focused on pre-separation counselling as part of retirement preparation. This cooperation with the Directorate of Human Resource Separation is critical.

Serving SANDF members thus have access to MilSW services throughout their tenure in the SANDF, during transition to veteran-status, and as veterans. During the transition process to veteran status, separating members are assessed and, where indicated, referred to appropriate services such as financial planning services or the Department of Military Veterans social work service.

In practice, post-separation social work services to veterans by the Directorate of Social Work focus on restorative interventions from position one of the MSWPM. Social workers in the Department of Military Veterans focus on services specified in the Military Veterans Act. Close cooperation between military social workers and Department of Military Veterans social workers ensures seamless service delivery.

10.6 Ethical Issues

A central source of tension in occupational social work is "Just who (or what) is the social worker's primary client?" (Smith and Gould 1993). In the SANDF, this question is viewed alongside an often-repeated military mantra, namely, "You are first a soldier and then a professional" with "professional" being any health care professional.

Within the MSWPM, this tension is fully acknowledged. While the model does not offer the impossible, namely, a simple solution to the tension, it does offer guidance in managing it. The model proposes that the tension must be accepted as normal. The model suggests that the social worker obtain clarity in her or his mind on who (or what) the client is defined as in any given circumstance. The identity of the client can therefore vary, with the social worker having to ensure that ethical dilemmas be dealt with based on the given identity as point of departure.

Professional ethical guidance in South Africa is provided through various rules and guidelines provided by the South African Council for Social Service Professions (South African Council for Social Service Professions n.d.).

Within the SANDF, military social workers are advised to consult with colleagues and, where needed, with military law officers regarding any ethical dilemmas faced. Only one instance of a unit commander charging a military social worker in terms of the Defence Act related to social work service delivery (position four) is known. In this instance, the military prosecution service withdrew the charges after the social worker provided proof that her actions followed consultation with colleagues and consideration of the best interests of the SANDF.

The concept of confidentiality is well understood within military hospitals. In military units outside of the SAMHS, the main issue lies around the understanding of the concept by commanders. A two-pronged approach is followed in terms of addressing this matter via educating commanders regarding confidentiality issues and obtaining informed consent from the soldiers before approaching their commanders in case of work-related issues that require intervention by the commanders themselves.

10.7   Military Social Work Education and Training

There are, at present, 16 universities with schools of social work in South Africa. The minimum requirement for registration as a social worker with the South African Council for Social Service Professions (SACSSP) is the completion of a 4-year bachelor's degree that meets the following course requirements (Department of Social Development 2011):

- At least 4-year courses in the subject Social Work, 1 year of which may be completed on post-graduate level
- A second major subject consisting of at least 3-year courses in any subject in human or economic sciences
- A third subject consisting of at least 2-year course in any subject in the human or economic sciences, which does not include the subject referred to in the second sub-category above

The Directorate of Social Work in the SANDF will currently only consider applicants for appointment as social workers who are registered with the SACSSP and who have completed either psychology or sociology as their 3rd-year level human sciences subject, and psychology or sociology as their 2nd-year level human sciences subject. This requirement is based on the fact that it was found that in practice in the SANDF social workers who did not possess these subjects found it difficult to perform to the requirements of the Directorate.

Some schools of social work offer coursework modules in occupational social work and health care social work respectively as part of their 4-year general social work education programmes. Where offered, these modules provide an introduction to the respective fields that focus on core theoretical concepts. No school of social work in South Africa offers specialised training in MilSW in their bachelor's courses or in postgraduate courses.

Fieldwork is required as part of all four-year social work courses mentioned above. The SACSSP requires registration as a student social worker from the second year of social work studies in order for the student to be placed for fieldwork. The Directorate of Social Work do accept a limited number of students for fieldwork placements, with the actual number of placements varying from year to year.

The University of the Witwatersrand in Johannesburg offers a master's degree in occupational social work and the University of Pretoria offers a master's degree in health care social work. These two institutions are the only ones in South Africa to offer the respective courses. Few military social workers hold these respective qualifications.

Military social workers are encouraged to pursue post-graduate studies in social work. To encourage this, military social workers can apply for studies at state expense for their post-graduate studies. Preference is given to funding military social workers wishing to pursue studies in occupational social work or health care social work. The number of military social workers pursuing post-graduate studies has shown a steady increase over the past 10 years.

To prepare social workers who are recruited into the SANDF for the practice of military social work, an in-house course on MilSW has been developed. The Basic Military Social Work Course consists of both theoretical and practical components followed by a formal assessment. A minimum of 6 months of exposure to the military setting is required as a precondition for acceptance on the course. Prior knowledge and experience play a prominent role in adaptation to the military setting. This course includes modules such as introduction to MilSW, report writing, resilience theory, and various policies within the SANDF.

Following the completion of the in-house MilSW course, all newly appointed social workers must undergo a minimum of 2 years of individually supervised practice irrespective of their prior experience in social work. The social work supervision process is semi-structured and aims at supporting social workers using professional development plans and supervision according to the unique needs of each individual.

The Directorate of Social Work designed and presents a Social Work Supervision Course. This course equips military social workers appointed in social work personnel development posts to fulfil their functions.

Two initiatives underway are the development of an Advanced Management Course and a post-graduate course in MilSW. The Advanced Management Course is aimed at empowering military social workers appointed in managerial positions to optimally perform their Position 6 functions.

It is envisaged that the post-graduate course in MilSW will be established with a university partner. The cooperation is likely to result in military social workers being able to obtain either a certificate-level post-graduate qualification or a master's degree qualification.

10.8   Vignette

A General officer reported that soldiers in a specialised unit in the SANDF under his command were deemed to be "over stressed". It was feared that if the situation was to continue, the military capability represented by the small, specialised grouping could be significantly degraded in the foreseeable future. This could not be allowed to happen. A team of social workers was dispatched to assess the situation at the unit. It was found that the majority of the soldiers in the small unit have been deploying on various missions over a number of years. The nature of the military tasks executed by the unit was such that deployments were highly unpredictable and mostly of short duration, with soldiers rotating in and out of deployment on a monthly basis. While part of the unit staff was deployed, the remaining unit members had to fulfil the normal routine unit functions of those deployed. On several occasions, the small unit had to accommodate multiple deployments simultaneously. The officer commanding the unit was one of the most frequently deployed members, leaving more junior ranking members to take over his role during deployments. This brought about conflict regarding leadership styles, as well as some role uncertainty and role conflict within the unit. Family members of some of the soldiers were asking the soldiers to start looking for alternative work opportunities, as they could no longer cope with the constant disruption of their family lives. Family members specifically mentioned that the actual deployment of their loved ones was not the primary disruptive force impacting on them, they experienced the homecoming process of the soldiers (family reintegration) as the most challenging. In response to the situation, the following were some of the interventions that took place:

- It was recommended to the General Officer that the unit commanders' deployments be reconsidered, as it had a detrimental impact on command, control, and leadership dynamics within the unit (Position 3 intervention). After consideration, this recommendation was accepted and immediately implemented.
- A support group for the wives of soldiers in the unit was created and facilitated by a social worker (Position 1 intervention). The group enabled the wives to foster mutual support, develop their own problem-solving strategies, and help one another cope with the demands of parenting the children.
- Post-deployment family reintegration seminars were presented within the unit (Position 2 intervention). This helped to normalise the family reintegration process and teach family members and soldiers skills and approaches that made reintegration easier to accomplish.
- It was recommended to the General Officer that the policy regarding the medium-term operational utilisation of the unit be revisited in order to provide the unit with an operational pause (Position 4 intervention). A decision on this recommendation could not be made at the level of the General Officer, the General Officer communicated the recommendation up the chain of command for consideration. Following the conclusion of a series of operational commitments, the unit was afforded an operational pause.

10.9   Conclusion

MilSW in South Africa has been shaped by both the history and contemporary needs of the SANDF. The adoption of a developmental social welfare and developmental social work approach by the government of the country was a further significant contributor thereto. In response to this, a unique practice model was developed to guide both thinking and practice of military social workers.

The primary challenge faced by MilSW in South Africa is to maintain its relevance through constant development and innovation. Two focal areas, in the near future, will be the training of military social workers and the development of Information and Communication Technology in support of service delivery.

References

Carbonato C (2019) Social work in health care in South Africa. In: Winnett R, Furman R, Epps D, Lamphear G (eds) Health care social work: a global perspective. Oxford University Press, New York

De Klerk M, Kruger A (1999) Military social work: a South African perspective. Unpublished document, Pretoria

Department of Defence (2003) Defence Act No 42, 2002. Government Gazette No. 24576. Republic of South Africa, Government Printer, Pretoria

Department of Defence and Military Veterans (2011) The Military Veterans Act. Government Gazette No. 34819. Republic of South Africa, Government Printer, Pretoria

Department of Social Development (2011) Regulations regarding the registration of social workers. Government Gazette No. 34020. Republic of South Africa, Government Printer, Pretoria

Department of Social Development (2020a) Proposed regulations pertaining to the registration of a speciality in occupational social work. Republic of South Africa, Government Printer. Pretoria

Department of Social Development (2020b) Proposed regulations relating to the requirements and conditions for registration of a speciality in social work in health care. Republic of South Africa, Government Printer, Pretoria

Department of Social Development (2020c) Regulations relating to the requirements and conditions for registration of a speciality in clinical social work. Government Gazette No. 43343. Republic of South Africa, Government Printer, Pretoria

Directorate Social Work (2021) Military social work practice model. Directorate Social Work, South African Military Health Service, Pretoria

Eatwell M (1982) Social work within the South African Defence Force: an evaluation of its role and position. Unpublished BA Social Work Degree Thesis, University of Port Elisabeth

Germain C, Gitterman A (1980) The life model of social work practice. Columbia University Press, New York

Kruger A, Van Breda A (2001) Military social work in the South African National Defence Force. Mil Med 166(11):947–951

Ministry of Welfare and Population Development (1997) White paper for social welfare. Available via https://www.gov.za/sites/default/files/gcis_document/201409/whitepaperonsocialwelfare0.pdf. Accessed 20 Feb 2021

Patel L, Hochfeld T (2013) Developmental social work in South Africa: translating policy into practice. Int Soc Work 56(5):690–704

Radebe C (2009) The mentoring of officers commanding in the South African Military Health Service (SAMHS): a military social work perspective. Unpublished Master's Degree Dissertation, University of Stellenbosch

Smith M, Gould G (1993) A profession at the crossroads: occupational social work – present and future. In: Kurzman P, Akabas S (eds) Work and well-being: the occupational social work advantage. NASW Press, Washington, DC, p 12

South African Council for Social Service Professions (n.d.) Policy guidelines for course of conduct, code of ethics and the rules for social workers. Available via https://socialdev.mandela.ac.za/socialdev/media/Store/documents/SACSSP-Code-of-Ethics.pdf. Accessed 10 May 2021

South African Military Health Service (2009) The fourth dimension: the untold story of military health in South Africa. Shereno Publishers, Pretoria

The Constitution of the Republic of South Africa (1996) Available via https://www.justice.gov.za/legislation/constitution/saconstitution-web-eng.pdf. Accessed 21 Feb 2021

Van Breda A (2012) Military social work thinking in South Africa. Adv Soc Work 13(1):17–33

Chapter 11
Military Social Work in the United Kingdom

Clare Low, Craig Richard Pearce, Richard Alan Leighton, Katherine Hillman, Ian Barber, Emma Mabbutt, Jennifer Brown, and Pauline Diane Bridgette Ross

11.1 Introduction

The United Kingdom (UK) is made up of four devolved nations: England, Scotland, Wales and Northern Ireland. The population of the UK as of 30 June 2020 was estimated to be 67 million (Office of National Statistics 2021) with a military size of 193,460 as of July 2020 (Ministry of Defence 2021).

C. Low (✉)
Army Welfare Service, UK Ministry of Defence, Tidworth, UK
e-mail: clare.low104@mod.gov.uk

C. R. Pearce
UK Ministry of Defence, Ilchester, UK
e-mail: Craig.pearce111@mod.gov.uk

R. A. Leighton
Defence Medical Services, Department of Community Mental Health, UK Ministry of Defence, RAF Digby, Lincoln, UK
e-mail: richard.leighton103@mod.gov.uk

K. Hillman
Army Welfare Service, UK Ministry of Defence, Chilwell, Nottingham, UK
e-mail: Katherine.Hillman101@mod.gov.uk

I. Barber
University of Central Lancashire, Lancashire Armed Forces Covenant Hub, Preston, UK
e-mail: IBarber@uclan.ac.uk

E. Mabbutt
Army Welfare Service, UK Ministry of Defence, Donnington, Telford, UK
e-mail: emma.mabbutt995@mod.gov.uk

J. Brown · P. D. B. Ross
Defence Medical Rehabilitation Centre, UK Ministry of Defence, Loughborough, UK
e-mail: Jennifer.brown482@mod.gov.uk; pauline.ross109@mod.gov.uk

© Springer Nature Switzerland AG 2023   151
M. A. Forgey, K. Green-Hurdle (eds.), *Military Social Work Around the Globe*,
Military and Veterans Studies, https://doi.org/10.1007/978-3-031-14482-0_11

11.2   History of Military Social Work

The 'professional' recognition of social workers in the UK was enshrined in law in 2002 (Cromarty 2018). Prior to this, many people practiced social work informally, supporting those in need, without a formal social work qualification. The 'professional' social worker in the UK evolved out of the philanthropic works of charitable organisations in the 1870s and the community-based works in the 1880s. These social workers offered philanthropic or community works, with those in need identified based on personal experiences, ability and perceived social position, underpinned by welfare courses. Academic social work learning in the UK began in 1908, with the University of Birmingham's one-year social studies courses which delivered knowledge and skills for social and philanthropic work.

The paucity of historical records of social workers in the British military reflects society's sense of practicing social work without formal recognition until the latter half of the twentieth century. Earlier, the wives of senior personnel were required to help out the less able/fortunate families of junior personnel, reflecting the UK's reliance on philanthropic welfare work. As social work within the civilian sector became more specialised, disbanding generic social work teams into adults and children specialisms in the 1980s, the social work profession was driven to have academically trained and qualified professionals. This led to more recognised formal welfare and eventually social work provision within the military.

The first iteration of professional social work within British military formations could be posited to be mental health social workers, with its roots in military hospitals. Military hospitals date back to the Crimean War, with some providing psychiatric services. Military hospitals were closed following defence reviews from the 1990s onwards, leading to the development of the Department of Community Mental Health (DCMH) with inpatient provision provided by a consortium of NHS (National Health Services) Trusts around the UK.

Over the years, a wide array of other services staffed by social workers were developed to support the British military each with their own set of influences. These included the following.

11.2.1   Defence Medical Services

Defence Medical Services (DMS) social workers are based at tri-service defence specialist rehabilitation centres, one of which is the Defence Medical Rehabilitation Centre (DMRC) Stanford Hall in the Midlands, operating since 2018. Prior to 2018, DMRC services were delivered at the Headley Court, Surrey, providing military rehabilitation services since the Second World War. The other rehabilitation centre is the Hasler Naval Service Recovery Centre (NSRC), which opened in 2014 for predominantly Naval Service personnel and some tri-service personnel. DMS social workers provide specialist clinical and welfare casework for patients during their admission to DMRC or NSRC.

11.2.2   Royal Navy Family and Personal Support Service

The Royal Navy took initiative from Lord Seebohm's report of Naval welfare provision (Ministry of Defence 1974), which included recommendations that led to welfare services reform in 1977, with an emphasis on the social work role. The Royal Navy Family and Personal Support Service has military and civilian social workers who provide case management and specialist welfare support with a social work management team responsible for the management and support of Royal Navy Welfare Workers.

11.2.3   Directorate of Children and Young People

The establishment of the Ministry of Defence (MOD) Directorate of Children and Young People in 2010 to oversee defence strategy, MOD schools abroad and the support to service families around school education matters led to the development of the MOD Global Safeguarding Team (social work team) for safeguarding concerns.

11.2.4   Polaris Children's Services

The Polaris Children's Services provide contracted overseas social work provision including the British Forces Social Work Services (BFSWS) (Polaris Children's Service, 2019), since 2014. Prior to this, SSAFA (Soldiers', Sailors', Airmen and Families Association) provided contracted social work provision for overseas command, dating from the late 1960s.

11.2.5   Soldier', Sailors and Airmen's Families Association (SSAFA)

The Soldiers', Sailors' and Airmen's Families Association (SSAFA) is a military charity that has provided contracted social work services for the Royal Air Force since 1990. SSAFA have historically managed and supported Army Welfare

Workers, until the Army Welfare Service (AWS) developed their own social work management roles.

11.2.6   The Army Welfare Service

The Spencer Report review of Army welfare provision (Ministry of Defence 1975) recommended social work provision, which was not implemented until 20 years later, following subsequent reviews and reform and the development of the Army Welfare Service. The Army Welfare Service has civilian social work managers responsible for managing and supporting Army Welfare Workers (non-social work) and social workers providing specialist welfare casework.

The Iraq and Afghanistan conflicts shaped the social work casework provision for the Army through the Army Welfare Service, with the development of Casualty keyworkers. They were a small civilian social work team based across military establishments around the UK, providing welfare expertise for those severely injured returning from conflicts. The conflicts led to the development of specialist recovery cells and units across the military to support wounded, injured or sick (WIS) serving personnel with complex needs. This enabled recovery units to manage WIS serving personnel until return to duty or discharge from service. The Army developed the Personnel Recovery Units (PRU) based across military establishments, where Casualty keyworkers became PRU social workers managed by a PRU social work manager.

11.3   Military Social Worker Qualification Requirements

Military social workers in the UK are required to have a social work qualification and post-qualifying experience to be eligible to apply for military social work roles. Social work qualifications are either a degree, three years for bachelor's or two years for master's, or postgraduate diploma, completed through universities or employer-sponsored programmes. University programmes typically include full-time academic study and two placements in health or social care settings. The first placement of 70–100 days depends on course requirements, and final placement of 100 days is ideally a statutory service. Employer-sponsored programmes fund the social work qualification, with the employee resuming work duties during the academic holidays and taking on a social work role within the organisation upon qualifying. Employer-sponsored programmes can be either a typical university degree programme or a specifically tailored university programme which includes an intensive and shortened curriculum and placements. Social workers must maintain their registration whilst training and post-qualifying according to the requirements of the regulatory bodies for each of the devolved nations.[1] There is variability in social work roles and training across the countries in accordance with legislation, policy and remit.

The Royal Navy is the only service with uniformed social workers working alongside civilian social workers in its welfare service. Uniformed military social work personnel are now required to be officer ranked and transfer into the welfare service to be eligible to complete their social work degree through the MOD. Naval officers complete the standard university programme of full-time academic study and two placements, returning to duty during the academic holiday periods.

11.4   Practice Settings

Military social workers are found in a range of settings, with the service or support provided determining the type of intervention. Predominantly, interventions delivered are with individuals or families in either the individual's or family's home, community-based setting or on military establishments.

In most instances, military social workers carry out visits to families and individuals, away from their workplace or the establishment. Social workers based at the Defence Medical Rehabilitation Centre (DMRC) and Department of Community Mental Health (DCMH) typically see service users where they are based, due to service users being an in-patient or benefitting from a clinical setting for support. Social workers at DMRC typically engage with service users for the length of their admission, with transfer of care if needed to a relevant agency, such as DCMH, or to a social worker in one of single service welfare teams. Due to the nature of the setting and service in which DMRC workers operate, engagement with family members has challenges, such as geographical distance from families and confidentiality in the medical arena.

The locations and number of military social workers in the UK vary across the three services based on numbers of serving personnel and geographical spread. For example, the Royal Navy has concentrated support near major ports and Naval air stations, whereas the Army has a greater spread across a larger range of establishments. There is usually a large presence of serving personnel and their families near major establishments, which enables good links with local agencies such as the local authority with statutory responsibilities for safeguarding, children and adult social care, police and non-statutory agencies such as charities and support groups. Uniformed social workers can be found in less conventional places than statutory agencies, for example, on establishments abroad such as Cyprus and Gibraltar. In

[1] Regulatory bodies for Social Work in the UK:
   Scotland – Scottish Social Services Council
   England – Social Work England
   Wales – Social Care Wales
   Northern Ireland – Northern Ireland Social Care Council

addition, only uniformed social workers go to sea, and during these deployments, they provide specialist welfare (practical and emotional) support for Naval personnel.

11.5 Military Social Work Roles and Interventions

Military social workers undertake a range of work at every level of practice, from direct client practice work to policy-level roles. Military social workers engage with core tasks that are common across the social work profession regardless of role/team. These include holistic assessments of needs, risk assessments and care/support plans to identify needs and support required.

11.5.1 Interventions with Military Personnel

Social workers do direct work with serving personnel and/or families. The exceptions to this are DCMH not being commissioned to work with families and DMRC requiring serving personnel's consent to involve families in their care. Referrals for social work service include a range of complex welfare issues such as health, housing, welfare benefits, and family situations such as safeguarding or additional needs.

Military social work is underpinned by a holistic approach to encapsulate the individuals' experiences/situations and those of their families/support networks. Simplistically, assessments might be framed within an 'exchange model' or 'constructive' approach, whereby service users are seen as experts in their own experiences, and the worker helps the service user to identify internal resources and potential (Smale et al. 1993).

Social workers draw upon a range of skills and knowledge due to the diversity of needs a service user may present, using skills from previous roles such as working in mental health. Social workers have understanding and knowledge of legislation, particularly safeguarding, and processes to engage health and social care services. The focus of work carried out with service users is a person-centred approach and empowerment to ensure that they are informed about their rights, entitlements and supports available.

Social workers use theories and models relevant to their practice and in accordance with the service user's needs. For example, DCMH practitioners deliver group work, and DMRC practitioners use psychodynamic theory (as endorsed by the MOD) in their practice. Those in non-clinical roles draw upon a variety of perspectives, such as a task-centred perspective supporting service users to develop strategies and timelines to achieve agreed goals (Reid and Epstein 1972). They will also use a range of techniques such as motivational interviewing to support service users with reframing their narrative of their situation (Miller and Rollnick 2002).

11.5.2   Interventions with Children

The British Forces Social Work Services (BFSWS) provide an overseas statutory children and families' safeguarding role following English legislation, where the Children's Act (1989) and Working Together to Safeguard Children (Department of Education 2020) underpin all welfare and safeguarding in relation to children, and the Care Act (2014) outlines safeguarding responsibilities for adults. Adult safeguarding concerns for those deployed are managed by the chain of command of the serving person and include mental health and sexual assault, with personnel being repatriated to the UK for appropriate support and care. The MOD Global Safeguarding Team provide support, advice and strategic guidance across defence for safeguarding children and young people of service families. They are responsible for children and adult safeguarding in overseas locations not covered by contracted social work providers.

11.5.3   Interventions Within the Organisation

Social workers deliver training to units and the wider military, such as safeguarding updates or delivering the Safe and Together model for domestic abuse (Safe and Together Model, 2019). There are some specific roles social workers have, such as the Royal Navy Family and Personal Support Service social workers delivering deployment briefs. The welfare services across the separate services have their own community teams who deliver community support to serving personnel and their families.

11.6   Practice Orientation and Approach

Military social workers for Army, Royal Navy and RAF have an occupational approach in their role. The work undertaken is to support the operational effectiveness of service personnel or with transition out of service.

Social workers based in mental health or rehabilitation teams have a clinical approach in their roles, as the teams are focused on medical/therapeutic interventions alongside welfare issues. The following vignette provides an example of how the military social worker may partner with local authority social work services to deliver comprehensive support to a member and family.

> **Vignette**
>
> Sgt S has a traumatic brain injury from a non-operational workplace fall, with secondary health-related issues (mental health, physical health and mobility issues), and is due to be medically discharged from the Army. He was referred to a PRU social worker as there have been recent incidents of concern. On one occasion, he was found wandering outside the home in his pajamas by a neighbour, in a confused state, and was assessed by his medical officer. On another occasion, he made an online purchase and does not recall why or what the product is, which was unusual for Sgt S. These incidents raised concerns for Sgt S and his wife/family about his mental health and well-being.
>
> Sgt S was referred to a brain injury support service, and his wife was referred to a carer's support service. A case conference was convened to discuss support needs from all MOD health and welfare professionals involved in his care. Sgt S was referred to the local authority for a social worker to conduct a needs assessment, including his wife's needs as a carer.

11.6.1 Influences on the Military Social Work Approach

There are a number of social, economic and political influences upon the approach of military social work. For example, following inappropriate behaviour found in the Wigston Review (Ministry of Defence 2019), recommendations were made to address such issues. As a consequence, the military has become more forward leaning towards those with protected characteristics such as members of the LGBTQI+ population as well as those with mental health concerns.

Several projects have also been set up to promote cultural change within the military, including an active LGBTQI+ network with regular conferences. Social workers sit on working groups to shape welfare practice, policy and procedures for issues such as domestic abuse and mental health to reflect current and best practices.

Despite some of the highlighted progress being made, there are still strides to be made within the military. A recent parliamentary report by the Defence Committee (2021) has identified that there remains a 'lad' culture within the army, with a high number of women subject to sexual harassment. The outcome of this report will have sweeping implications for the military and management of sexual assault cases.

11.7 MilSW Role in Military to Civilian Transition

Following discharge from the armed forces, UK ex-military personnel are known as veterans, and the UK government has defined this as 'anyone who has served for at least 1 day in Her Majesty's Armed Forces (regular or reserve) or Merchant Mariners who have seen duty on legally defined military operations' (Ministry of Defence 2017). The term veteran has been found to be problematic for female veterans, who associate the term with someone elderly and male (Jones 2018). There is currently no evidence to suggest impact to accessing support, but overlapping perceptions around gender and veteran identity leads to a complicated understanding of self-image and 'veteran' status (Jones, 2018, p. 131).

UK government data on military veterans shows their employment, education and health outcomes to be broadly comparable with non-serving counterparts (Office of Veterans Affairs 2020), with specific employment research showing higher rates of employment for veterans compared to the general population (Deloitte 2018). In recognition of the difficulties faced by some service personnel during their transition from the military, particularly those being medically discharged, military social workers across medical and Army/RAF/Navy welfare teams assist those most vulnerable to navigate military to civilian care pathways.

Post-discharge, the health- and social care needs of veterans are met by an amalgamation of statutory services, private organisations and the charitable sector. The charitable sector has dominated support provision with the rolling back of the contemporary welfare state, following the economic downturn of 2008 and subsequent austerity agenda (Herman and Yarwood 2015). The armed forces charity sector currently contains over 2000 charities providing a range of services, supplementing the infrastructure and support provided by the government.

Work has recently been undertaken to simplify engagement with service providers. The Confederation of British Service and Ex-Service Charities Organisations (COBSEO) provide coordination to its members and provide a single point of access to the sector for the government. Similarly, the Veterans' Gateway, created in 2017, is the single point of access to military charities for service users and professionals alike. In 2020, Op Courage was developed to simplify access to NHS mental health services for military veterans.

The UK government has further recognised the need to support the most vulnerable service leaders and subsequently created the Defence Transition Service in 2019 (Ministry of Defence and Veterans UK 2021). This service is delivered by non-social work welfare managers who connect service users to a range of support organisations, according to their needs and provision available where they reside.

These support activities and the mutual obligations between the UK government and its Armed Forces are laid out in the Armed Forces Covenant (Ministry of Defence 2021). The Covenant defines the need for service personnel to be treated fairly both during and after military service. Whilst it has been enshrined in UK law since its creation in 2011, a new Armed Forces Bill for 2022 is likely to place a legal obligation on public bodies to give due regard to the principles of the Covenant, to provide veterans and their families access to health care, housing and education services.

11.8 Ethical Issues

UK social work regulators set out within their professional standards, ethics and values expected both in and outside the workplace. Whilst ethical dilemmas are not unique to military social workers or the social work profession, working within a military organisation has its own ethical tensions.

A critical component of managing ethical tensions for MOD social work practitioners is having a clear understanding of who the client is. Often social workers need to manage the needs of service users, chain of command and the MOD as an employer of both worker and service user. Information sharing and privacy issues can cause significant challenges, as practitioners need to abide by the General Data Protection Regulations (Data Protection Act 2018) given the military is integrated in its personnel's personal and professional lives.

Social justice and human rights are core to social work practice, and as such, military law and policy also present ethical tensions for practitioners. It took until the year 2000, 33 years after the Sexual Offences Act (1967) legalized homosexual acts in England and Wales, for the military to allow service personnel who are openly LGBTQI+ to serve. Other tensions include the British Military continuing to enlist minors despite criticism from the United Nations Committee on the Rights of the Child; minimum recruitment age is 16 with parental consent, although soldiers cannot serve on operations below 18 years old.

In response to ethical challenges practitioners face, the British Association of Social Workers (BASW) developed a professional code of ethics and values to underpin practice (BASW 2014). Social workers are required to maintain their professional registration including evidencing knowledge of legislation and theory and considerations of personal and professional values. Military social workers utilise consent paperwork and codes of confidentiality to agree on information sharing with service users.

For serving uniformed military social workers, many ethical tensions emanate from the dual professional identity they hold. These include the rank of practitioners relative to service users, having military duties alongside social work responsibilities, and potentially integrated work/home lives alongside service users—a tension also often present for social workers who practice in smaller rural communities. There are mechanisms to help with conflicting identities such as training, liaising with civilian counterparts, reflective supervision and ethical principles to inform ethical decision-making.

For civilian military social workers, the focus on the operational effectiveness of service personnel to meet the military's requirement of protecting the nation's interests often conflicts with empowerment and person-centred social work ideals. Practitioners are also required to navigate an environment of orders, rank and military law, whilst striving to have their professional voice heard. The focus on operational effectiveness has led to a military provision for health and welfare support. It is noted that disparities exist between rank and military branches, and referrals for welfare support can vary according to knowledge and viewpoint of staff or which service the individual works for. Access to support can be congruent with increasing rank, although senior ranks may not want to be seen as needing support.

For workers to avoid the moral distress these ethical tensions may cause, the support from trusted social work colleagues is key. Shared reflection is considered to be an intrinsic tool to developing critical thinking and identifying and managing potential tensions (Shdaimah and Strier 2020). Workers have access to employee's wellbeing services, such as the Employee Assistance Programme for civil servants, or the appropriate welfare service for military personnel for counselling support as well as accessing clinical support. Additionally, an understanding of the core values and policies of the organisation enables workers to have a better understanding of how/when to advocate for their service users.

11.9 Major Challenges and Future Directions

Challenges within UK military social work often reflect those in wider social work practice. It is the authors' collective opinion that social work within the UK is not a widely respected or understood profession, including within parliament. In 2013, a government minister remarked that social work had been 'invaded by left-wing dogma' (McNicoll 2016). The negative perception of social work in the public is fuelled by the media and is evident within the military, leading to uncertainty about the role and value of social work. The UK media have at times vilified the profession, reducing it to a headline about removing children from their families, and social workers being blamed when there is a serious adverse incident (Doughty 2021).

As a result, service users are often anxious to engage with social workers, which impacts the building of rapport and partnership. The Social Work England, the profession's regulating body, has not undertaken campaigns to address the public perception of the profession. However, the British Association of Social Workers (BASW) regularly rallies the UK government to support social workers, notably during the Covid-19 pandemic. During times of war, there has been a greater sense of value placed on military social work roles due to the support provided to those injured on operational duty and for families of deceased personnel.

Within the military, the lack of a clear understanding of social work roles can lead to service users not receiving specialist support and units struggling to manage complex issues. To address these challenges, social work teams run briefings to units to broaden awareness of military social work roles and support available. Welfare and safeguarding policy now direct where social work referrals are to be made, and schemes such as 'OPSMART' (British Army 2020), a training programme for stress management and resilience training, are being implemented to enhance the mental health of military personnel.

The MOD and associated military charitable organisations offer a vast array of support to military personnel and their families, which can lead to inconsistencies in the support for service users. With military welfare support agencies having their own policies, procedures, agendas, thresholds and approaches to delivering welfare, it can be a challenge for social workers to even be made aware of those who would benefit most from their expertise.

As there is no centralised military social work team, this has resulted in a lack of streamlined services across the MOD, with clinical teams using a different IT system to those working in welfare and each military branch having its own recording systems. This causes problems with consistency in care and service users having to repeat sometimes difficult personal narratives. Mitigating these challenges in accordance with policy, practitioners utilise their professionalism to appropriately share information and promote partnership working with other agencies. Practitioners in clinical teams have the additional challenge of recording and storing social care information, so it is held securely and shared with health professionals on a need-to-know basis.

The UK remains in a period of austerity with continual budget cuts across government spending, with a current defence review in progress. Reviews and likely fiscal cuts raise concern about privatisation of military welfare provision and uncertainty around the focus of welfare work and role of workers. There has been significant impact from austerity cuts coupled with Covid-19 for charitable sector funding, leading to cuts in welfare support services and inconsistent support available for service users.

The Ministry of Defence made £1 billion of funding cuts during 2021, as part of cost-cutting measures following a National Audit Office report (2020). Recruitment of civil servants was paused, and reductions were made to training budgets, further impacting an already complex and time-consuming process of sourcing specialist training through specific funding requests. The MOD is currently conducting a Defence Welfare Review with recommendations unknown at present. It is likely to impact the welfare budgets and potentially training budgets for social workers, despite continuous professional development being a requirement of professional registration.

11.10   Covid-Related Challenges

For social workers working within a military environment, adaptability to ever-changing political priorities and global issues is par for the course. The most recent significant challenge has been the Covid-19 pandemic, which is likely to shape the future of the practice.

Where safe and appropriate, social work has been conducted remotely utilising digital communications to continue service provision. Remote working has had its issues; availability and guidance with digital platforms were mixed, initially because of security and confidentiality concerns, and then the additional challenge of workers trying to build rapport and trust with service users remotely.

Social workers have met these challenges by using transferrable skills to adjust to remote working, such as adapting information to be understood by service users and having regular supervision and team meetings. Service users at risk of significant harm or with considerable difficulties including communication difficulties continue to be seen in person, relying on clear safety measures and protective equipment for staff and service users to complete risk assessments.

During the pandemic, BASW rallied the government and succeeded in having social workers recognised as *keyworkers*. This enabled social workers to travel for work during nationwide lockdowns.

There have now been consultations with staff on working through the pandemic, with a hybrid model, a mix of face-to-face and remote working, being encouraged. Whilst social work requires face-to-face service user contact for many interventions, social workers reported that working from home benefitted their work/life balance, and service users reported that remote appointments saved money, energy and time. Some service users and families have preferred the flexibility that remote working creates, with meetings accommodating school hours, so childcare is not needed. Others have missed the rapport and relationship from face-to-face appointments. Remote working has enabled online training delivery to larger cohorts whilst reducing travel and subsistence costs.

The social work profession continues to adapt through the challenges it faces, as well as challenge policy and restrictions that do not benefit service users. BASW continues to campaign for not only better working conditions and funding for social workers but also for knowledgeable and skilled practitioners to perform effective, safe interventions.

11.11 Conclusion

The introduction of the military social work role across health and welfare services to support those most vulnerable with complex needs demonstrates how welfare provision in the UK Ministry of Defence has adapted and evolved to the needs of service users and the organisation, particularly during times of war and crisis.

The challenges for military social work are amplified by the inherent structure and hierarchy of the military, alongside the dichotomy of *service user need* versus *operational effectiveness*. Through their inherent understanding of multilevel systemic interactions, social workers are well placed to adapt to working in an ever-changing environment amidst defence spending cuts, wider community health and social provision being under pressure, and the recent Covid-19 pandemic further impacting on ways of working. The vision for UK military social work identity is a clear understanding of the role and scope of military social work across all levels of the MOD and greater awareness with military families and community services, who are often not aware of the military social work role. A MOD social work network for MOD social workers could provide a platform for the disparate social work teams to network through joint social work training and seminars.

References

British Army (2020) People: mental resilience. https://www.army.mod.uk/people/join-well/mental-resilience/. Accessed 05 Oct 2021

British Association of Social Workers [BASW] (2014) The code of ethics for social work: statement of principles. British Association of Social Workers, Birmingham

Cromarty (2018) Social work regulation (England). House of Commons Briefing Paper https://researchbriefings.files.parliament.uk/documents/CBP-7802/CBP-7802.pdf. Accessed 14 Oct 2021

Data Protection Act (2018) The Stationary Office, Norwich

Defence Committee (2021) Protecting those who protect us: women in the armed forces from recruitment to civilian life. https://publications.parliament.uk/pa/cm5802/cmselect/cmdfence/154/15402.htm. Accessed 14 Oct 2021

Deloitte (2018) Key findings. In: Veterans work: moving on. https://www.veteranswork.org.uk/wp-content/uploads/2020/01/Veterans-Work-Moving-On-Report.pdf. Accessed 15 Sep 2021

Department of Education (2020) Working together to safeguard children statutory guidance: a guide to inter-agency working to safeguard and promote the welfare of children. Department of Education, London

Doughty S (2021) Toddler was left at risk from 'cannibal' father by bungling social workers during three-year catalogue of mistakes in the case, court hears. https://www.dailymail.co.uk/news/article-9284539/Toddler-left-risk-cannibal-father-bungling-social-workers.html. Accessed 14 Oct 2021

Herman A, Yarwood R (2015) From warfare to welfare: veterans, military charities and the blurred spatiality of post-service welfare in the United Kingdom. Environ Plan A 47(12):2628–2644. https://doi.org/10.1177/0308518X15614844. Accessed 05 Oct 2021

Jones G (2018) Exploring the psychological health and wellbeing experiences of female veterans transitioning from military to civilian environments. Thesis, The University of Manchester. https://www.research.manchester.ac.uk/portal/en/theses/exploring-the-psychological-health-and-wellbeing-experiences-of-female-veterans-transitioning-from-military-to-civilian-environments(32c236b6-618b-494a-bd4c-b545d97a1a5c).html. Accessed 05 Oct 2021

McNicoll A (2016) Government must end 'unsubstantiated criticism' of social workers and engage on reforms – BASW. https://www.communitycare.co.uk/2016/05/18/government-must-end-unsubstantiated-criticism-social-workers-engage-reforms-basw/. Accessed 14 Oct 2021

Miller WR, Rollnick S (2002) Motivational interviewing: Preparing people for change. New York: Guilford Press

Ministry of Defence (1974) Report of the Naval Welfare Committee. Ministry of Defence, London

Ministry of Defence (1975) The Army Welfare Inquiry. Ministry of Defence, London

Ministry of Defence (2017) Veterans key facts. https://www.armedforcescovenant.gov.uk/wp-content/uploads/2016/02/Veterans-Key-Facts.pdf. Accessed 27 Sept 2021

Ministry of Defence (2019) Report on inappropriate behaviour. https://assets.publishing.service.gov.uk/government/uploads/system/uploads/attachment_data/file/817838/20190607_Defence_Report_Inappropriate_Behaviours_Final_ZKL.pdf. Accessed 14 Oct 2021

Ministry of Defence (2020) Quarterly Service Personnel Statistics 1st July 2020. https://www.gov.uk/government/statistics/quarterly-service-personnel-statistics-2020/quarterly-service-personnel-statistics-1-july-2020. Accessed 15 Oct 2021

Ministry of Defence (2021) The Armed Forces Covenant. https://www.gov.uk/government/collections/armed-forces-covenant-supporting-information. Accessed 05 Oct 2021

Ministry of Defence and Veterans UK (2021) Help for service leavers from Defence Transition Services. https://www.gov.uk/guidance/help-and-support-for-service-leavers-and-their-families. Accessed 05 Oct 2021

National Audit Office (2020) Departmental overview 2019-20: Ministry of Defence. DP Ref: 008063-001. National Audit Office, London

Office of National Statistics (2021) Population estimates. https://wwwonsgovuk/peoplepopulationandcommunity/populationandmigration/populationestimates. Accessed 15 Oct 2021

Office of Veterans Affairs (2020) Employment. In: Veterans Factsheet 2020. https://assets.publishing.service.gov.uk/government/uploads/system/uploads/attachment_data/file/874821/6.6409_CO_Armed-Forces_Veterans-Factsheet_v9_web.pdf. Accessed 20 Sept 2021

Polaris Children Services (2019). https://www.forcessocialwork.com/. Accessed 01 Oct 2021

Reid WJ, Epstein L (1972) Task-centered casework. Columbia University Press, New York

Safe and Together Model (2019). https://safeandtogetherinstitute.com/about-us/about-the-model. Accessed 01 Oct 2021

Shdaimah C, Strier R (2020) Ethical conflicts in social work practice: challenges and opportunities. Ethics Soc Welf 14(1):1–5. https://doi.org/10.1080/17496535.2020.1718848

Smale G, Tuson G, Biehal N, Marsh P (1993) Empowerment, assessment, care management and the skilled worker. HMSO, London

The Care Act (2014) The Stationary Office, London

The Children's Act (1989) The Stationary Office, London

The Sexual Offences Act (1967). https://www.legislation.gov.uk/ukpga/1967/60. Accessed 01 Oct 2021

Chapter 12
Military Social Work in the US Armed Forces with a Focus on Service Members and Military Organizations

Jeffrey S. Yarvis, Nickalous Korbut, and James A. Martin

12.1 History of Military Social Work in the US Armed Forces

Social work in a military setting was established in 1918 during World War I at the Plattsburgh Army Base in New York by civilian Red Cross volunteers in a US Army General Hospital (Washington 1957). Social workers proved their value by assisting medical officers in diagnosing, treating, and discharge planning of service members admitted for neuropsychiatric disorders from the war. By request of the Office of the Surgeon General (OTSG), the American Red Cross took full responsibility for social work services in military hospitals for over 20 years, providing psychiatric civilian social workers in hospitals across the US and overseas (Rubin and Harvie 2013). The birthplace of uniformed military social work as an occupational specialty occurred in 1942 at Fort Monmouth, New Jersey, when an Army psychiatrist assembled six professionally trained enlisted social work soldiers to perform social work duties. They demonstrated that soldiers could perform the same neuropsychiatric mission as the Red Cross volunteers, which led to the establishment of the Military Occupational Specialty (MOS 263) of psychiatric social worker.

J. S. Yarvis (✉)
School of Social Work, Tulane University, New Orleans, LA, USA

21st Combat Support Hospital. Colonel (Ret), Fort Hood, TX, USA
e-mail: jyarvis@fordham.edu

N. Korbut
Futures and Concepts Center, Army Futures Command, Fort Sam Houston, San Antonio, TX, USA
e-mail: nickalous.a.korbut.mil@army.mil

J. A. Martin
School of Social Work, Bryn Mawr College, Bryn Mawr, PA, USA
e-mail: jmartin@brynmawr.edu

© Springer Nature Switzerland AG 2023
M. A. Forgey, K. Green-Hurdle (eds.), *Military Social Work Around the Globe*, Military and Veterans Studies, https://doi.org/10.1007/978-3-031-14482-0_12

The value of the military social work profession and their contributions to the hospital mission became increasingly evident during and after World War II, and in 1946, the Army created a Commissioned Officer Psychiatric Social Worker Military Occupational Specialty (MOS). The establishment of uniformed social workers enabled a function that the civilian Red Cross volunteers did not perform, collocating with field units in a concept called the mental hygiene consultation service [MHCS] (Washington 1957). The MHCS provided field commanders' behavioral health (BH) services in their area of operations, reducing the time a soldier spent away from training and increasing the soldier's contribution to the mission. MHCS' embedded behavioral health services decreased hospital admissions, and this concept has stood the test of time across all military services and operational requirements (Washington 1957).

From 1942 to the present day, the MHCS concept of embedding uniformed social workers with service members has brought mental health services to Army divisions, naval ships, marine regiments, and airfields whether in garrison or in a combat zone. Today, most uniformed military social workers are utilized in some type of role consistent with the original MHCS concept of embedding with military units. Military social workers have a storied history of providing care in various settings by meeting their clients where they are, whether in a substance use clinic, in a medical center, or in a combat zone embedded with service members. The foundation of military social work was built upon the flexibility to meet the service member's needs, ranging from garrison settings to combat. The array of today's military social work roles is an evidence of the profession's value to our armed services.

12.2 Uniformed Social Work Roles and Responsibilities

Military social work in the US reflects military service's unique mandates and needs. Coupled with a rich and diverse array of human services associated with the requirements of military duties and the demands of a military lifestyle, it is emblematic of the health and human service requirements typical in US society. Military social workers (those in uniform, civilian government employees, and contract social workers) are present in all the active component branches of the US armed forces, including the National Guard and other Reserve Components. Social workers are the largest behavioral health provider population among the Department of Defense, comprised of over 40% of behavioral health specialties including psychologists, psychiatrists, and psychiatric nurse practitioners (Yarvis 2020) (Table 12.1).

Table 12.1 Military social worker

	Military	Civilian	Contract	Total
Army	273	1298	107	1678
Navy	51	89	66	206
Air force	231	143	117	491

Personnel by Service (Government Accountability Office 2015)

Military social workers serve in the continental US, Alaska, Hawaii, and the US territories. They are stationed overseas and deployed globally to support the full spectrum of operational missions both on land and at sea and in some future date in space.

Military social workers serve in traditional installation (military community) settings, hospitals, clinics, and various human service agencies. In addition, they support an array of military family and community issues (addressed in the companion Chap. 13 in this book). There are uniformed and civilian military social workers (including those with advanced rank and/or specialized training) in a variety of senior policies, program management, and research positions within each service branch, as well as in policy and program positions at the headquarters of the Department of Defense (DoD) and within subordinate defense agencies and activities.

While it is essential to recognize the presence and contributions of civilian military social workers in many of these support settings and roles, it is the uniformed military social worker who provides the best examples of the breadth and scope of military social work in both arenas. The greatest number of uniformed military social workers is engaged in direct practice behavioral health roles as members of military units, or they serve in direct service roles at installation agencies providing counseling and case management services to military members and consultation to their unit leaders. A smaller number of uniformed social workers, typically more senior in rank or with specialized education and training, perform a range of occupationally focused duties at various headquarters and other support agencies and organizations within the Active, National Guard, and Reserve Components. Examples of these services organizations and agencies supporting service members include various occupationally focused issues such as oversight of health-care delivery, policy development and program management, education and training, law enforcement and correctional duties, research and evaluation functions, and senior duties not directly associated with social work practice, like command and senior executive positions.

Typical duty assignments for military social workers include clinical social work counseling and case management services in various direct practice settings within military installation medical, behavioral health, and human service settings. Military social workers perform essential clinical social work and consultation roles as members of or in support of operational units sustaining the fighting force, promoting unit readiness, and ensuring the well-being of service members. Military social workers assigned to behavioral health teams with line units or ships provide service members and their combat leaders with direct support in addressing operational stress issues. They perform special behavioral health-related staff functions for commanders at all echelons of the armed forces.

Uniformed military social workers provide and supervise direct patient care in health and behavioral health settings, planning and executing numerous health and behavioral health programs that address physical and mental health wellness.

Interventions are focused on primary, secondary, and tertiary responses to various behavioral health issues including substance abuse, suicide, domestic and family violence, and sexual assault. Military social workers perform suicide assessments and other crisis intervention services. Many are also prepared to assist with disaster relief and provide support in domestic and overseas humanitarian missions.

Military social workers occupy teaching and training roles in various military health-care and leadership settings and engage in research on a wide array of issues and conditions of military importance. Uniformed military social workers supervise and participate in graduate medical education and the training of other medical personnel required to maintain a robust medical system during both peace and conflict. Uniformed military social workers engage in administration, consultation, research, and policy development across all levels of the service components and the Department of Defense.

Rank among uniformed social workers varies by military service branch, yet each rank can be related to a pay grade, as seen in the chart below. Uniformed social workers enter service as military officers in the pay grade of 0–1 and spend their first 4 years completing a master's degree and internship for licensure. Upon promotion to the 0–3 pay grade, they begin serving as independent practitioners and obtain assignments that provide direct patient care to service members and their families. Typically, around the tenth year of service, uniformed social workers are promoted to 0–4 and assume supervisory roles within behavioral health clinics. Upon promotion to 0–5 at around 17 years of service, they are utilized as department supervisors managing multiple clinics or working staff positions at the service-specific headquarters. To date in the Department of Defense, the highest pay grade uniformed social workers have achieved is 0–6, where they maintain senior executive assignments and staff positions in military hospitals. Occasionally, military social workers will assume command positions unrelated to their social work specialty (Table 12.2).

12.2.1 Embedded Social Work Officer Position

Uniformed social workers embedded within operational units exist across all the military services supporting the warfighter which is the most common role performed by uniformed military social workers. These positions exist because stress

Table 12.2 Military ranks by service

Pay grade	Army/Air Force/Marines	Navy
0–1	Second lieutenant (2LT)	Ensign (ENS)
0–2	First lieutenant (1LT)	Lieutenant junior grade (LTJG)
0–3	Captain (CPT)	Lieutenant (LT)
0–4	Major (MAJ)	Lieutenant commander (LCDR)
0–5	Lieutenant colonel (LTC)	Commander (CDR)
0–6	Colonel (COL)	Captain (CAPT)

and related mental health casualties are a significant military operational concern during periods of high operational tempo, especially in direct combat operations.

The members of an embedded Army division mental health team consist of a division psychiatrist, a brigade social worker, a brigade psychologist, and an assortment of enlisted behavioral health technicians. On deployment, these mental health officers and technicians represent a team supporting the division's brigade medical companies within the brigade support area. Social workers supervise behavioral health technicians and oversee combat stress casualty care in concert with higher-level uniformed social workers. These services typically occur within an assigned area of combat operations and as a component of the overall combat support structure and operational stress control campaign plan for the theater of operations. In combat and during all operational deployments, the division mental health team, including the uniformed military social worker, is ensconced in the deliverance of direct mental health services. The Navy began the embedded model in the 1990s, when uniformed social workers were first deployed onboard naval vessels, eating, sleeping, and living with the same sailors receiving their behavioral health services. During Operation Desert Shield/Storm, Navy social workers were first assigned to the hospital ships Comfort and Mercy (US Navy Medical Corps 1999). Their value was recognized and now has expanded their presence across the entire fleet of Navy ships assigned to combat zones. The principles of combat social work apply to most acute and chronic stress situations and need little modification in dealing with the various roles associated with other military operations. As with combat, refugee care requires rapid social work interventions and utilizes simple supportive treatments such as a focus on shelter, nutrition, and rest. A positive expectancy of normal functioning and eventual social stability must be maintained. Humanitarian support to the displaced person is a critical part of combat, peace enforcement, and peace-keeping missions. Rules of engagement often allow for social work support to displaced people and civilians impacted by military operations or located in areas that medical units are assigned to support. In addition, locus of control-related stressors can impact the service member as they bear witness to humanitarian crises but are empowered or resourced to intervene in some cases (Yarvis 2020).

When not deployed, the embedded social worker is typically performing various functions supporting soldiers and their leaders. In a garrison environment, the military has begun embedding more social workers to improve service member's well-being while the unit is preparing for its next missions. The primary mandate of embedded social workers in garrison is to improve the behavioral health of the force and their families by reducing the stigma associated with behavioral health support and by facilitating utilization and access to care (Dunigan et al. 2014). Behavioral health-care delivery is partially grounded on the assumption that service members are most comfortable seeking care from familiar providers. Social workers regularly consult with unit commanders to proactively identify and address behavioral health needs before these needs developed into severe issues. Social workers conduct classes on numerous behavioral health topics, attend military training, and share meals in units with the soldiers to enhance their identification with these soldiers and to promote behavioral health-care knowledge and utilization. The presence of an embedded social worker increases opportunities for primary prevention such as psychoeducation, traumatic event management, workshops for service members and their families, and leadership consultation. On occasion, these social workers serve dual roles as staff officers at battalion or brigade level. Their proximity to unit leaders increases the efficacy of their consultation relationship and further promotes their support for service members.

During the wars in Afghanistan and Iraq, Army leaders increased the number of behavioral health-care providers embedded within units deploying to these conflicts based in part on findings from Mental Health Advisory Teams (MHATs) deployed to assess mental health needs (Bliese et al. 2011). These teams with social work members repeatedly documented access challenges in the provision of behavioral health care among deployed service members. Such findings led to the recommendation in 2009 (MHAT IV 2009) to adopt a "dual-provider" model, which increased the number of organic social workers in a Brigade Combat Team (BCT) comprised of approximately 3500 soldiers. However, it is essential to note that considerably more behavioral health assets support the deployed warfighters who are not organic to the BCT. At its core, the inclusion of behavioral health providers within units was designed to increase access to care and promote early prevention and intervention (MHAT IV 2009). The efficacy of the social worker/leader relationship is observed in reducing stigma and barriers to care. Statistics show that service members in units with embedded social workers accessed care more often, reported victimization of sexual misconduct at higher rates, felt more comfortable discussing suicidal ideation, and had lower morbidity rates (Wright et al. 2009).

12.2.2 Hospital and Clinic Assignments

The Korean War became a catalyst for the Air Force's need to address the increase in psychiatric casualties by creating a social work military occupational specialty. Like their Army counterparts, Air Force social workers filled a crucial role during the war with assignments to multidisciplinary psychiatric teams within both inpatient and outpatient medical settings that provided treatment and assessment of Air Force service members. Over the last 60 years, military social workers across all services have transitioned from their origin as multidisciplinary team members to leading behavioral health services at hospitals, clinics, and airfields worldwide (Field Manual 8-51 1994; Jenkins 1999). Similarly, the history of Navy social work began with hospital assignments in the 1950s, with civilian social workers conducting psychosocial assessments, treatment plans, and group therapy sessions. The 1970s brought to the forefront the value of social work when only 29 civilian social workers across the Navy were charged with the overwhelming task of caring for the psychiatric demand from the Vietnam War. One social worker to every 170 physicians seemed insufficient, which forced the chief of naval operations to create the uniformed social work officer position (United States Navy Medical Service Corps 1999). July of 1979 marked the first uniformed social worker position in the Navy, with 11 more commissioned social workers joining the service that year to work in naval hospitals across the world (Kennedy 1999). Today, military social workers may find themselves assigned to military treatment facilities, medical centers, family advocacy clinics, substance abuse clinics, and family or community service centers worldwide. Through military medical social work, practitioners can further distinguish themselves in military family counseling, military-to-civilian transition support, crisis intervention, substance abuse counseling, outpatient mental health, and domestic violence counseling.

Military medical social workers serve as liaisons that interface with the civilian medical community and specialize in public and population health, geriatric, palliative, and inpatient medical or mental health care. They communicate and coordinate care with hospitals or other military and civilian specialized medical settings like trauma and substance abuse centers, nursing homes, rehabilitative care centers or related home care services (i.e., hospice), warrior transition units, partial hospitalization programs, intensive outpatient programs, and veteran treatment courts.

12.2.3   Military Substance Abuse Counselor

Service members returning from the Vietnam War demonstrated a new challenge with dramatic increases in substance use addictions to opiates, heroin, and marijuana (Rubin and Barnes 2013). Public Law 92-129 empowered the DoD to create a program to identify and treat service members with drug and alcohol addictions. Social workers working in substance use clinics became increasingly crucial to the nation's readiness when a policy change in the 1980s required a mandatory evaluation for any service member involved in a substance incident (Newsome 1999). Today, there are several areas where military uniformed military social workers assist those struggling with substance use and co-occurring behavioral health concerns.

Social workers help service members navigate the complex interplay of military life to include their combat experiences, adaptation patterns, co-occurring behavioral health conditions, and family problems. They assist service members to learn and functionally adopt coping mechanisms other than substance use to increase military readiness. Like embedded social workers, those in substance use disorder clinics work with service members as treatment providers while advocating for them to their command on their ability to function as warriors. The spectrum of care where military social workers can be found includes outpatient prevention and treatment services, intensive outpatient services utilizing individual and group modalities, partial hospitalization programs for co-occurring disorders, residential clinics, and inpatient hospitalization.

12.2.4   Policy and Advocacy Positions

Experienced senior military social workers serve in strategic-level assignments that impact the future of the military social work profession. Health-care leaders understand the value of having social workers and provide leadership at the policy level, and uniformed social workers hold staff officer billets at the Department of Defense Headquarters in the Pentagon and within the Defense Health Agency in Falls Church, Virginia. They provide resources and information and write policy to enhance social workers' capacity to improve the health of military beneficiaries, families, and communities. Uniformed and civilian social workers also hold essential billets in training and doctrine organizations, where they collaborate with other medical professionals to develop doctrine which delineates which units require social workers and how they operate within an organization. Their primary focus is the future of health-care delivery to shape the profession for future wars.

Uniformed social workers have opportunities to complete fellowships at the White House and Congress. The Army Congressional Fellowship Program is a 44-month program that includes pursuing a master's degree in Legislative Affairs at George Washington University, service on a Member of Congress staff, and utilization on the Army Staff in a congressional-related duty position. These social workers often then move on to top advisory positions to the Surgeon General of their respective military services and key staff positions at the Pentagon, addressing crucial issues such as suicide, military sexual trauma, violent crime, substance abuse, warrior reintegration, and family housing, to name a few. Social workers serve in research positions within military research programs across each of the services and have opportunities to conduct research addressing a variety of stress and well-being issues, including the efficacy of behavioral programs serving military communities. These coveted positions help shape the future of military social work and are desired positions within a military social worker's career.

12.2.5   Corrections of Social Work Officer

During the Korean War era, Army social workers saw their roles and responsibilities expanding to the military prison system. These are unique as each service has military-only correctional facilities on land and afloat (Keller et al. 2014). By creating these facilities, the US Surgeon General's Office's goal was rehabilitation, and the office published the Army Regulation 210–181, which implemented social workers leading the psychiatric evaluations of prisoners within their first couple days of confinement (Harris 1999). Social workers assigned to military prisons help delineate prisoners with a psychiatric disorder and provide treatment plans to challenge their behaviors. Social work in the prison system allows an added dimension of treatment and hope to the prisoners, where historically the goal was punishment and confinement. The 1957 Army Regulation advancing social workers in the prison system has ensured behavioral health as a mainstay in the over 50 Army correctional facilities and has provided a model for Navy and Marine brigantines and pretrial confinement facilities across all military services today (Habeck 1974).

12.2.6   Instructor Positions

Academic positions at every level of military service are considered prestigious assignments. The military places its best, brightest, and most experienced leaders in educational centers of excellence, and military social workers are no different. Just as experienced pilots become instructor pilots and former regimental commanders become doctrine writers and deans of programs, social workers do the same. Often military social workers can find themselves in training positions within the Medical Center of Excellence, which produces military occupational specialties. These positions train future warriors in behavioral health specialties, diverse medical specialties, and leadership positions across the services. They inform future leaders across the military of the importance of behavioral health and attack stigma before it becomes a problem in the popular imagination of these future leaders.

12.2.7   Educational Opportunities

During World War II, the necessity for an abundance of high-quality social workers led to the Army Surgeon General's Office establishing a military social work scholarship program. Service members interested in becoming social workers could apply for civilian schooling in exchange for a training tour at a large general hospital followed by a service contract (Washington 1957). This scholarship program continues to the present day at the Fort Sam Houston, Texas. Future Army and Navy social workers receive a Master of Social Work (MSW) degree and a 2-year internship at a military medical center in exchange for a service contract to help them meet the requirements in becoming a licensed clinical social worker (LCSW) (Freeman and Bicknell 2008). The Air Force operates a similar program by providing scholarships for students to receive their MSW at any accredited college or university, followed by their internship hours being completed at an Air Force hospital. Regardless of which schooling opportunity a military social worker takes, there are basic requirements across the services. All uniformed military social workers are commissioned officers who possess a master's degree from a program in social work accredited by the US Council on Social Work Education (CSWE). They must also obtain a current, unrestricted license for clinical social work practice from any one of the 50 US states by passing the Association of Social Work Boards examination, which is the regulatory organization ensuring safe and competent social work practice.

176 | J. S. Yarvis et al.

Table 12.3 Roles performed by military social workers in the US armed forces

Outpatient SW	Special operations
Inpatient SW	Support to civil-military operations
IOP and partial hospitalization	Disaster social work
Medical social work	Family advocacy and domestic violence
Embedded BH	Sexual trauma
Corps, division, and brigade social work	Child and adolescent SW
Primary prevention	Health-care policy and advocacy
Corps combat and operational stress control	Command consultation
Forensic SW	Social work and medical training
Aviation SW	Substance abuse
Research	Military education and training centers

Social workers also compete for PhDs and clinical fellowships. The PhD education opportunities are awarded through the Long-Term Health Education and Training Program and offer military social workers the opportunity to receive a fully funded PhD or DSW education at their school of choice or degree completion. The Army also offers a unique child and family social work fellowship at the Walter Reed National Military Medical Center in Bethesda, Maryland. This intense program provides advanced child and family clinical training comparable to the board certification training a psychiatrist gets to become board certified in child psychiatry. After completing a PhD or military fellowship, social workers often complete a utilization tour to apply and cultivate their recently attained skills.

In addition, certain assignments and specific roles often require advanced military or civilian training, professional education, or credentialing. During their career in the armed forces, uniformed military social workers attend "officer training" programs and professional military schools commonly required across all military allied health disciplines for promotion. Many military social work officers seek additional specialized social work education and advanced training/credentialing, reflecting advanced status within the social work profession (Table 12.3).

12.3 Interventions Utilized by Military Social Workers

Military social workers utilize evidence-based interventions throughout the military practice settings. Often social workers are placed at military installations with large concentrations of returning combat veterans, military medical complexes, or state-of-the-art trauma research facilities that study the efficacy of frontline interventions. In the mental health arena, these interventions include prolonged exposure therapy, cognitive processing therapy, and prevention programs such as Battlemind training (Montgomery 2009). Not only does this pair researchers with the number of military personnel necessary for large-scale studies, it means that social work investigators' expertise and innovative treatment programs are helping where they are needed most.

Social work researchers working with the military are conducting a broad array of clinical, exploratory, and preclinical trials and utilize specialized research to assess novel delivery methods of evidence-based posttraumatic stress disorder (PTSD) treatments (Reisman 2016). These delivery methods are adapted to meet the unique needs of active-duty military members, as well as veteran populations. Simultaneously, military social workers are striving to learn more about the biological factors involved in PTSD development and recovery, the influence of co-occurring physical and psychological ailments, and the interaction of cognitive-behavioral therapies and pharmacologic treatments. Social work investigators want to help returning warfighters live healthy, productive lives and prevent the development of chronic PTSD, traumatic brain injury, sleep disorders, family violence, community health, and related problems in a new generation of veterans (Lawrence-Wolff et al. 2021, Straud et al. 2021, Rauch et al. 2020, Taylor et al. 2020, Yarvis and Schiess 2008, Yarvis et al. 2005).

One example of an evidence-based program for service members and their families is Battlemind (Castro et al. 2006). This intervention was originally developed as a mental health post-deployment briefing and quickly evolved into a training system supporting soldiers and families across the seven phases of the deployment cycle (Huseman 2008). The Battlemind program is centered around the soldier's inner strength to face fear and adversity with courage. Key components include self-confidence: taking calculated risks and handling challenges and mental toughness, overcoming obstacles or setbacks, and maintaining positive thoughts during times of adversity. The intervention now includes separate pre-deployment training modules for soldiers, unit leaders, health-care providers, and spouses. Social workers deliver psychological debriefings in theater (country of deployment) and upon redeployment help normalize and manage expectations of changing behaviors due to their changed environment. There is also a post-deployment module for spouses and several post-deployment modules for soldiers. The significance of Battlemind in readiness or holistic social work systems theoretical context is that Battlemind skills help you survive in combat, but may cause you problems, if not adapted when you get home.

The Battlemind is an innovative concept that includes resiliency training for soldiers, leaders, and military families. It is incorporated in the training provided at formal leadership schools, offered as a part of deployment cycle training, and integrated into resiliency training for support populations throughout the military. Battlemind training augments existing soldier, leader, and unit strengths to create a more resilient military community.

12.4 Military Social Work Challenges

12.4.1 Ethical Tensions

Social workers regularly face ethical tensions as they have allegiance to their patients and the military organization. They are often required to choose between their patients' client-centered interests and military administrative regulations. Embedded social workers have the arduous task and pressure from commanders who seek to maximize combat readiness objectives, which could deter non-deployable treatment recommendations. Professional ethics bind military social workers to provide recommendations that prevent further harm to their patients, yet in doing so, they could impact the combat mission. Ethical conflict can occur during deployment when service members require evacuation for psychiatric reasons, yet the commander can override social work treatment recommendations to achieve the combat mission (Johnson et al. 2010). Social workers can struggle when the combat mission impacts the commitment to deliver the best clinical care. Successful military social workers are competent in adhering to their social work ethical code and the military regulations that govern the organization. They must have a thoughtful, ethical decision-making process to utilize when conflict impacts their ethics by balancing their client's best interests, coupled with military regulations to avoid causing harm to their patient.

Balancing organizational and patient needs can also lend to a conflict of interest when an embedded social work officer must engage in different relationships and roles within the organization. They often maintain dual role relationships, which can result in misunderstanding and discomfort. Military social workers socialize and work among their patient population in austere environments, which can cause blurred boundaries when administrative behavioral health decisions are required. An embedded social worker could unexpectedly enter into a clinical relationship with a co-worker who was previously considered a friend when a behavioral health evaluation or clinical support is required in an austere environment. Military social workers help mitigate these conflicts by assuming that every member of their organization could be a future patient, maintaining a neutral posture within the organization and limiting self-disclosure. If a service member of the organization does become a patient, ensuring immediate informed consent and providing need-to-know information help protect the relationship from the start (Johnson et al. 2010). Military social workers expect multiple role dilemmas as a dimension of their work and must navigate their careers by adhering to their professional ethical boundaries (Johnson et al. 2006).

12.4.2 Management of Deploying Social Work Providers

The Army has never had enough medical providers to simultaneously fill operational units, otherwise known as the Modified Table of Organization and Equipment (MTOE), and the medical treatment facilities (MTF), who support garrison soldiers, veterans, and their families. In 1986, the Professional Filler System (PROFIS) was developed, which assigned social workers at an MTF with the caveat that they must remain ready to deploy for operational needs (Sorbero et al. 2013). Key leadership positions within TOE units were filled organically, with a majority of TOE assignments reserved for the PROFIS system. This system highlighted various issues during the continuous deployment cycles of the Afghanistan and Iraq wars as predictability among the PROFIS officers became frustrating. PROFIS social workers constantly on ready status for an operational mission caused anxiety among military families and decreased family stability. Tensions existed with TOE units, as they would receive social workers from the PROFIS system whom they felt were not adequately trained in basic soldier skills because of their responsibilities serving patients in the MTFs. The MTFs struggled as they constantly had to shift resources when their PROFIS providers were pulled from their clinics to deploy (Sorbero et al. 2013). In 2019, OTSG developed a new MTOE assigned system, which effectively assigned each PROFIS provider to a permanent unit across the Army. Assignment to a unit increased deployment predictability which decreased strain on MTFs and families. The MTOE unit could now plan future training for their MTOE assigned providers based on the MTOE mission to ensure that their social workers were adequately prepared in their warrior tasks and drills. MTOE assignment is a relatively new concept that is still being developed but has made considerable strides since the 1980s, when the Army could not meet the provider needs of deploying operational units while ensuring garrison MTFs were supported.

12.4.3 Congressional Oversight into Social Work Delivery

Social work services often face mandates from the government on the delivery of care. Pressure from government officials was noticeable for the Family Advocacy Programs (FAP) founded by military social workers during the 1960s when child protection laws became an increasing concern within American culture (Military One Source 2020). As awareness increased, military social workers across all services began developing localized programs to identify and treat child abuse. However, Public Law 93-247 (Administration for Children, Youth, and Families 1985) forced military social workers to create standardized programs outlining specific guidelines for child maltreatment (Nelson 1999). The Air Force was the first to establish a formal Child Advocacy Program in 1975, and a year later, the Navy and Army all had service-specific programs to address child maltreatment among their military families. The Navy additionally included spouse abuse in its program, which highlighted a critical issue. In 1981, the Department of Defense (DoD) published Directive 6400.1 (2019), requiring social workers from each service to establish the Family Advocacy Programs (FAP) to address prevention, identification, reporting, treatment, and follow-up of child and spouse abuse (Military One Source 2020). This congressionally mandated program continues management at the DoD level today by requiring specific credentials each social worker must meet to oversee their service program and reporting requirements to ensure oversight. Social workers are bound to utilize protocols that adhere to the evolution of this congressionally standardized program. Congressional oversight into the delivery of social work can be challenging, as rules and regulations must be adhered to and impact clinical decisions, such as only doctoral-level trained social workers could conduct mental status exams despite licensure level (DoD 6400.1). This part of the DODI was later overturned; however, it is a good example of where policy and practice can clash in a military delivery system.

12.4.4 Social Worker Shortages Affect Access to Care

Behavioral health stigma has decreased since the turn of the century leading to an increased demand for military social workers. In 2020, the Senior Enlisted Advisor (SEA) to the Joint Chiefs Chairman spoke out about the need for service members to seek help and the struggle he endured for 15 years as he pushed off treatment (Association of the United States Army 2020). Senior leaders like the SEA are making considerable strides in normalizing behavioral health care delivered by social workers, increasing the demand. Unfortunately, the current demand already exceeds the capability within the military health system, which results in service members receiving delayed care. The inability to hire enough providers increases strain and provider burnout with military social workers who must attempt to meet the warfighter's needs. Technological advances in telemedicine (telehealth) have become an increasingly popular method to decrease this capability gap. Telehealth allows a social worker in any region of the world to provide virtual clinical care through smartphones, tablets, or laptops to a service member (Little et al. 2021). The telehealth method reduces access issues when a remote provider from another organization might have a decreased caseload and can virtually assist a needed population. Military social workers can now assist each other across the world by referring cases to the telehealth network when their demand exceeds the ability to meet their organization's behavioral health needs. These services are coordinated regionally by the regional medical commands that the providers are assigned to.

12.5   Conclusion

Social workers play a unique and vital role in providing care and support to military personnel and their families. Today, more than 2100 clinical social workers support the Department of Defense by conducting health assessments, providing evidence-based interventions, delivering case management services, advocating for the warfighter and their families, conducting research, writing policies, and administering programs. According to Military Health System Management Analysis and Reporting Tool (2018) data, approximately 1,301,273 behavioral health encounters were conducted by social workers in 2018 – more than any other behavioral health professionals (Military Health System 2018). Because of their impact on such a large population of the military community, health-care leaders understand the value social workers provide.

It is evident by the complex roles and responsibilities that have evolved since the military social work profession was founded in 1918 that social workers have a long and proud history of service in most branches of the US Military. Ever-evolving, today's military social worker represents the epitome of an agile and multifaceted leader-practitioner-scholar-educator-warrior, able to face challenges across a volatile, uncertain, complex, and ambiguous operational environment. When the smoke has cleared on the battlefield and the fog of war has lifted, when the physical wounds have healed, and when the psychological wounds remain, it is the military social worker of the US that persists, serving as a lightship in the darkness for our psychological casualties of war and trauma.

References

Administration for Children, Youth, and Families (1985) Child Abuse Prevention and Treatment Act. Public Law 93-247. Washington, DC. https://eric.ed.gov/?id=ED271674

Association of the United States Army (2020) Senior enlisted advisor talks about mental health. Association of the United States Army. https://www.ausa.org/news/senior-enlisted-adviser-talks-about-mental-health. Accessed 28 May 2022

Bliese PD, Adler AB, Castro CA (2011) Research-based preventive mental health care strategies in the military. In: Adler AB, Bliese PD, Castro CA (eds) Deployment psychology: evidence-based strategies to promote mental health in the military. American Psychological Association, pp 103–124. https://doi.org/10.1037/12300-004

Castro C, Hoge C, Cox A (2006) Battlemind training: building soldier resiliency. In: Human dimensions in military operations – military leaders' strategies for addressing stress and psychological support, p 42-1–42-6

DODI 6400.1 DOD INSTRUCTION 6400.01 (2019) Family Advocacy Program (FAP) Office of the Under Secretary of Defense for Personnel and Readiness Effective: May 1, 2019. https://www.esd.whs.mil/DD/

Dunigan M, Farmer CM, Burns R, Hawks A, Setodji CM (2014) Out of the shadows: the health and Well-being of private contractors working in conflict environments. Rand Health Q 3(4):5

Field Manual (FM) 8-51 (1994) Combat stress control in a theater of operations. Government Printing Office, Washington, DC

Freeman D, Bicknell G (2008) The Army master of social work program. U.S. Army Medical Department Journal 72(5):72–75

Government Accountability Office (2015) Additional information needed about mental health provider staffing needs. GAO Publication No. 13-255. U.S. Government Printing Office, Washington, DC

Habeck EJ (1974) Army corrections. Current trends in army social work: refinement of army social work programs to meet tomorrow's challenges. Academy of Health Sciences, Ft. Sam Houston

Harris J (1999) History of Army social work. In: Daley G (ed) Social work practice in the military. Routledge, New York, pp 3–19

Huseman S (2008) Battlemind prepares soldiers for combat, returning Home USAG Stuttgart Public Affairs Office. https://wwwarmymil/article/6829/battlemind_prepares_soldiers_for_combat_returning_home. Accessed 26 Aug 2021

Jenkins JL (1999) The history of air force social work. In: Daley G (ed) Social work practice in the military. Routledge, New York, pp 28–45

Johnson B, Bacho R, Heim M, Ralph J (2006) Multiple-role dilemmas for military mental health care providers. Mil Med 171(4):311–315

Johnson B, Grasso I, Maslowski K (2010) Conflicts between ethics and law for military mental health providers. Mil Med 175(8):548–553

Keller N, Franklin A, Galloway E, Whaley L, Lesniak J (2014) Directorate of treatment programs: providing behavioral health services at the US disciplinary barracks. U.S. Army Medical Department Journal Oct Issue

Kennedy D (1999) The future of Navy social work. In: Daley G (ed) Social work practice in the military. Routledge, New York, pp 317–327

Lawrence-Wolff KM, Higgs JB, Young-McCaughan S, Mintz J, Foa EB, Resic P.A, Kelly KM, Maurer DM, Borah AM, Yarvis JS, Litz B., Hildebrand B., Williamson DE, Peterson AL (2021) The prevalence of fibromyalgia syndrome in active-duty military personnel. Arthritis Care Res (in press). https://doi.org/10.1002/acr.24801

Little J, Schmeltz A, Cooper M, Waldrop T, Yarvis JS, Pruitt L, Dondanville KA (2021) Preserving continuity of behavioral health clinical care to patients using mobile devices. Mil Med 186(1):137–141. https://doi.org/10.1093/milmed/usaa281

Mental Health Advisory Team (MHAT-IV) (2009, May 8) Operation Iraq Freedom 07-09, chartered by the Office of the Surgeon General Multi-National Forces-Iraq and Office of the Surgeon General United States Army Medical Department, San Antonio

Military Health System [MHS] (2018) Management analysis and reporting tool. Office of the Army Surgeon General, Falls Church

Military One Source (2020) The Family Advocacy Program https://www.militaryonesource.mil/family-relationships/family-life/preventing-abuse-neglect/the-family-advocacy-program/. Accessed 17 May 2021

Montgomery N (2009) Study find 'Battlemind' is beneficial. https://www.army.mil/article/16986/study_finds_battlemind_is_beneficial. Accessed 26 Aug 2021

Nelson JP (1999) Development and evolution of the family advocacy program in the department of defense. In: Daley G (ed) The history of navy social work. Social work practice in the military. Routledge, New York, pp 317–327

Newsome R (1999) Military social work practice in substance abuse programs. In: Daley G (ed) Social work practice in the military. Routledge, New York, pp 91–98

Rauch SAM, Sripada R, Burton M, Michopoulos V, Kerley K, Marx CE, Kilts JD, Naylor JC, Rothbaum BO, McLean CP, Smith A, Norrholm SD, Jovanovic T, Liberzon I, Williamson DE, Yarvis JS, Dondanville KA, Young-McCaughan S, Keane TM, Peterson AL (2020) Neuroendocrine biomarkers of prolonged exposure treatment response in military-related PTSD. Psychoneuroendocrinology 119:104749

Reisman M (2016) PTSD treatment for veterans: what's working, what's new, and what's next. Pharm Ther 41(10):623–634

Rubin A, Barnes W (2013) Assessing, preventing and treating substance use disorders in active duty military settings. In: Rubin A, Weiss E, Coll J (eds) Handbook of military social work. Wiley, Hoboken, pp 191–208

Rubin A, Harvie H (2013) A brief history of social work with the military and veterans. In: Rubin A, Weiss E, Coll J (eds) . Handbook of military social work, Wiley, Hoboken, pp 3–19

Sorbero ME, Olmsted SS, Morganti KG, Burns RM, Haas AC, Biever K (2013) Improving the deployment of army health care professionals: an evaluation of PROFIS. RAND Corporation. https://wwwrandorg/pubs/technical_reports/TR1227html. Accessed 17 May 2022

Straud CL, Dondanville KA, Hale WJ, Wachen JS, Mintz J, Litz BT, Roache JD, Yarvis JS, Young-McCaughan S, Peterson AL, Resick P (2021) The impact of hazardous drinking among active-duty military with posttraumatic stress disorder: does cognitive processing therapy format matter? J Trauma Stress 34(1):210–220. https://doi.org/10.1002/jts.22609

Taylor DJ, Pruiksma KE, Hale WJ, McLean CP, Zandberg L, Brown L, Mintz J, Young-McCaughan S, Peterson AL, Yarvis JS, Dondanville KA, Litz BT, Roache JD, Foa EB (2020) Sleep problems in active duty military personnel seeking treatment for posttraumatic stress disorder: presence, change, and impact on outcomes. Sleep 43(10). https://doi.org/10.1093/sleep/zsaa065

United States Navy Medical Service Corps (1999) History of Navy social work. In: Daley J (ed) Social work practice in the military, Hawthorne Press, Binghamton, p 23–26. Previously published as, Medical Service Corp (1997) The clinicians. In: Many specialties, one corps: a pictorial history of the U.S. Navy, MSC. Washington, DC: Department of the Navy, p 151–153

Washington L (1957) The history and function of social work in the military service. Dissertation, Atlanta University

Wright M, Cabrera A, Bliese D (2009) Stigma and barriers to care in soldiers post-combat. Psychol Serv 6(2):108–116

Yarvis J (2020) The life of a combat social worker. In: Figley C, Yarvis J, Thyer B (eds) Combat social work: applying the lessons of war to the realities of human services. Oxford University Press, New York, pp 15–27

Yarvis J, Schiess L (2008) Subthreshold PTSD as a predictor of depression, alcohol use, and health problems in soldiers. J Work Behav Health 23(4):395–424

Yarvis J, Bordnick P, Spivey C, Pedlar D (2005) Subthreshold PTSD: a comparison of depression, alcohol and physical health problems in Canadian peacekeepers with different levels of traumatic stress. Stress Trauma Crisis 8:195–213

Chapter 13
History and Current Framework of Social Work Services Delivered to Families and Communities Within the US Military

René J. Robichaux and Keita Franklin

13.1 History of Social Work Services Delivered to Military Families and Communities

The US military supports and funds an array of social work-related services out of a desire to increase retention, reduce misconduct, and decrease stress distractors that endanger the military mission. In doing so, the military recognizes the important role of social work interventions delivered to individuals, couples, families, groups, and communities. Harris (1993) explicitly defined these services within the field of occupational social work, but according to Maiden (2001), military social work in the US has generally not been equated as such within the profession. Maiden attributed this lack of conceptual inclusion to the "association with uniformed personnel, soldiering, war, and defense" (2001).

Since the advent of social work state licensure and the decreasing presence of the field of occupational social work within the social work profession in general, military social work practice has been defined more and more as a form of clinical social work practice. While there are a small number of positions that do not require a Masters in Social Work (MSW) with an advanced clinical state license, most civilian-military social work positions and all uniform positions require the advanced clinical social work state license. While specific requirements for each state's clinical social work license vary, all require the passing of a written examination and several years of post-MSW supervised clinical practice experience. After

R. J. Robichaux (✉)
Social Work Programs, Army Medical Command, US Army (Ret), San Antonio, TX, USA
e-mail: rene.robichaux@yahoo.com

K. Franklin
Loyal Source Government Services, USA, New York State Psychiatric Institute, Columbia University, New York, NY, USA
e-mail: keitafranklin4@yahoo.com

© Springer Nature Switzerland AG 2023
M. A. Forgey, K. Green-Hurdle (eds.), *Military Social Work Around the Globe*, Military and Veterans Studies, https://doi.org/10.1007/978-3-031-14482-0_13

obtaining employment, licensed social workers are also required by each state to obtain a specified amount of continuing education hours. Social workers who practice in military medical settings (family advocacy, medical social work, and substance abuse) are privileged to practice using specific modalities by the medical commander, and their clinical competencies are reviewed annually. The credentialing process requires the provider to specify the procedures (individual, group, couples, etc.) that he/she is requesting privileges to practice within.

Each branch within the US military has a unique history in relation to the development of military social work. Below is a brief description of the beginnings of military social work within each branch of service.

13.1.1   US Army

The first civilian social workers supporting Army military service members and their families were psychiatric social workers, who worked in inpatient facilities providing psychosocial assessments and mental health status checks. These social workers were provided by the Red Cross in 1918. Eventually, the Red Cross expanded their support to include medical social workers who were civilians engaged in a broad range of support services across a hospital-based service delivery. American Red Cross social workers provided services in military hospitals from 1918 to 1945, numbering about 1000 during World War II. In 1951, the American Red Cross withdrew all Red Cross-funded medical and psychiatric social work functions from Army hospitals (National Association of Social Workers 1965).

The first uniformed social worker in the US Army was Major Daniel E. O'Keefe, chief of the Army's Psychiatric Social Work Branch, who assumed the position on July 1, 1945 (Camp 1951). Due to the very large number of neuropsychiatric disorders during both World Wars, the need for psychiatric social work preceded medical social work in the Army. During World War II, more than 545,000 troops were separated from the service for neuropsychiatric disorders, which accounted for 49% of all discharges for either physical or mental defects (Caldwell 1948). The Army brought Major Barbara B. Hodges onto active duty on July 2, 1951, as the first director of the Army's Medical Social Work Program (Harris 1999). This was significant because it shifted the mindset of social workers serving as individual assets providing services at local military installations to an established program with a director and assumingly a support structure to provide policy-level support, oversight, and advocacy for the profession.

It is also important to note that although the Red Cross workers were withdrawn from Army hospitals following the war, these workers continued to take care of the more functional aspects of post-discharge planning including pension rights, insurance conversion, and employment (Beck 1944). They also linked the service member to civilian psychiatric treatment, community resources, and job placement (Beck 1944).

Currently, in 2020, there are 312 active-duty social work officers in the US Army performing a variety of roles inside hospitals, embedded into units, and in community and support organizations (Humphries 2020). While the uniform social work positions have remained unchanged since the 1970s, the number of civilian social work positions has increased, now numbering well over 1000 within Army Medicine alone (Robichaux 2020). The increase in civilian positions is a direct result of increased caseloads stemming from the impact that the Global War on Terror has had on the mental health of service members. As the active-duty population shrinks due to overall force reductions, there will follow a similar decrease in uniformed social work positions. It is anticipated that civilian social work positions will not shrink as rapidly as uniformed positions will. Uniformed positions are always subject to trade-offs with other specialties, including combat arms positions. The only rationale for maintaining current levels centers around combat support roles in the theater of operations and current overall troop levels. As the Army downsizes, the uniformed social work positions will be reduced proportionally.

13.1.2 US Navy

At the end of World War II, the Navy Relief Society employed its first professional social worker to assist US Navy Sailors and their families with psychosocial problems. At the time, most professional social work activities were limited to training volunteers to extend assistance to Navy families. It was not until the 1950s and 1960s that civilian psychiatric social workers initiated clinical social work services at naval hospitals. In 1979, only 29 civilian social workers were employed in naval hospitals. The Bureau of Medicine and Surgery created social work departments and authorized the recruitment of uniformed social workers beginning in 1979. Lieutenant (junior grade) David Kennedy was commissioned as the Navy's first uniformed social worker in January 1980 (United States Navy Medical Service Corps 1999). According to the most recent data available, there were 51 active-duty social workers, 89 civilian social workers, and 66 contracted social workers in the Navy in 2015 (Government Accounting Office [GAO] 2015).

Navy social workers perform a variety of roles from providing treatment to children and their families who are struggling with family violence to offering community-based help to families facing deployment-related challenges that are common for military families. Most social work services provided for marines and their families are provided through the Navy Health Care system. However, throughout the Operation Enduring and Iraqi Freedom, the US Marine Corps took great strides to stand up several helping programs often staffed by social workers providing home visiting services to new parents, family violence prevention, and serving in units as part of an embedded prevention-focused program.

13.1.3   US Air Force

The US Air Force was established as a separate military department in 1947. Until 1967, Air Force social work remained predominantly psychiatric in nature. Mental health services have remained a primary practice function for social workers in the Air Force since that time. In 1967, Colonel Jack Davis was designated as the first associate chief of the Biomedical Sciences Corps for Social Work. At large medical facilities, the senior uniformed social worker was designated as the chief of social work services. By the 1970s, it was common for a single social worker to be assigned to a small medical facility, most often as a member of a multidisciplinary mental health team (Jenkins 1999). There are currently 251 active-duty social work officers, 120 government service civilian social workers, and 99 contracted social workers in the US Air Force (Collins 2020). Many of these social workers work to provide treatment for families struggling with intimate partner violence, child abuse, and even in sexual assault prevention and response programs.

13.2   Community Service and Family Support Centers

Community and family support services evolved out of a need to reduce the stress associated with military life. Relocation services included loan closets (which included lending of furniture and small appliances), financial assistance, and spouse employment services. Parenting education, stress management classes, and new parent support and home visiting services became standard prevention services.

The Army Community Services (ACS) traces its beginnings to 1965. Given the fact that 53% of enlisted members and officers are married and frequently separated from their families, the demand for social services had proven enormous (National Academy of Sciences 2019). The early mission of ACS was to establish the following:

> A centrally located responsive and recognizable service to provide information, assistance, and guidance to members of the Army community in meeting personal and family problems beyond the scope of their own resources, in order to reduce the man-hours consumed by commanders, staff officers and soldiers in seeking assistance for complex personal problems, and to improve personnel retention by increasing career satisfaction (Army Community Service Program 1965).

The Army initially authorized the establishment of 42 social work officers and 19 enlisted social work specialists, who were assigned to over 90 ACS centers worldwide. Social work officers assumed significant leadership roles at ACS centers and in Army headquarters level positions designed to provide both oversight and policy guidance for the operating forces. These early positions were eliminated in 1981. Some, but not all, leadership positions were filled by government service civilian social workers (Army Community Service Program 1965).

The Navy Family Support Program was established in 1979 to assist in improving combat readiness, job performance, and retention. The program was tasked with establishing Navy Family Support Service Centers (FSCs). A total of 62 centers were planned for the end of the fiscal year 1985 (O'Keefe 2019). In 2001, the Navy FSCs were renamed Fleet and Family Support Centers and exist at 81 Navy locations worldwide.

Air Force Family Service Programs were developed during the 1950s but were often filled by other helping professionals outside the social work profession. Historically, these programs were developed by laymen, administered by nonsocial workers, and implemented by volunteers (Jenkins 1999). These programs offered concrete services designed to help families struggling with the stressors of relocation and financial stress and to help military spouses find employment and engage in volunteer activities.

Since the beginning of the 2003 war with Iraq, the Department of Defense has funded the Military and Family Life Counselors (Military and Family Life Counseling Program 2020). These contracted providers have been placed in military units, in childcare centers, and in the family support programs to provide short-term outreach/counseling to service members and their families. The providers have included both licensed clinical social workers and psychologists. Interventions in these settings include individual counseling, group psychoeducational interventions (such as stress management and parenting skill-building), and organizational/community prevention briefings.

There have been numerous research projects that have informed and guided the preventative interventions applied to service members and their families. Much of this research is designed to uncover how heightened levels of risks impact military families and how to further build protective factors. The stress associated with deployment, life changes such as frequent moves, births, divorces, death, injury, and financial problems are all typical challenges facing military families today. Research that was conducted on an active-duty Navy population as far back as 1967 concluded that high levels of stress are associated with increased risk of illness, injury, or death (Holmes and Rahe 1967). More recently, research had confirmed previous research and correlated high levels of stress with a wide range of psychological and physical illnesses (Schneiderman et al. 2005).

Outreach and command consultation in the Army has been studied by researchers at Cornell University, revealing a positive correlation between briefings and unit commander attendance at meetings addressing service member problems, coupled with subsequent command support for recommended treatment plans (Leidy et al. 2015).

New parent support home visiting and prevention-focused services have been measured for effectiveness, and it was found that when families participate in home visiting education and support services, they are less likely to have a substantiated case of child abuse (Leidy and Thomas 2015). The Child Abuse Potential (CAP) Inventory is used as a risk screening tool (Milner 1986). The risk scores for child maltreatment are observed at the start of service and at case closure, and in both instances, the program has recorded very low rates of maltreatment for families that complete the program (Leidy and Thomas 2015).

13.3 Family Advocacy Services

Other types of assistance provided predominately by military social workers within all of the branches are services focused on family violence prevention and intervention. The military community is concerned about family violence for two primary reasons. First, and most obviously, family violence exacts physical and psychological harm upon the men, women, and children of America's military community. The second concern stems from an awareness among leaders that family stress degrades the readiness of the service member by distracting their focus away from the details that are required for them to perform their military mission safely. Overly stressed and distracted service members are a danger to themselves and to other members of units that depend upon them to be clear-minded and decisive in their actions. For these reasons, each branch of service has a requirement through its Family Advocacy Program (FAP) to prevent child and intimate partner maltreatment, protect victims, and provide treatment to those affected.[1]

The Army established a Child Advocacy Program in 1976 with the publication of AR608-18. The Army program is a split program with intervention, case management, and treatment services under the Surgeon General which is currently staffed by 300 government service social workers (Humphries 2020). Prevention activities are provided at the installation level and managed by a Family Advocacy Program manager working in the Army Community Service Center. Spouse and intimate partner violence was added to the regulation in the early 1980s, when the Armed Services became aware of the need that had previously remained somewhat hidden from view. The specific timeline for these spouse and intimate partner regulation and policy changes varied by branch as detailed by Bowen (1984).

The Navy Family Advocacy Program (FAP) was established in 1976 with the publication of BUMED Instruction 6320.53 and formally launched in 1979 (United States Navy Medical Service Corps 1997). Initially, the program was split in a similar way to the Army's program, between hospital FAP positions and Family Service Center positions and functions. In October 1997, the entire program was aligned under the Bureau of Naval Personnel and located in Family Support Centers (renamed in 2001 to Fleet and Family Support Centers).

In 1975, the Air Force published AFR168-38 and thereby became the first service to establish a Child Advocacy Program (Jenkins 1999). The Air Force Family Advocacy Program is managed within the Office of the Surgeon General and is

---

[1]The current family advocacy regulations in each branch are as follows: Army Regulation AR608-18, Department Air Force Instruction 40-301, and Navy instruction OPNAVINST 1752.2C.

currently staffed by 120 government service civilian social workers and 99 contracted workers (Collins 2020).

Social workers have played a central role throughout the evolution of the Family Advocacy Program. They are employed at all major command levels, and they have been responsible for policy development and execution of care delivery every step of the way. Social work training, with its person-in-environment/ecological perspective, has proven invaluable in meeting the demands and challenges of the job. At the individual case level, social workers have used their clinical skills and state clinical licenses to provide case assessments and treatment recommendations and to conduct individual, couple, family, and group therapy. On the prevention side of the Family Advocacy Program, social workers provide managerial guidance/supervision to education and prevention staff through delivering senior leader awareness briefings, stress management sessions, and parenting classes. They also supervise the activities of social workers and nurses who staff New Parent Support Services provided to at-risk families.

The military services have far outpaced their civilian counterparts in the standardization of definitions describing four types of child maltreatment, which include child neglect, physical abuse, emotional abuse, and sexual abuse. Similarly, definitions were developed for adult intimate partner physical abuse, emotional abuse, sexual abuse, and neglect (Heyman and Smith-Slep 2012).

The standardized definitions became the core of the case determination process, guided by a computer-based decision tree algorithm (DTA). The DTA ensures that all required criteria are considered. Committee members vote on each criterion. Published psychometric data indicates the use of both standardized definitions, and the DTA process increases the validity and reliability of determinations (Heyman and Smith-Slep 2009).

The Department of Defense (DoD) and the military services have continually worked on processes to improve treatment and assessment of domestic abuse. The DoD contracted university researchers to develop and test an actuarial domestic abuse risk assessment instrument, now known as the Intimate Partner Physical Injury-Risk Assessment Tool [IPPI-RAT] (Stith et al. 2016). It is designed to be used by FAP clinical providers to assess the likelihood that an active-duty military member or partner, who had been reported to FAP for an incident of domestic abuse, will have another incident of domestic abuse resulting in physical injury to the victim. The authors list the following key points regarding the tool:

- It is the first tool designed specifically for a military population.
- It is designed to predict physical injury in alleged intimate partner violence (IPV) cases (independent of allegation or whether the reported incident met criteria).
- It is one of the first tools to include perpetrator characteristics, victim characteristics, and relationship characteristics.
- It is one of only a few tools designed for both male and female offenders.

FAP services are available to any individual who qualifies for medical services at a military treatment facility. This extends services to retired service members and eligible family members, as well as active-duty service members and their families.

There are occasional ethical tensions that arise from the advocacy role assumed by social workers when they intervene in domestic violence cases. In the absence of physical injuries, the command group may be more inclined to believe the denials put forth by the active-duty member when they perceive the member to be an excellent performer with respect to his military duties. Command education has had a positive impact in mitigating such denials. In these situations, social workers have a strong victim advocacy orientation and would frequently appeal up the chain of command to obtain the desired safety outcome.

Perhaps the largest ethical challenge has presented at the program management level in that active-duty social work officers are assigned as chiefs of Family Advocacy Programs when they have not necessarily obtained sufficient knowledge and skills to work in this area. There have been instances where their lack of knowledge has resulted in poor decisions with regard to safety plans, and the outcomes have resulted in serious injuries. Another significant challenge occurs when senior officers ignore conflicts of interest and attempt to circumvent the process for soldiers with whom they have a personal relationship. In these instances, the offending officers have been investigated and held accountable after the fact.

13.4 Medical Social Work Services

Within the Department of Defense, civilian medical social workers assist military members, retired service personnel, and families in dealing with the psychological, social, and physical consequences of illness and injury. In the earlier section on the evolution and history of social work delivered services in the military, the early contributions of the American Red Cross in the period from World War I through World War II were noted. As the American Red Cross withdrew from serving patients in military hospitals in 1951, the Joint Commission on the Accreditation of Hospitals, under pressure from advocacy groups, required all hospitals to have a social work program (Cowen 1970). The Armed Services responded to these requirements for several decades, and by the 1980s, the medical social work role was well established and quite stable in military hospitals. Medical social work presented opportunities for rich and rewarding practice in areas that included nephrology, hematology/oncology, neonatal care, pediatric intensive care, rehabilitative medicine, and acute medical and surgical intensive care. Medical social workers focused their skills on working with military families around permanent nursing home placements, home health needs, psychosocial issues, crisis intervention, grief counseling, and problem/unplanned pregnancies. In the 1980s, special funding for the treatment of patients with HIV expanded the role of social work in response to this new area of practice. When newly diagnosed service members were brought to the Walter Reed Army Medical Center for staging and treatment, Captain Stan Piotroski, PhD, a medical social worker with extensive training in group psychotherapy, took the lead in facilitating the adjustment to illness and development of coping skills needed to deal with the many issues surrounding diagnosis for both the patients and the staff treating them (Piotroski and Chapin 2003). His skills in managing groups as large as 20 individuals were remarkable and set the standard for others responding to this first of many crises to follow.

The 1990s marked a significant era of change and variation in military health care. Managed care brought dramatic changes in the delivery of health care in general, as well as changes in the delivery of medical social work. In the present day, some hospital civilian medical social workers have been realigned as part of utilization management departments, and they have assumed roles that closely resemble case management roles of nurses in those same departments. They focus on discharge planning functions related to transitional facilities and durable medical equipment and have much less incentive or encouragement to explore the psychosocial aspects of illness and injury.

There are still opportunities for social workers in primary and specialty care clinics in military settings to practice within the scope of traditional medical social work, but the positions have decreased as occupational health psychologists have been hired in larger numbers to provide comparable services. The services provided are similar, but not entirely equal, as the psychologist's focus tends to be limited to the individual patient or at times may expand to group interventions. The broader social work view of systems and families may not be addressed or taken into consideration by other disciplines, further challenging the need for a holistic approach to managing complex health issues.

One of the significant roles performed by medical social workers is that of a discharge planner. It is in this capacity that barriers to continued recovery are anticipated and resources are brought into play to facilitate a smooth transition from hospital to home or from military service to civilian or Veterans Administration care.

Just as the number of medical social work positions were declining due to managed care, a new practice area opened in the military with the creation of social work positions within the Wounded Warrior Program/Army Recovery Care Program (United States Army 2022). The program was established in 2004, in response to the large number of casualties resulting from the Global War on Terror (GWOT). Approximately, 100 civilian behavioral health social workers were assigned to the Warrior Transition Units at 23 different active duty- and community-based locations organized at each medical treatment facility (Robichaux 2020). The Units provided a comprehensive behavioral health and psychosocial assessment for all Warriors in Transition, managed risk identified during the assessment interview, and documented the actions taken in the health-care record. They also ensure soldier and family member counseling/treatment using the appropriate modality, collaborate with other members of the treatment team (nurse case manager, primary care manager, and squad leader), and provide a variety of social services as indicated. The Licensed Clinical Social Worker (LCSW) uses a clinical evaluation tool developed by the Behavioral Health Division in the US Army Medical Command in conjunction with the Previdence Corporation. This web-based tool is known as the Psychological and Behavioral Health Tools for Evaluation, Risk, and Management (PBH-TERM) (Putnam 2017). Responses to questions are solicited from the soldier and cover eight areas associated with the risk to harm to self and/or others. The

LCSW conducts a more comprehensive interview based on the responses and the overall assessment of risk. Soldiers with elevated risk estimates are identified to the team, and a risk management plan is developed. High-risk soldiers are reevaluated weekly and all soldiers are reevaluated monthly. The risk assessment questionnaire comprises questions that are aligned under eight factor groups:

- Factor Group 1: Behavioral health (depression/suicide)
- Factor Group 2: Mental status/psychosis
- Factor Group 3: Anxiety/post-traumatic stress
- Factor Group 4: Anger/aggression/violence
- Factor Group 5: Substance abuse/use
- Factor Group 6: Psychosocial history/relationships
- Factor Group 7: Environment support system
- Factor Group 8: Health history/traumatic brain injury

The contributions made by Wounded Warrior Program social workers in determining the risk estimates for service members have been enormous. Social workers assigned to community-based Warrior Care Units were particularly sensitive to identifying inadequate discharge plans for wounded soldiers sent to live and recover in remote locations. These were often National Guard and Reserve soldiers who lacked the close unit support of active-duty soldiers. On more than one occasion, social workers drove to remote locations and found a severely injured soldier living in homes without running water and without electricity. They initiated immediate action to move the soldier to a more appropriate setting. A more rewarding area of practice for social workers does not exist within the military services.

13.5   Social Work Practice with Substance Use Disorders

Public Law 92-129 was enacted in 1971 and mandated a program for the identification and treatment of drug- and alcohol-dependent individuals in the armed forces (United States 92nd Congress 1971). Similar to civilian employee assistance programs, military substance abuse prevention and treatment programs are targeted at assuring work performance and force readiness. While each branch established their own prevention and treatment programs, they all shared a primary treatment model based on the 12-step model developed by the Alcoholics Anonymous (Alcoholics Anonymous 2022). Providers were most often selected based on their own recovery from substance abuse. Rehabilitative services were provided by paraprofessional counselors who performed the initial assessment.

In the Air Force in the 1970s, an active-duty social worker assigned to the base mental health clinic was responsible for any alcohol use disorder diagnosis. An individual receiving an alcohol dependence or abuse diagnosis was most often referred to a 28-day inpatient treatment program at one of the regional treatment facilities. Follow-up care was provided by paraprofessional staff with minimal direct involvement from mental health social workers (Newsome 1999).

In the early 1980s, the Air Force initiated a new policy mandating referral for evaluation following any incident in which substance abuse was suspected. The other services also adjusted their policies accordingly. The result was an increase in referrals across rank structures and an opportunity for earlier intervention in addressing the problem of substance abuse (Newsome 1999).

During the 1990s, military treatment programs emphasized outpatient treatment following brief inpatient stays when appropriate. Plans may have included issues such as current marital/family problems, family of origin concerns, physical and emotional/psychological well-being, and job skills. Initially, experienced addiction counselors, including some social workers, expressed concerns that such a broad focus could serve as a distraction from the primary problem of alcohol abuse. However, clinicians found that by using more comprehensive treatment plans, initial concerns subsided because tangible progress could be measured through tools and techniques that gauged the individual's progress in moving from denial to acceptance of the alcohol use disorder (Newsome and Ditzler 1993).

In 2013, the Institute of Medicine (known now as the National Academies of Science) published findings on substance use disorders in the US Armed Forces. The authors of the report were critical of the overall state of treatment but also identified some promising changes that had been piloted by the services. They identified the need for licensed clinicians including LCSWs, LPCs, and clinical psychologists to support service members with comorbid mental health and substance abuse disorders (Institute of Medicine 2013). Contained in the report was the recognition that unless the comorbid mental health disorder and existing marital/family stress were addressed along with the substance abuse disorder, the likelihood of treatment failure increased exponentially (Institute of Medicine 2013). The authors further noted that Air Force and Navy training manuals were outdated and did not address the use of evidence-based pharmacological and behavioral therapies and did not reference the VA/DoD Clinical Practice Guidelines for the management of substance abuse disorders (SUDs) (Institute of Medicine 2013). In addition, the authors noted that all branches had shortages of SUD counselors and that few physicians had received training in addiction medicine or addiction psychiatry (Institute of Medicine 2013). The authors of the study further contended that primary care clinics were missing the single largest opportunity in the military for early and confidential identification of and brief intervention in alcohol and other drug misuses (Institute of Medicine 2013). They urged DoD and the branches to better integrate care for SUDs with care for other mental health conditions and ongoing medical care.

During the study period, the Air Force was the first to integrate behavioral health (BH) into primary care. By the time the study was published, the Army had not only integrated behavioral health into primary and specialty care but had also developed integrated intensive outpatient programs (IOPs), where mental health conditions and SUDs could be addressed at the same time. These programs are staffed by both SUDs and BH clinicians. There are currently 450 government service civilian social workers working in substance abuse in the Army (Milliken 2020).

The report also singled out the Army's Confidential Alcohol Treatment and Education Pilot (CATEP) as an outstanding way to increase self-referral across a broad range of ranks (Gibbs and Olmstead 2011). During the pilot treatment, services were offered outside duty hours, so soldiers could participate anonymously or without informing the commander. In other words, they encouraged but did not require soldiers to disclose their participation to their commanders based on the belief that access to confidential brief counseling, treatment, and more intensive treatment promotes good care and builds resilience. The pilot was so successful that the Army moved forward with incorporating it into their program in their revised policy publication (Department of the Army 2020). The program was renamed Voluntary Alcohol-Related Behavioral Health Care.

13.6 Current Challenges

As medical social work positions in military settings have undergone significant challenges from both nurses and health psychologists, opportunities to expand their role in working with wounded soldiers have increased. Although these opportunities came about as an afterthought (social workers were not included in the original triad model of commander, nurse case manager, and squad leader), they soon proved their value in the management of behavioral health problems. The cast of leaders who developed the plan did not factor in the possibility of behavioral health problems and therefore did not see behavioral health clinicians as contributing to the possible solutions. However, many soldiers assigned to the Wounded Warrior Units manifested behavioral and mental health concerns that interfered with recovery from physical injury.

Civilian social workers have also found their place in expanded areas of practice within the embedded behavioral health units that support soldiers in garrison. The functions of these embedded teams were addressed in the previous chapter by Yarvis, Korbut, and Martin and include individual, couple, and family therapy interventions. Civilian social workers function as team members in all respects, except for the role of the social work officer in deploying with the supported units. Opportunities for social work positions within intensive outpatient programs (IOPs) have also enlarged their numbers within medical treatment facilities. Salaries for LCSWs tend to be less than PhD-level psychologists, and when social workers demonstrate to leadership that they can provide competent clinical services at a more reasonable cost, they will find that opportunities increase for expanding their role in the delivery of behavioral health services across programs and services.

With the exception of social work functions within the Wounded Warrior Program, such as discharge planning, the amount of transitional assistance provided by DoD social workers to veterans is minimal. This type of service is most likely provided by providers who accept responsibility for transitioning a patient from their care to a program or provider outside of the active military service.

13.7 Conclusion

Social work within a military setting provides a very broad and rewarding area of practice, not only at an individual, couple, and family level but also at a macro level, with opportunities to inform policy and educate military leaders about the many challenges that military life presents to families. Over the years, social workers have been able to present relevant research and data to advocate for improved staffing in support of programs such as family advocacy. Initially, the program relied on a significant number of contract social workers, and as the years went on, the vacancy rates increased, and the quality of contract providers decreased. Social work leaders asked for and received support to transition all contract positions to civilian government employees. The example highlights the potential of social work within the military but also demonstrates what leadership must do to communicate its value and ensure its place within the military's support structure.

References

Alcoholics Anonymous (2022) Twelve steps and twelve traditions. https://www.aa.org/twelve-steps-twelve-traditions. Accessed 19 May 2022
Army Community Service Program (1965) In Army Regulation 6081. Department of the Army, Washington, DC
Beck B (1944) The military social worker. Soc Serv Rev 18(4):461–468
Bowen GL (1984) Military family advocacy: a status report. Armed Forces Soc 10(4):583–596
Caldwell JM (1948) The problem soldier and the Army. Am J Psychiatry 105(1):46–51
Camp EW (1951) Psychiatric social work in the Army today. In: Maas HS (ed) Adventures in mental health. Columbia University Press, New York, pp 201–212
Collins P (2020) Air Force Family Advocacy Program Manager. Telephonic communication with the author about the number of active-duty AF social workers and Family Advocacy social workers
Cowen R (1970) Some new dimensions of social work practice in a health setting. Am J Public Health Nations Health 60(5):860–869
Department of the Army (2020) The Army Substance Abuse Program Army Regulation 600-85. Washington DC. ,https://armypubsarmymil/epubs/DR_pubs/DR_a/ARN30064-AR_600-85-000-WEB-1pdf. Accessed 19 May 2022
Gibbs DA, Olmstead KL (2011) Preliminary examination of the confidential alcohol treatment and education program. Mil Psychol 23(1):97–111
Government Accounting Office [GAO] (2015) Additional information needed about Mental Health provider staffing needs, GAO Pub, No. 13-255. U.S. Government Printing Office
Harris J (1993) Military social work as occupational practice. In: Work and well-being: the occupational social work advantage. NASW Press, pp 276–290
Harris J (1999) History of army social work. In: Daley JG (ed) Social work practice in the military. The Haworth Press, New York, pp 3–22
Heyman RE, Smith-Slep AM (2009) Reliability of family maltreatment diagnostic criteria: 41 site dissemination field trial. J Fam Psychol 23(6):905–910. https://doi.org/10.1037/a0017011
Heyman RE, Smith-Slep AM (2012) Decision tree algorithm and definitions for use within the Family Advocacy case review. Family Advocacy Program, U.S. Army Medical Command, Washington, DC

Holmes TH, Rahe R (1967) The social readjustment rating scale. J Psychosom Res 11(2):213–221

Humphries J (2020) Social Work Consultant to the U.S. Army Surgeon General, telephonic communication with author

Institute of Medicine (2013) Substance use disorders in the U.S. Armed Forces. The National Academies Press, Washington, DC. https://doi.org/10.17226/13441

Jenkins J (1999) History of Air Force social work. In: Daley JG (ed) Social work practice in the military. The Haworth Press, New York, pp 27–48

Leidy B, Thomas M (2015) The effectiveness of new parent support programs within the U.S. Army. Unpublished report delivered to Army Family Advocacy Program Manager's Annual Meeting

Leidy B, Thomas M, Enroth C, Lockwood K (2015) Command Support Study. Unpublished report delivered to Army Family Advocacy Program Manager's Annual Meeting

Maiden RP (2001) The evolution and practice of occupational social work in the United States. Empl Assist Q 17(1–2):119–161

Military and Family Life Counseling (2020) https://www.militaryonesource.mil/confidential-help/non-medical-counseling/military-and-family-life-counseling/. Accessed 27 May 2022

Milliken C (2020) Program Manager, U.S. Army Substance Abuse Program. Telephonic communication about current civilian social workers employed within Army Substance Abuse

Milner JS (1986) The child abuse potential inventory: manual, 2nd edn. Psytec, Webster

National Academies of Sciences, Engineering, and Medicine; Division of Behavioral and Social Sciences and Education; Board on Children, Youth, and Families; Committee on the Well-Being of Military Families, Le Menestrel S, Kizer KW (eds) (2019) Strengthening the military family readiness system for a changing American Society. National Academies Press (US). https://pubmed.ncbi.nlm.nih.gov/31600043/

National Association of Social Workers (1965) Mental health and psychiatric services. National Association of Social Workers, New York

Newsome RD (1999) Military practice in substance abuse programs. In: Daley JD (ed) Social work practice in the military. The Haworth Press, New York, pp 91–106

Newsome RD, Ditzler T (1993) Assessing alcoholic denial: further examination of the denial rating scale. J Nerv Ment Dis 181(11):689–694

O'Keefe A (2019) Launching the Navy family support program: a heartfelt blend of history and memoir. Amazon Kindle Direct Publishing

Piotroski S, Chapin MG (2003) Human immunodeficiency virus social work program at the Walter Reed Army Medical Center: a historical perspective. Mil Med 168(9):698–701. https://doi.org/10.1093/milmed/168.9.698

Putnam KD (2017) Behavioral health risk assessment and estimation: validating an integrated, multi-risk factor approach aided by technology. Dissertation, University of Houston

Robichaux RJ (2020) Social Work Programs Manager, Behavioral Health Division, U.S. Army Medical Command. Internal Reports generated for Command briefings

Schneiderman N, Ironson G, Siegel SD (2005) Stress and health: psychological, behavioral, and biological determinants. Ann Rev Clin Psychol 1:607–628

Stith SM, Milner JS, Fleming M, Robichaux RJ, Travis WJ (2016) Intimate partner physical violence risk assessment in a military sample. Psychol Violence 6(4):529–541. https://doi.org/10.1037/a0039969

United States 92nd Congress (1971) HR 6531, Public Law 92-129: an act to amend the military selective service act of 1967; to increase military pay; to authorize military active duty strengths for fiscal year 1972; and for other purposes. U.S. Govt Printing Office 85:348–362 https://www.govtrack.us/congress/bills/92/hr6531

United States Army (2022) Army Recovery Care Program (ARCP) (formerly known as Army Wounded Warrior Program (AW2). https://myarmybenefits.us.army.mil/Benefit-Library/Federal-Benefits/Army-Recovery-Care-Program-(ARCP)-(formerly-known-as-Army-Wounded-Warrior-Program-(AW2)). Accessed 25 May 2022

United States Navy Medical Service Corps (1999) History of Navy Social Work. In J Daley, Social
    work practice in the military, Hawthorne Press, Binghamton, p 23–26. Previously published as,
    Medical Service Corp (1997) The clinicians. In: Many specialties, one corps: a pictorial history
    of the U.S. Navy, MSC. Washington, DC: Department of the Navy, p 151–153

Chapter 14
Equipping Uniformed and Civilian Military Social Workers for Service: Efforts of Civilian and Military Education Programs in the United States

Dexter R. Freeman, Christopher Flaherty, and Jill J. Henderson

14.1 Introduction

After over two decades of war in Afghanistan and Iraq, countless bodies and minds have returned to America's shores broken and maimed forever. It is a known fact that those who served in this war, just as those who served in previous conflicts, will need the assistance of professionals who understand the military worldview and can help service members and their families give a voice to their hidden wounds of war. Service members require the aid of social workers who possess a unique set of skills. These skills include having the ability to advocate and challenge bureaucratic rules and policies that may hinder service members' ability to get their needs fulfilled. Furthermore, these social work practitioners must also be compassionate listeners who are capable of ascertaining the therapeutic needs and psychological damage that service members have experienced. Other times, these providers must be able to assess service members' environmental and family strengths that promote resiliency and reintegration upon returning from deployment. Lastly, providers must demonstrate a deep level of understanding and awareness of the military culture that enables them to understand their responsibility to assist service members

D. R. Freeman (✉)
University of Kentucky, US Army Medical Department Center of Excellence,
Fort Sam Houston, San Antonio, TX, USA
e-mail: dexter.r.freeman.civ@army.mil

C. Flaherty
College of Social Work, University of Kentucky, Lexington, KY, USA
e-mail: chris.flaherty@uky.edu

J. J. Henderson
College of Social Work, University of Kentucky, Fort Sam Houston, San Antonio, TX, USA

Social Work Consultant to the Army Surgeon General, Falls Church, VA, USA
e-mail: jill.j.henderson.mil@army.mil

© Springer Nature Switzerland AG 2023
M. A. Forgey, K. Green-Hurdle (eds.), *Military Social Work Around the Globe*,
Military and Veterans Studies, https://doi.org/10.1007/978-3-031-14482-0_14

while supporting the readiness of the force. This skill set is indicative of the characteristics that well-trained and competent uniformed and civilian military social workers bring to the military practice setting. Wooten (2015) described military social work as a specialized area of practice that differs from social work practice in civilian communities. This chapter will primarily focus on uniformed social workers who serve in the active-duty military, with a responsibility to support military service members, organizations, commanders, and families in accomplishing the overall mission. It will also address the ways in which civilian social workers are educated and equipped within colleges and universities to serve military populations.

14.2 History of Military Social Work Education

Civilian universities have been educating social workers who have gone on to serve military service members since 1918 (Freeman and Bicknell 2008). Initially, military social work services were primarily conducted by Red Cross civilians treating military service members. It was not unusual to find a Red Cross social worker providing casework services to soldiers in the Mental Hygiene Clinic or a military hospital (Beck 1944). Red Cross social workers provided a valuable service to the military, and the Army began relying upon services that professionally trained social workers were providing the military force. In an effort to increase the number of social workers available to meet the needs of the Army, the Department of the Army created a Military Occupational Specialty (MOS) for commissioned social work officers in 1943 (Beck 1944). This MOS was established to enable the Army to take advantage of the unique skills that social workers brought to the organization.

From 1918 until 2008, civilian universities assumed responsibility for educating and developing social workers who would serve in the military alongside service members they would be treating. In order to increase the number of trained uniformed social workers, the Department of the Army established a two-pronged social work procurement program that was designed to recruit and develop future uniformed psychiatric social workers (Camp 1948). At the time of this program's inception, the Army had grown to rely upon the expertise of hospital social workers and psychiatric social workers to meet the case management, family, and discharge planning needs of military service members and their families (Greenberg 1951; Whitney 1951).

The Psychiatric Social Work Program procured uniformed social workers by providing funds that would enable academic eligible commissioned Army officers to attend civilian education institutions of their choice. The Army Medical Department authorized eight educational training slots for regular Army officers to attend civilian universities of their choice (Camp 1948). During the first year of this program, three regular Army officers pursued their social work degrees at the New York School of Social Work, the Pennsylvania School of Social Work, and the University of Chicago.

An alternate route to serve as a uniformed social worker was through attending a 26-week sub-professional training program for commissioned officers with a college degree, who were interested in fulfilling the duties of a psychiatric military social worker (Camp 1948, 1951). Commissioned officers who completed this program were trained and equipped to serve as nonprofessional social workers in mental hygiene units, combat divisions, neuropsychiatric hospitals, or convalescent hospitals. They were not only taught the role of the social worker but were equipped to understand cultural, organizational, and professional challenges they might encounter as a member of a treatment team that was often led by a psychiatrist who viewed the social worker as their assistant (Whitney 1951). The Army recognized that civilian-trained social workers, while valuable to the services because of their professional knowledge, lacked knowledge and awareness of the military culture. The knowledge and cultural sensitivity that comes with serving in the military is essential to being an effective uniformed social worker, no matter if one is serving in 1950 or in 2021. The 26-week psychiatric social work program attempted to ensure that uniformed social workers were not only technically competent as social workers but that they were also culturally sensitive and capable of engaging military service members in their roles as social workers.

While it was inviting for regular military officers to have the opportunity to take off their military uniforms and become immersed into the practice of social casework in a civilian environment, an unforeseen knowledge deficit was not being addressed (Camp 1948, 1951): how to adapt civilian social casework practice methods to a military environment when uniformed social workers would have to balance their role as a soldier with that of a practitioner (Rockmore and Greving 1951). The knowledge gap between what civilian education systems were doing to equip future uniformed social workers to practice and what they were actually required to do as social workers in a military environment continued until most recently.

Simmons and DeCoster (2007) surveyed uniformed military social workers to explore the level of preparation they received to practice as uniformed social workers during their civilian education. A majority of the social workers surveyed expressed feeling they learned very little about how to practice social work in a military community during their graduate social work program (Simmons and Decoster 2007). Even though civilian programs were expected to equip social workers with unique knowledge and skills to practice in the military, it was not until recently that the social work profession truly acknowledged military social work as a distinct area of social work practice.

In 2012, the National Association of Social Workers [NASW] published practice standards for serving military service members, their families, and communities. They identified 12 practice standards that uniformed and civilian social workers should adhere to when serving military and veteran clients (NASW 2012). These standards involved recognizing the importance of adhering to the ethics and values of the profession, ensuring that uniformed and civilian social workers are qualified to practice social work with military clients, and highlighting the basic knowledge that uniformed and civilian military social workers must have to effectively serve this unique population. The standards explain what is involved when conducting an assessment with military clients and what is relevant to all fields of social work, highlighting the importance of offering a multisystems approach when intervening or providing clinical treatment, discussing the importance of professional development, and emphasizing the essentialness of being culturally humble and competent. The NASW standards also articulated the importance of supervision, documentation, and advocacy when providing social work intervention to military clients and organizations. Moreover, the NASW standards of practice also require that social workers who provide support to military service members and families possess a core set of knowledge and basic qualifications. In addition, clinical social workers serving a military population must be knowledgeable about the physical, mental health, and psychosocial stresses that service members and veterans experience. They should also be competent to provide counseling in areas such as grief, depression, post-traumatic stress, substance abuse, separation, and loss. Furthermore, it is essential that military social workers have basic knowledge about military culture, resources, and awareness of some of the challenges that military families encounter. These standards have been a positive step toward identifying military social work as a unique area of social work practice that requires special training and knowledge to perform competently.

To further solidify the establishment of military social work as a specialty area of practice, the Council on Social Work Education (CSWE) revised the ten core competencies from the 2008 Educational Policies for Accreditation Standards (EPAS) for undergraduate and graduate social work programs that were offering military social work educational concentrations (CSWE 2010). Furthermore, in 2018, CSWE published a detailed curriculum guide to provide resources and guidance to educational programs that are offering concentrations and certification training to current and future uniformed and civilian military social workers (CSWE 2018).

Military social work is defined as direct social work practice with military service members, families, organizations, and diverse communities that consists of providing clinical practice, program management and development, policy practice, social advocacy, and research and development (CSWE 2010, 2018). The social work profession now recognizes that competent military social work practice demands that one be knowledgeable and capable of demonstrating specific skills to engage individuals, families, communities, and organizational systems within military communities at the micro, mezzo, and macro levels of practice (Wooten 2015). This chapter will describe some of the efforts that have been taken in social work graduate education in military-affiliated and nonmilitary-affiliated (civilian) programs within the United Sates to educate both future uniformed and civilian military social workers.

14.3   Military-Affiliated Social Work Educational Programs: Growing Their Own

In 2006, five years after the United States began major military operations in Afghanistan and Iraq, the Army was suffering from a shortage of qualified social workers to serve the needs of service members and their families. In response, the Army Surgeon General approved the establishment of a military-delivered Master of Social Work (MSW) program that would be affiliated with a degree-granting civilian higher education institution and would be conducted in a military environment, at the Army Medical Department Center and School, now referred to as the Army Medical Center of Excellence (MEDCoE). Students must meet the admission standards of the selected educational institution and every instructor selected to teach in the Army MSW Program to have direct social work practice experience within the military healthcare system as a uniformed or civilian-military social worker. These qualifications would enable each instructor to take on an active role as a mentor as well as an instructor to students in the program.

In 2007, the Army solicited proposals from CSWE-accredited social work programs to establish a partnership with the MEDCoE. Fayetteville State University (FSU) was awarded the initial contract with the US Army MEDCoE in 2008. Brown and Freeman (2010) describe the program selection process and criteria that were considered in determining the appropriate university partner, as well as the benefits of the partnership for FSU. A major consideration in the Army selecting a university partner was that the university must have demonstrated a commitment to educating military service members and their families. For more details on the establishment of this partnership, see Freeman and Bicknell (2008).

The Army MSW Program contract was for five year increments, and after the third solicitation, the University of Kentucky, a proven military-friendly institution with a demonstrated commitment to serving the military, was selected as the university partner for the MSW Program in November 2016. After a one year transition and start-up period, the first Army-University of Kentucky cohort of 24 MSW students enrolled in January 2018.

14.3.1   Gatekeeping: Ensuring Suitability

When the Social Work Consultant to the US Army Surgeon General proposed the plan to increase the number of social workers who would be equipped to meet the needs of soldiers and their families, the expectation was that these social workers would be culturally competent, independently licensed to practice, deployable, and they would be prepared to join the military force in half the amount of time that civilian higher education systems would typically take (Freeman and Bicknell 2008). Some concerns were how effective would the Army be at growing their own? How competent and committed would these behavioral health providers be as uniformed military social workers and leaders? How suitable would the fit be between soldiers admitted to the Army MSW Program and the social work profession?

To address these concerns, professional gatekeeping became paramount in the Army Master of Social Work (MSW) program. Every faculty member, program administrator, and member of the Army social work community assumes a gate-keeping role in the student development, evaluation, and selection process. Staff and faculty have learned to embrace their responsibility for ensuring that every graduate of the Army Social Work program be equipped to meet the needs of soldiers and their families.

GlenMaye and Bolin (2007) describe gatekeeping as a responsibility fulfilled by an educator to determine if students are suitable and appropriate to practice in a select field or profession. Over the years, higher education has primarily viewed gatekeeping as a procedure to determine if a student applicant had the intellect and personal characteristics that would make them suitable for entering the profession. As such, historically, most social work educational program's gatekeeping efforts took place during the admission phase of their programs (Lafrance et al. 2004). Thus, many programs assumed that once a student was admitted to a program, the educator's responsibility as a gatekeeper ended, and their primary responsibility was to do all they could to ensure a student's academic success. As a result, many educational programs use graduation and passing ratios as indicators of their program's success.

The Army MSW Program extends gatekeeping beyond GlenMaye and Bolin's (2007) conception of gatekeeping and views gatekeeping as a process of considering the goodness-of-fit between the military soldier and social work and the prospective professional's competency to practice (Hylton et al. 2017). Thus, the Army MSW Program begins the process of gatekeeping during the application and admission phase and concludes the process with the successful completion of a 26-month post-MSW internship. Each applicant's educational readiness, military awareness, leadership potential, and expressed commitment to serve as a military social worker are examined during the application and admission phase of the program. Moreover, those components, along with the student's demonstrated competency to practice social work in a military setting, are continuously evaluated throughout the MSW Program degree granting and post-master's internship phase. The post-MSW internship phase allows the Army MSW Program to evaluate potential uniformed military social workers' competency to practice social work in an array of military environments and assess their military professionalism and ability to function as military officers.

14.3.2   Admission Process

Applicants for the Army-University of Kentucky MSW Program undergo a two-step application process. First, they apply through the US Army Recruiting Command to become commissioned officers in the Army Medical Service Corps and to attend the MSW Program at the MEDCoE. An applicant must meet the legal, physical, and academic requirements of the Army and the MSW Program to be considered by a board of active-duty social workers for selection. Once an applicant is recommended for selection by the Recruiting Command selection board, they then must apply for admission to the University of Kentucky College of Social Work. Once an applicant has been approved by the Army and University of Kentucky, they and their families relocate to the MEDCoE to complete the MSW Program.

14.3.2.1   Pre-requisite Military Training

To ensure that each applicant has foundational knowledge about military customs, organizations, policies, and procedures, all students must complete basic officer leadership training prior to beginning the MSW Program. Those who enter the program with no previous military experience must attend a four week military familiarization course at Fort Sill, Oklahoma, titled the Army Medical Department Direct Commission Course [AMEDDCC] (AMEDDCC 2021). This course offers basic knowledge on what it means to be a commissioned officer in the Army Medical Service Corp. Graduates must effectively demonstrate an awareness of the Army values, the warrior ethos, the military tactics, the components of military leadership, and the commitment to maintaining physical and mental fitness. Upon completion of the pre-commission-level course, all newly commissioned officers must complete the Army Medical Service Corp Basic Officer Leadership Course.

14.3.2.2   Program Orientation

Once students have completed these initial requirements, they are now prepared to enter the Army MSW Program, where they will develop competencies to practice social work within a military environment. However, prior to beginning formal graduate classes, each cohort of students receives a two week orientation to the program and military social work as detailed below.

Week 1 During the first week of orientation, students are alerted that this program will not be delivered the same as typical civilian-based undergraduate and graduate programs they may have attended. Students are informed that the academic phase of the program is a fast-paced, intense 14-month phase that typically takes two years to complete. They are reminded that the accelerated nature of this graduate program is reflective of most military assignments they will be given to accomplish as military social workers. Unlike civilian education programs, students are expected to present as soldiers first. Student cohorts are structured and organized as a military unit. As such, the MSW Program director selects a student from each cohort to serve as the class leader (comparable to a military unit commander) and another student to serve as the assistant class leader. Other students are placed into leadership positions in which they are expected to ensure accountability; display military bearing; promote adherence to following military rules, regulations, and policies; and encourage everyone to work as a cohesive team.

Each student takes a pre-assessment instrument called the Foundation Curriculum Assessment Instrument (FCAI), which was developed by the Social Work Educational Assessment Project [SWEAP] (SWEAP 2021). The FCAI is a 64-item pre- and post-assessment that evaluates the foundational intellectual competency of entry-level graduate social work students in seven curricular SW areas of social work: practice, human behavior in the social environment, policy, research, ethics and values, diversity, and social and economic justice. These results can then be compared with other foundation-level graduate social work students.

Results from the FCAI have consistently revealed that students in the military MSW Program score higher than the national average on the pre- and post-assessments in a majority of the curricular areas. This confirms that students who have entered the Army MSW Program are intellectually suitable for entering the social work profession.

Week 2 The second week of orientation focuses on orienting new military social work graduate students to the profession of social work and the various venues in which military social workers practice. Students explore the congruence that may exist between their values and beliefs, the values and perspectives of the military culture, and the values and principles of the social work profession. Since the program began in 2009, each student has completed a social work values assessment to examine the extent to which personal values are congruent with the core values of social work. The social work values scale is a ten-item questionnaire based on the core values detailed in the NASW Code of Ethics (2021). The questionnaire was developed by the author, Dexter Freeman, and each statement corresponds with a social work core value. Students respond to statements: "I believe it is important to care for the vulnerable and oppressed," and "I should use my skills and knowledge to help others voluntarily." The results indicate that across cohorts, military students have placed great importance on being competent, promoting the dignity and worth of others, displaying integrity, and serving others. The reliability of the scale is 0.77 when used with a military population. Furthermore, the results from the values scale provide students additional confirmation that they have chosen a profession that is consistent with their personal and military values system.

14.3.3   Overview of the Curriculum

Throughout the MSW Program, students are closely monitored, evaluated, challenged, and required to demonstrate their ability to integrate their knowledge of social work with their understanding of military culture. During the foundation phase of the program, students gain a thorough indoctrination to social welfare policy in the civilian community and transpose that knowledge onto the military to examine how it influences military family policies. Students learn how to conduct generic mental health assessments as a social worker and how military social workers conduct assessments in austere military environments. They learn about the process of conducting social work research and then develop military-related social work research proposals. Every social work class during the foundation and advanced practice phase of the curriculum is taught from a military-focused perspective, and students are constantly reminded that their preparation during the MSW degree phase of the program is designed to prepare them for their postmaster's internship.

Graduates of the Army-University of Kentucky MSW Program enter the Army's 26-month Social Work Internship Program (Howard 2014), which is a structured, rotational internship at one of ten select military installations. Interns in the Social Work Internship Program (SWIP) go through several 3–6-month rotations in substance abuse, family violence, embedded military behavioral health, and other areas of interest to the intern (Howard 2014). During the SWIP, interns practice under the supervision of a licensed clinical social worker and complete the requirements to become a state-approved licensed independent clinical social worker. Prior to beginning the SWIP, each student is required to take the initial master's level social work licensing exam to demonstrate their intellectual competency to practice social work at the master's level. Since the inception of the military MSW Program, 94% of the graduating students have passed this exam. This is another example of how gatekeeping is performed throughout the program to ensure the safety of society and the competency of students who have matriculated through the MSW Program.

In summary, the Army MSW Program has built upon the work that was started by NASW and CSWE, by narrowing the focus on what it takes to practice military social work as a uniformed military social worker. It is one thing to provide clinical social work support to a service member who is not directly influenced by the military system, and it is a completely different perspective to advocate for social justice in a military system when one has committed to upholding the values of that system. As such, military students in the Army MSW Program are taught to recognize their roles as change agents who must learn to balance their allegiance to the social work profession with their allegiance to the military profession. They are reminded that as social workers, their primary mission is to enhance the well-being of all, especially the vulnerable and oppressed, through service, advocacy, policy practice, research, and at times challenging the military system to promote social justice. This is the perspective the Army MSW Program takes when it recruits and trains future uniformed military social workers.

Every social work class is taught from a military perspective, using military scenarios, with the objective of preparing students to apply social work principles and processes in a variety of military environments. For example, students in the Army MSW Program do not just learn about social work ethical decision-making. They interview current active-duty military social workers regarding their experiences with ethical dilemmas and demonstrate their ethical decision-making skills using contemporary military examples. Graduate students in the Army MSW Program learn from an explicit curriculum that requires that every student demonstrate the intellectual competency to apply social work values, practice concepts, and principles in a variety of military situations. Their competency and suitability to practice are evaluated via their performance on pre- and post-assessments in the classroom, a national curriculum assessment instrument, and a national master's entry-level social work licensing examination. In addition, they must also complete 1000 hours of field education supervision training under the supervision of a licensed social worker.

Graduate-level field placements are conducted in civilian- and military-affiliated counseling and healthcare agencies. To further ensure students' readiness to practice independently as uniformed military social workers, graduates of the MSW Program complete a structured, rotational post-master's social work internship program. During the SWIP, they receive a minimum of 3000 hours of clinical supervision from an independently licensed uniformed clinical social worker, complete four to six clinical rotations, and receive an array of military-focused evidence-based trainings to further hone their clinical skills as military social workers.

The military social work program began as a pilot program for the US Army in 2009, and today, it has become the US Army's primary means for developing and multiplying the force. Over the years, many military specialty areas have been reduced due to budget cuts. However, military social work has grown and is continuing to grow. Originally, the Army MSW Program was primarily designed for active-duty Army social workers. Today, the program has also become the program of choice for the US Air Force and the Army National Guard.

14.4   Educating Civilian Military Social Workers

Social workers have served military and veteran populations in various capacities since World War I, and today's largest employer of social workers is the Department of Veterans Affairs (Harris 2000; NASW 2012; Wooten 2015). Smith College was the trailblazer in educating social workers to treat returning veterans. Smith college was founded with the expressed purpose of accomplishing this mission, which laid the groundwork for veteran-focused education to follow in the United States (Jacobs 2009).

Despite social workers' long history of serving the active-duty and veteran population, and some of the early publications outlining the unique knowledge and skillset required (e.g., Beck (1944)), it has only been within the last decade that the social work profession has acknowledged the uniqueness of social work practice within a military culture and context. Moreover, it is only recently that the profession has recognized the specialized training that social workers must have to be prepared to attend to the specific needs of service members, their families, and veterans within the context of the military's unique culture (CSWE 2010; DuMars et al. 2015; Martin et al. 2017). In 2010, the CSWE published standards for advanced practice in Military Social Work. These military-specific practice behaviors are associated with the CSWE's ten core advanced practice competencies (CSWE 2008).

The War on Terror created an onslaught of war victims who were physically and psychologically maimed thus, increasing the demand for universities to prepare social workers to serve military populations. Moreover, numerous schools of social work began developing or expanding specialized curricula to address the needs of military service members, a problem that had become prevalent within many American communities. Early leaders in these efforts include Smith College, the University of Southern California, the University of Texas at Arlington, Boston University, West Virginia University, the University of Missouri, and the University of South Carolina (Wooten 2015).

Military-specific social work education has been incorporated into undergraduate, graduate, and doctoral programs. Offerings range from individual courses, undergraduate and graduate certificates, and doctoral specialization tracts. Civilian educational programs have also developed and designed an array of continuing education workshops and classes, from as little as three continuing education credits to as much as 60 continuing education credits. A wide range of subjects are addressed in these military-focused trainings and workshops, such as understanding military culture, post-traumatic stress, evidence-based practice models used to treat military service members, neuroscience fundamentals and depression in military service members, substance use and abuse, and other topics relevant to the needs of social workers who may be treating and serving military service members, veterans, and their families (Smith-Osborn 2015). Typical civilian educational programs have a limited number of military-affiliated instructors and/or practitioners. Thus, many civilian educational programs will contract with military organizations who may bring in retired military social workers, military guest lecturers, or military personnel to share their experiences with students to provide relevant and realistic education. This will also enhance the cultural competency of future military social workers. The following is a description of the iterative process that has been used to develop and expand military social work educational opportunities at the University of Kentucky.

14.4.1 An Identified Need

Canfield and Weiss (2015) discuss the need to educate students who may seek to serve as social workers within the Veteran's Association (VA); however, there is also a need to educate and equip future social workers who plan to work within the

Department of Defense and with agencies and organizations that serve service members and their families who seek behavioral health services within the civilian community. Therefore, social work graduates who work within DoD and civilian agencies that serve military populations must be knowledgeable about military culture and pertinent systems of care. Hall (2011) points out that in order for a healthcare provider to be effective in engaging members of the military community, they must acknowledge and respect the unique family, organizational, and community perspective that these military families bring to a relationship. Secrecy takes on an entirely new meaning in the military community. In military organizations, the culture embraces the importance of remaining loyal to the hierarchical structure and mission-first mentalities. These organizational loyalties can, at times, even trump family priorities. Service members are also conditioned to minimize defects while keeping problems within the unit, family, or the military organization. Therefore, when a service member refuses to discuss their problems in counseling, it is not always resistance; at times, this may be reflective of the closed military society that the service member and the military family represent.

For many years, civilian social work educational programs treated social work practice within the military as synonymous to social work in any other organization. However, as previously identified, the NASW (2012) and CSWE (2010) have acknowledged the uniqueness of providing social work practice within a military context. This exclusivity is amplified for uniformed social workers, as social work officers must balance their role as a professional social worker with their role as a military officer who must also uphold a distinct set of values, responsibilities, and policies as a member of a military organization. Civilian educational programs must not only teach practice guidelines and principles; they must also help future uniformed military social workers to understand the challenges and nuances involved when practicing as a uniformed social work officer in a military environment.

14.4.2 Understanding Military and Veterans 101

Through various formal and informal interactions with students, the University of Kentucky MSW Program faculty identified a curricular need for a course covering topics related to social work practice with military and veteran populations. In the summer of 2014, the college launched a course titled Responding to Military and Veteran Populations. The course was designed by a college faculty member, who is a retired US Air Force social work officer, and a full-time Army National Guard social work officer/social work doctoral student.

Planning this course involved numerous discussions and reviews of primary duties, competencies, and skills needed to serve within military and VA systems of care. Hall (2011) identified three areas of cultural competence that are necessary to effectively practice social work with military populations: become aware of one's own behavior, values, biases, preconceived notions, and personal limitations; understand the worldviews of culturally diverse clients without negative judgment; and actively develop and practice appropriate, relevant, and sensitive strategies for this work.

Frey et al. (2014) conducted a survey of community-based licensed clinical social workers regarding the perceived needs of providers who serve military families. The primary needs identified revolved around the need to understand the implications of the military culture and learning how to coordinate services within the military and civilian community. These data, along with practice knowledge of the primary course developers, drove decisions around course content.

Course developers steered students to work in community agencies such as community mental health centers, substance misuse services, domestic violence shelters, and community-based programs to address homelessness. An important criterion that each agency must meet was that it served a substantial number of military-related clients.

It was determined, through discussions with local experts working within military and VA systems, that a substantial portion of the course would focus on understanding and appreciating the military culture and its impact on behavioral health, as well as attitudes toward seeking behavioral health services. Much has been written about the negative impact of stigma on receptiveness to receiving behavioral health services (Chu et al. 2021; Hernandez et al. 2016; Hipes et al. 2015). The first 2 weeks of the course focus exclusively on the multifaceted nature of military culture. Cultural considerations are also interwoven throughout all other course topics, which include an overview of the specific individual and family stressors associated with military life, commonly experienced psychiatric conditions, and DoD and VA systems of behavioral healthcare.

The course has been a success, in terms of student interest and enrollment. In the first 2 years, approximately 160 students completed the course. Students demonstrate related competencies through reflections, assignments, a quantitative examination, and quizzes, as well as a small group presentation examining the experience of a particular population (e.g., women veterans, military spouses, racial/ethnic minority service members). Finally, students complete a major writing assignment examining a macro- or micro-social problem currently or historically relevant to military and/or veteran populations. Some examples of macro-level issues include integration of minority groups into the military, economic hardship, and geographic mobility and reintegration into the civilian workforce. Some examples of micro-level issues include substance use disorders, conflict-specific injury, and family dysfunction. However, it was clear to faculty that the course provided only the most preliminary foray into military social work. Plans ensued to establish a graduate certificate in military behavioral health to further serve students who wish to extend their competency in this practice arena.

14.4.3 Interdisciplinary Graduate Certificate in Military Behavioral Health

Following the lead of some of the early innovators mentioned above, the University of Kentucky College of Social Work in cooperation with the Department of Family Sciences and the Student Veterans Resource Center developed a 12-credit-hour graduate certificate in Military Behavioral Health (MBH) in 2015. The goal was to provide additional training beyond the single course, directed primarily for graduate students who plan to seek careers in military healthcare systems (e.g., DoD, VA). The certificate was designed to be available and applicable to students in behavioral health disciplines such as family therapy, clinical psychology, rehabilitation counseling, and social work. The certificate consists of 12 hours of coursework, which typically includes four (three-credit-hour) classes. These courses consisted of Responding to Military and Veteran Populations, Counseling Military Families (a Family Science course), and an individual student capstone project. The remaining three credit hours are assigned to an elective course, approved by the certificate director that is relevant to military behavioral health practice. Some students gain additional training from field practicum placements within the local hospital. Although these placements are valuable, they are not available in sufficient numbers to accommodate all interested students. Therefore, the capstone course was designed to provide certificate seekers an opportunity to delve deeply into an area of military social work. Individual projects examine specific historical events that have had an impact on service members, families, and veterans, the consequences of these events, lessons learned for practice and policy, and recommendations for future research in the arena. An example would be the impact of the Vietnam War on substance use patterns within the ranks, the subsequent policy and practice responses within the DoD and VA care systems, and the relative success of the response. Students develop a portfolio around the topic, including a list of governmental and civilian resources currently available to impacted populations.

Unlike stand-alone courses, the graduate certificate was not immediately sought by large numbers of students. Examination of the college's various MSW Program models showed that obtaining the certificate required an additional semester of enrollment for many students, including those matriculating through the advanced standing track. Adjustments, such as counting certain required clinical courses toward the elective requirement, improved accessibility. Currently, approximately five students complete the credential per year, with enrollment steadily increasing as more students within the college's many newly established Doctor of Social Work program seeking the Military Behavioral Health Certificate.

In addition to the efforts taken at the University of Kentucky to equip future military social workers, there are a number of other certificate programs that have been developed at other universities. These certificate programs offer realistic exposure to the military context either through military-specific internships or through focused individual study, so that future military social workers might understand what it is like to offer social work services within a military environment. The course offerings include topics such as assessing, understanding, and treating post-traumatic stress within the military, as well as evidence-based treatment for mild traumatic brain injury, working with military families, substance use disorder prevention and treatment within the military, and post-deployment reintegration and military resiliency (Wooten 2015).

14.5 Discussion

The Council on Social Work Education (CSWE) took a major step forward in identifying military social work as a unique specialization when it promulgated advanced standards of practice for social work with military-affiliated clients (CSWE 2010). Even though higher education had been educating and equipping social workers who served the needs of military service members since World War I, it was not until the NASW (2012) and CSWE (2010) developed and began promoting the unique practice standards that are necessary to serve military clients that military social work was accepted a social work specialty.

Thus, today there is a proliferation of individual courses at the undergraduate and graduate level and military certificate programs available to ensure that social workers are competent to meet the needs of active-duty service members within the military and veterans in their communities who may be suffering from the wounds of war and/or the operational stressors of military life. When CSWE established standards for social work practice with the military, it was apparent that they wanted military social work to be viewed as a social work specialty that would be used to meet the needs of a diverse population. CSWE (2010) asserts that military social work is direct practice, research, policy, and advocacy that is conducted with active and retired members of the Department of Defense, as well as members of the Department of Homeland Security, Public Health Service, National Oceanic, and Atmospheric Administration, and individuals participating in disaster relief and humanitarian missions.

Graduate students in the Army MSW Program are shaped and molded by an intense implicit curriculum that involves being part of a strict military community that requires them to maintain high physical, mental, and emotional standards of living on a daily basis. They are reminded that they are always military officers and must uphold the standards and values of the military in all situations. These students not only recognize that missing class without an excuse is unprofessional social work behavior, but they also realize that this is a violation of the military regulation with the potential for negative consequences. The military context in which the Army MSW Program is delivered is what makes it unique and effective at equipping tomorrow's uniformed social workers to practice when they leave this educational program.

Given the diverse populations and various venues in which military social work is practiced, it is imperative that a plethora of educational and training opportunities continue to be offered to equip tomorrow's social workers to meet the current and emerging needs of this diverse client population.

References

Army Medical Department Direct Commission Course [AMEDDCC] (2021). https://sill-www.
    army.mil/30ada/amedd_dcc.html. Accessed 12 Dec 2021
Beck BM (1944) The military social worker. Soc Serv Rev 18(4):461–468. https://www.jstororg/
    stable/30014258. Accessed 18 May 2022
Brown TM, Freeman DR (2010) Distance education: a university's pioneering Master of Social
    Work program partnering with the U.S. Army. Planning for Higher Education, July-September
    pp 35–43
Camp EW (1948) The army's psychiatric social work program. Soc Work J 29(2):76–78. https://
    www.jstor.org/stable/23705044
Camp EW (1951) Psychiatric social work in the army today. In: Maas HS (ed) Adventure in mental
    health: psychiatric social work with the armed forces in World War II. Columbia University
    Press, New York, pp 202–220
Canfield J, Weiss E (2015) Integrating military and veteran culture in social work education:
    implications for curriculum inclusion. J Soc Work Educ 51:S128–S144. https://doi.org/10.108
    0/10437797.2015.1001295
Chu KM, Garcia SMS, Koka H, Wynn GH, Kao T (2021) Mental health care utilization and
    stigma in the military: comparison of Asian Americans and other racial groups. Ethnic Health
    26(2):235–250. https://doi.org/10.1080/13557858.2018.1494823
Council on Social Work Education (CSWE) (2008) Educational policy and accreditation stan-
    dards, Alexandria
Council on Social Work Education (CSWE) (2010) Advanced social work practice in military
    social work, Alexandria
Council on Social Work Education (CSWE) (2018) Specialized practice curricular guide for mili-
    tary social work, Alexandria
DuMars T, Bolton K, Maleku A, Smith-Osborne A (2015) Training MSSW students for military
    practice and doctoral students in military resilience research. J Soc Work Educ 51(1):117–127.
    https://doi.org/10.1080/10437797.2015.1001294
Freeman DR, Bicknell G (2008) The Army master of social work program. Army Med Depart J,
    July–September 72–75
Frey J, Collins KS, Pastoor J, Linde L (2014) Social workers' observations of the needs of the
    total military community. J Soc Work Educ 50(4):712–729. https://doi.org/10.1080/1043779
    7.2014.947904
GlenMaye LF, Bolin B (2007) Students with psychiatric disabilities: an exploratory study of program
    practices. J Soc Work Educ 43(1):117–131. https://doi.org/10.5175/JSWE.2007.200404112
Greenberg I (1951) Neuropsychiatric hospital. In: Mass HS (ed) Adventure in mental health:
    psychiatric social work with the armed forces in World War II. Columbia University Press,
    New York, pp 63–77
Jacobs C (2009) The response of schools of social work to the return of uniformed service
    members and their families. Smith Coll Stud Soc Work 79(3/4):453–463. https://doi.
    org/10.1080/00377310903130258
Hall LK (2011) The importance of understanding military culture. Soc Work Health Care 50:4–18.
    https://doi.org/10.1080/00981389.2010.513914
Harris J (2000) History of army social work. In: Daley JG (ed) Social work practice in the military.
    The Haworth Press, New York p3–22
Hipes C, Lucas JW, Kleykamp M (2015) Status and stigma related consequences of military ser-
    vice and PTSD: evidence from a laboratory experiment. Armed Forces Soc 41(3):477–495.
    https://doi.org/10.1177/0095327X14536710
Hernandez SHA, Morgan BJ, Parshall MB (2016) A concept analysis of stigma perceived by mili-
    tary service members who seek mental health service. Nurs Forum 52(3):198–195. https://doi.
    org/10.1111/nuf.12187

Howard RW (2014) The army social work internship program: training today's uniformed social worker. Army Med Depart J, January –March:35–38

Hylton ME, Manit J, Messick-Svare G (2017) Gatekeeping and competency-based education: developing behaviorally specific remediation policies. J Teach Soc Work 37(3):249–259. https://doi.org/10.1080/08841233.2017.1313359

Lafrance J, Gray E, Herbert M (2004) Gate-keeping for professional social work practice. Soc Work Educ 23(3):325–340. https://doi.org/10.1080/0261547042000224065

Martin J, Albright D, Borah E (2017) Expanding our understanding of military social work: the concept of military and veteran-connected populations. J Fam Soc Work 20(1):5–8. https://doi.org/10.1080/10522158.2016.1237919

National Association of Social Workers (2021) Code of ethics. https://www.socialworkers.org/About/Ethics/Code-of-Ethics/Code-of-Ethics-English

National Association of Social Workers (2012) NASW standards for social work practice with service members, veterans, & their families. https://www.socialworkers.org/LinkClick.aspx?fileticket=fg817fIDop0%3D&portalid=0

Rockmore MJ, Greving FT (1951) Adapting civilian practice to military settings. In: Maas HS (ed) Adventure in mental health: psychiatric social work with the armed forces in World War II. Columbia University Press, New York, pp 3–23

Simmons CA, DeCoster V (2007) Military social workers at war: their experiences and the educational content that helped them. J Soc Work Educ 43(3):497–512. https://doi.org/10.5175/JSWE.2007.200600054

Smith-Osborne A (2015) An intensive continuing education initiative to train social workers for military social work practice. J Soc Work Educ 51(Suppl. 1):S89–S101. https://doi.org/10.1080/10437797.2015.1001290

Social Work Education Assessment Project (SWEAP) (2021). https://www.sweapinstruments.org. Accessed 12 Dec 2021

Whitney F (1951) Convalescent hospital. In: Mass HS (ed) Adventure in mental health: psychiatric social work with the armed forces in World War II. Columbia University Press, New York, pp 78–98

Wooten NR (2015) Military social work: opportunities and challenges for social work education. J Soc Work Educ 51(1):S6–S25. https://doi.org/10.1080/10437797.2015.1001274

Chapter 15
Current Status of Military Social Work in Japan

Kengo Tanaka and Kazushige Nakano

15.1 Outline of Japan's Self-Defense Forces

Before discussing the current status of military social work (MilSW) in Japan, this chapter provides a brief explanation of the Japan Self-Defense Forces (JSDF). Japan's legal system presupposes that it has no "army" capable of any offensive force. Article 9 of the Japanese Constitution declares that the Japanese people forever renounce war. However, based on the self-defense right granted by the United Nations, the JSDF exists as an organization for self-defense, and it conforms to the "exclusively defense-oriented policy." This fundamental concept of self-defense in Japan is the major difference from the United States and most other countries' militaries. The exclusively defense-oriented policy is thought to prohibit the possession of aircraft carriers, bombers, ballistic missiles, and other offensive arms, assuming that offense and defense are mutually exclusive and clearly distinguishable in military affairs. Considering these facts, Japan's exclusively defense-oriented policy may be defined as "adopting passive self-defense strategies in the spirit of the Constitution, such as using defensive force only in the event of an armed attack and limiting the extent and level of defensive force use to the minimum necessary for self-defense" (The House of Representatives 1946).

According to Kawano (2015), the JSDF has dispatched its members for various international cooperation activities over the past years, including the United Nations peacekeeping operations in Mozambique, humanitarian aid in Rwanda, and

K. Tanaka (✉)
School of Social Work, St. Catherine University, Matsuyama City, Ehime Prefecture, Japan
e-mail: tanakak0816mildefsw@gmail.com

K. Nakano
Faculty for the Study of Contemporary Japanese Society, Kogakkan University, Ise, Mie, Japan
e-mail: k-nakano@kogakkan-u.ac.jp

© Springer Nature Switzerland AG 2023
M. A. Forgey, K. Green-Hurdle (eds.), *Military Social Work Around the Globe*,
Military and Veterans Studies, https://doi.org/10.1007/978-3-031-14482-0_15

emergency assistance for those affected by a hurricane disaster in Honduras. These operations are based on the Law Concerning the Dispatch of the Japan Disaster Relief Team (1987) (Kawano 2015). After the terrorist attacks in the United States on September 11, 2001, and onward, it has also been dispatching its members to various other international operations.

Senda (2015) reported that no other countries' military personnel have been killed by the JSDF, and none of its military members have been killed by the act of fighting since the end of World War II. However, Senda further reported that of the JSDF members dispatched to the Indian Ocean to guard the oil supply under the Japanese Act on Special Anti-terrorism Measures, and those dispatched to Iraq for the Humanitarian and Reconstruction Assistance Project under the Japanese Act on Special Measures for Humanitarian Relief and Reconstruction Assistance in Iraq, a total of 56 military members died by suicide during their term of duty. This included 21 of the Ground, 8 of the Air, and 27 of the Maritime JSDF.

Another notable point is that new tasks were assigned to the JSDF, including dispatching emergency security guards to remote areas at the request of other countries when Japan's Legislation for Peace and Security was introduced in 2015, resulting in increased risk for each JSDF member and high expectations placed on the JSDF by Japanese civilians (Japan's Legislation for Peace and Security 2015). These new tasks included dispatching assistance for disaster relief and emergency management assistance for natural disasters attributed to climate change and expanding peacekeeping operations. In short, the authors contend that the risks and expectations have increased for each JSDF member due to legislative changes and subsequent dispatch mission requirements.

15.2   Special Characteristics of Social Work in Japan

As a basis for identifying challenges in making MilSW take root in Japan, this section briefly explains the history of social work within Japan. The term "social work" was used for the first time in Japan after World War II. Noting the necessity of trained social work professionals in social welfare measures, the General Headquarters (GHQ) and the Supreme Commander for the Allied Powers opened a school for social work in Tokyo in 1946 (Simura 2021).

Additionally, Shigeo Okakura, a Japanese scholar of social welfare, translated the literature on social work he read at the GHQ Library, paving the way for the dissemination of this area in Japan (Matsumoto 1999). In his paper, Okamura (1956) defined social workers as "life advisors of social welfare facilities" and discussed residential social work as his central theme. In his work, "residential social work" refers to the "life support" provided in social welfare facilities such as nursing homes and facilities for people with disabilities, and in this context, "life support" refers to the assistance provided to residents in managing their daily lives.

The widespread recognition of social work as residential social work in Japan, and a welfare service system centered upon administrative "placements" performed by government workers until 2000, has resulted in dividing the profession and leaving generic social work undeveloped in Japan (Simura 2021). Consequently, social work has developed mostly as residential social work in Japan, and supporting vulnerable residents living in group life became the main focus in these facilities. Kensaku Ohashi, a famous Japanese scholar of social welfare, noted with regard to such a consequence that social work in Japan after Okamura has developed without a consensus on how to define the concept of social work and its function (Ohashi 2005).

Although a legal system to certify professional social workers was established with the occupational title "Certified Social Workers," these workers' position as professionals remains low. The Japanese Association of Certified Social Workers is a nationwide organization of social workers that could address this issue. However, the number of members is limited to 41,731, accounting only for about 20% of the 233,517 certified social workers as of March 2019, revealing the poor recognition of these professionals among the general public (Japanese Association of Certified Social Workers 2019). Considering such a situation, the government of Japan attempted to ensure a sufficient quality of social work services by revising the law, but it was determined that practical experience for a given period of time is the only requirement to take the national social work licensure examination, despite repeated demands from social workers in actual welfare settings.

15.3   JSDF and Military Social Work

Japan's national security services protect the lives of its people and the nation and contribute to international disaster relief efforts. The JSDF is addressing areas of need where military social workers provide support in other countries, such as suicide prevention and family support. Yet to date, there are no professional social workers allocated to the JSDF, unlike the militaries of other countries, such as those that have contributed chapters to this book. There has also been insufficient academic exchange between social welfare workers and the JSDF to explore how social work expertise could support the security assurance role of the military system. Further, the lack of exchange between the JSDF, academics, and practitioners is also limiting the development of MilSW studies in Japan.

In order to resolve these difficulties, it may be necessary to distinguish MilSW as a new domain of social work in the study of social welfare and promote recognition of its usefulness among JSDF members. As a first step in this process, it will be important to study the need for MilSW in Japan from the available data. The following section summarizes the current status of the JSDF services in areas in which social work expertise could be beneficial but does not currently exist, including (1) suicide prevention measures, (2) support for members dispatched overseas and their families, and (3) family support for service members in domestic assignments.

15.3.1   Suicide Prevention Measures

The JSDF has identified suicide as a serious concern among its members. In 2000, an investigative committee on JSDF members' mental health was organized to address an increasing number of suicide cases. This report by the Ministry of Defense (2000) provided a basis for establishing the current suicide prevention system.

Although detailed information regarding the causes of suicides among JSDF members have not been made public in recent years, a member of the House of Representatives provided the following data when fielding questions in 2015 in relation to the total number of suicide deaths and causes among JSDF members within the period between 2003 and 2014. According to the data, the following factors that were deemed to be causes for suicide were identified: suffering from diseases, 32; debt, 159; family issues, 118; professional issues, 123; mental disorders, 289; others, 95; and unclear, 228 (House of Representatives 2015).

When trying to understand the conditions that may exacerbate the risk of suicide within the JSDF, the missions that JSDF members are required to participate in must be taken into consideration. The first type of mission involves *disaster relief operations* to help areas affected by major disasters that periodically occur and are attributed to climate change and the natural features of Japan, such as typhoons and earthquakes. The second is the increased prevalence of *overseas dispatches* based on the exclusively defense-oriented policy specific to the JSDF.

The number of *disaster relief operations* performed by the JSDF in recent years is as follows: 2018, 501 (a total of approximately 2.03 million members dispatched); 2019, 443 (1.19 million members dispatched); and 2020, 449 (1.15 million members dispatched) (Ministry of Defense 2020a). The JSDF began to dispatch its members overseas in 1991. The total number of *overseas dispatches* within the 30-year period until March 2020 was 55, and the frequency of dispatches during the first decade was once a year. The majority of these dispatches were reportedly based on the United Nations Peacekeeping Operations Act (Nihon Keizai Shimbun 2021).

Over the past two decades, in response to the rise in the incidence of suicide of military members which became apparent in 2000, the JSDF has implemented multiple strategies to maintain its members' mental health under these conditions and has allocated clinical psychologists to perform a range of intervention and prevention activities (Ministry of Defense/Self-Defense Forces 2020), which include the following:

- Expanding its counseling system, such as providing consultations by telephone on a 24-hour basis and allocating clinical psychologists to military bases
- Promoting awareness-raising activities, such as mental health education for commanders and general members
- Setting "mental health promotion periods," instructing supervisors to clarify the emotions of their subordinates who experience environmental changes due to relocations, and distributing various types of reference materials

Since mental health specialists have been focusing on suicide prevention efforts, the number of suicide deaths has changed according to the data published by the Ministry of Defense as demonstrated by the following figures: 2010, 83; 2011, 86; 2012, 83; 2013, 82; 2014, 69; 2015, 73; 2016, 65; 2017, 90; 2018, 62; and 2019, 60 (Ministry of Defense 2021a).

15.3.2 Support for Members Dispatched Overseas and Their Families

Similar to the militaries of other countries, the JSDF also dispatches its members overseas and has adopted a range of strategies including the provision of adequate rest and addressing mental disorders and PTSD (posttraumatic stress disorder) through cooperation among physicians, counselors, and unit chiefs to maintain the mental health of those dispatched overseas.

As part of the Iraq Humanitarian and Reconstruction Assistance Project, which took place from December 2003 to February 2009, mental health care for JSDF members and support for their families were provided at various stages such as in "preparation for dispatch," "reconstruction assistance," and "withdrawal." As a lesson from this experience, the effectiveness of mental health care for JSDF members was reported as follows:

> Mental health care for JSDF members before, during, and after their dispatch is effective to develop overall perspectives on their mental status. In order to provide appropriate counseling for JSDF members with mental problems at appropriate times, it is effective to dispatch these members with counselors. (Ground Staff Office 2008, p. 106)

Some proposals on mental health care emphasize the necessity of allocating several counselors and inserting periods of downtime, as well as "the importance of providing mental health care for families of dispatched JSDF members and examining required measures" (Ground Staff Office 2008, p. 91).

Support measures for families of dispatched service members include securing means of direct contact for the families of members dispatched overseas (such as e-mail and Skype), helping them send additional comfort articles to the members, holding family meetings to provide various types of information, organizing family support centers for the families of dispatched members, and opening web pages for families to manage consultations from them (Ministry of Defense 2020b). The need to provide psychoeducation and other preventative services to family members of dispatched service members has also been recognized in the psychiatric and psychological literature (Tanichi et al. 2019). However, there is no mention in this literature or in any defense reports about the role that social work could play in supporting military members and their families in their daily lives and living environments or in providing support to individual service members and their families through the use of Japanese social welfare legislation and services.

15.3.3 Family Support for Families of Service Members in Domestic Assignments

JSDF established a system to provide family support for members engaged in domestic assignments, rather than overseas deployment, based on the US Army Family Support Program (Ground Staff Office 2008, p. 106). In the aforementioned Iraq Humanitarian and Reconstruction Assistance Project, family support was also evaluated as "effective and necessary measures for the recovery of performance and mental health, including the removal of stressors," while suggesting the standardization of these measures should be "a requirement of long-term dispatches with environments in dispatch destinations taken into consideration" in future JSDF dispatch activities (Ground Staff Office 2008, p. 91).

The peacetime family support activities that the JSDF is promoting for members engaged in domestic assignments include the organization of family support centers and family counseling rooms, with trained members as nonprofessional supporters. Furthermore, the Ground and Maritime SDFs entered into agreements for cooperation to support family members with private organizations represented by JSDF veteran groups and families' associations in 2017 (Japan Ground Self-Defense Force 2017) and 2019 (Japan Maritime Self-Defense Force 2019), respectively. Specifically, these organizations support the families of dispatched JSDF members by providing information regarding caregiving and parenting support and promoting the provision of advice/guidance for married couples of JSDF members with children by providing childcare professionals in temporary daycares in military posts or dispatching childcare professionals.

Similar to the cases of other countries, JSDF members and their families are frequently relocated for work purposes. To support the relocation process, the Ground SDF has created a support guide for each military post. This guide helps JSDF members and their families in moving from other communities to obtain information regarding everyday life in their new communities, specifically information regarding areas surrounding military posts and available social resources to reduce their anxiety about daily life due to relocation. However, as these resources are provided by trained general JSDF members (rather than social workers), the information provided tends to be general (Japan Ground Self-Defense Force 2020).

In summary, while there are programs in existence within the JSDF to respond to suicide and the stressors of deployment and domestic assignments for both the service members and their families, there have been no social workers hired to address these concerns, unlike other foreign militaries. The next section develops future perspectives on MilSW in Japan under such a situation.

15.4 Outlook on the Potential for Development of Military Social Work in the JSDF

As previously mentioned, Japan has no army capable of any offensive force, as Article 9 of the Japanese Constitution declares that the Japanese people forever renounce war (The House of Representatives 1946), and there are no professional MilSW activities in JSDF bases in charge of defenses.

Japan's legal systems related to welfare were developed after World War II to address each life-related challenge, and comprehensive support has been promoted since the 2000s. However, social work in occupational settings, such as the JSDFs' so-called occupational/labor social work, has remained insufficient with methodologies having yet to be established.

Furthermore, the enactment of Japan's Legislation for Peace and Security Military in 2015 seems to have further increased the burdens on JSDF members in the future. Dispatches of emergency security guards to remote areas at the request of other countries, based on the exclusively defense-oriented policy which is one of the tasks additionally assigned by the Cabinet Office, are likely to markedly change JSDF members' regular activities and training.

Once actually dispatched, these guards may use weapons in some internationally sanctioned, high-risk, and potentially life-threatening situations which may increase JSDF members' risk. Therefore, in the future, the JSDF may also need to establish systems of support for physical/psychological issues that JSDF members may face, similar to other countries where military social workers provide such support.

In addition to increasingly being assigned high-risk tasks, there are also concerns about the increased workload on JSDF members that has resulted from decreased personnel levels. In March 2020, the total quota fill rate of the Ground, Air, Maritime SDFs, and General Staff Office was 92.0%, but the rate of members working on-site was reported to be as low as 77.0% (Ministry of Defense/Self-Defense Forces 2021b). Despite efforts to increase the quota fill rate such as raising the upper limit of the enlistment age, extending the retirement age, and increasing the rate of female JSDF members, the JSDF has not yet found fundamental solutions to this issue.

Based on evidence of the value that MilSW brings to systemically supporting and enhancing operational effectiveness and sustainability of a country's military forces as outlined in the chapters of this book, it is the authors' opinion that the development of MilSW in Japan should be strongly considered by the JSDF. To provide more effective support, and improve the quality of life of JSDF members' and their families, the following strategies are recommended to increase the likelihood of MilSW in Japan becoming more of a reality:

- Strategically sharing the value of established systems of international MilSW practices and studies with the JSDF Ministry of Defense, with a view to introducing a pilot program of social workers working with the JSDF. For example, this could include the initial provision of more proactive support to partners and family members who experience challenges associated with the JSDF lifestyle, including the implementation of psychoeducation programs, the development of community support groups, and more formalized social support activities.

- Collaborating with other countries where MilSW has been established in order to develop a culturally appropriate MilSW training course for social workers within the community who are already supporting JSDF members and their families. In addition, an education program for nonprofessionals engaged in support activities within the JSDF could also be considered.
- Stimulating the interest of Japan's social work researchers in this untapped area of research and the possibilities for national and international significance. For example, researchers and practitioners could codevelop programs which could be piloted and evaluated to ascertain outcomes of social work interventions in specific tasks.
- In order for the JSDF to understand the necessity of social work, it is necessary to enhance the function and role of social work in Japan and to further expand the areas of expertise to which social work responds. In addition, the lack of a common understanding of social work's expertise and breadth of roles is an issue that needs to be resolved in order for MilSW to become a reality in Japan.

15.5 Summary

In summary, the JSDF has characteristics different from those of other countries. Therefore, for MilSW to be successfully developed and implemented in Japan, the professional identity must be strengthened. At the same time, it will also be important to analyze the organization of the JSDF to determine where the role of social work would be best placed to achieve positive outcomes for the JSDF, for military members, and for their families. In addition, it is necessary to closely examine the preceding research and practical activities of MilSW in other countries and to construct a unique MilSW model of practice in accordance with the characteristics of the culture and organization of the JSDF and the profession of social work in Japan. As noted by Nakano (2020) based on the results of a study by Dobashi (2020), it may also be necessary to consider "the possibility of military social work in Europe and the United States being ineffective to support the mental health of JSDF members if applied without adjustments."

References

Dobashi K (2020) Risk factors of suicide among U.S. Army soldiers: the Army STARRS project and its review of suicide researches. National Defense Medical J 67(1–2):1–9

Ground Staff Office (2008) History of the reconstruction work in Iraq. Chapter 3. Reconstruction support activities

House of Representatives (2015) Cabinet question No.189-246, from a Member of the House of Representatives: Tomoko Abe: Answers to questions about SDF members' suicide and line of duty death. https://www.shugiin.go.jp/internet/itdb_shitsumon.nsf/html/shitsumon/b189246.htm. Accessed 15 Sept 2021

Japan Ground Self-Defense Force (2017) Central Agreement Signing Ceremony for Cooperation to Support Families of JSDF Members among the Ground SDF, Families' Association, and Veterans. https://www.mod.go.jp/gsdf/news/train/2017/20170526.html. Accessed 1 Sept 2020

Japan Ground Self-Defense Force (2020) Message for the Families of Japan Ground Self-Defense Force personnel. https://www.mod.go.jp/gsdf/family/gsdf_family/. Accessed 1 Sept 2020

Japanese Association of Certified Social Workers (2019) Number of members by prefecture. https://www.jacsw.or.jp/introduction/kokaijoho/shibubetsukaiin.html. Accessed 10 Apr 2021

Japan's Legislation for Peace and Security September 19, 2015. https://www.mofa.go.jp/fp/nsp/page1we_000084.html

Japan Maritime Self-Defense Force (2019) Japan maritime self-defense force mission. https://www.mod.go.jp/msdf/family/img/0806-01.pdf. Accessed 1 Sept 2020

Kawano H (2015) Self-defense forces and family support cultural anthropology of the military. Fukyosha:95–135

Law Concerning the Dispatch of the Japan Disaster Relief Team September 16, 1987 (amended on December 22, 2006). https://www.mofa.go.jp/policy/emergency/assistance1.html

Matsumoto H (1999) Principal social welfare theory. Sangaku Publishing, pp 2–3

Ministry of Defense/Self-Defense Forces (2000) Summary of recommendations regarding the mental health of SDF personnel. https://warp.da.ndl.go.jp/info:ndljp/pid/11591426/www.mod.go.jp/j/approach/agenda/meeting/materials/mental/houkoku/hokoku01.html. Accessed 3 Dec 2021

Ministry of Defense/Self-Defense Forces (2020) Defense of Japan (annual white paper). https://www.mod.go.jp/j/publication/wp/wp2020/html/n41103000.html. Accessed 7 Sept 2021

Ministry of Defense/Self-Defense Forces (2020a) Defense of Japan 2020. https://www.mod.go.jp/j/publication/wp/wp2020/html/ns014000.html. Accessed 1 Sept 2020

Ministry of Defense/Self-Defense Forces (2020b) Defense of Japan 2020. https://www.mod.go.jp/j/publication/wp/wp2020/html/n41103000.html. Accessed 15 Apr 2021

Ministry of Defense/Self-Defense Forces (2021a) Updating the number of suicides of SDF personnel. https://www.mod.go.jp/j/press/news/2020/10/30c.pdf. Accessed 10 Apr 2021

Ministry of Defense/Self-Defense Forces (2021b) Personnel composition of the Ministry of Defense and the Self-Defense Forces. https://www.mod.go.jp/j/profile/mod_sdf/kousei/. Accessed 8 Sept 2021

Nakano K (2020) Consideration of stigma and Japanese shame in military social work. Separate volume general human science 2:51–60

Nihon Keizai Shimbun (2021) 55 JSDF Overseas dispatches in 30 years: PKO ratio declining https://www.nikkei.com/article/DGXZQOUA04E0B0U1A600C2000000/?unlock=1" https://www.nikkei.com/article/DGXZQOUA04E0B0U1A600C2000000/?unlock=1. Accessed 20 Sept 2021

Ohashi K (2005) In search of a theory of social work in Japan. Studies on social work Aikawa Shobo 31(1):4–19

Okamura Shigeo (1956) General comments on social welfare. Shoten, Shibata

Senda K (2015) Focus politics. Weekly Toyo Keizai:110–111

Simura K (2021) Japanese association for social work education, foundations of social work and the profession. Chuo Hoki Publishing Co, pp 166–168

Tanichi M, Nagamine M, Shigemura J, Yamamoto T, Sawamura T, Takahashi Y, Obara A, Saito T, Toda H, Yoshino A, Shimizu K (2019) General psychological distress among Japan Self-Defense Forces personnel dispatched on United Nations peacekeeping operations and their spouses. Psychiatry Clin Neurosci 73(2):77–83. https://doi.org/10.1111/pcn.12806

The House of Representatives (1946) The constitution of Japan Chapter II renunciation of war. https://www.shugiin.go.jp/internet/itdb_english.nsf/html/statics/english/constitution_e.html. Accessed 20 Sept 2021

Chapter 16
Slovakia: The Newest Country to Develop Military Social Work – A Description of the Planning and Development Process

Pavel Czirák

16.1 Historical Review

16.1.1 The Armed Forces of the Slovak Republic

The Armed Forces of the Slovak Republic (AFSR) were established on January 1, 1993, at the same time as the Slovak Republic. Sťahel (2002) states that at the time of establishment, there were 27,000 professional soldiers and 26,000 compulsory service soldiers. In addition to personnel, the AFSR had 995 tanks, 1370 APC (armored personnel carriers) and armored transporters, 1053 artillery systems, 146 combat aircraft, and 19 combat helicopters (Segeš et al. 2007). The ASFR was a conscription force with a focus on territorial defense. For comparison in 2020, the AFSR had 13,140 professional soldiers (Štatistická ročenka personálu OSSR 2020) in its all volunteer Armed Forces, and in 2021, combat equipment included 31 tanks, 95 APC and armored transporters, 63 artillery systems, 12 combat aircraft, and 23 multipurpose helicopters (Ministry of Defense of the Slovak Republic, 2021). Although the numbers of personnel have reduced since the abolition of conscription, issues faced by soldiers requiring social care and support have continued.

P. Czirák (✉)
Human Resources Department, Social Policy Division, Social Analysis Section, Ministry of Defense of the Slovak Republic, Bratislava, Slovakia
e-mail: czirakp@outlook.com

© Springer Nature Switzerland AG 2023
M. A. Forgey, K. Green-Hurdle (eds.), *Military Social Work Around the Globe*,
Military and Veterans Studies, https://doi.org/10.1007/978-3-031-14482-0_16

16.1.2 The Profession of Social Work in Slovakia

Social work as a scientific profession was established in Slovakia in 1989 during a period of important social changes[1] that significantly affected the everyday life of the inhabitants of Slovakia. Over the course of 30 years, social work in the Slovak Republic has developed a relatively successful path to professionalization and standardization of the quality of its performance. This was helped in particular by the systematic education of social workers at several universities, which formally began in Slovakia in 1991, with the opening of the first Department of Social Work at the Faculty of Education, Comenius University in Bratislava. There are presently 11 Slovak universities that have an accredited Department of Social Work. Universities are also among the most important scientific research institutions at which independent research in social work is carried out.

Laws regulating individual areas of their performance relevant to the professionalization of social work include the Social Protection of Children and Social Guardians (Ministry of Labor, Social Affairs and Family of the Slovak Republic, 2005), Social Services (Ministry of Labor, Social Affairs and Family of the Slovak Republic, 2008). A breakthrough milestone was the elaboration and approval of the Act on Social Work (Ministry of Labor, Social Affairs and Family of the Slovak Republic, 2014), which regulates the conditions for the exercise of the profession in the sector of work, social affairs, and family. Important benefits of this professional law include the establishment of the necessary qualification requirements and the establishment of the Slovak Chamber of Social Workers and Social Work Assistants.

To fulfil professional competencies for social work, one must have completed higher education in the field of social work and continue to undertake further education for maintaining, improving, and supplementing the knowledge and skills necessary for the performance of social work.

16.1.3 The Development of the Military Social Work Role in the AFSR

After the establishment of the AFSR in 1993, the areas of what may be considered to be social work tasks were covered mainly by *andragogists*,[2] cultural workers, and psychological and spiritual counselors. These services were focused mainly on the care of soldiers of compulsory service. Following the gradual transition of AFSR to a professionalized voluntary armed forces, these employees were based within personnel management, where they still work until today.

In 2013, a new organizational element of the Ministry of Defense of the Slovak Republic (MDSR) was created outside the structures of the Armed Forces, that is,

---

[1] The transformation of the socialist economy into a market economy and socialism into democracy
[2] Adult educators.

the Human Resources Department. This department develops strategic materials in the field of personnel and social policy of the MDSR, focusing on the social security system of professional soldiers, the care of war veterans and military retirees, and the quality of life of professional soldiers and their families, in particular. Legislation amendments and the creation of this new department created preconditions for sustainable care of professional soldiers and their families to develop (Ministry of Defence of Slovak Republic, White Paper, 2016) and subsequently for the inclusion of social work services to be initially considered as part of a sustainable system of care.

16.2   Factors that Support the Development of Social Care for Professional Soldiers and Their Families

The first step in the direction of establishing Military Social Work (MilSW) was the establishment of a specialization in the form of social services and consulting experts as identified in the Defence of Slovak Republic, White Paper, 2016. In addition, legislative developments and research were also important factors that supported the development of the specialty.

16.2.1   Key Legislative Developments

The military organization provides professional soldiers with binding (mandatory) and nonbinding (optional) care. Binding care is regulated mainly by Act No. 281/2015 on the state service of professional soldiers (Ministry of Defense of the Slovak Republic, 2014), as amended; Act No. 328/2002 on social security for police officers and soldiers, as amended (Ministry of Interior of the Slovak Republic, 2002); and Act No. 463/2003 on war veterans (Ministry of Defense of the Slovak Republic, 2003).

Under the aforementioned legislation, the mandatory care of a professional soldier is divided as follows (Czirák 2018):

1. General care (the basic responsibility of the commander for creating the appropriate conditions to satisfy the cultural, recreational, and physical needs and interests of professional soldiers, to ensure health care, the equipment of workplaces, cooperation with the families of professional soldiers)[3]
2. Health care (military hospital, polyclinics, garrison ambulances)

---

[3] § 120 of Act no. 281/2015 Coll.

3. Preventive rehabilitation (a set of preventive, physical education, sports, and medical measures, which are aimed primarily at strengthening and consolidating the physical and mental health of a professional soldier)[4]
4. Special conditions for the performance of civil service (protective measures for pregnant professional soldiers; professional soldiers, women caring for a child under one year of age; and lone professional soldiers, men who permanently care for a child under eight years of age)[5]
5. Social security (sickness insurance, accident insurance, retirement insurance, and social security services)[6]
6. Caring for war veterans (health care, recreational care, spa care, pension for war veterans)[7]

In addition, nonbinding (optional) care for professional soldiers will be provided in the following areas:

1. Care of families of professional soldiers sent to perform tasks outside the territory of the Slovak Republic
2. Psychological care of professional soldiers
3. Spiritual care of professional soldiers
4. The program for gender mainstreaming in the defense sector
5. Programs for the prevention of socially undesirable phenomena in the defense sector, that is, crime, extremism and radicalism, mobbing, corrupt practices, alcoholism, and other manifestations of substance misuse

This legislation is an integral background to appropriate support services being developed.

16.2.2 Research Support for the Need for Military Social Work (MilSW)

Regular research among professional soldiers makes it possible to find out their views on current social and occupational issues. This research shows that the care of professional soldiers and their families is one of the most important sources of satisfaction of professional soldiers, in addition to satisfaction with the financial reward of the work of a professional soldier (Czirák 2018).

---

[4] § 126 of Act no. 281/2015 Coll.
[5] § 128 of Act no. 281/2015 Coll.
[6] Act No. 328/2002 Coll.
[7] Act No. 463/2003.

There has been a shift in the care of families, as well as in matters of social assistance[8] to soldiers themselves, and this area is gaining importance in the whole spectrum of quality of life of professional soldiers (Matis, 2016). The year 2021 can be considered a turning point, when the Minister of Defense of the Slovak Republic approved the "System of care for professional soldiers and their families." On the basis of this document, for the first time in 2022, funds were set aside for the harmonization of work and family life, such as day camps for the children of professional soldiers. In 2022, the Ministry of Defense launched a new field social work project for war veterans in cooperation with the NGO Czechoslovak Legionary Community (Československá obec legionářská) on the basis of this document. In the long term, it will be possible to identify through empirical research the needs of professional soldiers for the provision of social assistance services, such as the following:

- Support and assistance required in their arrival in the new unit. This may include assistance in finding housing, employment for family members, and schools for children.
- Military career planning. Greater empirical understanding of the issues will result in better knowledge of one's career in the short- and medium term and subsequently greater stability in the place of service.
- Assistance in leaving the AFSR in the transition from military role to the civilian labor market. Professional soldiers have also shown interest in the possibility of retraining, and this will be an important consideration in the transition process.
- Gaining vocational training in the transition to the labor market. It is understood that professional soldiers would welcome the introduction of measures to promote the reconciliation of work and family life, which would include forms of care for dependent children, such as the construction of kindergartens (children's corners) or the organization of day camps for children.

Looking to the future, a deeper understanding of these issues will enable social workers and researchers to ensure that services are tailored to meet the emerging and current needs of soldiers and their families across the course of their military career.

---

[8] Social assistance according to Act No. 195/1998 Coll. aims to alleviate or overcome, with the active participation of the citizen, social deprivation; to prevent the causes of the occurrence, deepening, or recurrence of disorders of mental development, physical development, and social development of the citizen; and to ensure the integration of the citizen into society. It is implemented in the form of social prevention, social counseling, and social services.

16.3   Rationale for the Development of Military Social Work (MilSW)

Nowadays, personnel management focuses mainly on personnel administration tasks.[9] However, it is the author's opinion that it lacks a pillar that focuses on the quality of life of professional soldiers, and it is suggested that this quality of life pillar could be established through the development of MilSW. This idea is also a part of the Manifesto of the Government of the Slovak Republic for 2020–2024 (Government of the Slovak Republic, 2020).

The introduction of the social care (or MilSW) for professional soldiers is based on the awareness that a number of their personal problems arise in direct connection with their work, that is, with the performance of military service in the AFSR for the benefit of the state. Human worries and problems (and the resulting stress and tension) may stem from military service and can relate to job security, level of remuneration, satisfaction with caring for an employee (professional soldier), health, and relationships with other people. Due to the nature of the civil service, professional soldiers' personal problems may sometimes be solved by addressing the conditions for carrying out work, for example, the granting of leave or leave to care for children, parents, or a sick household member, or advice on how to solve a problem so as to minimize its impact on the workplace.

Černáková and Čukan (2019) suggest that the key aims of establishing a system of MilSW, including the expected benefits of its implementation for the military organization, would be the impact on the stabilization of performance and efficiency of the military force and military personnel.

According to Martinská and Matis (2011), social work in the military organization can be defined as specific services aimed at solving the problems arising from factors such as the following:

- Unique culture of the military leadership and management of a military organization and leadership of soldiers
- Special type of communication (orders and regulations, command technique) in combat
- Special social structure, organizational climate, and also social mobility
- Impact of the service on the individual and on social behavior (combat and training)
- Hierarchical system of superiority and subordination and its social impacts
- Social and psychological aspects of service and combat conflicts
- Consolidation of the military family
- Care of members during and after active service

---

[9] Creation of personnel materials, issuing of decisions, licenses, confirmations, creation of normative acts (SOP), elaboration of plans, requirements for selection, rotation and fulfillment of personnel and their evaluation, management and statistics, and others General Staff of the Armed Forces of the Slovak Republic (2008)

Empirical research carried out in the defense sector has also shown that there is considerable interest among professional soldiers in the provision of services for the care of soldiers and their families, and at the same time, they consider the current situation to be very unsatisfactory (Czirák 2018). Existing care programs cover mainly psychological care during the deployment and return phase of professional soldiers in international crisis management operations.

Some of the military service and lifestyle difficulties that will be addressed include transition to a new military base, sending a professional soldier to perform tasks outside the territory of the Slovak Republic, return of a professional soldier from the performance of tasks outside the territory of the Slovak Republic, deployment of professional soldiers to military education and training, leaving a military career, and life after the end of a military career.

Military social work is a young and exciting developing scientific discipline within the AFSR. Its establishment will assist commanders with personnel management by providing professional soldiers with social work support to manage difficulties that may arise in relation to military service. It will be important, however, for the command corps to see MilSW as an integral element of personnel management which aims to keep their military unit combatable. AFSR has been building MilSW work from the ground up, although it follows a rich tradition of providing services for the benefit of soldiers.[10]

16.4 Care Programs for Professional Soldiers and Their Families

The direction of care for professional soldiers and their families will be organized into three program areas as the following:

1. *Individual care for professional soldiers* which involves supporting the adaptation of professional soldiers and their families to the new environment when they arrive at the new military base, supporting professional soldiers after returning from tasks outside the territory of the Slovak Republic, and supporting professional soldiers before the end of their military career
2. *The care program for families of professional soldiers* which includes care for the families of professional soldiers sent to perform tasks outside the territory of the Slovak Republic, support for the harmonization of family and work life, and support for the community way of life of professional soldiers and their families

---

[10] We are thinking in particular of the organizational structures for education and culture (andragogists, cultural workers), who did social support, especially for soldiers of compulsory service until 2005, and the organizational structures of the quality of life of personnel management, which were devoted to the care of professional soldiers and their families until 2009 (but they were still not social workers).

3. *The program of care for war veterans and retirees* which includes building community centers with social and health services and providing guesthouse accommodation for war veterans.

In addition to defining the needs, content, and scope of care programs, the introduction of a systemic approach to the care of professional soldiers and their families requires the establishment of mechanisms for their application in practice. These mechanisms are intended to ensure the professionalization and centralization of support activities and services for professional soldiers and their families, which will help them to overcome the socially unfavorable and stressful situations arising during their military career.

16.5 Plan for the Implementation of Military Social Work (MilSW)

The entire system of care for professional soldiers and their families will be provided and managed by the expert in social services and counseling, that is, a MilSW professional, with the exception of specialized programs under the auspices of the psychological, medical, and spiritual services. Caring for professional soldiers and their families will be a part of a comprehensive system of social services and counseling.

The functions of experts in social services and counseling will be established at battalion level (and their equivalents) for civil servants and from the level of the brigade for professional soldiers. All employees and professional soldiers in these functions will undergo a modular training course at the Academy of the Armed Forces gen. M. R. Štefánik in Liptovský Mikuláš (military academy), where they will gain knowledge with relevant legislation and from the military environment. The education process will use methods that should bring them closer to the real situations they may encounter in their future practice and provide them with practical procedures for how they can be addressed.

The centralization of care programs and their transition to a new entity with professional competence will ensure the streamlining of the entire system of care for professional soldiers and their families. When providing care programs, the expert for social services and counseling will also use and develop cooperation with representatives of regional self-government and public administration, as well as with nongovernment organizations with a professional relationship with AFSR. It is anticipated that the implementation process will involve working more closely with nongovernmental organizations to ensure that the legitimate interests and needs of professional soldiers are considered and working collaboratively to improve the conditions of state service, health, and social and cultural conditions, including conditions for the use of leisure time.

The Ministry of Defense is preparing conceptual material for the management of MilSW including establishing a further set of education requirements for military social workers and developing a pilot project in selected military units, where these care programs will be tested. The implementation of MilSW in the AFSR will be broadly focused on the development of the following areas: monitoring of social processes in military units and proposals for measures to the commander, provision of counseling services and care programs, and culture and education management.

In the initial implementation period in late 2022, the broad and important main tasks for MilSW will be to identify processes within military bases that may have socially adverse effects on professional soldiers and their families, identify risk groups of professional soldiers, implement a social welfare program, and convince commanders of the benefits and importance of MilSW for the sustainability and development of their military units in the context of other support services, such as psychological and spiritual service.

In the next phase, emphasis will be placed on increasing the professionalism of the staff, with an emphasis on the pursuit of social work as a regulated profession and on optimizing what will be required to establish MilSW practice.

16.6   Conclusion

The vocation of an AFSR professional soldier demands a high degree of self-discipline, mental and physical endurance and fitness, and physical and mental vitality. Optimal mental condition of the individual soldier is reflective of the level of cognitive abilities, specifically the quality of thinking and responses that are required to adapt to each situation when performing complex tasks in challenging circumstances.

The introduction of social care programs and the services of military social workers with professional soldiers is based on the awareness that personal and professional issues may impact military service performance within the AFSR, which in turn may impact on military capability and stability. Subsequently, the primary goal of the introduction of MilSW is to build and stabilize performance and efficiency of the network of professional personnel. It is expected that the implementation of MilSW in the ASFR in 2022 will ultimately help the military organization to address the soldiers' challenges through the use of targeted and planned strategies.

The Armed Forces await the exciting process of establishing a new executive element that will support the combat potential of military units and show the human side of caring for professional soldiers and their families during and after their military careers. Successful establishment of MilSW in the AFSR will be an important example of good practice in the field of employee care and also an inspiration for public administration or the commercial sphere. The establishment of MilSW in Slovakia will be a significant milestone not just for nation but also for the current and emerging international MilSW community.

References

Černáková D, Čukan K (2019) Starostlivosť o profesionálnych vojakov a ich rodiny v kontexte manažmentu vojenského personálu (Care of military professionals and their families in context of military personnel management). In: Belan L, Petrufová M, Kmošena M, Martinská M, Nagyová L, Revajová E (eds) Human resources management in the armed forces, security and rescue corps. The International Scientific Conference, Liptovský Mikuláš, May 2019. edn. Akadémia ozbrojených síl generála Milana Rastislava Štefánika, p 64–75. http://www.aos.sk/struktura/katedry/ksvj/dokum/zborniky/konf2019.pdf. Accessed 15 Aug 2020

Czirák P (2018) Vplyv úrovne starostlivosti o profesionálnych vojakov a ich rodiny na stabilitu vojenského personálu (The Impact of the level of care for professional troops and their families on the stability of military personnel). In: Matis J, Nagyová L (eds) Aktuálne otázky regrutácie a stabilizácie personálu v ozbrojených silách, bezpečnostných a záchranných zboroch Medzinárodná vedecká konferencia: Liptovský Mikuláš, May 2018. edn. Akadémia ozbrojených síl gen, M. R. Štefánika Liptovský Mikuláš, p 64–81. http://www.aos.sk/struktura/katedry/ksvj/dokum/zborniky/konf2018.pdf. Accessed 15 Aug 2020

General Staff of the Armed Forces of the Slovak Republic [GS AFSR] (2008) Doctrine of Personnel Management of the Armed Forces of the Slovak Republic - SVD 10 (B) Internal material, edn. GS AFSR, Bratislava

Government of the Slovak Republic [GSR] (2020) Programové vyhlásenie vlády Slovenskej republiky na obdobie rokov 2020–2024 (Manifesto of the Government of the Slovak Republic for 2020 to 2024). https://www.nrsr.sk/web/Dynamic/DocumentPreview.aspx?DocID=494677. Accessed 25 Aug 2021

Martinská M, Matis J (2011) Rodovo orientovaná sociálna práca vo vojenskej organizácii (Gender - oriented social work in a military organization). edn. Akadémia ozbrojených síl gen, M. R. Štefánika, Liptovský Mikuláš

Matis J (2016) Soldiers and their families in the Slovak Republic: a report on quality of functioning from the empirical perspective. Curr Issues Pers Psychol 4(2):118–124. https://doi.org/10.5114/cipp.2016.60099. Available via https://www.termedia.pl/Soldiers-and-their-families-in-the-Slovak-Republic-a-report-on-quality-of-functioning-from-the-empirical-perspective,75,27640,0,1.html. Accessed 24 June 2021

Ministry of Interior of the Slovak Republic [MISR] (2002) Zákon č. 328/2002 Z. z. o sociálnom zabezpečení policajtov a vojakov (Act no. 328/2002 Coll. on social security for police officers and soldiers)

Ministry of Defense of the Slovak Republic [MDSR] (2003) Zákon č. 463/2003 Z. z. o vojnových veteránoch (Act no. 463/2003 Coll. on war veterans)

Ministry of Labor, Social Affairs and Family of the Slovak Republic [MLSAFSR] (2005) Zákon č. 305/2005 Z. z. o sociálnoprávnej ochrane detí a o sociálnej kuratele (Act no. 305/2005 Coll. on the social legal protection of children and on social guardianship)

Ministry of Defense of the Slovak Republic [MDSR] (2014) Zákon č. 281/2015 Z. z. o štátnej službe profesionálnych vojakov (Act no. 281/2015 Coll. on the state service of professional soldiers)

Ministry of Defense of the Slovak Republic [MDSR] (2016) White Paper on Defence of the Slovak Republic. https://www.mod.gov.sk/data/WPDSR2016_LQ.pdf. Accessed 25 Aug 2021

Ministry of Defense of the Slovak Republic [MDSR] (2021) Celkové početné stavy vojakov a zamestnancov a počty hlavných druhov vojenských zbraní, vojenských zbraňových systémov a bojovej techniky v Ozbrojených silách Slovenskej republiky v súlade s potrebami zabezpečenia obrany Slovenskej republiky a bezpečnosti štátu a v súlade s medzinárodnými zmluvami, ktorými je Slovenská republika viazaná a rozmiestnenie zväzkov, útvarov, úradov a zariadení Ozbrojených síl Slovenskej republiky k 31. Decembru 2021. (Total number of soldiers and personnel and numbers of main types of military weapons, military weapons systems and combat equipment in the Armed Forces of the Slovak Republic in accordance with the needs of defense security of the Slovak Republic and state security and in accordance with international treaties by which the Slovak Republic is bound and deployment of unions, units, offices and establishment of the Armed Forces of the Slovak Republic as of 31 December 2021). https://rokovania. gov.sk/RVL/Material/25601/1. Accessed 12 Oct 2021

Ministry of Labor, Social Affairs and Family of the Slovak Republic [MLSAFSR] (1998) Zákon č. 195/1998 Z. z. o sociálnej pomoci (Act no. 195/1998 Coll. on social assistance)

Ministry of Labor, Social Affairs and Family of the Slovak Republic [MLSAFSR] (2008) Zákon č. 448/2008 Z. z. o sociálnych službách (Act no. 448/2008 Coll. on social services)

Ministry of Labor, Social Affairs and Family of the Slovak Republic [MLSAFSR] (2014) Zákon č. 219/2014 Z. z. o sociálnej práci a odborných činností v oblasti sociálnych vecí a rodiny (Act no. 219/2014 Coll. on social work and professional activities in the field of social affairs and the family)

Personálny úrad ozbrojených síl SR (2021) Štatistická ročenka personálu OS SR 2020 (Statistical yearbook of personnel of AFSR 2020). Liptovský Mikuláš. https://personal.mil.sk/data/ att/95956_subor.pdf. Accessed 12 Oct 2021

Segeš V, Baka I, Cséfalvay F, Čaplovič M, Dangl V, Maskalík A, Purdek I, Štaigl J, Štefanský M (2007) Slovensko Vojenská kronika (Slovakia Military Chronicle) edn. Perfekt, Bratislava

Sťahel R (2002) Reforma zvýšila prestíž Ozbrojených síl SR (The reform increased the prestige of the Armed Forces of the Slovak Republic). Hospodárske noviny. https://dennik.hnonline. sk/servisne-prilohy/23041-reforma-zvysila-prestiz-ozbrojenych-sil-sr. Accessed 7 Sept 2020

Chapter 17
The Status of Military Social Work in Ukraine: Current Efforts to Develop This Role and the Obstacles Encountered[1]

Nataliia Gusak

17.1 The Status of Military Social Work in Ukraine: Current Efforts to Develop This Role and the Obstacles Encountered

The armed conflict in Eastern Ukraine has been ongoing since 2014 and reveals systematic gaps in professional support of active-duty service members, veterans, and their families. The Ukrainian government refers to the conflict as aggression by Russia against Ukraine, and it is officially called Anti-Terrorist Operation (ATO)/ Joint Forces Operation (JFO) by the Ukrainian government.

Prior to 2014, Ukraine had not been involved in military conflicts since the end of World War II, except for taking part in the Soviet military operation in Afghanistan in 1979–1989 as a part of the Soviet Union (Sklokina 2015). There also had not been internal conflicts on the Ukrainian territory in the last few decades, and therefore public services, as well as specialists, were not ready to deal with the provision of social support to active-duty servicemen, veterans, and their families in the country.

Semigina and Gusak (2015) highlight that the aggression by Russia in 2014, and resulting conflict, has raised issues for Ukraine in terms of welfare policy, social services, and the responsibilities and the level of professionalism of those delivering these services. Volunteers with or without relevant education and training became the first-line responders involved in services provision to war-affected populations. Most volunteers were not trained in methods of working with mental health, substance

---

[1] This chapter was written prior to the Russian invasion of Ukraine in February 2022.

N. Gusak (✉)
School of Social Work, National University of Kyiv-Mohyla Academy, Kyiv, Ukraine
e-mail: gusakny@ukma.edu.ua

© Springer Nature Switzerland AG 2023
M. A. Forgey, K. Green-Hurdle (eds.), *Military Social Work Around the Globe*,
Military and Veterans Studies, https://doi.org/10.1007/978-3-031-14482-0_17

abuse problems, trauma, disability, or family conflicts and knew nothing about the military culture, occupational therapy, or veterans' transition to civilian life.

In Ukraine, there are no professional social workers officially employed in the military and the Armed Forces, and the Ministry of Veterans Affairs (established in 2018) does not oversee issues related to military social work (MilSW) practice. To fill this gap in national policy and governmental services, numerous social workers are employed in nongovernmental organizations and have been providing different services to servicemen, veterans, and their family members since 2014.

This chapter presents the prerequisites for MilSW development in Ukraine and the prerequisites for future directions to address the needs of active-duty service members, veterans, and their families.

17.2 Active-Duty Service Members and Veterans' Needs

17.2.1 Active-Duty Service Members

In this chapter, active-duty service members are defined as citizens of Ukraine who perform active military service in the Armed Forces of Ukraine and other troops in accordance with Ukrainian legislation.

After the collapse of the Soviet Union, Ukraine inherited one of the largest armies in Europe, about 780,000 troops. However, due to the economic crisis and military reform at the beginning of 2013, the Ukrainian military had downsized compared to its Soviet predecessor, comprising 184,000 soldiers (Kiryukhin 2018). In 2014, the Ukrainian army began to recover from a state of complete degradation that followed the Soviet collapse. Now there are 361,313 (1% of the total population) active-duty service members in Ukraine. According to the national legislation, up to 215,000 of them are employed by the Armed Forces (On Number of the Armed Forces of Ukraine 2015), 60,000 by the National Guard (On The National Guard of Ukraine 2014), 52,000 by the State Border Service (On the State Border Service 2003), 27,000 by the Security Service (On General Structure and Number of the Security Service of Ukraine 2006), 4010 by the Intelligence Service (On the Foreign Intelligence Service of Ukraine 2006), 2694 by the State Protection Department (On General Structure and Number of the Department of State Protection of Ukraine 2006), and 6095 by the State Service for Special Communications and Information Protection (On Total Number of the State Service for Special Communications and Information Protection of Ukraine 2016). The real number of active-duty service members in Ukraine, however, may vary.

As of September 2020, there were 398,491 officially employed service members in Eastern Ukraine, and more than 7000 of them were servicewomen (Martsenyuk et al. 2019). Also, there were paramilitary troops who volunteered to fight in the armed conflict without official enlistment in the military (the so-called dobrovolci). Paralysis and failure of the state to prevent the annexation of Crimea by the Russian Federation in 2013 encouraged volunteer mobilization to protect Ukrainian sovereignty. These were highly motivated "patriots" who left their jobs and families to defend Ukrainian territorial sovereignty. *Dobrovolci* were not assigned to the Armed Forces of Ukraine, the Ministry of Internal Affairs of Ukraine, the National Guard of Ukraine, and other military forces nor law enforcement agencies established under the laws of Ukraine (Kulak 2016). They had almost complete freedom to do what they wanted to do in the early stages of the conflict. The government both encouraged them and also punished them for war crimes if necessary. Starting from 2015, the state was effectively competing for volunteers and recruited them to the National Guard. Some of them were integrated into "special police battalions" and continued to serve in the police forces after returning home (Käihkö 2018).

Existing research data on active-duty service members and their families' needs remains limited. Recent studies mainly explore service members' mental health and their needs following discharge. According to Pinchuk et al. (2017), 941 combatant servicemen were admitted to psychiatric hospitals in 2015 due to mental disorders caused by severe stress reaction and adjustment disorders (AD); 70.9% suffered from posttraumatic stress disorder (PTSD), 21.5% from short depression episodes, and 4.8% from an acute stress reaction. One hundred percent of servicemen with PTSD participated in combat operations and 51.5% with AD (Pinchuk et al. 2017). Suicidal ideations included 19.6% persons with PTSD and 20.6% with AD (Pinchuk et al. 2017). The results of deaths by suicide analysis showed that the main suicide mode was gunshot at 61%, while 46% servicemen at the moment of suicidal attempt were intoxicated with alcohol or drugs (Pinchuk et al. 2017). Additionally, the Armed Forces reported that from 2015 to April 2018, around 550 ATO combatants have died by suicide.

Tackling the mental health needs in the broader scope including employment, benefits, and self-fulfillment are important prerequisites for service members following discharge. Martsenyuk et al. (2019) highlight specific needs of servicewomen for a peaceful life, including high-quality medical and social services, decent employment, respectful attitude from the society, and official recognition of combatant status.

17.2.2 Veterans

In this chapter, we define veterans as those who served in active military services and who were discharged or released under a condition other than dishonorable.

The number of veterans is much higher than the number of active-duty personnel; currently, there are around 1.2 million veterans which is almost 4% of the total population (The Legal Hundred 2018). However, according to the national legislation, there are 21 groups of persons with veteran status in Ukraine, and not all of them have been served in the military. The first cluster includes 847,882 veterans of war, 427,046 combatants, 111,768 persons with disabilities due to war, and 436,068 war participants. The second includes people with special status: 161,302 family members of the war victims, 433 participants of the Revolution of Dignity, 21,000 persons with disabilities resulting from the liquidation of the consequences of the 1986 Chernobyl nuclear plant disaster, and volunteers. The third cluster includes 191,335 persons who have served in the military for more than 25 years, persons fighting for the independence of Ukraine in the twentieth century, and labor veterans (The Legal Hundred 2018). Meanwhile, the Ministry of Veterans Affairs of Ukraine (2020) officially recognize only war veterans and their family members.

The number of studies on veterans' needs is steadily increasing since 2014 when the armed conflict started. However, the most recent research covers only those 370,000 veterans who participated in the 2014 conflict and focused on employment and stigmatization (Martsenyuk and Kvit 2019).

A number of studies emphasize employment as veterans' core need associated with successful reintegration into peaceful life. Martsenyuk et al. (2019) highlighted that decent employment is often related to financial sustainability, self-realization, and meaningful contribution to society's development. Meanwhile, every fifth veteran has money to buy only food and links unemployment to injuries or illnesses sustained during military services (International Organization for Migration 2020). The same study reported that one-third of the men and almost half of the women veterans who had a job before military service returned home to find that they were no longer employed at their previous place of work, due to employers not expected to hold the job open until the return of the military member.

While many veterans eventually found paid jobs (67%), started their own business, or registered as private entrepreneurs (11%), others cited a need for retraining and support in finding income opportunities. It seems difficult for some of them to find a new job due to stigmatization because of their mental health and behavior issues. Meanwhile, only every third veteran would like to receive psychosocial support (International Organization for Migration 2020).

Some studies highlighted that veterans felt they were excluded from society, while having a strong sense of self-identification with their reference group, and almost half of them experienced discrimination or biased treatment at least once (International Organization for Migration 2020). However, the public opinion survey results show that a positive attitude toward veterans predominates (Kvit and Martsenyuk 2020), and Ukrainians have higher trust in veterans than in the Armed Forces or even in the president (Sociological Group Rating 2019). Some studies also stress that people think that ATO/JFO veterans are heroes and patriots (InfoSapiens 2019).

Very few publications are devoted to veterans with disabilities. It is estimated that at least 5500 former combatants now have a disability. Nevertheless, the data on their status and needs remains limited.

17.3 Governmental, Civil Society, and International Organizations' Response

17.3.1 Governmental Benefits

Ukraine inherited a post-Soviet system of benefits for active-duty service members, veterans, and their families. So far, about 36 benefits are mentioned in Ukrainian legislation and financed by the government.

According to the Law of Ukraine "On Social and Legal Protection of Servicemen and their Families (1992)," servicemen and their family members are entitled to different social benefits covering annual financial aid for recreation and living arrangements, free housing from the state, uniforms and other service-related materials, paid annual leave, financial aid for relocation, free lunches in working days, free medical aid in medical facilities for military, annual recreation in facilities for military, free education in higher education institutions, and retirement benefits.

The Law of Ukraine "On Status of War Veterans, Guarantees of Their Social Protection (1993)" guarantees war veterans' coverage of different social benefits, priority provision of housing land plots, loans for housing construction, discounts on payments for housing and utility services, free public transport, and provision of various health-care services.

The most popular among beneficiaries are free travel in public transport and reduced ticket price for railway, air, and other travel, priority land allocation (right to obtain 10 acres of land for personal needs), and subsidies for rent and utilities (Organization for Security Cooperation in Europe 2016). Around 71–89% of veterans are satisfied with these benefits. However, there are several challenges they meet in the labor market, in health care, in social protection institutions, and in everyday life to obtain other state benefits. According to the International Organization for Migration study (2020), veterans have limited access to priority housing, long-term educational loans, and free legal service.

At the beginning of the armed conflict, it became obvious that the current needs of active-duty service members, veterans, and their families cannot be covered by the existing efforts, especially in a "closed" military system with its specific cultural context (Bulakh et al. 2017). Governmental organizations were not ready to react immediately, and the vacuum was partly filled by the new government bodies established on the national level. In addition to the Ministry of Veterans Affairs, the Ministries for Temporarily Occupied Territories and Internally Displaced Persons was established shortly after the beginning of the conflict. But despite these efforts, there are 33 committees in different ministries at the national level overseeing the implementation of over 30 policies on reintegration; it remains a big challenge to fill the services gap by implementing various projects and programs (International Alert 2019).

17.3.2 Nongovernmental Services

A crucial role in conflict response was allotted to international and intergovernmental agencies. The United Nations Development Programme (UNDP), the North Atlantic Treaty Organization (NATO), the Liaison Office, the Organization for Security Co-operation in Europe (OSCE), and others have implemented initiatives aimed at supporting service personnel directly, including both long-term initiatives for service personnel and more recent initiatives focusing specifically on veterans, as well as former service personnel more broadly (International Alert 2019).

At the beginning of the conflict, numerous people organized themselves to protect Ukraine, including newly established groups of combatants (*dobrovolci* that were not employed as active-duty service members), doctors and nurses, psychologists, chaplains, cooks, etc. They created an independent network to protect the country, while state military and other governmental structures were not able to react immediately when the armed conflict started (Bulakh et al. 2017). Due to the armed conflict, a mass volunteer movement was born to defend the country and its defenders. In 2014–2015, an unprecedented number of self-organized combatants (*dobrovolci*) took part in the war instead of, or together with, active-duty service members. Later, most of them were officially employed by the military. As of 2019, volunteers have registered in almost 1000 nongovernment organizations since the beginning of the conflict to support combatants, veterans, and their family members (Martsenyuk and Kvit 2019).

In line with volunteers, veterans have developed peer-to-peer networks and nongovernmental organizations in order to support each other. This armed conflict also "challenged the very existence of the transnational identity of the former Soviet-Afghan War veteran," as the majority of veterans in the Russian Federation and Ukraine took opposite sides in this conflict (Sklokina 2015). As of 2019, there have been 55 all-Ukrainian organizations of ATO/JFO veterans that are working together for the creation of a coherent narrative of a continuous Ukrainian national struggle for freedom and peer-to-peer support (Kvit and Martsenyuk 2020).

To date, there are three main areas covered by different service providers who focus on veterans: (1) mental health and psychosocial support, (2) employment, and (3) peer-to-peer support.

17.3.2.1 Mental Health and Psychosocial Support

Mental health and psychosocial supports are implemented by several projects and service providers to reduce the severity of common mental health problems, such as depression, post-traumatic stress, impaired functioning, anxiety, and substance use problems. An intervention known as "Common Elements Treatment Approach" has been tested and implemented (Murray et al. 2018). There are also mobile teams delivering psychosocial support for veterans and their family members that include social workers (UNFPA 2020), with national and professional suicide prevention and mental health support helplines having been established (Lifeline Ukraine

2021). Several projects provide training for mental health professionals and volunteers who work with service members, veterans, and their families.

17.3.2.2 Employment

Programs and projects supporting veterans' employment and vocational training provide training on employment skills, advocate for private and public sector employees to hire veterans, and facilitate the hiring of veterans. Currently, about 20 of the 55 all-Ukrainian initiatives provide such services at the local level in different areas including security, cybersecurity, information technologies, social entrepreneurship, and psychosocial support.

17.3.2.3 Peer-to-Peer Support

Almost all of 55 all-Ukrainian organizations of veterans provide peer-to-peer support through their networks. Some of them encourage veterans' representation in policy at the national and local levels to support each other and advocate for the veterans' rights (Kvit and Martsenyuk 2020). However, the current programs are not systematically coordinated, and the risks of duplication are high. Thus, comprehensive analysis, monitoring plan, planning, and staff training should be completed before implementing reintegration policies and programs (International Alert 2019).

17.4 Prerequisites for Military Social Work Establishment in Ukraine

Social work by itself is a new profession that has existed in Ukraine for only around 30 years. It was established as an academic discipline in 1990, with the support from a range of international projects, universities, and nongovernmental organizations, including from the United Kingdom, Germany, Portugal, Belgium, the US, and Canada (Boiko and Kabachenko 2016). So far, the process of social work professionalization in Ukraine is still ongoing, based on Weiss-Gal and Welbourne's (2008) indicators that include (1) public recognition of professional status, (2) professional monopoly over specific types of work, (3) professional autonomy of action, (4) possession of a distinctive knowledge base, (5) professional education regulated by members of the profession, (6) an effective professional organization, (7) codified ethical standards, and (8) prestige and remuneration reflecting professional standing (Semigina and Boiko 2014).

The armed conflict revealed a pervasive misunderstanding about the role of social work. Many other professionals, including army workers, see the role of social workers merely as carers or social inspectors responsible for social benefits. For instance, in an article by Bespalko and Shumeiko (2019), military personnel described potential tasks for social workers within the military as the following:

- "Protection of social norms and guarantees of military personnel following existing legislation
- Implementation of measures to reduce the social tension of military collectives
- Research of social processes in military collectives
- Creation of prerequisites for the formation and maintenance of high combat activity of personnel
- Adaptation of military personnel to changing conditions, work with families of military personnel"

The contextual paradox is that although there is no established precise definition of MilSW either among academics and practitioners or in the Ukrainian legislation, a semblance of MilSW has been practiced in various settings in the country during the recent 6 years, with the main focus on veterans. However, existing practice is still developing and has not been institutionalized as MilSW.

Considering the development of uniformed or civilian MilSW, the latter is already semiorganized as social work practice with veterans and families, but practice with active-duty personnel by uniformed or civilian social workers has not been introduced. Numerous nongovernmental organizations in Ukraine provide services to veterans and their families to support them within civilian life. As mentioned already, these services combine psychosocial support, peer-to-peer-support, and employment to reintegrate veterans into civilian life. Accordingly, almost all service providers include psychosocial support in their programs. In line with evidence-based interventions specifically adopted and implemented in Ukraine for veterans (i.e., Common Elements Treatment Approach (CETA), cognitive behavior therapy (CBT), narrative therapy, first psychological aid for the vulnerable population (i.e., WHO Mental Health Gap Action Programme (mhGAP), problem management plus (PM+), and resilience- and strength-based approaches, there is a potential to strengthen social work with active-duty personnel and their families. Social workers could employ existing evidence-based interventions, since many of them are already trained in it and have unique experience in providing such services in their practice. Thus, there are specific roles that could be covered by social workers including case management, assisting with obtaining social benefits, providing individual and family psychotherapy and psychological support, preventing and supporting those impacted by intimate partner violence and/or substance abuse, and assisting with employment and reintegration of veterans, as well as community development to prevent stigma and discrimination.

Meanwhile, uniformed social work needs more professional discussion and consultations with key stakeholders in the military sector. A major challenge is the education and training of military social workers. Currently, around 80 higher education institutions in Ukraine teach social work generalists without any specializations, such as community social work, child and school social work, clinical work, or MilSW. On the one hand, it helps social workers to employ relevant knowledge from multiple disciplines and be flexible in resolving diverse potential issues related to war-affected populations at different levels (Williams 2016). On the other hand, social work as a profession has been underestimated in such well-developed areas of practice such as health, military, or even psychotherapy. For example, governmental military structures do not recognize social workers as qualified professionals, since there are no special educational programs for them or professional organizations to advocate for them. Furthermore, no higher educational institution is currently teaching MilSW, even though numerous social workers in nongovernmental organizations provide services for active-duty service members, veterans, and their families. One course in MilSW will be introduced by the School of Social Work at the National University of Kyiv-Mohyla Academy for the master's students in the 2021/2022 academic year. It covers mostly topics related to the military culture, ethics, active-duty service members, veterans, and their family needs, evidence-based interventions, benefits, and service provision. Also, numerous trainings have been provided by international and national organizations and projects that focused on employment, psychological aid, resilience, and working with trauma. These trainings need to be integrated into the official curricula. According to Trubavina et al. (2021), the core themes in the curricula should cover digital tools for teaching social work, theoretical foundations of social work with servicemen and their families, and practice of social work with servicemen and their families in the community.

17.5   Conclusion

Military social work is still not developed in Ukraine, and social worker's professional competency and areas of practice are still misunderstood. In addition, there is a gap between social work education and practice, as social work generalists are not trained to provide services within the military. The only trainings that exists are provided by nongovernmental organizations and address services to veterans.

Priority steps are needed to develop MilSW in Ukraine, including the identification of roles and tasks that social workers can perform within the military and the creation of specialized education and training in MilSW. Additionally, meetings with military representatives to provide evidence about the role of MilSW would be beneficial for recognizing the potential of the social work profession within the military.

References

Bespalko A, Shumeiko A (2019) Bases of military-social work in the Ukraine Armed Forces and the world leading countries army. Bulletin of Taras Shevchenko National Uni Kyiv, Soc Work 1(5):6–10. https://doi.org/10.17721/2616-7786.2019/5-1/1

Boiko O, Kabachenko N (2016) Social work formation in Ukraine. Int J Transf Soc Pol Pract 1:35–40

Bulakh A, Senkiv G, Teperik D (2017) First on the front lines—the role of volunteers in countering Russia's military aggression against Ukraine. Report. Tallinn, Estonia. Available via International Centre for Defence and Security. https://icds.ee/wp-content/uploads/2018/ICDS_report_First_on_the_front_lines_ukraine.pdf. Accessed 21 Mar 2021

InfoSapiens (2019) Doslidzhennia vrazlyvykh group (Study on vulnerable population groups). https://sapiens.com.ua/ua/publication-single-page?id=101#. Accessed 5 Mar 2021

International Alert (2019) Policy Brief March 2019, What's next for veterans in Ukraine? Promoting inclusion to improve the reintegration architecture for former combatants. https://www.international-alert.org/sites/default/files/Ukraine_Whatsnextforveterans_%20EN_2019.pdf. Accessed 18 Mar 2021

International Organization for Migration (2020) Life after conflict: survey on the sociodemographic and socioeconomic characteristics of veterans of the conflict in eastern Ukraine and their families. https://ukraine.iom.int/resources/life-after-conflict-survey-sociodemographic-and-socioeconomic-characteristics-veterans-conflict-eastern-ukraine-and-their-families-january-2020. Accessed 8 May 2021

Käihkö I (2018) A nation-in-the-making, in arms: control of force, strategy and the Ukrainian volunteer battalions. Def Stud 18(2):147–166. https://doi.org/10.1080/14702436.2018.1461013

Kiryukhin D (2018) The Ukrainian military: from degradation to renewal. Eurasia Program. https://www.fpri.org/article/2018/08/the-ukrainian-military-from-degradation-to-renewal. Accessed 16 June 2021

Kulak NV (2016) Actual'ni pytannia pravovoho statusu dobrovolchych formuvan' v Ukraini (Current issues of legal status of paramilitary troops in Ukraine). Chasopys Kyivskoho Uni Prava 4:84–88

Kvit AS, Martsenyuk TO (2020) Attitudes towards ATO/JFO veterans and their political activism in Ukraine. Ukr Soc 2(73):172–184. https://doi.org/10.15407/socium2020.02.172

Lifeline Ukraine (2021). https://lifelineukraine.com/en. Accessed 14 Mar 2021

Martsenyuk T, Kvit A (2019) Zaluchennia veteraniv do hromadskogo i politychnoho zhyttia: shliakh vid viiskovykh peremoh do osobystyh (Veteran's involvement to social and political life: the way from military victory to personal). Available via Google Docs. https://drive.google.com/file/d/1h4jHcYtPs62tdyWoYrvVLkFGpyUuGPML/view. Accessed 15 Apr 2021

Martsenyuk T, Kvit A, Hrytsenko A, Vasylenko L, Zviahintseva M (2019) Invisible battalion 2.0: women veterans returning to peaceful life: sociological Research. https://www2.unwomen.org/-/media/field%20office%20eca/attachments/publications/2019/11/invisible%20battalion%2020eng.pdf?la=en&vs=3417" https://www2.unwomen.org/-/media/field%20office%20eca/attachments/publications/2019/11/invisible%20battalion%2020eng.pdf?la=en&vs=3417. Accessed 8 Apr 2021

Ministry of Veterans Affairs of Ukraine (2020) Ukraine, Kyiv. https://mva.gov.ua/ua/pro-ministerstvo/polozhennay-pro-ministerstvo-u-spravah-veteraniv-ukrainy. Accessed 28 May 2021

Murray LK, Haroz EE, Doty SB, Singh NS, Bogdanov S, Bass J, Dorsey S, Bolton P (2018) Testing the effectiveness and implementation of a brief version of the Common Elements Treatment Approach (CETA) in Ukraine: a study protocol for a randomized controlled trial. Trials 19(418). https://doi.org/10.1186/s13063-018-2752-y

On General Structure and Number of the Department of State Protection of Ukraine (2006) Law of Ukraine. Official web-portal of the Parliament of Ukraine. https://zakon.rada.gov.ua/laws/show/3106-15#Text. Accessed 28 May 2021

On General Structure and Number of the Security Service of Ukraine (2006) Law of Ukraine. Official web-portal of the Parliament of Ukraine. https://zakon.rada.gov.ua/laws/show/3014-15#Text. Accessed 28 May 2021

On Social and Legal Protection of Servicemen and their Families (1992) Law of Ukraine. Official web-portal of the Parliament of Ukraine. https://zakon.rada.gov.ua/laws/show/2011-12#Text. Accessed 28 May 2021

On Status of War Veterans, Guarantees of Their Social Protection (1993) Law of Ukraine. Official web-portal of the Parliament of Ukraine. https://zakon.rada.gov.ua/laws/show/3551-12#Text. Accessed 28 May 2021

On the Foreign Intelligence Service of Ukraine (2006). Law of Ukraine. Official web-portal of the Parliament of Ukraine. https://zakon.rada.gov.ua/laws/show/3160-15#Text. Accessed 28 May 2021

On the National Guard of Ukraine (2014). Law of Ukraine. Official web-portal of the Parliament of Ukraine https://zakon.rada.gov.ua/laws/show/876-18?lang=en#Text. Accessed 28 May 2021

On the Number of the Armed Forces of Ukraine (2015). Law of Ukraine. Official web-portal of the Parliament of Ukraine. https://zakon.rada.gov.ua/laws/show/235-19#Text. Accessed 28 May 2021

On the State Boarder Service (2003) Law of Ukraine. Official web-portal of the Parliament of Ukraine. https://zakon.rada.gov.ua/laws/show/661-15#Text. Accessed 28 May 2021

On Total Number of the State Service for Special Communications and Information Protection of Ukraine (2016) Law of Ukraine. Official web-portal of the Parliament of Ukraine. https://zakon.rada.gov.ua/laws/show/932-19#Text. Accessed 28 May 2021

Organization for Security Cooperation in Europe [OSCE] (2016) Report on the results of the study of the social protection system of struggle participants and family members killed in the ATO. Available via Google Docs. https://docs.google.com/document/d/1Upa4reZ77sULPE5_MUxLs4Lkkr-bFImtUbVV5MgTLOY/edit?usp=drive_open&ouid=0. Accessed 14 Mar 2021

Pinchuk IY, Yachnik IV, Ladyk-Bryzgalova AK, Bulakhova LO (2017) Psychological recovery and social integration of veterans in Ukraine. Arch Psychiatry 23(1):6–10. http://www.irbis-nbuv.gov.ua/cgi-bin/irbis_nbuv/cgiirbis_64.exe?I21DBN=LINK&P21DBN=UJRN&Z21ID=&S21REF=10&S21CNR=20&S21STN=1&S21FMT=ASP_meta&C21COM=S&2_S21P03=FILA=&2_S21STR=apsuh_2017_23_1_3

Semigina T, Boiko O (2014) Social work education in post-socialist and post-modern era: case of Ukraine. In: Noble C, Strauss H, Littlechild B (eds) Global social work education- crossing borders blurring boundaries. Sydney University Press, pp 257–269

Semigina T, Gusak N (2015) Armed conflict in Ukraine and social work response to it. Soc Health Commun Stud J 2(1):1–24

Sklokina I (2015) Veterans of the Soviet–Afghan war and the Ukrainian nation-building project: from perestroika to the Maidan and the war in the Donbas. J Sov P-Sov Politics Soc 1(2):133–168

Sociological Group Rating (2019) Assessment of the situation in Ukraine. http://ratinggroup.ua/en/research/ukraine/ocenka_situacii_v_strane_19-22_oktyabrya_2019_goda.html. Accessed 10 Apr 2021

The Legal Hundred (2018) Bila knyga. Analis systemy derzhavnoi pidtrymky veteraniv ta ikh simej (White Book. Analysis of the system of state support for veterans and their families in Ukraine). Iiurydychna Sotnia, Ukraina

Trubavina I, Medvid M, Cwer AM, Petryshyn L, Meshko H (2021) Substantiation of the advanced training program "Social work with military personnel and military-social work in the context of sustainable development goals." E3S Web of Conferences, 280(04007). https://doi.org/10.1051/e3sconf/202128004007

UNFPA (2020) Effectiveness of models of assistance of mobile brigades of social and psychological assistance on the way of reintegration of participants of hostilities in anti-terrorist operation / environmental protection and members of their families to a peaceful life in the Nikolaev and Kiev areas by RBM methodology. https://ukraine.unfpa.org/sites/default/files/pub-pdf/mt_jfo_report_final_compressed_1.pdf. Accessed 21 Mar 2021

Weiss-Gal I, Welbourne P (2008) The professionalization of social work: a cross-national exploration. Int J Soc Welf 17(4):281–290. https://doi.org/10.1111/j.1468-2397.2008.00574.x

Williams DJ (2016) The future of effective social work practice: broadening multidisciplinary collaboration and increasing flexibility. Soc Work 61(4):363–365. https://doi.org/10.1093/sw/sww054

Chapter 18
Strengthening Military Social Work Through the Development of a Global Understanding of Practice Similarities and Differences

Mary Ann Forgey and Karen Green-Hurdle

18.1 Introduction

Prior to this book, little was known about Military Social Work (MilSW) within most of the countries represented in this publication or that social work practice within the military was also a global phenomenon. Furthermore, when other professionals not associated with the military, or the general public, first learn about social workers practicing within defense organizations, questions are often raised as to their purpose and role and how a social worker can uphold the values and principles of the profession while working directly for a military authority. This book aims to increase understanding about this specialized MilSW role through each country's subject matter experts' descriptions of how MilSW came to be in their country, "what" military social workers do within their defense organizations, and "how" they do it.

In this last chapter, the cross-country commonalities and differences found in relation to the described evolution of MilSW and current scope of practice will be highlighted including the common ethical tensions encountered in MilSW practice across countries. The extent to which military social workers within a defense organization work with former military members in their adjustment to civilian life will be described and the differences will be examined. What was learned about the extent of MilSW education and training and its limited availability in most countries will also be discussed. Lastly, the common challenges ahead will be identified, with

M. A. Forgey (✉)
Graduate School of Social Service, Fordham University, New York, NY, USA
e-mail: forgey@fordham.edu

K. Green-Hurdle (✉)
Department of Veterans Affairs, Open Arms Veterans and Families Counselling (North Queensland), Townsville, QLD, Australia
e-mail: greenhurdle@gmail.com

© Springer Nature Switzerland AG 2023
M. A. Forgey, K. Green-Hurdle (eds.), *Military Social Work Around the Globe*,
Military and Veterans Studies, https://doi.org/10.1007/978-3-031-14482-0_18

the hope of creating a sense of unity and shared mission among these specialized international groups of social workers who work within their country's defense organization providing support to military service members and their families.

18.2 History of Military Social Work

As shared by the chapter authors within this book, MilSW within defense organizations first emerged in the 1940s following the conclusion of World War II in Australia, Canada, and the US. Denmark followed in the 1950s, and in the 1960s, MilSW gained status in Israel and South Africa. While the South Africa Defence Force employed social workers as early as 1968 during the era of apartheid, MilSW in the integrated military system of the South African National Defence Force (SANDF) did not begin until 1998. Contemporary MilSW supporting all branches of the Netherland's military began in the 1980s; however, the roots of social work in this country began when support was needed for "resistors" after World War II. MilSW began in Finland in the late 1970s and in Ireland in the 1990s, and in 2000, New Zealand introduced social work services within their military system. It is also important to note that for countries where both civilian and uniformed MilSW exist, those roles did not develop simultaneously. For example, in the US, uniformed social workers were first utilized and civilian were hired later. Low and colleagues in Chap. 11 describe a paucity of historical records in the UK about social workers in the British military, which they see is indicative of the lack of formal recognition of the social work profession in general until the latter half of the twentieth century.

As the preceding chapters illustrate, MilSW did not just develop spontaneously within each country. Rather it developed as a result of multiple components coming together, including the recognition of the value of social work in addressing the unmet needs of the military community. While each country's story of MilSW origin is unique, there are common factors reported among some of the represented countries. Following are some of these common elements, along with unique ones, that facilitated the development of MilSW practice within the defense organization of the country.

World War II and the recognition of the devastating psychosocial impact of that war on service members and their families were integral to the development of a social work role within the militaries of Australia, Canada, the US, and the Netherlands. Equally important however was the fact that the profession of social work in each of these countries was at a stage of development in which it could respond to the needs identified. Furthermore, social work was also recognized by the military of these countries as the appropriate profession to address the specific support needs that were emerging.

Another common factor after World War II that deserves recognition for the part that it played in the development of the MilSW in the US and Australia is the Red Cross service. In both countries, it was this organization that had initially provided medical and psychiatric social work services within the military hospitals. By pioneering this role, the Red Cross developed the blueprint for many of the functions that would eventually be taken over by civilian military medical and psychiatric social workers hired directly by the defense organizations.

There were also some powerful individual advocates for the role of social work in addressing the particular needs of active-duty service members and their families. One such voice discussed by Bailey and colleagues in Chap. 3 was Stewart Sutton, a civilian social worker in Canada, who wrote to the nation's prime minister in 1939 and described his concerns for the morale of soldiers serving in theaters of war and his vision for social work service within the military. In his letter, he advised that he was concerned about how the soldiers' problems would be dealt with at home and the impact this may have on them. He suggested that a form of social service underpinned by confidentiality was needed to support soldiers and help them communicate about and manage family-related problems (Blackburn 2015). He subsequently joined the Army, achieving the rank of Lieutenant Colonel, and set up the first social service corps (McCullagh et al. 2002). As further discussed in Chap. 3, Sutton was instrumental in establishing the Division of Special Services in 1942, which is considered the beginning of MilSW in Canada.

Another compelling advocate for MilSW later in the century was Gabi Weissman. Weissman was the first social worker in the Israeli Defence Forces (IDF), and he reportedly played a significant role in the development of MilSW in Israel in 1962. As detailed by Zitronblat in Chap. 7, Weissman was instrumental in highlighting the strengths of the social work response to the IDF and his military psychiatric colleagues and in particular its ability to work on all system levels to develop more effective coping within the military environment. To this day, as described in Chap. 7, the IDF has maintained a systemic community approach within its entire mental health array of services, and this is credited to the vision of Gabi Weissman.

Interestingly in Ireland, it was not a social worker's voice who sounded the call for the profession's development within the military. Fallon and Hickey in Chap. 9 affirm that it was the chaplains who expressed their concern in 1981 "regarding the growing number and diversity of problems affecting the lives of service personnel and the failure of those in authority to adequately address the solution" (p. 2). This concern, combined with their advocacy for a defense policy that attended to all aspects of the person, including the soldier's family and environment, led to the first head social worker within the Irish Defence Forces being hired in 1991. Today, when integrated support services can be compromised by interdisciplinary competitiveness to maintain an individual professional's own foothold, the early advocacy work by Irish chaplains for MilSW demonstrates the strength of interdisciplinary respect and collaboration and the positive impacts for clients when each profession values and draws on the unique qualities of another profession in service of client needs.

Within Finland, as reported by Seppanen and Maijanen in Chap. 5, the needs of service personnel and conscripts that would eventually be within the purview of military social workers were identified from the volunteer committees of full-time service personnel and conscripts within each garrison. The volunteer Social Welfare Committees concerned itself with the well-being and service conditions of the full-time military personnel and the volunteer Conscript Committees on the well-being and conditions of the conscripts. As a result of the work on these committees, the well-being needs of full-time service members and conscripts were regularly and systematically identified and communicated to the commander. The duties of the first social worker hired in 1976 endure to the present day and entail working in collaboration with these committees to address the needs identified.

In South Africa, a major impetus for MilSW development came from the need for organizational change within the military itself, following the fall of Apartheid and the creation of the South African National Defence Force (SANDF) in the 1990s (Van Breda 2012). Social work was integral to the successful integration of the seven military systems of the SADF into the SANDF. Key to this process, according to Potgieter and Pitse in Chap. 10, was the Psychological Integration Program (PIP), which saw military social workers being called upon to support the organizational change process and to use their knowledge and training in multisystemic interventions grounded in the values of social justice. There are important lessons to be learned from the way in which military social workers effectively engaged with the racial integration tasks in South Africa about the potential part MilSW can play in addressing social justice issues within military organizations.

The above examples of the origins of MilSW may seem quite disparate; however, it is important to recognize the role that each played in the development of MilSW from a global perspective, as they may provide a pathway forward for its development in countries where it does not yet exist, as well as strategies to further its growth in countries where it does exist. What is clear from the histories shared about MilSW development is that in some countries, the impetus for its development was in part a response to the consequences of geopolitical events such as World War II, whereas in other countries, such as South Africa, part of the impetus was in response to organizational changes needed within the military itself. In addition, strong advocacy for the specific needs of service members and for a social work response to these needs also played a critical role in MilSW development. This advocacy occurred through various channels. In Finland, it was through service members themselves, in Ireland, it was the chaplains, and in Canada and Israel, it was from powerful voices from within the social work profession. What was also evident from the histories shared is that when events occur and the need for social work within a country's military was identified, the social work profession understood their capability and embraced the challenge to respond.

18.3 Military Social Work Scope of Practice

18.3.1 Overview of Military Social Work Roles

As detailed in the previous chapters, military social workers perform a range of roles on the micro, mezzo, and macro levels. All participating countries with MilSW described the provision of direct support services to individual service members, most of which were short term. The majority of the countries also reported that military social workers provided services on a group and family level for clinical or psychoeducational purposes, although the extent of family level services varied greatly by country and will be discussed later in this section in more depth. While all countries reported some work at the organizational level, major differences among the countries were found. Command consultation was the most commonly reported role on the organizational level, although this role was often case specific rather than consultation about broader issues impacting the military unit as a whole. Fewer countries reported that military social workers were involved in policy development, management, and education/training. Research as a designated MilSW task was undertaken by only a few of the countries; however, it was identified by many as an area needing greater attention by military social workers. It is noted that South Africa had the most defined MilSW research role, having a separate social work research department devoted to this.

Across countries, the uniformed or civilian status of a military social worker had a certain impact on the type of roles performed. In summarizing the "uniformed" and the "civilian" status of social workers in countries that contributed to this book, it is noted that 4 of the 11 countries have solely civilian military social workers, and the remaining 7 countries have both uniformed and civilian military social workers.

South Africa, Israel and the Netherlands report having more uniformed than civilian military social workers within their defense organization, whereas the US reports having substantially more civilian military social workers than uniformed social workers. It is also important to note that in the countries with uniformed military social workers, all were reported to be commissioned officers, with the highest rank most commonly achieved being colonel. One exception however is South Africa (see Chap. 10), where the highest ranking uniformed social worker holds the impressive rank of brigadier general.

In comparing the roles of uniformed and civilian military social workers across countries, one of the major similarities found was that only uniformed social workers (who have the dual role of being a military officer and a social worker) were deployed to combat zones and embedded with the military unit while on deployment. As discussed by Yarvis and colleagues in Chap. 12, the uniformed social work role in this embedded context requires an even more specialized MilSW knowledge and skill set to intervene effectively with acute combat and deployment stressors on an individual and unit level. This involves not only knowledge of the types of stressors but also agility in developing and managing the trust of the unit members and the command leadership while also navigating the dual identity and loyalty tensions that can emerge as a uniformed social worker (Simmons and DeCoster 2007; Simmons and Rycraft 2010).

There were also some countries where civilian military social workers, although not embedded within military units, are also assigned to noncombat zones outside their country in support of military missions. For example, as described by Robichaux and Franklin in Chap. 13, civilian military social workers from the US defense organization hold positions in multiple duty stations worldwide providing support to US military personnel and their families. In addition, as reported by Fallon and Hickey in Chap. 6, Ireland has sent civilian military social workers to countries where Irish peacekeeping missions have been undertaken.

Another key difference in the MilSW roles found among the countries included in this book was the extent to which the military social workers worked with families. In some countries such as the US, Australia, and Canada, there was an extensive array of services provided by the defense organization to military families and delivered for the most part by civilian military social workers. The recognition of the importance of the family to the military mission and a greater understanding of the impact of family stress and crisis including child abuse and intimate partner violence on performance were factors that propelled the development of these services. Robichaux and Franklin in Chap. 13 describe a large array of family advocacy services with the US military focused specifically on the prevention and intervention of child abuse and neglect and intimate partner violence which were fueled by an avalanche of research in the 1970s and 1980s on the national prevalence of child abuse and spouse abuse and its consequences (Aronson et al. 2017; Bowen 1984; Milner 2015; Stith et al. 2016; Wichlacz et al. 1975).

Specialized support following the death of a service member is another example of the type of MilSW support provided for families. As noted in Green-Hurdle and Siebler in Chap. 2, the Bereavement Support Team (BST) that is activated in Australia following the death of a current serving military member provides a potentially valuable model for consideration in countries where a formalized family support process for this issue has not yet been established. In Chap. 7, Zitronblat describes how the Array of Casualties Team within the Israel Defense Forces promotes education and care for families of soldiers that have died and cares for those that have been wounded in war. Social work has a training role in this team which encompasses notification processes and being culturally responsive in mourning processes.

There were also several countries where direct family work was provided to a much lesser extent or not at all. Some of the differences in family service provision may be related to the extent to which conscription of young recruits characterizes the majority of a country's military population, as well as the availability of universal social welfare and health systems that address family support needs. In Israel, as explained by Zitronblat in Chap. 7, due to conscription, the majority of service members are young and single, and therefore family services are focused more on career personnel. In Finland, which also has conscription and therefore a younger-aged defense force overall, there are no direct family services provided, according to Seppanen and Maijanen in Chap. 5. If a family of a conscript or a career personnel needs assistance, they can be referred to civilian social security services available to all citizens as a result of a generous welfare state.

Most recently in Denmark, as reported by Birk and Christensen in Chap. 4, military social workers have begun focusing on the needs of families, and in 2020, a Family Center was created with specialized child counselors, with the service seeing an increase in the number of cases being referred. Being able to meet this increased demand with the current supply of social workers was identified as an ongoing challenge for MilSW in Denmark.

18.3.2 Military Social Work Practice Settings

Across countries, the chapter authors described a range of MilSW practice settings located on the military installation or within the civilian community. These practice settings include military units, military mental health/behavioral health clinics, social service centers, occupational social work services center, veteran services center, rehabilitation centers, and hospitals. In addition to having the largest number of uniformed and civilian military social workers, the US also has the most diverse types of practice settings, including embedded military units, behavioral health clinics, social service centers, hospitals, military prisons, Department of Defense (DoD) schools, substance abuse programs, and Master of Social Work degree programs within military-sponsored university settings, as described in Chaps. 12, 13, and 14.

In reviewing the different practice settings in which military social workers work across countries, there were some settings that appeared to have a particular impact on the social work role performed, as well as on the MilSW identity. The following is a closer look at some of these specific settings and the impact of practicing in this type of setting on the MilSW role and identity.

18.3.2.1 The Military Unit as the Practice Setting

While multiple countries reported having uniformed social workers embedded in specific military units when deployed to a combat zone, as discussed earlier, some countries such as Ireland (Chap. 6), New Zealand (Chap. 9), Finland (Chap. 5), South Africa (Chap. 10), and the US (Chap. 12) reported having uniformed and/or civilian social workers also assigned to a military unit as their practice setting when units were not deployed. When the practice setting was the military unit, whether in a deployed context or not, the approach to social work practice revealed some important differences. For example, in this type of practice setting, the military social worker must establish, build, and maintain relationships with not only individual members of the unit but with the unit leadership and the unit as a whole. In Chap. 6, Fallon and Hickey describe the importance of relationship building and how the civilian military social workers go about establishing trust on all system levels within this context. Being consistently and authentically present in all interactions, whether in formal meetings or when attending a less formal event such as the barrack's Christmas party, was described as integral to building trust and a social work presence. In South Africa, the social work services provided to military units are described by Potgieter and Pitse in Chap. 10 as ones that focus on services from the occupational social work perspective and cite the Department of Social Development definition of Occupational Social Work in South Africa as "a specialized field of social work practice which addresses the human and social needs of the work community" and uses "a variety of interventions which aim to foster optimal adaption between individuals and their environment." Seppanen and Maijanen in Chap. 5 describe the military social worker in Finland as being "part of the garrison's psychosocial support group and is involved in the organization of the crisis work." They also describe how military social workers work in close collaboration with the conscript committees within each garrison "to provide information on work and study matters and study counselling for conscripts."

The impact of providing services from within an embedded unit context also has empirical evidence of effectiveness. A recent study in Israel (Shelef et al. 2019) cited by Zitronblat in Chap. 7 found a 50% reduction in suicides within the IDF following the implementation of a multipronged suicide prevention strategy which included reducing access to weapons, psychoeducation, and recruiting a mental health officer (MHO) to be an organic member of the fighting unit. Increased accessibility to the MHO, including follow-up and maintaining of chain of care, appears to have reduced the stigma of seeking assistance and contributed to the reduction of suicides. Yarvis and colleagues in Chap. 12 also call attention to the findings on preventative mental health strategies in the military reported by Bliese et al. (2011) that led to the increased numbers of behavioral health providers, including social workers, to be embedded within deployed units.

18.3.2.2 Mental Health Clinic Setting

Another major difference found in relation to MilSW practice settings among the countries participating in this book was the extent to which military social workers practiced within designated mental health settings as part of the medical services delivery system. In some countries such as the US and Canada, many military social workers can be found practicing within mental health settings (e.g., behavioral health clinics), alongside mental health and medical professionals employing evidenced-based intervention protocols for a range of psychological diagnoses. The expansion of military social workers into mental and behavioral health care within certain countries has been driven by multiple forces including the increased societal understanding and acceptance of mental health as noted by Bailey and colleagues in Chap. 3. This movement of social workers in certain countries into mental health-focused settings within the medical services delivery system is also not a phenomenon specific to the military but is somewhat emblematic of the "medicalization" response to mental health issues in general (Maturo 2012). The force driving the medicalization of mental health issues within these countries is beyond the scope of this chapter given its complexity, but the impact of these trends on how and in what settings MilSW is practiced must be acknowledged and more systematically examined.

18.3.2.3 Interdisciplinary Practice Settings

Many of the previous chapters describe military social workers working in close collaboration with other disciplines to provide support to service members and their families. In some of these countries, the interdisciplinary support services operate under one organizational structure. An example of this is in Finland, as described by Seppanen and Maijanen in Chap. 5, where the Human Performance section of the Education and Training Division branch includes multiple disciplines that support the various aspects of the physical, psychological, social, and ethical factors of human performance. Within this framework, military social workers work collaboratively with the other disciplines but are specifically responsible for matters related to the service member's psychological and social performance. Other examples of where MilSW practice is organized in a way that maintains a clear MilSW role but facilitates interdisciplinary practice include the Veteran Services Center in Denmark, as described by Birk and Christensen in Chap. 4, and in the camps in New Zealand, described by Nicholson and colleagues in Chap. 9. In these interdisciplinary settings, the military social workers have clear professional boundaries and distinct roles as social workers. This type of professional boundary-keeping is considered an important factor in maintaining a professional social work identity and one that can be at risk in interdisciplinary practice if roles are unclear due to, for example, generic titles and role descriptions (Abbot 1995; Webb 2016).

Interestingly in Israel, according to Zitronblat in Chap. 7, military social workers work in an interdisciplinary community mental health setting alongside psychologists and psychiatrists and share the generic title of Mental Health Officers (MHO). While this type of generic title could be a risk for boundary erosion and loss of a social work identity, Zitronblat describes a very systemic approach to the way in which all of the MHOs practice community mental health, regardless of their professional discipline. So, while their job title in the IDF is not "military social worker," their internal identity and way of practicing remain in consonance with social work, which may be indicative of their numbers (approximately 60% of MHOs are social workers), as well as the respect and status the profession has within the organization. Nonetheless, it is important to recognize that the absence of "social worker" from the professional title of the role within a military organization, where social workers have other titles (such as MHO in Israel or Behavioral Health Officers in the US), could potentially be a risk to maintaining a social work identity and practicing in a way that is more reflective of another discipline, such as psychology.

There were also some countries in which the MilSW services are not delivered from within an interdisciplinary structure but rather from within a social work-specific organizational structure. For example, Kruishaar and Hulskamp (Chap. 8) report that in the Netherlands, MilSW services are delivered under the auspices of the Occupational Social Work Service Center. In South Africa, according to Potgieter and Pitse (Chap. 10), MilSW services are delivered from within the Directorate of Social Work and headed by a military social worker with the rank of Brigadier General. In both of these countries, this type of organizational structure supports MilSW having a strong presence and much visibility within the defense organization. This may be an important structural consideration for countries struggling to develop or maintain their MilSW identity.

18.3.2.4 Theoretical Perspective

The majority of MilSW approaches described in this book spanned from a generalist approach with an emphasis on working systemically with the person in the environment on all system levels to narrower clinically and psychologically focused
approaches. The countries that explicitly identified themselves as having occupational social workers described, for the most part, a more generalized approach to
their practice. These countries not only described how they worked on an individual
level, using interventions such as solution-focused, crisis intervention, and case
management, but also described interventions including preventative and psychoeducational strategies on a family, group, and community level. For those describing a more clinically oriented approach to practice, individually oriented
evidence-based interventions such as cognitive behavior therapy, prolonged exposure therapy, eye movement desensitization and reprocessing (EMDR), and hypnosis were identified as being used. Several authors including Yarvis and colleagues
(Chap. 12) and Bailey and colleagues (Chap. 3) described the use of both a generalist and clinical theoretical approaches within the US and Canadian military, respectively, depending on the type of setting in which the MilSW practice was occurring.

Only South Africa has developed a specific practice model of MilSW practice
(Van Breda 2012) which is described in detail by Potgieter and Pitse in Chap. 10.
The model makes explicit the integrated way in which the military social worker
works and interacts with the various system levels within the military environment
from different social work "positions." The metaphor of "binocular vision" is used
to explain how ecosystemic thinking is operationalized in practice. In essence, binocular vision bridges the dichotomy between micro and macro practices and allows
the social worker "to focus on the military organization, soldiers and their families
simultaneously, thereby seeing the system as one, rather than viewing the component parts separately." This then facilitates a focus on the transactions between systems as the points for social work intervention.

While not a specific model of MilSW practice, the overt importance that was
authentically placed on the use of a cultural lens in MilSW interventions in New
Zealand is also notable. Nicholson and colleagues in Chap. 9 describe the use of the
indigenous model called "Te Whare *Tapa Whā*" in the practice of MilSW. According
to the New Zealand authors, Te Whare Tapa Whā provides a Māori perspective on
health based on the four cornerstones of well-being developed by Durie in 1984 and
includes (1) *taha tinana* (physical health), (2) *taha hinengaro* (mental health), (3)
taha wairua (spiritual health), and (4) *taha whānau* (family health) (Durie, 1998).
In acknowledging the importance of practicing in a culturally safe manner, and in
recognition of the significance of considering mental, spiritual, and social well-
being in addition to physical health, it provides points of reflection for other MilSW
services across the globe to consider ways in which they could become more inclusive of or advocate for the inclusion of indigenous culture in day-to-day practice.

The application of a human development theoretical perspective was also very
prominent in several countries that have conscription, namely, Israel and Finland as
described in Chaps. 7 and 5. This perspective provided an increased understanding

of the potential stressors that young adult conscripts may encounter as a result of their mandatory service occurring during their early stage of adulthood and developmentally appropriate interventions. Countries without conscription did not describe this type of developmental focus or emphasis on preventative services for young single adults. While the reason for this difference is not known, it may be due to an assumption that voluntary enlistment in service does not produce the same stressors as mandatory service. While this may be true for some voluntary recruits, for others, it may feel "involuntary" due to the circumstances of their enlistment. For example, some voluntary recruits may have enlisted to overcome financial stress or family challenges. Others may begin to question their decision to enlist after they do so, resulting in a feeling of being "involuntarily" bound to fulfill their service obligation for the prescribed period of time. Subsequently, countries without conscription may benefit from learning about the array of services provided to young conscripts in Israel and Finland and what is being done to prevent and address the stressors they encounter.

18.3.2.5 MilSW Identity

Another important difference to highlight among the countries was the way in which the military social workers defined themselves. In several countries including the Netherlands, Ireland, New Zealand, and South Africa, chapter authors reported that military social workers defined themselves explicitly as occupational military social workers and emphasized their responsibility to address the fit between the service member and the military "work" environment. Within these countries, there also was a stronger tradition of occupational social work reported within the social work profession itself. In other countries, such as the US, Canada, and the United Kingdom, the occupational social work role and the clinical social work roles were described as being carried out somewhat separately depending on the context. It was only in South Africa through the application of the MilSW model of practice, discussed earlier, where these two roles were more integrated within MilSW practice.

Low and colleagues in Chap. 11 also identified challenges associated with how MilSW is viewed by the general public and subsequently understood by the military community. The authors suggested that the negative public perception of social work, fueled by media reports about adverse child safety events, has contributed to a sense of uncertainty and misunderstanding about the role and value of social work in the military environment.

Another important issue, although not directly explored in this book, arose from informal discussions with chapter authors who shared perspectives about the potential practice advantages and disadvantages of being a uniformed or civilian social worker within a defense organization and how military or civilian status can impact perceptions of effectiveness. The field of MilSW could benefit from more focused inquiry across countries about effective practice strategies for developing trust and addressing mistrust stemming from the uniformed or civilian status of the military social worker.

18.4 MilSW and Military to Civilian/Veteran Transition Support Services

Pedlar et al. (2019) state that it is well accepted that the process of transitioning from military to post-service civilian status is a critical period in a military member's life. The authors further suggest that "transitions are times of both opportunity and vulnerability characterized by adjustments to cultural shifts that require management of relationships and social identity" p. 25. Given the importance of the transition process to health and well-being outcomes for the service member, as well as their family, the question of "What do military social workers within defense organizations (within each country) do to assist with the military to civilian transition?" was an important area of inquiry.

In reviewing the MilSW roles described across countries, major differences were identified about the extent to which the military social workers, particularly those working within defense organizations, provide services to assist the active-duty members in their transition and adjustment to post-service life. Surprisingly, despite the goodness of fit of social work in supporting personnel and families to navigate complex issues and systems at a critical transition point in their lives, the role and responsibilities of military social workers within defense organizations in relation to this transition process varied greatly across countries. In addition, the extent to which active-duty military and veteran systems of care were integrated varied from low to moderate to high levels of integration.

The US, the UK, and New Zealand described very limited involvement of the military social workers employed by the defense organization in the provision of military to civilian transition support to active-duty members nearing discharge either through direct service provision or linking them to services provided by separate veteran organizations. In these countries, there was also a relatively low level of integration as two very separate systems of care were described. One system of care provided support services for active-duty service members (and their families) through the defense organization, and another totally separate system of care provided support services for the veteran population. For example, in the US, the separate system of care for veterans is provided mainly by the US Department of Veteran Affairs (VA) (US Department of Veterans Affairs 2022) and in New Zealand by the national department of Veterans' Affairs – Te Tira Ahu Ika A Whiro (New Zealand Veterans Affairs 2022).

Some transition services do exist within these countries but most are geared toward seriously disabled service members. For example, in the US, the DoD and VA jointly created the Disabled Transition Assistance Program (DTAP) which offers disabled service members' guidance about VA services as well as rehabilitation and employment services (Coll and Weiss 2013). Robichaux and Franklin in Chap. 13 also describe the Warrior Transition Units that have been created. Within these units, military social workers make up part of the team assisting veterans with disabilities in returning to active duty or if it is determined that this is not possible assisting them with their transition out of the military. This may involve coordination with the VA to ensure that they receive the services and benefits to which they are entitled. In addition, for service members who do not have a disability, the Transition Assistance Program (TAP), a joint DoD, and a VA initiative provide workshops at selected installations about employment and benefits (Coll and Weiss 2013). Similar workshops for personnel leaving military service were also noted to be provided in other countries; however, the specific role of MilSW in relation to these programs is not clear and requires further exploration.

Concern has been raised about the narrow focus of the US military's transition assistance program, and proposed changes have included the need for service members to have more holistic and individualized assessments prior to discharge, the development of individualized transition plans, and procedures to assure a "warm handover' from the DoD to the VA (Whitworth et al. 2020). The need for greater understanding in how to "more effectively educate, guide, and bolster active-duty member prior to leaving active-duty service so they are knowledgeable about where to get support and for what programs they are eligible" has also been highlighted (Aronson et al. 2019, p. 645). While military social workers within the defense organization would be well equipped to carry out these needed assessments, case management, and education roles, what their involvement would be, if any, was not addressed in any of these proposed changes.

Countries such as South Africa, Canada, and Australia appeared to have a more moderate level of integration between the systems of care focused on the military to civilian transition. Although the systems of care for military personnel and veterans are separate, strategies are in place to support the military to civilian process. In these countries, social workers working within the defense departments have the capacity to assume more responsibility to facilitate linkages between the systems of care for service members and their families as they transition to veteran status in the civilian community. Potgieter and Pitse in Chap. 10 reported that close cooperation between South African National Defence Force (SANDF) military social workers and those in the Department of Military Veterans results in seamless service delivery. In Chap. 3, Bailey and colleagues highlight the establishment of the Canadian Armed Forces Transition Group (CAFTC) in 2018 to assist military personnel and their families to navigate the challenges that arise when exiting military service and the issues that may impact on social, emotional, and financial well-being. The social workers in the CAFTC, together with social workers from the Military Family Services and the Canadian Armed Forces (CAF) Health Service, provide a range of services to support personnel and families in the military to civilian transition process. Much collaboration is also reported to exist at the local and national levels to ensure that services are both coordinated and complementary. In Australia, transition support provided by military social workers in the defense organization can include practical planning and emotional support, short-term counselling, goal setting, psychoeducation related to adjustment and health and well-being, and referral to relevant community resources. In 2020, following a Productivity Commission's report, titled, "A Better Way to Support Veterans," a Joint Transition Authority (JTA) was created in Australia to improve the integration of services and share information (Department of Veterans Affairs 2021). Although the systems of care

are separate, there is now a systemic focus on increasing cooperation between departments, including DVA (Department of Veterans Affairs) having a presence on military bases, and appropriately sharing information to better support the transition process (Department of Veterans Affairs 2022).

Military social workers within defense organizations in Israel and Ireland also take on explicit responsibilities in relation to military to civilian transition support. In Israel, according to Zitronblat in Chap. 7, personnel who have completed their military service and sustained an injury while serving, which resulted in PTSD, can be treated within the Combat Stress Reaction Unit, a special unit staffed by IDF MHOs. And while Ireland does not have a separate government agency for veterans, the defense organization takes some responsibility for assisting service members as they transition out of the military. For example, Fallon and Hickey in Chap. 6 describe a program called "The Friday Club" which is run monthly on the military installation. It is a place where veterans can interact with others and get direct assistance and advice from defense organization military social workers in relation to issues such as housing, entitlements, physical and mental health issues, and bereavement support.

Countries that can be characterized as having a high level of system integration include the Netherlands and Denmark as their systems of care for service members and veterans are overseen and coordinated by one overarching organization. In the Netherlands, as reported by Kruishaar and Hulskamp in Chap. 8, both active-duty service members and veterans receive services through the Occupational Social Work Service Center which is part of the National Care System for Veterans. Within the Service Center, there are social workers specifically designated to serve the veteran population. Likewise in Denmark, according to Birk and Christensen in Chap. 4, both active-duty service members, veterans, and their families are provided with services through the Veteran Center.

In comparing the extent of the military to civilian transition support services available within countries represented in this book, it is also important to note that countries with conscription along with an extensive military reserve requirement following their mandatory service, such as Israel and Finland, have a very different military to civilian pathway. In these countries with conscription and extensive reserve requirements, their service does not abruptly end. In addition, as suggested by Fossey et al. (2019) in countries with conscription, military, family and societal relationships are intimately connected. The authors purport that in these countries, there are generations of shared experiences and expectations of what military service entails, and subsequently, there is a population that is aware of the post-service issues that personnel may face and the support that may be needed to and adjust to critical transition points. The transition challenges, therefore, facing service members in countries with a volunteer force (as opposed to veterans from countries with conscription and long reserve requirements) may be very different and need to be taken into consideration when comparing the transition support needs across countries.

Another important factor to consider when comparing the military to civilian transition services across counties is the availability of health and welfare services to the general public within a country. As pointed out by Seppanen and Maijanen in Chap. 5, although Finland does not have a separate system of care for veterans, Finnish veterans' care is provided by a range of national services including the State Treasury, with other veteran associations providing welfare support, in addition to public and private social welfare and mental health services. Veterans and their families can also contact the military social worker in the Pori Brigade for advice and support.

Other countries that contributed to this book also have universal health care including Australia, Canada, Denmark, Finland, Israel, the Netherlands, New Zealand, South Africa, and the UK (World Population Review 2022). This means that citizens, including veterans, in those countries, have access to an extensive array of services that are well known to all social workers due to their wide availability. In these countries, veterans may not be as dependent on a separate system of care as they are in countries such as the US where the array of support services available to the general public is more limited due to stricter eligibility requirements.

As has been outlined, integration and coordination of services between the systems of care for active-duty service members and veterans were recognized as an ongoing challenge and one that was in need of improvement by many of the countries. Chapter authors from Australia, Canada, the US, and the UK indicated that there are initiatives in place to improve the coordination of services between the formal systems of care for service members and for veterans. In the US for example, there is a joint interagency task force involving the Department of Defense and Department of Veteran Affairs and Health and Human Services which aims to ensure that service members, veterans, and their families have access to needed mental health services and support. Structurally this task force has the potential to address some of the specific military to civilian transition concerns identified earlier (SAMHSA n.d.).

Pedlar et al. (2019) describe a range of theoretical military to civilian transition (MCT) frameworks that have been developed in the UK, Canada, and the US and also provide a comprehensive overview of the common features and considerations of these conceptualizations which are underpinned by the life course model. These concepts present a fertile foundation for international MilSW consideration. Military social workers understand military culture and lifestyle impacts, experience of assessments in the context of working between family and organizational systems, the skills to navigate these systems, and ability to advocate for vulnerable clients. In addition, theoretical understanding and application of the life course model in relation to managing adjustment to life changes are all within the skill set of the military social worker and can be drawn upon to develop and implement initiatives and policies. This ensures that they are well equipped to take a more active role to support the MCT process at micro, mezzo, and macro levels. The potential for the development of the MilSW role in the MCT space will be dependent on a range of factors within the military and national context of each country and again is an area for further exploration and research.

18.5   Ethical Tensions

There were two common ethical challenges described by most of the chapter authors. The first was the tension between the responsibility to the individual service member's well-being as a client and the responsibility to the military mission. The second relates to the issues that arise between the service member's right to privacy and confidentiality as a client and the command's need to know in the context of maintaining operational capability. In countries with conscription, such as Finland, the chapter authors also discussed the difficult decisions involved in assessing conscripts' conscientious objections to service.

The process in which ethical tensions were resolved was also addressed by several authors. In New Zealand, for example, Nicholson and colleagues mentioned the importance of good communication and mutual respect and an understanding of the social worker and command role. They also discuss how ethical tensions may be experienced differently and somewhat more intensely for a uniformed social worker than a civilian social worker who does not hold rank and can advocate without fear of consequences within the hierarchal system. Yarvis and colleagues in Chap. 12 discussed the ethical conflicts that can arise in an embedded situation given the potential for boundary issues and the need to prepare for this. The importance of well-articulated privacy laws, reporting regulations and robust policies, and access to supervision were also seen as ways to prevent, or at least reduce, the development of ethical tensions.

In relation to the ethical issues that arise for social workers when confronting social justice issues within the military, it is important to note that during the writing of this book, the Black Lives Matter (BLM) movement gained international support following the outrage caused by police brutality that led to the death of George Floyd in the US (Black Lives Matter, 2020). The global BLM protests against racial injustice thrust racism into the forefront of the public arena and demanded that the issues be systemically addressed. The response of military social workers in South Africa in 1991 provides a hopeful vision of the type of response that MilSW is capable of within a defense organization when it has a clear understanding of the profession's unique strengths and capabilities (Van Breda 2012; Turton and Van Breda 2020).

Military social workers are especially well equipped to address unfair or oppressive organizational policies toward marginalized populations and have made efforts in this regard in relation to increasing LGBTQ service members' inclusion within the military (Alford and Lee 2016; Milano 2019; Pelts et al. 2014). It is imperative that social workers in military practice settings consistently honor the values of the profession and assume a leadership role in working strategically to create meaningful and sustainable transformational change to eliminate unjust, harmful policies, practices, and behaviors in defense organizations.

In reviewing the MilSW literature, several US-based articles were found that specifically addressed ethical issues in relation to the MilSW role itself (Olson 2014, 2018; Simmons and Rycraft 2010). Olson's articles explored discrepancies between the values of the social work profession and the military and recommended ways in which curricula in MilSW could better integrate a social justice perspective. Simmons and Rycraft (2010) reviewed the unique ethical challenges faced by uniformed social workers who were deployed in a wartime mission. In addition, overviews of the kinds of ethical issues encountered within the US military can be found in chapters in edited text books on US MilSW practice (Daley 2013; Tallant and Ryberg 1999).

18.6   Military Social Work Education and Training

Among the countries with MilSW described in this book, the US is the only country that has a military-sponsored Masters of Social Work program to educate uniformed social workers and an array of specialized MilSW certificate programs and courses offered at degree-granting schools of social work. Freeman and colleagues in Chap. 14 describe the history of MilSW education in the US and the educational approaches currently being utilized within schools of social work to prepare uniformed and civilian social workers to work with military service members, veterans, and their families. The US is also the only country that has promulgated educational standards through the Council of Social Work Education and that has developed a MilSW curriculum guide (Council on Social Work Education 2017).

From what was reported by the authors of chapters in this book from outside the US, specialized MilSW educational initiatives do not currently exist in their countries, although plans to develop a specialized course in MilSW were reported to be underway in New Zealand, Israel, and South Africa. And according to Gusak in Chap. 17, a MilSW course was introduced by the School of Social Work at the National University of Kyiv-Mohyla Academy in 2021. Tragically, this course implementation plan was abruptly thwarted by the Russian invasion of Ukraine in February 2022; however, it is noted that online classes recommenced in May 2022.

The factors responsible for the lack of specialized MilSW curricula across countries have not been systematically examined. It could be speculated that the smaller numbers of MilSW jobs in these countries and the size of each country's military force (compared to the US) may result in less demand for this specialized training within social work degree programs. Authors from the Netherlands, South Africa, and Ireland also describe how existing specialized course work in the Occupational Social Work prepare the students within their schools of social work in MilSW as these courses specifically teach the knowledge and skills necessary to work with clients within their work environments.

Several countries, in addition to the US, provide education opportunities for uniformed military officers to obtain their social work degree from civilian universities while serving in the military. Zitronblat in Chap. 7 and Low and colleagues in Chap. 11 describe such programs in Israel and the UK, respectively; however, unlike the US, they do not receive any MilSW-specific education within the academic program itself. The Israeli Defense Force, according to Zitronblat in Chap. 7, does have a robust on the job training programs for these students while they are attaining their social work degree consisting of a very structured three-year training program in basic theory and skills (e.g., interviewing, diagnosis).

Freeman and colleagues in Chap. 14 also describe the MilSW field component that exists for those training to be uniformed social workers within the Army Master of Social Work Program and for those training to be civilian military social workers within the University of Kentucky program. Hickey and Fallon in Chap. 6 also indicate that MilSW field opportunities exist within the Irish Defense Force. A limited number of students are also accepted each year for fieldwork placements within the Directorate of Social Work within the SANDF according to Potgieter and Pitse in Chap. 10 and Nicholson and colleagues in Chap. 9 describe plans to develop military field placements in New Zealand.

The US also leads in the literature being produced in relation to MilSW education. Since the commencement of the Iraq Afghanistan War, there has been an explosion of literature within the US that specifically addresses MilSW education and training needs, most of which occurred following the calls to action by two deans of schools of social work for more specialized MilSW training (Jacobs (2009) & Flynn and Hussan 2010). The literature produced during this period addresses MilSW education approaches in general (e.g., Wooten (2015), Frey et al. (2014)), MilSW teaching issues (e.g., Williams-Gray (2016), Rishel and Hartnett (2015), Forgey and Young (2014), Newell (2012), Hall (2011)), the application of MilSW competencies (e.g., Brand and Weiss (2015), Daley et al. (2015), Humphries and Howard (2014), and Whitworth et al. (2012)), SW values and ethics in MilSW education (Olson 2014, 2018; Simmons and Rycraft 2010), and continuing education (Smith-Osborne 2015). One article specifically addresses the teaching of doctoral students on how to conduct military research (DuMars et al. 2015). Several articles focus specifically on the education needs of civilian military social workers (Yarvis 2011; Savitsky et al. 2009) and several others on the education needs of uniformed military social workers (Freeman and Bicknell 2008; Simmons and DeCoster 2007). Field education issues in the Army Master of Social Work program (Howard 2013, 2014) and in a civilian program (Esqueda et al. 2014) are also addressed.

A small amount of literature from other countries that addresses MilSW education issues has also been identified; Sakarya and Şahin (2019), Tanaka (2014), and Runesu (2016) discuss the need for specialized curricula in MilSW in Turkey, Japan, and Zimbabwe, respectively. And Jen der Pan et al. (2008) describes a supervision method for training military social workers in Taiwan. Additionally, Al-Qahtani (2017) proposes educational and training requirements for MilSW social workers in Saudi Arabia.

The need to adequately prepare social workers to work competently with military service members and their families is an ongoing challenge for all countries. One approach, led by the US, has been to develop specialized curricula and specializations in this area of practice. However, this approach may not be realistic for many schools of social work both within the US and in other countries due to resource limitations. An alternative approach that has the potential for MilSW content deemed crucial by CSWE (2017) to reach more students involves the infusion of content relative to service members, veterans and their families, and communities into the required social work curriculum. So, for example, when teaching about cultural competence in social work practice, the military would be included as a separate culture that needs to be understood and respected in the same way as cultures shaped by race/ethnicity, gender, sexual orientation, etc. Or when teaching about family systems, the cycle of deployment and its impact on the family would be included. Canfield and Weiss (2015) present a strong argument for the infusion approach along with a myriad of other examples of relevant content that could be infused within social work theory, practice, policy, and research courses.

Field placements in MilSW, particularly in practice settings serving active-duty service members and their families, are another area of potential growth in MilSW education. The growth however will require the formation of stronger partnerships between schools of social work and defense organizations. If this growth did occur and more military field placements existed in schools of social work across countries, more opportunities could be developed for students to connect internationally using an "internationalization at home" approach (Hendriks et al. (2008)) which would allow them to develop a more global understanding and appreciation for international MilSW. Forgey et al. (2013) describe an example of this type of virtual international student education exchange. While the example presented is a virtual international education exchange among social work students in a foundation practice course, parts of the model itself could be adapted for social work students in military field placements.

Continuing education offered virtually is another educational approach that holds much promise for effectively preparing social workers internationally to work with military service members and their family members in their own countries. This is currently an initiative being pursued by the International Military Social Work (IMilSW) Consortium in collaboration with PsychArmor (2021). The initiative involves a series of webinars focused on MilSW education topics that would be of interest to military social workers worldwide.

18.7   Future Directions and Challenges Ahead for International Military Social Work

Based on the descriptions of MilSW among the various countries contributing to this book, military social workers perform a wide range of roles in various practice settings within the military environment and vary in the extent to which they work with the individual, the family, and the military environment directly. While this variety could be a strength if understood and applied within a theoretical framework, it can lead to identity confusion if this theoretical underpinning does not exist.

South Africa is the only country that has a theoretical model of MilSW that operationalizes individual, family, organization, and community practice and how they work in synergy with each other within the military. Through the use of "binocular vision," the South African model demonstrated how the core social work principal of "person in environment" is practiced. In the absence of this type of unifying model of practice, MilSW risks becoming fractured and divided into camps where MilSW gets defined in alternate ways, for example, as "clinical social work" or as "occupational social work" and not as "military social work."

Many countries described concerns in relation to the lack of a strong MilSW identity and the negative impact on practice effectiveness. Given this, it is critical that military social workers within each country do the conceptual work of developing and operationalizing their model of MilSW practice. While the descriptions of MilSW practice in each country contained in this book are a start in this direction, the development of a model of MilSW practice within each country will require an examination of current practices and critical reflection on what makes these practices social work. While this process will not lead to all countries having the same exact model of MilSW practice, they will have a deeper understanding of how they are operationalizing their practice as military social workers and what they are doing to facilitate the fit between the "person in environment." And in so doing, their social work identity will be strengthened leading to increased understanding and recognition of the value of their role by clients and other disciplines.

This conceptual and operationalization work will also aid countries that are interested in developing MilSW as it will provide a clearer road map as to how to get there. These countries need strong voices from within, but they also need to be able to point to other countries as examples of what social work is capable of within the military and how this is being accomplished in other countries.

A stronger conceptualization of MilSW and understanding of how it can be operationalized will also better ensure that social workers are placed in roles that utilize their full knowledge and skill set. Military social workers, both uniformed and civilian, with their education and training in working on multiple levels, have much to offer in many of the roles or potential roles that require this type of approach. One such practice setting is the embedded unit which requires the ability to work with the individual service member, the unit as a whole, and the unit leadership (Hoyt 2006). The value of this type of practice setting is increasingly being recognized and empirically validated for its effectiveness, particularly in relation to help-seeking behaviors and stigma reduction (e.g., Pierce et al. (2020), Rapley et al. (2017)). As the challenges of working in an embedded context for uniformed and civilian practitioners in both deployed units and non-deployed units are also examined, including the ethical conflicts that can emerge when practicing in a nontraditional informal setting as described by Hryshko-Mullen et al. (2022), military social workers need to be more at the forefront of this type of practice, given their history and experience in working in nontraditional environments.

Military social worker's multilevel practice expertise is also desperately needed to assist service members as they prepare to transition to civilian status. Social workers have the education and training to assess the psychosocial needs of service members preparing for discharge, develop individualized plans, and assist with navigating and accessing new systems of care within the civilian sector. As the demand for positions requiring multilevel interventions increases in response to need, military social workers must be prepared to embrace the challenge of stepping up to ensure that the fit of the profession for these roles is explicitly recognized.

To successfully develop an international perspective and knowledge base in International Military Social Work (IMilSW), practitioners, both uniformed and civilian military social workers, and academics, including educators and researchers knowledgeable about MilSW, must also work in partnership. The IMilSW Conference at West Point and this book represent a beginning in forming this type of academic/practitioner partnership in IMilSW, but much more needs to be done to unlock the possibilities of this specialization. Going forward, it will be critical to continue to have research projects that involve both academics and practitioners with knowledge and experience in uniformed and civilian social work roles. The next major project planned for the IMilSW consortium is a series of IMilSW themed webinars and IMilSW webpage in collaboration with PsychArmor (2021). The success of the webinar and web page will depend on the joint involvement of both academics and practitioners in the planning subcommittees. The formation of an ongoing joint writing group involving practitioners and academics is also an initiative that should be considered as it has been shown to be an effective way to disseminate practice experience and contribute to the development of a field of practice (Boddy et al. 2012).

Time and again the contributors to this book, along with other participants in the IMilSW virtual meetings, speak of the importance of coming together again for an event like the West Point Conference in 2019. Being in the presence of other military social workers from around the world strengthened a sense of identity and fueled an ongoing interest to learn more about practice in other countries. To come together annually, or every second year, however will require the IMilSW consortium to be accommodated within an international professional social work organization and to have a more formal structure. Finding a "home" for IMilSW is an ongoing challenge as the existing international social work professional organizations, for example, IASSW and IFSW, are currently organized by geographic region and not by practice areas and focus more on either academic participants or practitioner participants. To strengthen international dialogue within social work practice areas, including MilSW, international social work professional organizations need to address this structural barrier and create more opportunities through their organizations for regular international dialogue within practice areas throughout the year and at annual conferences.

Another potential strategy for increasing global partnerships and cross-cultural understanding of MilSW issues could be through the development of an international exchange or immersion program. A model, such as that which is provided through the annual eight-week "Mount Sinai International Enhancement of Social Work Leadership Program" in New York City, could provide a foundation for considering this innovation. In this program, social workers from different countries participate in a semi-structured program where they have opportunities to meet with leaders from hospitals, community-based organizations, and graduate schools of social work, "to enhance their leadership ability, strengthen management and research skills, and build upon global social work relationships" (Gordon et al. 2018

p. 406). There is also literature from the nursing profession indicating that global immersion programs provide professional and personal development opportunities for participants to exchange ideas about practice, research, and education (Turner et al. 2019). The logistical, coordination, and practical issues that would need to be attended to are beyond the scope of this chapter; however, the concept and the potential mutual benefits of an exchange or immersion program are worthy of future consideration.

This book has identified several research topics in relation to how military social workers manage issues such as the COVID pandemic and social justice issues; however, there will be many others that will also require more in-depth exploration. Other examples include the research needed to understand new and emerging MilSW roles that are being implemented worldwide and how countries may be working together to support those who are developing or refining MilSW practice models.

One of the major limitations of this book is that it does not include all countries that have MilSW as it only includes only 11 of the 29 total countries confirmed to have MilSW either through contact with the professional organization within that country or through the literature. Efforts were made to reach out to the countries initially confirmed to have MilSW from the 2016–2017 exploration study and to identify at least one subject matter expert. In some cases, there was no response, and in others, the invitation to participate was declined with reasons left unknown or that the country was unable to participate due to organizational restrictions. In addition to the 18 countries confirmed to have MilSW but not included in this book,[1] as outlined in Table 18.1 in Chap. 1, there may exist many more countries with MilSW with similarities and differences in terms of development, current practices, and educational efforts that future research can identify. Having an ongoing presence of a MilSW practice group within an international social work organization could also be an effective avenue for involving more countries in this research and identifying additional countries where the MilSW status is currently unknown.

18.8   Conclusion

Defense forces around the world work tirelessly carrying out an ever-widening range of roles and responsibilities. In addition to their core responsibility for defense of the country from outside threats, service members are increasingly being called to assist domestically, as seen most recently in their role as part of the frontline COVID response, in supporting rebuilding efforts following the impact of significant weather and climate events on communities and in providing care for refugees fleeing to their countries. Defense forces are also being deployed on humanitarian

---

[1] Brazil, Bulgaria, Czech Republic, Germany, Jordan, Nigeria, Romania, Russia, Saudi Arabia, Singapore, Slovenia, South Korea, Spain, Switzerland, Taiwan, Trinidad and Tobago, Turkey, and Zimbabwe

Table 18.1 Civilian and uniformed military social workers

Civilian only MilSW	Uniformed and civilian MilSW
Australia	Canada
Denmark	Finland
Ireland	Israel
New Zealand	The Netherlands
	South Africa
	UK
	US

missions to assist other countries struck by natural disasters and on multinational peacekeeping missions to countries that have been ravaged by war. In whatever role the military members of a country find themselves, whether it involves carrying out their role on a combat mission or engaging in a humanitarian or peacekeeping mission, the psychological and social stability of the defense force is paramount to maintaining their effectiveness and humanity.

Military social workers play a critical role in ensuring the well-being of service members and thereby contributing to the effectiveness of a stable and humane defense force. First and foremost, this requires attention to both the concrete and psychosocial needs of the service members and their families. It may also require intervention on the organizational level or within the military community as a whole in support of programmatic or policy changes needed to more effectively respond to the needs of service members and their families.

A global military social work partnership will allow robust international conversations about how to care for military service members and their families that strike at the core values of social work. This type of international collaboration will ensure that military social workers are at the forefront of contributing to the national and international bodies of knowledge on best practices in supporting an effective and humane defense force. "Military Social Work Around the Globe" is needed now, more than ever.

References

Abbot A (1995) Boundaries of social work or social work boundaries? Soc Serv Rev 69:545–562

Alford B, Lee SJ (2016) Toward complete inclusion: Lesbian, gay, bisexual, and transgender military service members after repeal of don't ask, don't tell. Soc Work 61(3):257–265. https://doi.org/10.1093/sw/sww033

Al-Qahtani MAM (2017) Professional requirements for applying social service in the military field. Naif Arab University for Security Sciences, College of Social Sciences, Department of Psychology

Aronson KR, Perkins DF, Morgan NR, Cox CA, Robichaux R (2017) Military family advocacy in the US army: program service outcomes and family participation. J Child Fam Stud 27(1):218–226. https://doi.org/10.1007/s10826-017-0864-8

Aronson KR, Perkins DF, Morgan N, Bleser J, Davenport K, Vogt D, Copeland LA, Finley EP, Gilman C (2019) Going it alone: post-9/11 veteran nonuse of healthcare and social service programs during their farly transition to civilian life. J Soc Serv Res 45(5):634–647. https://doi.org/10.1080/01488376.2018.1493410

Black Lives Matter (2020). https://blacklivesmatter.com/about/

Blackburn D (2015) Social work in the military – considering renewed scope of practice. Canadian Military Journal 16(1):34–43

Bliese PD, Adler AB, Castro CA (2011) Research-based preventive mental health care strategies in the military. In: Adler AB, Bliese PD, Castro CA (eds) Deployment psychology: evidence-based strategies to promote mental health in the military. American Psychological Association, pp 103–124. https://doi.org/10.1037/12300-004

Boddy J, Daly M, Munch S (2012) The writing series project. A model for supporting social work clinicians in health settings to disseminate practice knowledge. Soc Work Health Care 51(3):246–270. https://doi.org/10.1080/00981389.2011.619860

Bowen GL (1984) Military family advocacy: a status report. Armed Forces Soc 10(4):583–596

Brand MW, Weiss EL (2015) Social workers in combat: application of advanced practice competencies in military social work and implications for social work education. J Soc Work Educ 51(1):153–168. https://doi.org/10.1080/10437797.2015.979094

Canfield J, Weiss E (2015) Integrating military and veteran culture in social work education: Implications for curriculum inclusion. J Soc Work Educ 51(sup1):S128–S144. https://doi.org/10.1080/10437797.2015.1001295

Coll JE, Weiss E (2013) Transitioning veterans into civilian life. In: Rubin A, Weiss E, Coll J (eds) Handbook of military social work, 1st edn. Wiley, Hoboken

Council on Social Work Education (2017) Specialized practice curricular guide for Military Social Work. Alexandria. https://www.cswe.org/getattachment/Education-Resources/2015-Curricular-Guides/CSWE-Gero-Curricular-Guide.pdf

Daley JG (2013) Ethical decision making in Military Social Work. In: Rubin A, Weiss EL, Coll JE (eds) Handbook of military social work. Wiley, Hoboken

Daley JG, Carlson J, Evans P (2015) Military social work as an exemplar in teaching social work competencies. J Soc Work Educ 51(sup 1):S76–S88. https://doi.org/10.1080/10437797.2015.1001288

Department of Veterans Affairs (2021) Improving transition for ADF members and their families. Australian Government 22 July 2021. https://www.dva.gov.au/newsroom/latest-news-veterans/improving-transition-adf-members-and-their-families. Accessed 2 Apr 2022

Department of Veterans Affairs (2022) How DVA can help you transition to civilian life. Australian Government. https://www.dva.gov.au/sites/default/files/revised_next_stage_brochure_-_fas_cleared.pdf. Accessed 2 Apr 2022

DuMars T, Bolton K, Maleku A, Smith-Osborne A (2015) Training MSSW students for military social work practice and doctoral students in military resilience research. J Soc Work Educ 4:117

Durie M (1998) Whaiora Māori health development. Oxford University Press, Auckland

Esqueda MC, Cederbaum JA, Pineda DM, Malchi K, Benbenishty R, Astor RA (2014) Military social work field placement: analysis of the time and activities graduate student interns provide to military-connected schools. Child Sch 36(1):41–50. https://doi.org/10.1093/cs/cdt043

Flynn M, Hussan (2010) Unique challenges of war in Iraq and Afghanistan. J Soc Work Educ 46(2):169–173

Forgey MA, Young SL (2014) Increasing military social work knowledge: an evaluation of learning outcomes. Health Soc Work 39(1):7–15. https://doi.org/10.1093/hsw/hlu003

Forgey MA, Loughran H, Hansen J (2013) Employing video conferencing to introduce an international perspective in foundation social work practice. J Teach Soc Work 33(4/5):449–456. Special Issue: Distance Learning and Online Education in Social Work.

Fossey M, Cooper L, Raid K (2019) The transition of military veterans from active service to civilian life: impact of transition on families and the role of the family, support, and recognition. In:

Castro CA, Dursun S (eds) Military veteran reintegration. Academic Press, pp 185–213. https://doi.org/10.1016/B978-0-12-815312-3.00009-7

Freeman D, Bicknell G (2008) The army master of social work program. US Army Medical Department Journal. pp 72–75. http://citeseerx.ist.psu.edu/viewdoc/download?doi=10.1.1.884.4815&rep=rep1&type=pdf#page=75

Frey JJ, Collins KS, Pastoor J, Linde L (2014) Social workers' observations of the needs of the total military community. J Soc Work Educ 50(4):712–729. https://doi.org/10.1080/10437797.2014.947904

Gordon E, Green K, Whitwam L, Epstein I, Bernstein S (2018) The Mount Sinai international enhancement of social work leadership program: the past and the future. Soc Work Health Care 57(6):406–421. https://doi.org/10.1080/00981389.2018.1439134

Hall LK (2011) The importance of understanding military culture. Soc Work Health Care 50(1):4–18. https://doi.org/10.1080/00981389.2010.513914

Hendriks P, Kloppenburg R, Gevorgianiene V, Jukutiene V (2008) Crossnational social work case analysis: learning from international experience within an electronic environment. Eur J Soc Work 11(4):383–396. https://doi.org/10.1080/08841233.2013.829550

Howard RW (2013) The Army Internship Program: enhancing mission readiness for uniformed army social workers. J Hum Behav Soc Environ 23(6):812–816. https://doi.org/10.1080/10911359.2013.795088

Howard RW (2014) The army social work internship program: training today's uninformed social worker. US Army Medical Department Journal. pp 35–38. https://www.thefreelibrary.com/The+army+social+work+internship+program%3A+training+today%27s+uniformed...-a0361848304

Hoyt GB (2006) Integrating mental health within operational units: opportunities and challenges. Mil Psychol 18(4):309–320. https://doi.org/10.1207/s15327876mp1804_5

Hryshko-Mullen M, Behnke SH, Ogle AD, Rogers TE, Tubman DS, Rowe KL, Dunkle AN (2022) Embedded behavioral health in the US Air Force: addressing the ethics of an expanding area of practice. Prof Psychol Res Pract 53(1):59–68. https://doi.org/10.1037/pro0000423

Humphries JL & Howard RW (2014) Developing effective leadership competencies in military social workers. US Army Medical Department Journal. pp 3–7. https://www.researchgate.net/publication/274400857_Developing_effective_leadership_competencies_in_military_social_workers

Jacobs C (2009) The response of schools of social work to the return of uniformed service members and their families. Smith Coll Stud Soc Work 79(3/4):453–463. https://doi.org/10.1080/00377310903130258

Jen der Pan P, Deng L-YF, Tsai S-L (2008) Evaluating the use of reflective counseling group supervision for military counselors in Taiwan. Res Soc Work Pract 18(4):346–355. https://doi.org/10.1177/1049731507313981

Maturo A (2012) Medicalization: current concept and future directions in a bionic society. Mens Sana Monogr 10(1):122–133. https://doi.org/10.4103/0973-1229.91587

McCullagh J, Aitken G, Bellamy DF (2002) A legacy of caring. A history of the children's aid society of Toronto. Toronto, Dundurn Press

Milano AP (2019) Inclusion and readiness: in support of LGBTQ affirming military health care. Columbia Social Work Review X. https://doi.org/10.7916/cswr.v17i1.1828

Milner JS (2015) Child maltreatment in United States military families: the military Family Advocacy Program has given increased attention to the prevention of family violence. Child Abuse Negl 47:102–113. https://doi.org/10.1016/j.chiabu.2015.05.008

New Zealand Veterans' Affairs (2022) Te Tira Ahu Ika A Whiro. https://www.veteransaffairs.mil.nz/

Newell J (2012) Addressing the needs of veterans and military families: a generalist practice approach. J Baccalaureate Soc Work 17(1):53–68. https://doi.org/10.5555/basw.17.1.0246624pj1051014

Olson MD (2014) Exploring the ethical dilemma of integrating social work values and military social work practice. Soc Work 59(2):183–185. https://doi.org/10.1093/sw/swu010

Olson MD (2018) Exploring military social work from a social justice perspective. Int Soc Work 61(1):119–129. https://doi.org/10.1177/0020872815606792

Pedlar D, Thompson JM, Castro CA (2019) Military-to-civilian transition theories and frameworks. In: Castro CA, Dursun S (eds) Military veteran reintegration: approach, management, and assessment of military veterans transitioning to civilian life. Elsevier Academic Press, pp 21–50. https://doi.org/10.1016/B978-0-12-815312-3.00003-6

Pelts MD, Rolbiedki AJ, Albright DL (2014) Wounded bonds: a review of the social work literature on gay, lesbian, and bisexual military service members and veterans. J Soc Work. https://doi.org/10.1177/1468017314548120

Pierce KE, Broderick D, Johnston S, Holloway KJ (2020) Embedded mental health in the United States Marine Corps. Mil Med 185(9–10):1499–1505. https://doi.org/10.1093/milmed/usaa076

PsychArmor (2021). https://psycharmor.org/. Accessed 8 Apr 2022

Rapley J, Chin J, McCue B, Rariden M (2017) Embedded mental health: promotion of psychological hygiene within a submarine squadron. Mil Med 182(7):1675–1680. https://doi.org/10.7205/MILMED-D-16-00269

Rishel CW, Hartnett HP (2015) Preparing MSW students to provide mental and behavioral health services to military personnel, veterans, and their families in rural settings. J Soc Work Educ 51(sup1):S26–S43. https://doi.org/10.1080/10437797.2015.1001278

Runesu E (2016) An overview of military social work: the case of Zimbabwe. Afr J Soc Work 6(1):14–21. https://www.ajol.info/index.php/ajsw/article/view/148768

Sakarya H, Şahin F (2019) In: The army of social service academicians' thought for army and social services in Turkey: The place and future of the field in social service education. Commun Soc Work 30(2):538–554. https://doi.org/10.33417/tsh.572220

SAMHSA (n.d.) Substance abuse and mental health services administration. https://www.samhsa.gov/smvf-ta-center/collaboration/military-veterans. Accessed 7 Apr 2022

Savitsky L, Illingworth M, DuLaney M (2009) Civilian social work: serving the military and veteran populations. Soc Work 54(4):327–339. https://doi.org/10.1093/sw/54.4.327

Shelef L, Nir I, Tatsa-Laur L, Kedem R, Gold N, Bader T, Ben Yehuda A (2019) The effect of the Suicide Prevention Program (SPP) on the characteristics of Israeli soldiers who died by suicide after its implementation. Eur Psychiatry 62:74–81. https://doi.org/10.1016/j.eurpsy.2019.08.007

Simmons CA, DeCoster V (2007) Military social workers at war: their experiences and the educational content that helped them. J Soc Work Educ 43(3):497–512. https://doi.org/10.5175/JSWE.2007.200600054

Simmons CA, Rycraft JR (2010) Ethical challenges of military social workers serving in a combat zone. Soc Work 55(1):9–18. https://doi.org/10.1093/sw/55.1.9

Smith-Osborne A (2015) An intensive continuing education initiative to train social workers for military social work practice. J Soc Work Educ 51(sup 1):S89–S101. https://doi.org/10.1080/10437797.2015.1001290

Stith SM, Milner JS, Fleming M, Robichaux RJ, Travis WJ (2016) Intimate partner physical violence risk assessment in a military sample. Psychol Violence 6(4):529–541. https://doi.org/10.1037/a0039969

Tallant ST, Ryberg RA (1999) Common and unique ethical dilemmas encountered by military social workers. In: Daley JG (ed) Social work practice in the military, 1st edn. Hawthorne Press, Binghamton

Tanaka K (2014) A consideration on military social work training course and military culture. Kagoshima International University Faculty of Welfare and Sociology. Retrieved from: https://translate.google.com/translate?hl=en&sl=ja&u =https://core.ac.uk/download/pdf/235934905.pdf&prev=search&pto=aue

Turner L, Lau V, Neeson S, Davies M (2019) International exchange programs: professional development and benefits to oncology nursing practice. Clin J Oncol Nurs 23(4):439–442. https://doi.org/10.1188/19.CJON.439-442. PMID: 31322625.

Turton YJ, Van Breda AD (2020) The role of social workers in and after political conflict in South Africa: reflections across the fence. In: Duffy J, Campbell J, Tosone C (eds) International perspectives on social work and political conflict. Routledge, pp 128–141. https://doi.org/10.4324/9781315150833-11

US Department of Veteran Affairs (2022). https://www.va.gov/. Accessed 2 Apr 2022

Van Breda AD (2012) Military social work thinking in South Africa. Adv Soc Work 13(1):17–33. https://doi.org/10.18060/1890

Webb SA (2016) Professional identity in social work. In: Dent M, Bourgeault IL, Denis JL, Kuhlmann E (eds) The Routledge companion to the professions and professionalism. Routledge, London, pp 355–370

Whitworth JD, Herzog JR, Scott DL (2012) Problem-based learning strategies for teaching military social work practice behaviors: review and evaluation. Adv Soc Work 13(1):112–131. https://doi.org/10.18060/1876

Whitworth J, Smet B, Anderson B (2020) Reconceptualizing the US military's transition assistance program: the success in transition model. J Veterans Stud 6(1):25–35. https://doi.org/10.21061/jvs.v6i1.144

Wichlacz CR, Randall DH, Nelson JH, Kempe CH (1975) The characteristics and management of child abuse in US Army Europe. Clin Pediatr 14(6):545–548. https://doi.org/10.1177/000992287501400606

Williams-Gray B (2016) Teaching BSW students effective practice with returning military personnel: a strengths-based resiliency framework. J Baccalaureate Soc Work 21(1):1–11. https://doi.org/10.18084/1084-7219.21.1.1

Wooten NR (2015) Military social work: opportunities and challenges for social work education. J Soc Work Educ 51(sup. 1):S6–S25. https://doi.org/10.1080/10437797.2015.1001274

World Population Review (2022) Countries with universal healthcare. https://worldpopulationreview.com/country-rankings/countries-with-universal-healthcare. Accessed 7 Apr 2022

Yarvis JS (2011) A civilian social worker's guide to the treatment of war-induced PTSD. Soc Work Health Care 50(1):51–72. https://doi.org/10.1080/00981389.2010.518856

Index

© Springer Nature Switzerland AG 2023
M. A. Forgey, K. Green-Hurdle (eds.), *Military Social Work Around the Globe*,
Military and Veterans Studies, https://doi.org/10.1007/978-3-031-14482-0

CPSIA information can be obtained
at www.ICGtesting.com
Printed in the USA
LVHW050845220623
750206LV00020B/100